Titles in the IBM McGraw-Hill Series

BEHRSIN, MASON, and SHARPE • *Reshaping I.T. for Business Flexibility: The I.T. Architecture as a Common Language for Dealing with Change*

COLLEDGE • *The Advanced Programmer's Guide to AIX 3.x*

DOWN, COLEMAN, and ABSOLON • *Risk Management for Software Projects*

ELDER-VASS • *MVS Systems Programming*

GERAGHTY • *CICS Concepts and Uses: A Management Guide*

GOODYER • *OS/2 Presentation Manager Programming: Hints and Tips*

GRAY • *Open Systems and IBM: Integration and Convergence*

HARRIS, CLIVE • *The IBM RISC System/6000*

HARRIS, ROBERT • *The CICS Programmer's Guide to FEPI*

HASTINGS • *The New Organization: Growing the Culture of Organizational Networking*

HOGBIN and THOMAS • *Investing in Information Technology: Managing the Decision-Making Process*

LEAVER and SANGHERA • *The IBM RISC System/6000 User Guide*

ROSS • *Dynamic Factory Automation: Creating Flexible Systems for Competitive Manufacturing*

SIMS • *Business Objects: Delivering Cooperative Objects for Client-Server*

SMITH • *Commonsense Computer Security Second Edition: Your Practical Guide to Information Protection*

TURNER • *PC User's Guide: Simple Steps to Powerful Personal Computing*

Writing OS/2® REXX Programs

Ronny Richardson

McGraw-Hill, Inc.

New York San Francisco Washington, D.C. Auckland Bogotá
Caracas Lisbon London Madrid Mexico City Milan
Montreal New Delhi San Juan Singapore
Sydney Tokyo Toronto

OS/2 Accredited logo is a trademark of International Business Machines Corporation and is used by McGraw-Hill, Inc. under license. *Writing OS/2® REXX Programs* is independently published by McGraw-Hill, Inc. International Business Machines Corporation is not responsible in any way for the contents of this publication.

McGraw-Hill, Inc. is an accredited member of the IBM Independent Vendor League.

Library of Congress Cataloging-in-Publication Data

Richardson, Ronny.
    Writing OS/2 REXX programs / by Ronny Richardson.
        p.   cm.
    Includes index.
    ISBN 0-07-052372-X (p)
    1. REXX (Computer program language) 2. OS/2 (Computer file)
I. Title.
QA76.73.R24R53   1994
005.265—dc20   94-913
                                                          CIP

    2 3 4 5 6 7 8 9 0   DOC/DOC   9 9 8 7 6 5

ISBN 0-07-052372-X

The sponsoring editor for this book was Brad Schepp, the book editor was Kellie Hagan, and the production supervisor was Katherine G. Brown. This book was set in Century Schoolbook. It was composed in Blue Ridge Summit, Pa.

For more information about other McGraw-Hill materials, call 1-800-2-MCGRAW in the United States. In other countries, call your nearest McGraw-Hill office.

Contents

Foreword   xiii
Preface   xiv
Acknowledgments   xv
Introduction   xvii

Chapter 1. Getting Started   1

Before You Can Use REXX   1
On-Line Information   3
OS/2 Enhanced Editor   4
  It's ASCII   7
  Starting the Enhanced Editor   8
  Basic editing   10
  Intermediate editing   13
  Advanced editing   16
  Keeping it simple   17
Executing a REXX Program   18
  Creating a subdirectory and modifying your path   18
  Using the command line   18
  Using an Icon   18
More on Icons   23
  The Icon Editor   24
  Installing an icon   27
Summary   30

Chapter 2. Language Overview   31

Components of a REXX Program   32
  Tokens   32
  Literal strings   32
  Operators   32
  Symbols   33
  Special characters   33
  Command words   33
  Clauses   33
  Statement   36
  File   36

More on Clauses	37
Statement Tokenization	39
Summary	41

Chapter 3. Writing Simple Programs   **44**

Variables and Branching	44
Logic Testing and Looping	46
Subroutines	47
Summary	48

Chapter 4. Interactive REXX   **49**

REXXTRY.CMD	49
PMREXX.EXE	53
Summary	55

Chapter 5. Introduction to Variables   **56**

Creating Variables	56
Assigning Values to Variables	56
Assigning hexadecimal values to variables	58
Assigning binary values to variables	59
Getting Information from the Command Line	61
Taking Information from Another Variable	64
Asking the User for Data	65
Getting multiple characters from the user	66
Getting a single character from the user	68
Performing a Mathematical Calculation	68
Performing a String Manipulation	68
Variable Arrays	68
Summary	71

Chapter 6. Communicating with the User   **72**

Basic Communication	72
Advanced Communication	73
Positioning the cursor	73
Pausing a program	74
Clearing the screen	75
Nonvisual Communication	76
Summary	76

Chapter 7. Including Non-REXX Commands   **77**

Running Batch Commands in REXX	78
CALL batch subcommand	78
CHOICE batch subcommand	78
ECHO batch subcommand	79
The errorlevel	79
FOR batch subcommand	80
GOTO batch subcommand	80
IF batch subcommand	81

PAUSE batch subcommand   81
REM batch subcommand   81
SHIFT batch subcommand   82
Running External Programs   82
Summary   84

Chapter 8. Working with Strings   85

Variable Typing   86
String Definition   87
String Concatenation   88
Additional String Power with Functions   90
Summary   92

Chapter 9. Working with Numbers   93

Display Rounding   94
Precision   94
Exponential Notation   95
Whole Numbers   95
Mathematical Operations   96
Mathematical Precedence   96
Fuzziness   98
Errors   98
Additional Mathematical Power with Functions   99
Summary   100

Chapter 10. Logic Testing and Looping   101

IF   101
Logical Statements   101
Another Look at the IF Statement   106
Multiple instructions   106
Multiple IF tests   107
Multiple IF statements using the SELECT statement   107
Looping   108
DO/END block   108
Looping a fixed number of times   108
Counting the loops   109
Leaving the loop early   111
Looping forever   113
Looping until a condition is met   114
Altering the loop counter   114
Nesting DO loops   114
More on altering loops   115
Summary   116

Chapter 11. Built-in Functions   117

Syntax   118
Application Programming Interface Functions   118
RxFuncAdd   120
RxFuncDrop   120

RxFuncQuery	120
RxQuery	120
Function search order	121
Bitwise Functions	121
BitAnd	121
BitOr	122
BitXOr	123
Exception Handling	124
Condition	124
ErrorText	125
SourceLine	125
Trace	125
File Management	125
CharIn	126
Chars	127
CharOut	127
LineIn	128
LineOut	129
Lines	130
Stream	130
Format-Conversion Functions	131
B2X	132
C2D	132
C2X	133
D2C	133
D2X	134
X2B	134
X2C	134
X2D	135
Mathematical Functions	135
Abs	135
Max	136
Min	136
Digits	136
Form	137
Format	137
Fuzz	138
Random	138
Sign	138
Trunc	139
Miscellaneous Functions	139
Address	139
Beep	140
Date	140
DataType	141
Queued	142
Symbol	142
Time	143
Value	144
XRange	144
String Functions	145
Abbrev	146
Arg	146
Center/Centre	148
Compare	148
Copies	148
DelStr	149
DelWord	149

Insert   150
LastPos   150
Left   151
Length   151
Overlay   151
Pos   152
Right   152
Space   153
Strip   153
SubStr   154
SubWord   154
Translate   155
Verify   155
Word   156
WordIndex   156
WordLength   156
WordPos   157
Words   157

Chapter 12. External Functions   **158**

Function Review   158
Application Programming Interface Function Review   159
  RxFuncAdd   159
  RxFuncDrop   160
  RxFuncQuery   160
  SysDropFuncs   160
Function Search Order   160
Controlling the Screen   161
  RxMessageBox   161
  SysCls   162
  SysCurPos   163
  SysTextScreenRead   164
  SysTextScreenSize   164
Dealing with Objects   164
  SysCreateObject   165
  SysDeregisterObjectClass   166
  SysDestroyObject   166
  SysQueryClassList   166
  SysRegisterObjectClass   167
  SysSetObjectData   167
Disk and File Management   167
  SysDriveInfo   168
  SysDriveMap   168
  SysFileDelete   169
  SysFileSearch   169
  SysFileTree   170
  SysMkDir   171
  SysRmDir   171
  SysSearchPath   172
  SysTempFileName   172
Extended Attributes   173
  SysGetEA   173
  SysPutEA   174
Miscellaneous Functions   174
  SysGetKey   174
  SysGetMessage   175

SysIni	175
SysOS2Ver	175
SysSetIcon	176
SysSleep	176
SysWaitNamedPipe	176
Summary	177

Chapter 13. Keyword Instructions — 178

ADDRESS	178
ARG	180
CALL	180
Arguments used with the CALL instruction	181
Calling functions	181
Executing internal and external routines	182
Exception handling	182
Search order	182
DO	182
DROP	184
EXIT	184
IF	185
INTERPRET	185
ITERATE	185
LEAVE	186
NOP	186
NUMERIC	186
OPTIONS	187
PARSE	187
Parsing template	188
PROCEDURE	191
PULL	191
PUSH	191
QUEUE	191
RETURN	192
SAY	192
SELECT	192
SIGNAL	192
TRACE	193
Summary	193

Chapter 14. Internal Subroutines — 195

Types of Subroutines	195
Introduction to Internal Subroutines	195
A simple example	196
Improving the example	198
Adding a second subroutine	198
Internal Subroutine Advantages	199
Goto with SIGNAL	200
Leaving a Subroutine	200
Internal Subroutine Rules	201
Saved Information	201
A More Realistic Example	201

Variable Management in Internal Subroutines   203
  Using local variables   204
  Mixing local and global variables   205
  Local and global variables in nested subroutines   206
  Transferring data without global variables   207
Summary   209

Chapter 15. External Functions   210

Advantages of External Subroutines   210
  Accessibility   210
  Cohesion   211
When Is an External Subroutine Desirable?   211
Anatomy of an External Subroutine   212
Getting the Input   212
Calling the External Subroutine   213
Returning a Value   214
Summary   214

Chapter 16. Using the External Data Queue   216

Three Demonstrations   216
  GETDATA.CMD and SENDATA.CMD   217
  GETDATA.CMD then SENDATA.CMD   217
  SENDATA2.CMD   217
Understanding External Data Queues   217
Managing the External Data Queue   218
  Creating a new queue   218
  Making a queue active   219
  Putting data into a queue   219
  Putting data into a queue from the command line   219
  Getting data from a queue   220
  Finding the active queue   221
  Deleting a queue   221
Avoiding Conflicts   222
Summary   222

Chapter 17. Exception Handling   223

What Is Exception Handling?   224
Do You Always Need Exception Handling?   224
Types of Exceptions   225
Types of Exception Handling   226
  Default exception handling   226
  Type I exception handling   226
  Type II exception handling   226
Enabling and Disabling Exception Handling   227
Defining Exception Handling   227
EXCEPT-1.CMD   228
EXCEPT-2.CMD   230
EXCEPT-3.CMD   230
Selecting Between Type I and II Exception Handlers   231
Information Available to Exception Handlers   232
Summary   233

Chapter 18. Debugging   234

  Introduction to Debugging   234
    Passive tracing   235
    Interactive tracing   237
  Summary   238

Appendix A. Programs in the Book   239

Appendix B. Programs on the Disk   315

Appendix C. REXX Error Messages   350

Appendix D. Icons   359

Glossary   381

Index   386

Foreword

IBM UK and McGraw-Hill Europe have worked together to publish the IBM McGraw-Hill Series, which addresses information technology and its use in business, industry, and the public sector.

The series provides an up-to-date and authoritative insight into the wide range of products and services available, and offers strategic business advice. Some of the books have a technical bias and others are written from a broader business perspective. What they have in common is that their authors—some from IBM, some independent consultants—are experts in their fields.

Apart from assisting where possible with the accuracy of the writing, IBM UK has not sought to inhibit the editorial freedom of the series, and therefore the views expressed in the books are those of the authors, and not necessarily those of IBM.

Where IBM has lent its expertise is in assisting McGraw-Hill to identify potential titles whose publication would help advance knowledge and increase awareness of computing topics. Hopefully, these titles will also serve to widen the debate about important information technology issues of today and of the future—such as open systems, networking, and the use of technology to give companies a competitive edge in their markets.

IBM UK is pleased to be associated with McGraw-Hill in this series.

Sir Anthony Cleaver
Chairman
IBM United Kingdom Limited

Preface

Personal computer operating systems have long been bundled with some sort of programming language. For instance, MS-DOS comes with BASIC and DR DOS comes with GWBasic. I expect that this is because the developers of these operating systems realize that users are always going to want more power than the raw operating system offers. While Windows lacks a built-in programming language, OS/2 has REXX.

My first exposure to REXX was when I wrote my book on OS/2 batch files, *Writing OS/2 Batch Files To Go*, from Windcrest/McGraw-Hill. I needed a way to write some batch file utilities and none of the languages I was familiar with had versions for OS/2. After doing a little research, I discovered REXX. While BASIC under DOS lacks the interface to the environment and errorlevel to write anything other than simple batch utilities, REXX proved up to the task of writing every one of the batch file utilities I needed for my book. That sold me on REXX.

With that exposure, I set out to learn more about the language. I went to the bookstore and purchased all the REXX books I could find. REXX runs on a variety of platforms and I found about six books on the subject, but none on just OS/2 REXX. Also, none of the books I found had a lot of examples or a disk with programs I could experiment with.

For those reasons I decided to write this book, which is aimed at the beginning to intermediate REXX programmer. I don't try to duplicate all the information in the OS/2 on-line REXX documentation. If you're running REXX under OS/2 then you already have access to this information. Instead, I try to give you a fresh approach to the information.

While REXX will never replace C++ or Pascal as the language of choice among professional programmers, there are good reasons for every OS/2 user to learn about it. Any time you have a problem just a little too complicated to solve with a batch file, it's likely that REXX can easily solve the problem. Any time you need to write a macro or perform some repetitive task, it's likely that REXX can do it for you.

Acknowledgments

Personally, I want to thank my wife, Cicinda, my son, Tevin, and my daughter, Dawna. Without the love and support they've given me, none of this would be possible.

Professionally, there are three people I want to especially thank: Gary Murphy, Charles Daney and Dick Goran.

Gary Murphy of Hilbert Computing provided a number of sample programs and invaluable help. Gary is the author of Chron, a multithreaded OS/2 Presentation Manager application that schedules other DOS, Windows, and OS/2 programs for execution at a predetermined time with a predetermined frequency. The ability of REXX to automate many "housekeeping" chores within OS/2, and the ability of Chron to schedule those programs for execution after hours make a powerful combination for automating many of the routine tasks in an OS/2 environment.

Charles Daney is the author of *Programming in REXX*, available from McGraw-Hill. He's also the author of Personal REXX, a software package that lets you run REXX programs under DOS. There's also a version for Windows. Charles sent me a free copy of Personal REXX so I could continue to work on my REXX programming while I was working in real DOS. He also answered numerous questions that I posted on CompuServe, where he showed a vast knowledge of REXX. His *Programming in REXX* book is more advanced than this book and is an excellent follow-up. It is not, however, OS/2-specific. If you like REXX but are a confirmed DOS user, then his Personal REXX packages are wonderful. *Programming in REXX* should be available in any bookstore. If not, write McGraw-Hill at 1221 Avenue of the Americas, New York, NY 10020. For Personal REXX, contact Quercus Systems at (408) 867-REXX.

Dick Goran is the author of the *REXX Reference Summary Handbook*, an excellent quick-reference guide to REXX. Dick answered countless numbers of questions I posted on CompuServe. His knowledge of REXX shows up both in the quality of the answers he provided me and the high quality of his handbook. Every reader of this book would benefit from having a copy. For ordering information, call CFS Nevada at (702) 732-9616 or contact Dick on CompuServe at 72200,347.

Let me put in a major plug for the REXX area of the OS/2 forum on CompuServe (GO OS2SUPPORT). As I was writing this book, I posted hundreds of questions and discussions in the OS/2 forum on CompuServe. Without the answers and discussions this forum provided, writing this book would have taken much, much longer. Dozens of REXX experts helped me debug syntactical problems, understand confusing (to me) commands, and develop better approaches to problems. If you have a question or problem as you read this book, the REXX area of the OS/2 CompuServe forum is the best place you can turn to for help. You never know, you might even run into me there.

In addition to Gary Murphy, I'm indebted to the following individuals, who let me include copies of programs they had written with this book so you could see the great efforts of other REXX programmers: Robert Reynolds, Mercer H. Harz, and Gerald W. Amende.

At the risk of leaving someone out, I want to thank the following individuals from the REXX area of the OS/2 CompuServe forum for their invaluable help and discussion: Gregory Czaja, Alan Newman, Brian Jongekryg, Jim Standley, Lee Hite, Seymour Metz, Robert Briggs, Dion Gillard, Bruce Marshall, David Bailey, Steve Moore, Steve Price, Jerry Stuckle, Ron Watson, Ron Beauchemin, Ron Hester, Bill Hinkle, Randy Wheeler, Fred Cantwell, Tom Carlson, Laurie Chan, Lawrence Edditt, Robert Mahoney, Bob Price, Terry Roller, Namir Shammas, Irv Spalten, and Gary Williams. Thanks guys!

Introduction

Your local bookstore has many books intended to introduce you to PC-compatible computers and the OS/2 operating system. All of these books spend a lot of time explaining OS/2. Then they usually spend about one chapter explaining the basics of REXX programs—if that much. One chapter is probably enough to convince you that REXX programs are very powerful tools, but it isn't enough to teach you how to use them effectively, much less how to write really powerful REXX programs. That is where this book comes in, explaining in detail what those other books just gloss over.

Who This Book Is For

This book will help you learn to use the power of REXX programs. In writing this book, I'm assuming you have a general understanding of OS/2. You don't have to be a computer whiz, but you should know how to boot the computer, format a disk, erase and rename files, and generally use the graphical user interface. You should also know how to make, delete, and change directories on your hard disk. Finally, you should know how to access the OS/2 command line and enter some simple commands. In general, you should feel comfortable performing simple tasks using the OS/2 operating system. If this isn't the case, start with a general book first.

I'm also going to assume that you know how to program in some other language, be it C++, Pascal, BASIC, or any other language. In fact, knowledge of batch file programming will likely be enough of what you need to know for this book. When I mention that a command is used for looping and then I jump into the syntax of that command, you're going to have to know what a programming loop is and what it's used for. REXX is a fairly easy language so this knowledge doesn't have to be in-depth, but you must be familiar with the general concepts of programming using some other language in order to get the maximum benefit from this book.

REXX Background

REXX was written by Mike Cowlishaw of the IBM System Assurance Laboratory between 1979 and 1982. It was originally called REX because Mike thought that was a nice sounding name. He later changed the name to REXX, which stands for *restructured extended executor*, to eliminate a conflict with another name.

You might think that IBM had an idea for a new language that they then sat down and developed, but that wasn't the case at all. Mike's job wasn't writing languages, but he saw a need and had a vision of a solution. While developing the language, Mike communicated a great deal with the people using the language and then improved it based on their comments.

IBM didn't market REXX right away. It might have never been marketed but for the reputation it developed within the IBM organization. It speaks highly of the language that IBM decided to market it because of the reputation it developed among IBM professionals.

REXX was made available commercially with the third release of the IBM VM/CMS operating system in 1983. It's now available on a number of platforms, including OS/2 and DOS. When IBM announced its Systems Application Architecture (SAA for short) in 1987, REXX was included as its standard procedural language.

Since OS/2 is a graphical user interface, this will seem strange at first, but REXX is a command-line program. That is, programs are designed to issue series of commands rather than interacting with graphical elements. You place a series of commands in an ASCII file, launch the program from either the command line or the WP shell, and REXX executes the commands one at a time. A REXX program is often called a *procedure*, so I'll use the terms *program* and *procedure* interchangeably. REXX programs can also be used inside other programs, like the Enhanced Editor, so you might also hear them called *macros*. REXX has a number of advantages:

System independence. A REXX program written for VM/CMS will generally run with only minor modifications under OS/2, and this is true across all platforms. While most people rarely need to run the same program on multiple platforms, many users have to. Since the programs are very similar, switching between platforms is easy.

General-purpose extension language. REXX was designed as an extension to its host operating system. As a result, it's extremely easy for REXX to issue a command to the host operating system. In fact, issuing an operating-system command in REXX is almost as easy as it is in a batch file.

No typing. Many languages require you to type variables in advance. REXX avoids all that. All variables are character or string variables, so you don't need to do any typing. Additionally, REXX doesn't require you to declare a variable in advance. If you need a variable, you just begin using it.

No reserved words. REXX has no reserved words, so there are no special words to avoid using in your programs. That makes writing programs easier and avoids the hard-to-find problem in other languages of naming a variable something that turns out to be a reserved word.

Decimal mathematics. REXX performs mathematical calculations using decimal calculations. Additionally, the precision is controlled by the programmer rather than the language.

A minimum of overhead.   Some other languages place a burden on the user in terms of formatting and special punctuation. That is not true with REXX; the programmer can generally write the programs using whatever style he or she finds most advantageous.

REXX also has a few disadvantages, but they're fairly minor. The dynamic nature of REXX means that programs typically run slower than they do under other languages. Its decimal mathematics adds another speed penalty. This would be a bigger problem if REXX were used to write massive programs, but it's typically used to write smaller programs where a slight speed penalty isn't a problem.

REXX is also a "personal" language. That is, it doesn't have strong tools for pulling together modules written by different programmers into one larger program. This makes it hard for more than one person to work on a REXX program, which is exacerbated by the freedom REXX gives you in the way you program and format your code. This freedom can make it harder for one programmer to read and follow the code of another programmer.

In spite of these slight disadvantages, I'm sure you'll find REXX to be both a powerful and easy-to-learn language.

Hardware and Software

Writing a computer book is difficult. I never know what type of hardware and software readers have, and I don't even know what version of the operating system they're using. In writing about REXX programs, I'm more fortunate than many writers. Most REXX programs will run on any hardware configuration that supports OS/2. While I wrote this book using OS/2 2.1, most of the programs should run under OS/2 2.0 and many of them will even run under earlier versions of OS/2. For most of the examples in this book, I assume that the files supporting external commands like FORMAT and BACKUP are either in the current subdirectory or in the path when an example REXX program requires one of them.

Writing the Book

I wrote this book using a Gateway 2000 486/66 using DeScribe 4.0. I edited programs and other ASCII files with the Enhanced Editor that's built into OS/2. Finally, I created all the tables using QuarkXPress for the Macintosh running the Tableworks Plus extension. The screen shots were captured using the OS/2 Presentation Manager screen-capture program PMCamera by Jürg Von Känel.

Conventions

You should keep a few important pieces of information in mind when reading this book:

- The numbered function keys on the keyboard are shown as F1 through F12. Most older keyboards have ten function keys on the left side of the keyboard, labeled from F1 to F10. Newer keyboards have twelve function keys, F1 to F12, generally along the top of the keyboard.
- Enter stands for the Enter or Return key, which can also be represented on the keyboard as Rtrn or a bent arrow. Most other named keys, like Del or Tab, are also

referred to by their name. The directional keys are simply up, down, right, and left arrow.

- Information you type into the computer and pieces of programs broken out from the regular text are in a monospaced typeface. The names of keys you hit, like F6 or Enter, and explanatory text is in regular type.

- The caret symbol, ^ , generally means that you hold down the Control, or Ctrl, key and then tap the following key. So ^Z means hold down the Ctrl key and press the Z key. This type of key combination is shown as Ctrl–Z or ^Z.

- Any command inside brackets, [ ], is optional. Brackets are generally used when I'm giving the syntax for a command. In *DIR [/P]*, for example, the /P switch is optional. It causes the listing to pause each time the screen is full. Pressing any key restarts the listing.

- Most of the commands in this book are shown in uppercase when shown on a command line. For the most part, OS/2 doesn't care. Entering DIR, dir, or DiR on the command line are all the same to OS/2.

Since this is a programming book, a lot of programs will be used as illustrations. These illustrations will be shown in one of four ways. First, when a program is fairly short and easy to follow, the entire program will be listed in the text. It will be offset from the regular text and printed in the monospaced font, like this example program from chapter 2:

```
/* NAME:      HIWORLD.CMD
   PURPOSE:    Demonstrate Adding Comments To REXX Programs
   VERSION:    1.00
   DATE:       October 25, 1993
   COPYRIGHT: 1994 McGraw Hill */
SAY "Hello World! I'm A New REXX Program"
```

Second, when the programing concept takes only a line or two out of a program to fully demonstrate, just the lines of interest will be shown. For example, the following line is used in chapter 2:

```
SAY Say Don't I Know You
```

Of course, this is not a complete example. In fact, it won't even run as written since all REXX programs must start with a comment—something this programming segment doesn't do. Third, when a longer example is required to illustrate a point and the full program is important to the illustration, that program will be presented in a table with the source code on the left side and a line-by-line explanation on the right side. Many of the example programs that are referenced more than once are collected together in appendix A. Fourth, many of the programs referenced in the book are for additional illustration. They're included on the disk that comes with this book. You can look at them with an editor and experiment with them, but they aren't printed in the book.

Chapter Summaries

This book contains the following chapters, appendices, and reference material:

Chapter 1: Getting started. Before you can write REXX programs, you need to have REXX installed and you need to know how to use an editor, run the programs, and use the REXX help system. This chapter covers all those preliminary details. Experienced OS/2 users might want to skip this chapter.

Chapter 2: Language overview. This chapter discusses the basic structure of a REXX program. You'll learn the difference between a token, clause, and statement, and how these concepts interact with REXX. When you finish, you'll better understand how REXX looks at your finished code to figure out how to execute it. If you're fairly new to REXX, you might want to skip this chapter and come back to it later after you've had more experience with REXX and are interested in learning more about its inner workings.

Chapter 3: Writing simple programs. This chapter introduces REXX programming by giving you a very quick tour of the power of the language.

Chapter 4: Interactive REXX. The program REXXTRY lets you enter REXX commands one at a time and see their results. Results even carry forward to future commands, so a variable created with one command can be used by the next command. The program PMREXX lets you run REXX programs interactively and scroll through the results on the screen. Both make learning to use REXX and debugging REXX programs much easier. This chapter explains how to use both programs.

Chapter 5: Introduction to variables. OS/2 allows you to store information in variables and later use that information almost any place text or numbers would be used in a REXX program. This chapter explains how to use variables.

Chapter 6: Communicating with the user. REXX includes commands to display information for the user to read and get information from the user. This chapter explains how to use these features.

Chapter 7: Including non-REXX commands. REXX programs can run internal OS/2 commands, OS/2 batch files, other REXX programs, and external programs—in addition to REXX commands. This chapter explains how to include these in your REXX programs.

Chapter 8: Working with strings. Unlike batch files, REXX has some very capable string-processing features. This chapter shows you how to use them.

Chapter 9: Working with numbers. Unlike batch files, REXX has moderate mathematical abilities. It's not equal to C or BASIC but it can add, subtract, multiply, divide, and perform a few other operations. This chapter shows you how to use mathematics in programs.

Chapter 10: Logic testing and looping. REXX allows you to perform advanced logic testing. Additionally, it has come with very advanced looping features. This chapter explains how to use these features.

Chapter 11: Built-in functions. REXX has a number of built-in functions. These functions perform common procedures, like finding the largest of a series of numbers or stripping off a substring. This chapter explains how to use these functions.

Chapter 12: External functions. The RexxUtil dynamic link library adds a number of additional functions to the REXX language. This chapter explains how to use these additional functions.

Chapter 13: Keyword instructions. Prior chapters have introduced some of the REXX keywords. This chapter discusses the remaining keywords and briefly reviews those that have already been covered.

Chapter 14: Internal subroutines. A *subroutine* is a REXX procedure that's called by another REXX procedure. An *internal subroutine* is one that is stored inside the main program. REXX has some very advanced subroutine abilities and this chapter shows you how to use them.

Chapter 15: External functions. Sometimes there are advantages to making a subroutine external to the program, in its own .CMD file. This is especially true when the subroutine is complex or when it can be accessed by several different programs. This chapter shows you how to use external subroutines.

Chapter 16: Using the external data queue. REXX programs can perform a form of advanced piping by pushing data into the input queue for other programs to pull out. This chapter explains how to use this advanced feature.

Chapter 17: Exception handling. This chapter describes how REXX programs can deal with the unexpected.

Chapter 18: Debugging. Errors, called *bugs*, will occasionally creep into your programs. This chapter shows you how you can spot these bugs and get rid of them.

Appendix A: Programs in the book. This appendix contains tables listing the longer programs discussed in the book.

Appendix B: Programs on the disk. This appendix documents all the programs that are included on the disk that comes with this book.

Appendix C: REXX error messages. This appendix lists the REXX error messages and explains what they mean.

Appendix D: Icons. The disk that comes with this book includes a number of different icons you can use with the REXX programs you write. This appendix lists those icons.

Glossary. This section defines common REXX terms used in the book.

Let Me Know!

If this book causes you to develop a nice REXX program or raises a REXX-related question not currently answered in the book, write to me in care of McGraw-Hill and let me know. While I can't always respond to individual letters, your hint or question just might show up in the next edition of this book. The address is:

Ronny Richardson
c/o McGraw-Hill, Inc.
P.O. Box 40
Blue Ridge Summit, PA 17294-0850

Your letters will get to me more quickly if you make sure to include the name of the book in the letter. If you're active in the on-line community, you can also reach me via CompuServe, where my address is 70322,3100.

Writing this book has taken up a large portion of my waking hours over the past four months. I hope you enjoy reading it as much as I enjoyed writing it. Have fun!

Getting Started

If you're an experienced OS/2 user, this chapter will be a review you might want to skip entirely. In this chapter I discuss installing REXX, accessing the on-line help system, using the Enhanced Editor, and using templates to install REXX programs on the desktop or in a folder once they're running. If you've installed REXX already and are familiar with these other topics, feel free to go to chapter 2.

Before You Can Use REXX

Unlike the OS/2 batch language, support for REXX programs isn't automatically installed when you install OS/2. You have to physically select it. If you haven't installed REXX, you need to go back and add it to your installation. The steps are:

1. Find your installation diskettes or CD-ROM.
2. Close all programs and command prompts. This isn't required to install REXX, but it's a good idea for any installation. Besides, you're going to have to restart OS/2 to use REXX so you might as well shut everything down now.
3. From the desktop, open the OS/2 System folder.
4. Open the System Setup folder.
5. Double-click on the Selective Install icon. This will bring up the screen shown in Figure 1.1 for installing hardware. Click on OK to move to the next screen.
6. Click on the REXX button, as shown in Figure 1.2. As you can see, REXX takes less than 400K. You get a lot of power for that 400K!
7. Click on the Install button.
8. Insert the diskettes requested by the installation program.
9. Once the installation is finished, shut down and restart OS/2.

   You now have REXX installed and ready to use.

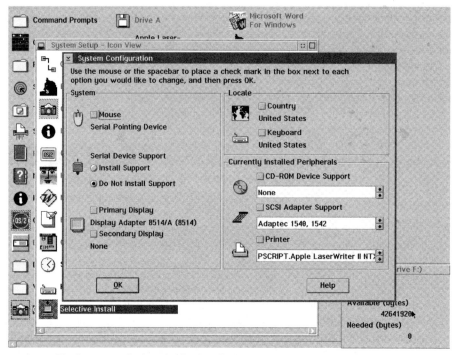

Figure 1.1 The first screen in the selective installation program.

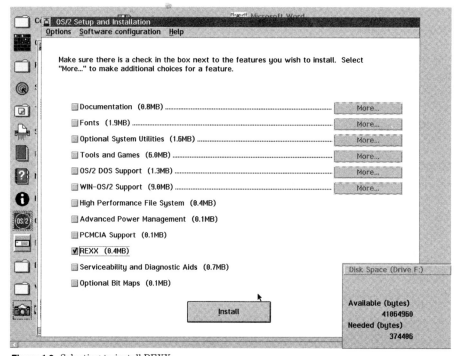

Figure 1.2 Selecting to install REXX.

On-Line Information

One of your best tools—besides this book—is the on-line documentation for REXX, which is installed at the same time you install REXX. It documents all the features and syntax of the REXX language. Because this information is so readily available, I haven't tried to duplicate the same information in this book.

The REXX on-line information is located in the Information folder. You'll access this information a lot while learning and using REXX, so it's a good idea to make the on-line documentation more accessible by making it available from the desktop. The easiest way to do this is to create a "shadow" of the REXX Information program in the Information folder and keep that shadow on the desktop. To do this, click on the REXX Information icon using the right mouse button and select Create Shadow from the menu. When it asks you for a location, select the desktop.

I'm going to take a few minutes to review how to use the on-line help system. Since it's used just like the OS/2 on-line documentation, you might want to skip this discussion if you're familiar with OS/2 documentation already.

When you first open the on-line documentation, you'll see the contents page, as shown in Figure 1.3. This is the page you'll use to access the particular information you're looking for. Notice that all the topics, except the first one, have a plus sign beside them. This means that subheadings are available. To see a subheading, move the black bar to that topic and press the plus sign, as shown in Figure 1.4. Once you've

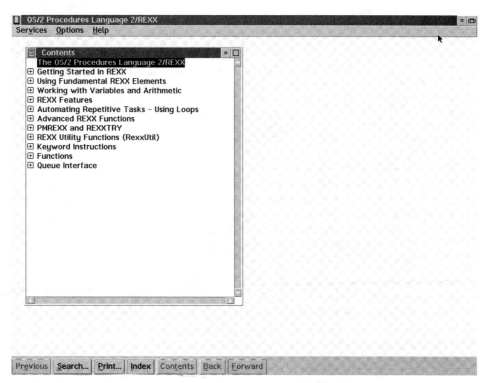

Figure 1.3 The Contents Page of the OS/2 online documentation for REXX.

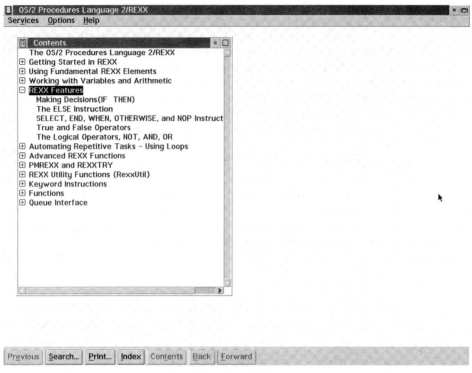

Figure 1.4 Expanding the topics under the REXX Features heading using the plus key.

found the particular heading or subheading you're interested in, you can press Return to see the information under that topic (see Figure 1.5). When a word or phrase is highlighted, as shown in Figure 1.5, you can double-click on that highlighted information to display additional information. Some of the REXX topics also have Example buttons you can double-click on to see one or more examples of REXX code using the concept being discussed.

Many times you'll find it easier to search for a phrase or command than to look through the contents. To do that, first click on the Search button, which will bring up a dialog box where you can enter the word or phrase to search on (see Figure 1.6). Once the search is finished, it will show you a list of topics that contain the word or phrase you entered (see Figure 1.7). You can then select any of these topics to review. If you find that you're using a few topics a lot, you can insert a "Bookmark" to let you jump to that section quickly. First find the text to mark and select Bookmark from the Services menu. Make sure the Place button is selected and enter the name for the bookmark, as shown in Figure 1.8. You'll use this same menu option to quickly display existing bookmarks as well as delete them once you don't need them anymore.

OS/2 Enhanced Editor

Before you can begin to write REXX programs, you need a tool with which to write your programs. OS/2 comes with the perfect tool, its Enhanced Editor in the Pro-

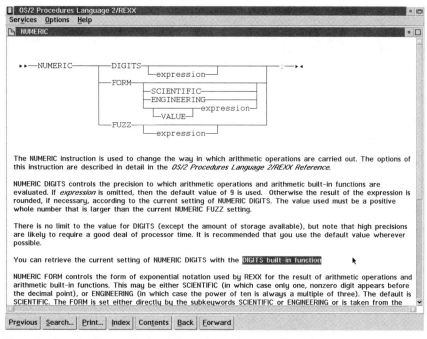

Figure 1.5 Pressing Return displays information under a specific topic.

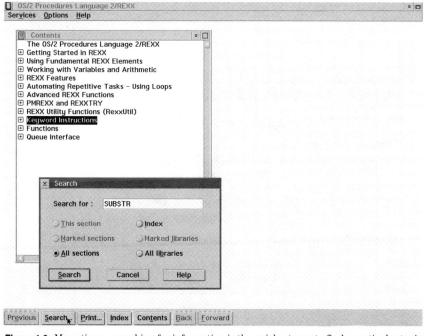

Figure 1.6 Many times, searching for information is the quickest way to find a particular topic.

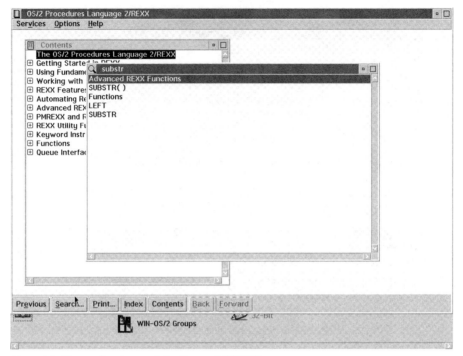

Figure 1.7 The results of a search for the word *SUBSTR*.

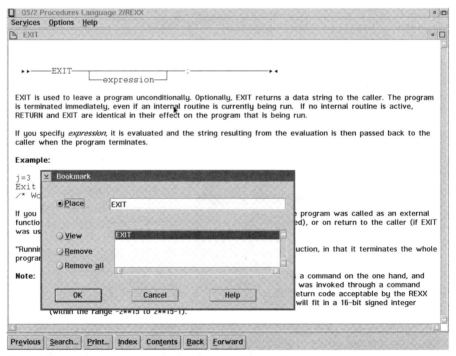

Figure 1.8 A bookmark can help you jump to information quickly.

ductivity folder. This section presents a brief tutorial on starting and using the OS/2 Enhanced Editor. It concentrates on those features most useful for writing REXX. For more information on all its features, see your OS/2 documentation.

Before I cover the OS/2 Enhanced Editor, let me say a few words about alternatives. Almost any word processor or editor—no matter how simple or advanced it is—can be used to write REXX programs. REXX programs must be saved as unformatted text. Any editor or word processor that can save unformatted text (also called ASCII or plain text) can write REXX programs. If you aren't sure about your editor, try creating a small REXX program with it and saving it as unformatted text. Then try to run that program. If it runs, then your editor is fine.

I've found that DeScribe 4.0 using the ASCII template works very well for writing REXX programs. Its one drawback is you must close the program file in DeScribe before you can run it from the command line. This is a limitation of DeScribe and not OS/2 or REXX.

The Enhanced Editor is a fairly powerful editor. It offers features like search and replace, moving text, word wrap, and multiple file editing. In fact, if your needs are simple, you could use the Enhanced Editor for all your word processing.

If you're experienced with editors in general, you might want to skip the first few subsections. If you're already familiar with the OS/2 Enhanced Editor or you plan on writing your REXX programs with your word processor or another editor, you might want to skip the rest of this section altogether and jump ahead to the section *Executing a REXX program*, later in this chapter.

It's ASCII

To help you understand the file format used by the Enhanced Editor, let's try an experiment first. Create a small file (say one or two paragraphs) with the word processor you normally use. Be sure to format all the text like you normally would. When you've finished, save the file and exit your word processor. Now drop out to the OS/2 command prompt and change to the subdirectory containing your file. Once you've done that, issue the command TYPE MYFILE.TXT, only change MYFILE.TXT to the name you used to save your file.

This command will cause OS/2 to display the contents of your short file to the screen. You should see most of the text you entered in the file. However, you should also see a lot of characters you didn't type. These characters contain the formatting information your word processor adds to the file. Some word processors, like Microsoft Word, add file summary information to files and you'll see these characters as well.

While this information is useful to your word processor and helps make your file look attractive when it's printed, it's poison to a REXX program. REXX programs must be saved containing the text you enter and nothing else. This format is called ASCII. The Enhanced Editor creates ASCII files automatically. To see this, create a small file with the Enhanced Editor, save it, and then exit to the OS/2 command prompt and type that file to the screen with the command TYPE MYFILE.TXT, again using your filename. This time you won't see any extra characters.

Because of the Enhanced Editor's limited formatting abilities, it's not the best choice for serious word processing. However, it's one program where it's safe to format your REXX programs for printing since it stores all formatting information in the Extended Attributes file. In addition to writing REXX programs, it's great for editing system files like your CONFIG.SYS file, keeping simple todo lists if the OS/2 Todo program isn't to your liking, and for writing brief memos or notes to yourself. It's also a good way to view the documentation files that come with more shareware packages even if you have no intentions of making any modifications to these files.

Starting the Enhanced Editor

The Enhanced Editor is stored in the Productivity folder, which is stored inside the OS/2 System folder. The steps and figures below assume that you left the Enhanced Editor in that location. If you've moved, you'll have to alter these steps. Figure 1.9 shows a typical OS/2 desktop. Move the mouse cursor inside the OS/2 System icon (on the left near the top) and press the left mouse button twice very quickly, called *double-clicking*. This will open the OS/2 System folder. Your system should look something like the one shown in Figure 1.10.

Next, move the mouse cursor over the Productivity folder and again double-click the left mouse button. This will open the Productivity folder. Your system should look something like the one shown in Figure 1.11. Move the mouse cursor over the Enhanced Editor icon and once again double-click. This will open the editor with a blank file ready to accept characters, shown in Figure 1.12.

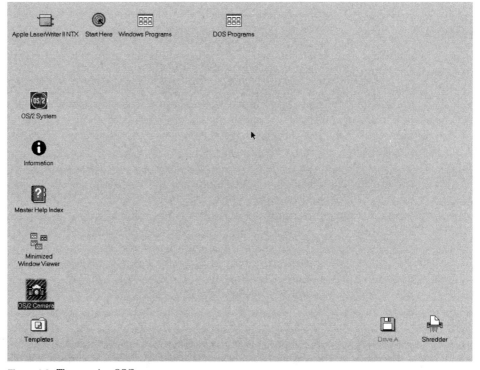

Figure 1.9 The opening OS/2 screen.

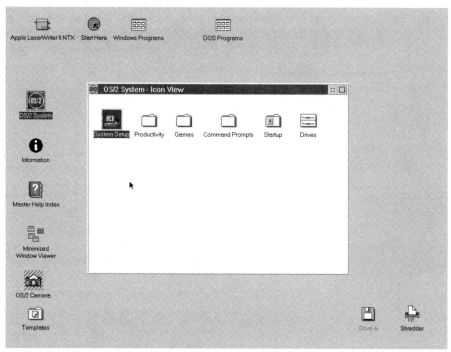

Figure 1.10 Opening the OS/2 System folder.

Figure 1.11 Opening the Productivity folder.

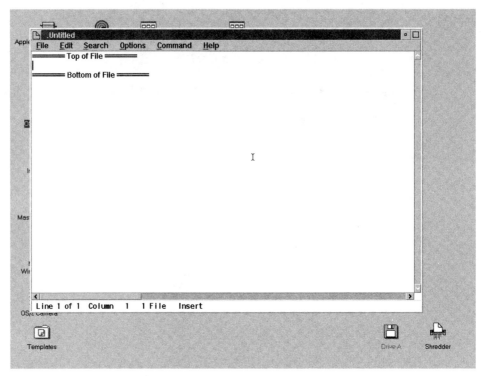

Figure 1.12 Starting the OS/2 Enhanced Editor.

Notice in Figure 1.12 that there's a line =====Top of File===== at the top and
=====Bottom of File===== at the bottom. These are there as markers. You cannot delete them and they aren't saved as part of the file you're creating. Also notice
in Figure 1.12 that the Enhanced Editor has a status line at the bottom of the screen,
a menu along the top of the screen, and a title bar above the menu screen.

I'll explain the menu bar later, but let's take a minute to review the status line at
the bottom of the screen and the title at the top. Figure 1.13 shows the Enhanced
Editor being used to edit an early draft of this chapter. At the time I took this screen
shot, I was editing line 67 of 67, so the file had 67 lines in it and I had the cursor on
the last line of the file. The cursor was near the right side of the screen in column
110. I had only this one file loaded into memory so the status bar showed 1 File. I had
the Enhanced Editor in insert mode so if I moved the cursor to the middle of the file
and started typing, the new characters would be inserted rather than overwriting existing characters. Finally, the file had been modified since the last time I saved it, so
the status line displayed Modified. From the top of the screen, you can see that the
name of the file I was editing was D:\BOOK11\EDITOR.DOC.

Basic editing

If you haven't yet done so, start the editor so you can follow along with this example.
Notice that there's a flashing vertical black line on the screen. This is the cursor. It's

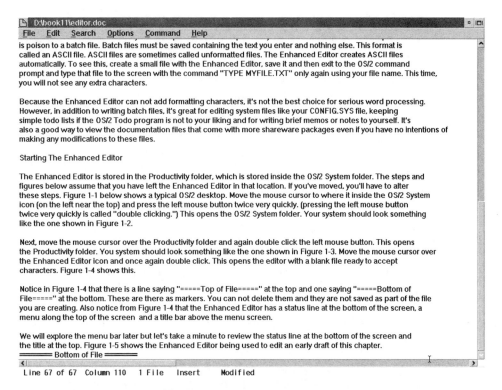

Figure 1.13 Editing a file in the OS/2 Enhanced Editor.

always located on the space where the next character will be inserted into the file. The line and column numbers on the status line refer to the position of this cursor.

One of your most common editing activities is to move this cursor around to different locations on the screen in order to insert or delete text. The up, down, left, and right arrow keys move the cursor one space in the appropriate direction. The Ctrl-left arrow and Ctrl-right arrow key combinations move the cursor one word left and right. PgUp and PgDn move the file one page up and down. Ctrl-PgUp moves the cursor to the top of the current page, while Ctrl-PgDn moves it to the bottom of the current page. Home moves the cursor to the beginning of the current line, while End moves it to the end of the current line. Ctrl-Home moves the cursor to the beginning of the file and Ctrl-End moves it to the end of the file. Table 1.1 summarizes this.

TABLE 1.1 Enhanced Editor Cursor-Movement Keystrokes

Keystroke	Action
Ctrl-End	Moves the cursor to the end of the file.
Ctrl-Home	Moves the cursor to the beginning of the file.
Ctrl-left arrow	Moves the cursor to the left one word.
Ctrl-PgDn	Moves the cursor to the bottom of the current page.

Table 1.1 (Continued)

Keystroke	Action
Ctrl-PgUp	Moves the cursor to the top of the current page.
Ctrl-right arrow	Moves the cursor to the right one word.
Down arrow	Moves the cursor down one line.
End	Moves the cursor to the end of the line.
Home	Moves the cursor to the start of the line.
Left arrow	Moves the cursor to the left one character.
PgDn	Moves the cursor down one page.
PgUp	Moves the cursor up one page.
Right arrow	Moves the cursor to the right one character.
Up arrow	Moves the cursor up one line.

Moving around with these keys can be cumbersome when you need to move the cursor up 12 lines and over 8 words. Fortunately, the Enhanced Editor has a speedier way. In addition to the text cursor, you should see a mouse cursor. It looks like a large capital I with the top bars bent up and the bottom bars bent down. If you move it outside the editing area, it changes to an arrow. To move the text cursor quickly to any point on the screen, move the mouse cursor there and click once.

You can also use the mouse cursor to easily scroll around the file. The small gray bar along the right side of the screen is called a *mouse elevator*. A smaller gray box inside the bar indicates the current position in the file. Clicking above this box works just like pressing PgUp, while clicking below it is just like pressing PgDn. Notice that there's also a mouse elevator above the status bar for moving the file to the left or right when it's too wide to fit on a single screen.

Go ahead and create the following five-line REXX program by entering the text using the Enhanced Editor:

```
/* Simple REXX Program */
SAY "This Is A Simple REXX Program Example"
SAY "The Name Of This File Is SAMPLE.CMD"
SAY "You'll Use SAMPLE.CMD To Illustrate"
SAY "Using Enhanced Editor"
```

Save the file by pressing the F2 key and using the name SAMPLE.CMD. This is a simple OS/2 REXX program. The SAY command causes the text that follows it to be displayed on the screen. I'll cover the commands in a later chapter so don't worry about that now; this is just a sample exercise so you can learn to use the Enhanced Editor.

To see how to insert text, move the text cursor to the left of the REXX on the first line. Check the status bar to make sure the Enhanced Editor is in insert mode (if you see Replace, then press the Ins key to toggle to insert mode). Now type in OS/2. See how the text to the right of the cursor moves over to make room for the new text. Now move the cursor to the You on the third line and press the Ins key to toggle to overstrike mode. Notice that the Insert at the bottom of the screen changes to a `Replace` and the text cursor changes to a black box that covers one character. The character it's covering is the one that is about to be replaced. Type `We` to replace `You` and press the Del key to delete the remaining character.

As I mentioned above, the Del key is one way to delete characters. In replace mode (also called overstrike mode), pressing the Del key deletes the character inside the cursor. In insert mode, it deletes the character to the right of the text cursor. In either replace or insert modes, pressing the Backspace key deletes the character to the left of the text cursor key.

There are two other ways to delete text that you'll generally use on larger blocks of text. With both of these approaches, you begin by highlighting the text to delete. To highlight with the mouse cursor, move the mouse cursor to the first character to delete, press and hold the right mouse button, and drag the cursor to the last character to delete. As you do this, everything you're highlighting will be shown inside a black box. To highlight text with the cursor key, move the text cursor to the first character and hold down the Shift key while using any of the cursor movement keys to move the text cursor to the last character to delete. Using either method, once the text is highlighted you can press the Del key to delete it or simply begin typing. The first letter you type will be placed in the file and all the highlighted text will automatically be erased.

I should mention that some keyboards have trouble selecting text using the keyboard method. My Gateway 2000 computer will do so using only the cursor arrow keys next to the letters. The cursor pad on the far right of the keyboard enters numbers when you press the Shift key. If you have trouble with your keyboard, you might want to experiment with different cursor keys, turning on the NumLock key, and trying both Shift keys.

Intermediate editing

Like most OS/2 programs, you have two ways to access the Enhanced Editor's menus. The first way is to move the mouse cursor to the desired menu and click once. You can also use the keyboard. First, press the Alt key, which causes the File menu to be highlighted. Then use the arrow key to highlight the desired menu and then press Enter to bring up that menu. If you're using a mouse, you can point to the option you want from a menu and click on it to execute it. If you're using the keyboard, move the highlight to the desired option and press Return. Figure 1.14 shows an early draft of this chapter with the File menu pulled down.

To save a file, pull down the File menu and select the Save option. Notice that this option has an F2 shown beside it. That indicates that pressing the F2 function key is a keyboard shortcut that lets you save a file quickly without having to use the menus. Any menu option that has a keyboard shortcut will display it on the menu as the Save command does. If you use the Enhanced Editor a lot, you'll want to learn to use a few of the more common keyboard shortcut keys.

To open a file that already exists on the disk to either edit, print, or read, bring up the File menu and use the Open command. If you want to start a new file without having to exit the Enhanced Editor first, bring up the File menu and use the New command. The File menu will offer the following additional commands:

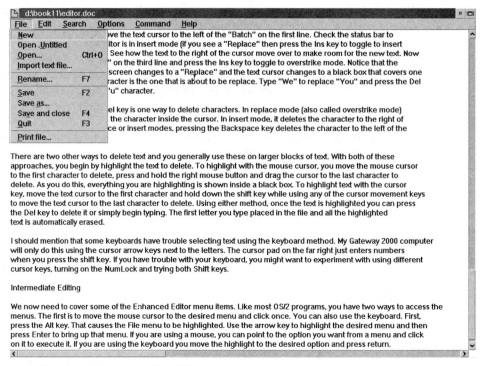

Figure 1.14 Using the menus in the OS/2 Enhanced Editor.

Open.untitled. The New command removes the current file from memory before starting a new file. This command keeps the current file in memory and available for editing while starting a new file for you to work on.

Import text file. This command inserts the contents of text file on disk into the current file at the cursor position. Think of it as a merge command.

Rename. This lets you change the name of the file you're currently working on.

Save as. This lets you save the current file to a new name on the disk.

Save and close. This saves the current file and exits the Enhanced Editor.

Quit. This exits the Enhanced Editor. If your file has been modified since the last time you saved it, the Enhanced Editor will warn you and give you the option of saving it first.

Print file. This sends the current file to the printer.

The Edit menu is used primarily for working with blocks of text. Recall from the previous discussion that you can select text by using either the keyboard cursor keys or the mouse cursor. Once that block is selected, in addition to deleting it you can use the Edit menu to operate on it. Selecting Copy from the Edit menu places a copy of the text in the paste buffer without disturbing the original text. The paste buffer is a special holding area for text. Only one block of text can exist in the paste buffer at a time, so if there's already text in the paste buffer then selecting the Copy command will replace that text with the highlighted text. If you select Cut rather than Copy, then the text is placed in the paste buffer but it's also removed from the file.

Once there's text in the paste buffer, you can move the text cursor to any location you like and copy that to the file using the Paste command. Doing this doesn't disturb the text in the paste buffer so you can make as many pastes of the same text as you like. Cutting and then pasting is how to move text around in a file. Copying and pasting is how to make copies of text in a file. The text remains in the paste buffer as you move between files (but not when you quit the Enhanced Editor), so this is an easy way to copy or transfer text between different files.

Another function of the Edit menu is to let you undo or reverse changes you've made. It offers two options for doing this, Undo line and Undo. The Undo line command lets you reverse any changes you've made to the current line. Once you move the cursor off the current line, the Undo line command no longer works. If you select the Undo line command by accident, you can select it again to reverse the undo operation.

The Undo command lets you undo commands even after you've moved off that line. When you select the Undo command, it brings up a dialog box with a mouse elevator. As you click on the mouse elevator, successive actions are reversed. You should be able to see the changes taking place on the screen underneath the dialog box. This box allows you to reverse multiple changes.

The Enhanced Editor offers a search as well as search-and-replace function. Go back to the original SAMPLE.CMD program and move the cursor to the top of the file with the Ctrl–Home command. Select the Search menu and then the Search command from that menu. This will bring up a dialog box where you can enter the text to search for and, optionally, the text you want to replace it with. For practice, try searching for the text *name* without replacing it with anything. Once the Enhanced Editor locates the text, it draws a circle around it. Had you misspelled a command, you could have the Enhanced Editor go ahead and replace the misspelling with the proper spelling by entering it in the replace field.

There are five option buttons for a search or search and replace:

Ignore cases. This causes the Enhanced Editor to ignore capitalization, so *Ronny* matches *RONNY* and *ronny.*

Marked area. If you highlight text prior to entering the Search command, this causes the action you select to be confined to the highlighted area and text outside that area is unaffected.

Reverse search. This causes the computer to search starting at the bottom of the file and move towards the top. The default is to start at the top.

Grep. This is an advanced (and confusing) pattern-matching option. If you're interested, check out the Help function.

Change all occurrences. This makes the changes for you without asking you about each one.

Once you've entered your search text and optionally your replace text, there are six different buttons at the bottom you can use to start the process:

Find. This locates the next occurrence of the text you entered in the Search field.

Change. This locates the next occurrence of the text you entered in the Search field and replaces it with the text you entered in the Replace field.

Change, then find. This does exactly what the Change command does, then it finds the next occurrence of the text you entered in the Search field.

Change, cancel. This locates the next occurrence of the text you entered in the Search field and replaces it with the text you entered in the Replace field, and then exits the Search dialog box.

Cancel. This exits the Search dialog box without performing any action. Pressing Escape does the same thing.

Help. This brings up the Help menu. Pressing the F1 function key does the same thing. The final REXX program should look like this:

```
/* Simple REXX Program */
SAY "This Is A Simple OS/2 REXX Program Example"
SAY "The Name Of This File Is SAMPLE.CMD"
SAY "We'll Use SAMPLE.CMD To Illustrate"
SAY "Using Enhanced Editor"
```

Advanced editing

It's often useful, when writing a new REXX program, to have an existing program handy in order to copy some of the syntax. The Enhanced Editor allows you to scroll between several different files. You can copy the commands you're interested in from the existing file and paste them into the new file. The Enhanced Editor also gives you several different ways that you can look at both files at once.

The first way is to put both files on the screen. To do that, load the existing file into the Enhanced Editor. Then move the mouse cursor to the very right of the screen. It will turn into a two-sided arrow. Press the left mouse button and drag the border to the middle of the screen. If you need to reposition the smaller screen, you can move the mouse cursor to the title bar and, while holding down the left button, move the window to where you want it. Next, use the Open command to open the next file (or the New untitled command to start a new one) and use the same technique to size it and place it beside the original screen. Using this approach, you can look at both files at once. Use the mouse cursor to click on one or the other to make that screen the active screen for editing the file.

If you want to switch between different files for editing but don't need to see more than one at a time, then ring editing is a better approach since it lets you use the entire screen for one file. First, pull down the Options menu and move to the right of the Preferences menu. Move the cursor down to the Ring enabled menu and press Return. Two buttons that look like rings will appear near the top right of the screen. Next, pull down the File menu. It will now have a new option, Add file. This lets you insert another file to edit into the ring of files. Use the Quit command from the File menu to remove the current file from the ring.

There are two different ways to switch between the various files in the ring. The first is to click on either of the two rings at the top of the screen, which will move you in different directions through the ring. The second method is to use the List ring command from the Options menu. This lists the titles of all the files. To switch to one, highlight it and click on the Switch button.

The Enhanced Editor has one annoying habit that I find really gets in the way of writing REXX programs. It knows that certain REXX commands require multiple components and it tries to help you by automatically adding these components when you start entering a command. For example, if you enter IF at the beginning of a line, REXX will automatically expand it so you have:

```
IF then
else
```

DO and other multiline commands are similarly expanded. If you find this useful, then by all means leave it in place. I find it distracting and I use a different capitalization scheme, so I end up typing over it anyway.

You can turn it off for a single session by selecting the Command menu, then Command dialog . . . and entering the command EXPAND OFF on the command line. This affects only the current session.

To turn command expansion off permanently, create a file called PROFILE.ERX in the subdirectory containing EPM.EXE, the Enhanced Editor program. This is usually C:\OS2\APPS, but you can use the FF.CMD program that comes with this book to find its location on your system. This file should contain the following two lines:

```
/* EPM Profile */
EXPAND OFF
```

Now, on the Command dialog . . . command line, enter the command PROFILE ON. Then select the Options menu and Save options to save this configuration. Command expansion will now be turned off for all future sessions.

Keeping it simple

If you find learning the Enhanced Editor too much just to create a few REXX programs and you're looking for something simpler, OS/2 has just the thing for you. It's called the System Editor. It's much like a stripped-down Enhanced Editor. Under the File menu, you'll find New, Open, Save, Save as, Autosave, and nothing more. Under the Edit menu, you'll find an Undo button, the block commands of Cut, Copy, and Paste, a Clear command to erase the highlighted block, and the Find and Select all commands. The Option menu lets you set the color and font and turn word wrapping on and off. That's it, nice and simple.

Executing a REXX Program

OS/2 offers you two different ways to start your REXX programs. In this chapter, I'll show you both ways, using the SAMPLE.CMD program. If you didn't create SAMPLE.CMD, you'll find a copy of it on the disk included with this book. Just to refresh your memory, SAMPLE.CMD is as follows:

```
/* Simple REXX Program */
SAY "This Is A Simple OS/2 REXX Program Example"
SAY "The Name Of This File Is SAMPLE.CMD"
SAY "We'll Use SAMPLE.CMD To Illustrate"
SAY "Using Enhanced Editor"
```

Creating a subdirectory and modifying your path

SAMPLE.CMD needs to be copied to a subdirectory that's in your path. As a general rule, it's a good idea to collect all your REXX programs together into a single subdirectory (I use F:\REXX on my system) and to include that subdirectory in your path.

To create a subdirectory to store your REXX programs in, open the OS/2 System folder and then the Command Prompts folder. Double-click on the OS/2 Full Screen icon to get to the OS/2 command line. Move to the root directory with the CD\ command. Now, create the subdirectory with the MD REXX command. You can change to this subdirectory with the CD\REXX command. Copy SAMPLE.CMD from its current location with the COPY command. Finally, use EXIT to return to OS/2.

Now you need to add this subdirectory to your PATH command. Unlike DOS, OS/2 keeps its PATH command in its CONFIG.SYS file. This is stored in the root directory of the drive containing OS/2. Open this file with either the System Editor or the Enhanced Editor. You'll see a line for the PATH command. Append the new subdirectory by adding a ;C:\REXX to the end. Of course, you should use the drive and subdirectory appropriate to your system. This change will take effect the next time you start OS/2. Make sure to restart OS/2 before going on to the next section.

Using the command line

The easiest way to run a REXX program is to get to an OS/2 command prompt and just enter the name of the program on the command line. If the subdirectory containing the REXX program is in your path, you can run the REXX program from any location on your hard disk. Figure 1.15 shows SAMPLE.CMD running in an OS/2 window.

Using an icon

OS/2 is a graphical user interface and it naturally seems backwards to go to a command line to run a program. Fortunately, OS/2 makes it easy for you to install a REXX program as an icon either on your desktop or in a folder. That way, all you have to do is double-click on the icon to run the REXX program.

The first step is to open the Templates folder. OS/2 uses templates to install new items. Figure 1.16 shows a desktop with the Template folder open. As is the case with all these screen shots, your screen might look different depending on how you installed OS/2.

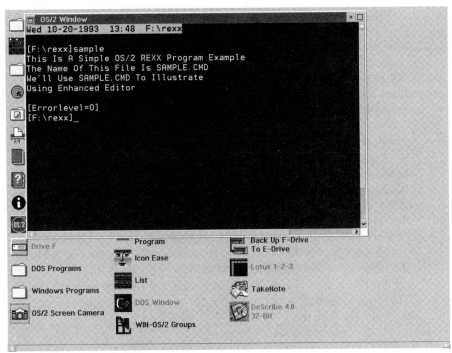

Figure 1.15 Running the REXX program SAMPLE.CMD in an OS/2 window.

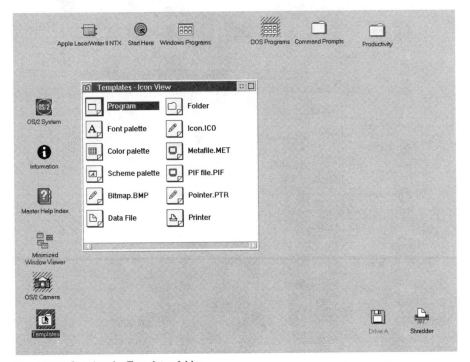

Figure 1.16 Opening the Templates folder.

Next, move the mouse cursor over the Program icon and press and hold down the right mouse button. Drag the icon out of the folder and onto the desktop. With templates, this creates a new copy at the location. To position the icon inside a folder, drag the Program icon to it. As soon as you release the right mouse button, OS/2 brings up the first page of the dialog box you fill out for every new program. On this Program page, enter the path to the REXX program and its name. Optionally, you can enter parameters to pass to the program and the subdirectory it should start working in. Figure 1.17 shows this.

The next page is the Sessions page, as shown in Figure 1.18. Here you tell OS/2 what type of session to run and how to handle the window when the program terminates. Notice that some of the options are grayed out. Since OS/2 knows from the extension that SAMPLE.CMD is an OS/2 REXX program or an OS/2 batch file, it doesn't give you the option of running it in a DOS or Windows window. The next page is the Association page (Figure 1.19) and this is used to link data files to programs. This page isn't generally used for REXX programs.

The next page is the Window page, shown in Figure 1.20, which is used to control the behavior of the OS/2 window while the program is running. It too isn't generally used for REXX programs. The final page is the General page, shown in Figure 1.21. This page is used to enter a title for the icon and optionally redesign the icon to appear any way you want it to look.

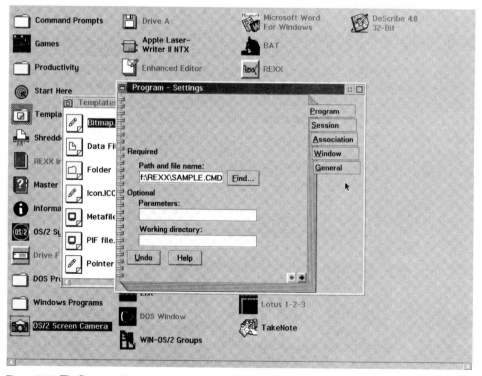

Figure 1.17 The Program sheet of the Program Settings notebook.

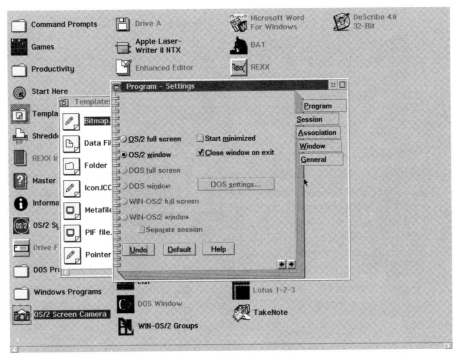

Figure 1.18 The Session sheet of the Program Settings notebook.

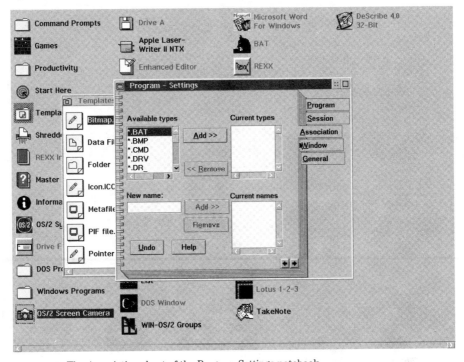

Figure 1.19 The Association sheet of the Program Settings notebook.

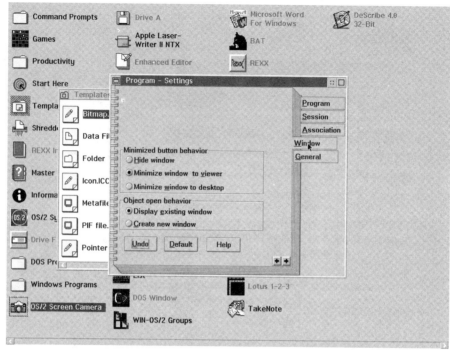

Figure 1.20 The Window sheet of the Program Settings notebook.

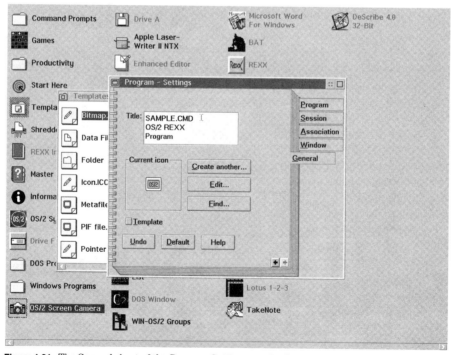

Figure 1.21 The General sheet of the Program Settings notebook.

Once you've filled in the necessary information, you can close this dialog box and the icon is ready to use. Figure 1.22 shows an OS/2 desktop with an icon to run SAMPLE.CMD installed. To run the REXX program, just double-click on its icon. From that point on, it will run just like it would if you had run it from an OS/2 command line.

More on Icons

Each program you want to run by double-clicking on it from the desktop needs an icon. Icons need to have three characteristics. They must be:

Distinctive. If all your icons look the same, then you lose the main feature of a graphical user interface since you can't quickly identify the function of each icon. To see this problem in action, start up Windows and look at the main screen. Every folder looks the same. That forces you to either try to remember the location of specific folders or read the titles below the folders. OS/2 folders initially have this same problem but since you can alter the appearance of your folders under OS/2 you can eliminate this problem.

Attractive. You don't want ugly icons on your screen, even if they're distinctive. Depending on your screen resolution, your icons are limited to at most 64×64 pixels, with each pixel limited to sixteen colors. One of the things you quickly find out is that this small size greatly limits your artistic abilities when creating icons.

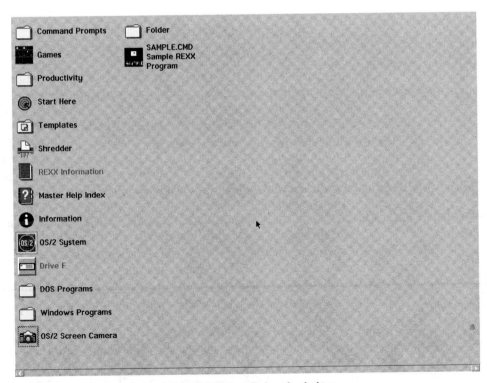

Figure 1.22 The REXX program SAMPLE.CMD installed on the desktop.

Simple. Icons are limited to 64×64 pixels, but most of them are actually 32×32. They're generally shown on the screen very small, so you have to keep the artwork simple in order to be able to make it out on the screen.

While these three characteristics might seem limiting at first, you'll quickly find that it's still possible to create some very artistic icons for your programs. There are three different ways to create icons:

Load them from a file of existing icons. I'm not very artistically inclined, so this is my favorite way. The disk for this book contains a collection of public-domain icons you can look through for your REXX programs and any programs you want to use under OS/2. They're also shown in appendix D.

Draw them yourself. If you're artistic, then drawing your own icons can be both fun and rewarding. If you have access to CompuServe or an OS/2 bulletin-board system, you might want to share your icon creations with others.

Modify existing icons. Often the easiest way to develop an icon exactly like the one you want is to take an existing icon and modify it. I have an icon of a floppy disk I'm always modifying for other purposes. With all the icons on the enclosed disk, you have a good many choices of icons to modify.

The Icon Editor

To draw your own icons or modify existing icons you need to use the OS/2 Icon Editor, so let's take a moment to explore this program. This isn't a complete tutorial on the Icon Editor, but it will tell you enough to work with REXX program icons. For more detailed information, consult your OS/2 on-line documentation.

There are three ways to start the Icon Editor. The first is to double-click on the program, which is stored in the Productivity folder. The other two require you to select the Settings menu and the General page, and then click on either Edit or Create another beside the picture of the existing icon. The Edit button loads the existing icon into the Icon Editor, but all three methods take you to the same screen.

You might want to start the Icon Editor now to follow along. Once you start the Icon Editor, your screen will look like Figure 1.23. Along the top of the Icon Editor, you'll see the main menu. Below that, you'll see several pieces of information:

Form size. This shows you the size of the icon. Typically, icons are 32×32 pixels. The first number is the width of the icon in pixels and the second is the height of the icon in pixels. You can also use the Icon Editor to edit bitmapped files of different sizes. When you use it to create a bitmapped file, the Icon Editor first prompts you for its size.

Pen location. This is the current location of the "pen" used to edit the icon. As with Form Size, the first number represents the width coordinate and the second represents the height coordinate. The bottom left corner is 0,0; the top left corner is 0,31 (the numbers go 0–31 not 1–32); the top right is 31,31; and the bottom right is 31,0.

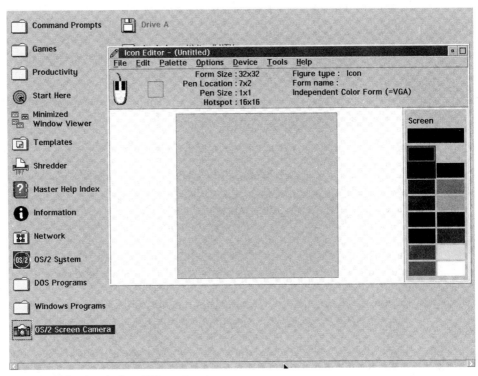

Figure 1.23 Starting the Icon Editor program.

Pen size. The pen normally alters a single pixel at a time, thus the 1×1. Using the Option menu, you can change the pen size to a 2×2, 3×3, and so on, up to 9×9.

Hotspot. The hotspot is the portion of the icon that the mouse pointer must be touching when you double-click.

Figure type. With the Icon Editor, you can edit icons, pointers, or bitmapped files. This tells you what type of file is being edited.

Form name. Once you've saved and named an icon, it shows here.

Independent Color Form (=VGA). This line shows the format that's used to store the icons. All icons on the disk are stored in the Independent Color Form (=VGA) format, at 32×32 pixels. Other available formats include:

- Independent BW Form (=1.1 format) at 32×32 pixels.
- Independent Form (1.2 format) at 64×64 pixels.
- 8514 16 colors at 40×40 pixels.
- 8514 at 40×40 pixels.

- 8514 (1.2 format) at 64×64 pixels.
- CGA at 32×16 pixels.
- EGA at 32×32 pixels.
- VGA (1.2 format) at 32×32 pixels.

The File menu has four options that are particularly useful for editing REXX program icons. They are:

New. This lets you start a new icon with a clean slate.

Open. This lets you open an existing icon and move it into the editor for manipulation.

Save. Use this to save your work to a disk file. If you're saving a new icon file for the first time, the Icon Editor will prompt you for the name to use.

Save as . . . This lets you save an already saved file to another name. It's useful when you want to modify an existing icon. Load the existing icon using the Open option and then save it to a new name using the Save as . . . option. It's best to save the icon to the new name before you begin modifications so you don't forget and save the modified icon back to the original name and overwrite that icon.

The Edit menu has seven options that are particularly useful for editing REXX programs icons. They are:

Undo. This reverses the last changes that were made.

Cut. This removes the selected portion of the icon (or the entire icon) from the file and places it in the paste buffer. The removed portion of the icon is replaced with a screen-colored background.

Copy. This copies the selected portion of the icon (or the entire icon) to the paste buffer without disturbing the icon.

Paste. This copies the icon or portion of icon in the paste buffer to the icon you're working on. Icons or icon fragments loaded into the paste buffer remain there until they're replaced by new material or until the Icon Editor is removed from memory. The Icon Editor has its own paste buffer that it doesn't share with other programs, so using Cut, Copy, and Paste in other programs doesn't affect the Icon Editor.

Clear. This erases the selected area and replaces it with a screen-colored background.

Select. Selecting this menu option converts the mouse cursor from a pen to a selection tool. Use this tool to select an area to cut or copy to the paste buffer.

Select all. This quickly selects the entire icon. You generally use this to copy the entire icon to the paste buffer.

Under the Tool menu, you'll find a Color fill option. This replaces the pen cursor with a tiny paint can. Everywhere you click the cursor, the pixel you click on and every other pixel of the same color connected to that pixel is changed to the currently selected color. This is a quick way to fill the interior of items in your icons.

Now that you've finished this quick tour of the Icon Editor and its more important menu items, I'll show you how to draw an icon. The Icon Editor lets you work with a palette of sixteen colors, shown to the right of the work area. Additionally, you'll see a color labeled Screen and Inverse. The screen color always displays as the same color as the OS/2 desktop screen and makes your icons look professional by giving them an invisible background. The inverse color is the color that contrasts best with the desktop color.

The Icon Editor allows two colors to be active at once. Move your mouse cursor to one color and press the left button. That is the color that will be painted while you hold down the left button. Now, move the pointer to another color and press the right button. That is the color that will be painted while you hold down the right button. I normally set the left button as the color I'm working with at the time and the right button as the background color for the area I'm working in. That way, if I click in the wrong spot using the left button, I can quickly erase my mistake by clicking on the same spot with the right button.

Now you're ready to edit. The best way to think of an icon is a matrix with 32×32 dots. All you're going to do is change the color of some of the dots in this matrix. You can do this by moving the mouse cursor to a particular pixel and clicking the mouse button or holding down either mouse button and dragging the mouse cursor across the screen.

By way of an example, let's draw an icon of a 5¼-inch floppy disk. This size floppy disk is mostly a black square with holes in it, so begin by drawing a black square (shown in Figure 1.24). There are two notches at the front of the disk (one pixel each) and one larger notch (four pixels) on one side of the disk. You'll see these added in Figure 1.25. There's a large hole in the middle for the disk hub, a smaller hole near the front of the disk where the disk is read, and a tiny hole (one pixel) near the large center hole (see Figure 1.26). Finally, the hole in the front is entirely filled with gray to indicate the center platter of the disk, and some of that platter is visible in the large hole in the center. You'll see these added in the final version of the icon in Figure 1.27. Save the icon to a disk file and you're ready to use it.

Installing an icon

OS/2 gives you four different ways to install an icon for a REXX program. You can have a disk file ready, create a new icon from the General page of the Settings notebook, paste an existing icon from the paste buffer in the General page of the Settings notebook, or drop and drag an icon. Let's look at each of these in more detail:

Have a disk file ready. An icon file is a file created with the Icon Editor that contains one icon and has an .ICO extension. If an icon file exists in the same subdirectory as a program and has the same name, when you use a template to install that program to the desktop or to a folder OS/2 will automatically use that icon for the program.

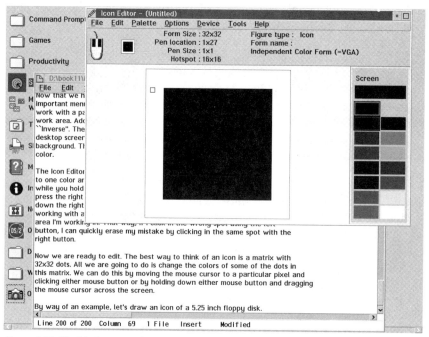

Figure 1.24 The black square that forms the basis of a floppy disk icon.

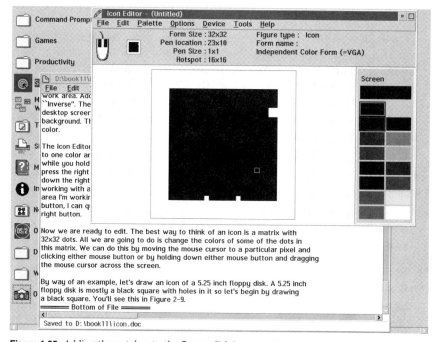

Figure 1.25 Adding the notches to the floppy disk icon.

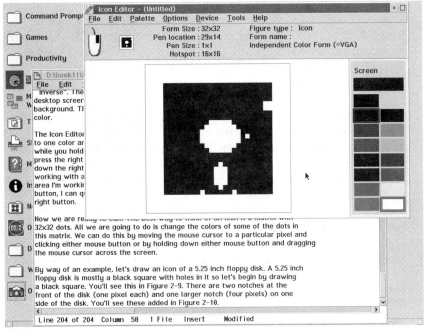

Figure 1.26 Adding the holes to the floppy disk icon.

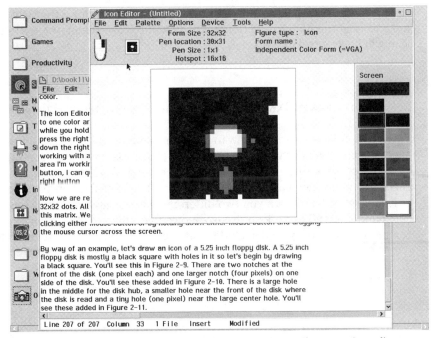

Figure 1.27 Adding shading to the floppy disk icon to represent the magnetic media you can see from the outside of the disk.

For example, assume you have a REXX program called SAMPLE.CMD in your C:\REXX subdirectory that you're planning to add to your REXX folder. Just use the Icon Editor to create SAMPLE.ICO and save it to your C:\REXX subdirectory. Now when you install SAMPLE.CMD, OS/2 will automatically use SAMPLE.ICO as its icon. You must create the icon before installing the program, if you want OS/2 to automatically use that icon.

Create a new icon. If you don't have a previously created icon, you can click on the Create another button on the General page of the Settings notebook. This will take you to the Icon Editor and automatically start you working on the icon for the program you're installing. If you just want to modify the default folder icon used for folders or the box icon used for programs, just click on the Edit button rather than on the Create another button.

Paste an existing icon. If you've previously used the Icon Editor and have copied an existing or modified icon to the paste buffer, you can use that icon to replace the default icon for a program. Just click on the Create another button (the Edit button won't work for this) on the General page of the Settings notebook to go to the Icon Editor. Then select Paste from the Edit menu to paste the icon in the paste buffer into the Icon Editor.

Drop and drag an icon. If another item on your desktop uses the same icon you want to assign to an item, then making that assignment is as easy as dragging the icon and dropping it in place. First, bring up the Settings Notebook for the item that's to have its icon changed and change to the General page. Then click on the item that has the icon you want to use, using the right mouse button. Hold down the right mouse button and drag the item to the General page and release the mouse button. The new icon will be dropped into place.

Summary

Before you can use REXX, you must install it. This chapter has briefly outlined how to install REXX and access the on-line help.

The chapter also explained how to use many—but not all—of the features of the Enhanced Editor. Rather than trying to cover all of its features, I've concentrated on those you're most likely to use while creating and editing REXX programs. To learn more, check the on-line documentation for OS/2 or pick up a general-purpose OS/2 book.

This chapter has shown you two different ways to run REXX programs: from the command line and as an icon. It also showed you how to store your programs in a common subdirectory and include that subdirectory in your path statement so they'll run from any subdirectory.

Language Overview

A complete and operational REXX program can consist of as few as two lines, for example:

```
/* Comment */
SAY "Hello World! I'm A New REXX Program"
```

OS/2 uses the same .CMD extension for REXX programs as it does for its native batch files, so simply looking at the extension isn't enough to tell OS/2 if the file contains a batch file or a REXX program. To overcome this, OS/2 requires that all REXX programs begin with the two characters /*.

This isn't as strange a requirement as it first seems. REXX delimits the beginning of a comment with the /* characters. Everything following them is ignored as a comment by REXX until it encounters a set of */ characters. Comments can span across lines. For example, the following would be a valid beginning for the simple program shown above:

```
/* NAME:     HIWORLD.CMD
   PURPOSE:  Demonstrate Adding Comments To REXX Programs
   VERSION:  1.00
   DATE:     October 25, 1993
   COPYRIGHT: 1994 McGraw Hill */
SAY "Hello World! I'm A New REXX Program"
```

Even though it now spans five lines, everything between the /* and the */ is treated as a comment by REXX and ignored. The SAY on the last line is a REXX command. It's the same as the ECHO command in a batch file, and it tells REXX to display information on the screen.

Two comments about this example are in order. First, REXX programs are designed to run under multiple platforms with a minimum of translation. That REXX programs begin with a comment is a requirement of OS/2 and not REXX itself. If you receive a REXX program from another platform, it might not begin with a comment. In that case, you'll have to add a comment to the top of the program. Second, the requirement to use the .CMD extension is also an OS/2 requirement. The naming conventions for other platforms might be different.

Components of a REXX Program

A REXX program consists of the following components:

Tokens

The most basic unit of a REXX program is a token. In its simplest form, a token is a unit of a REXX program that it doesn't make sense to break down any further. For example, the line:

```
SAY "Hello World! I'm A New REXX Program"
```

contains two tokens, the SAY instruction and the character string it displays on the screen. This instruction could also be written as:

```
SAY"Hello World! I'm A New REXX Program"
```

with no space between the SAY instruction and the phrase, so there are only two tokens. If the instruction were written as:

```
SAY Hello World! I'm A New REXX Program
```

without the quotation marks, REXX would display the phrase in all uppercase. Now, the space between the SAY instruction and Hello is required because REXX wouldn't know what SAYHello meant. However, any spaces on this line after the Hello are simply for human readability and aren't required by REXX, so the line has three tokens: the SAY instruction, the space after the SAY instruction, and the phrase Hello World! I'm A New REXX Program. REXX has four different types of tokens:

Literal strings

These are phrases that begin with a single or double quotation mark and continue until a matching quotation mark is reached. A literal string can also be implied without quotation marks, as illustrated in the previous example. These function just as if they had been defined using quotation marks. There are three types of literal strings: character or ASCII, hexadecimal, and binary.

Operators

Any group of operator characters counts as a single token, even when they're separated by spaces. Operators are characters like –, +, and *.

Symbols

Any group of characters that isn't a literal string is a symbol. Numbers, variable names, and reserved words are examples of symbols.

Special characters

REXX uses a few symbols for special purposes. For example, text to be displayed with the SAY instruction can be split across multiple lines with a comma. These special character symbols count as a token.

Command words

A command word is a special token, a word that has a special meaning to REXX. For example, the SAY instruction in the previous example is a command word. Command words have a special meaning only at the beginning of a clause, so the following would be a valid program line:

```
SAY Say Don't I Know You
```

The second Say isn't at the start of a clause, so it's just part of the message this REXX program will display on the screen. Since the message is not in quotation marks, REXX will display it in all uppercase. REXX is much more lenient than other programming languages. You might think that the instruction:

```
SAY = 123
```

would use the SAY reserved word to display = 123 on the screen. However, REXX tries to anticipate what you're trying to do and, in doing so, creates a variable called Say containing = 123. This is, of course, very bad programming practice. If you really wanted to display = 123 on the screen, you could use the instruction:

```
SAY "= 123"
```

and everything would work correctly.

Clauses

A few tokens, like the EXIT instruction, make sense by themselves. However, most tokens must be combined with other tokens to form a complete instruction. When several tokens are combined together to form a complete REXX instruction, that instruction is called a *clause*. An entire clause is executed if it's error-free. If a clause contains an error, none of it is executed.

In general, a clause consists of one or more tokens and zero or more spaces (which are ignored). A clause can begin with one or more spaces. If a clause begins with spaces, they're ignored. For example, the following two instructions:

```
SAY "Hello"
    SAY "Hello"
```

are identical. Clauses end with a semicolon, but REXX adds them automatically to the end of most lines, so most OS/2 REXX programmers leave them out of their programs.

Under OS/2, clauses are limited to a maximum length of 500 characters. Cowlishaw doesn't specify a maximum length, so this is implementation-specific. For example, the Personal REXX version from Quercus has a maximum length of 1,000 characters.

When REXX encounters a clause, it scans it from left to right and performs a process called *tokenization*. It is this "tokenized" clause that REXX executes. I'll discuss this in more detail later in the chapter.

Since comments are removed from a clause before it's executed, you can include them anywhere in a statement. For example, the following program segment stores a value to a variable and then performs a logic test on that variable:

```
X = 7
IF X=7 THEN SAY "X Is 7"
```

This code would execute identically to the following code:

```
X = 7
IF X=/* Comment */7 THEN SAY "X Is 7"
```

even though the second code has a comment in the middle. They execute the same because tokenization removes /* Comment */ from the second code segment, leaving it the same as the first segment. Programmers often use this fact to add comments to the end of lines of code that might take a little explanation to understand. However, including comments inside code, as was done in the example, is bad programming form. It works, but it makes your programs very hard to follow. The code that follows is a much better approach to documenting specific lines:

```
X = 7                      /* Assign A Value  */
IF X=7 THEN SAY "X Is 7"   /* Test That Value */
```

There are four types of clauses:

Label. A label is a symbol followed by a colon, e.g., END:. A label is used merely to mark a location in a program; the line itself does not execute. It might be used to jump to a line, like a GOTO command in a batch file, or it might represent the name of a subroutine. Notice that batch files place the colon at the beginning of the label while REXX programs place it at the end of the label.

Assignment. Any clause that begins with a symbol token followed by an equal sign is an assignment clause. The contents of the token following the equal sign is assigned to the variable name in the token preceding the equal sign, for example:

```
X = "Ronny"
Y = 100
```

If the first token isn't a legal variable name nor a variable name at all, then, while the clause is still an assignment clause, it contains an error. For example, the following are all invalid assignment clauses:

```
1 = "Ronny"   /* 1 Is Not A Valid Variable Name   */
"X" = 7       /* "X" Is A Literal, Not A Variable */
```

Since an assignment clause begins with a variable name and not a command word, the instruction:

```
SAY = 123
```

is valid because REXX treats SAY as a token containing a valid variable name and not a token containing an instruction.

Instruction. When the clause isn't an assignment clause and the first token is a valid REXX instruction (command word), then the clause is an instruction clause.

OS/2 command. When the clause isn't an assignment clause and the first token isn't a valid REXX instruction, then the command is passed to OS/2 for execution. In this fashion, REXX programs can execute other programs as easily as any batch file. The command is fully evaluated by REXX first, so the second command in the following:

```
Message = "Hello From A REXX Program"
ECHO Message
```

would be passed to OS/2, but not before the variable Message had been expanded, so the command to OS/2 would be:

```
ECHO Hello From A REXX Program
```

As you've seen, a clause is a series of tokens, usually ending at the end of a line. However, there are four different situations that can end a clause:

- The end of a line, unless the last token on the line is a comma. Since the comma is the continuation punctuation, lines that end with a comma are generally treated as though they continue on the next line.

- A semicolon.

- The keyword THEN, provided the first token is an IF or WHEN instruction. Note that the THEN is treated as a separate clause and not part of the clause it ends. The keywords ELSE and OTHERWISE are also treated as clauses unto themselves when they occur in the appropriate place.

- A colon when it's the second token and therefore used to identify a label.

As complex as this sounds, it's generally true that the end of a line marks the end of a clause.

Statement

I defined a clause as "several clauses combined together to form a complete REXX instruction." Another way of looking at this is that a clause is a complete line ending with an actual or implied semicolon. However, not all REXX instructions are complete when made up of just a single line. For example:

```
X = 7
IF X = 7 THEN
    SAY "X Is 7"
ELSE
    SAY "X Is Not 7"
```

consists of five lines and five clauses, but not five logically independent actions. The first line is clearly an independent action; it assigns a value to a variable. It would make sense in a program by itself. The two SAY lines would also make sense in a program by themselves. However, the IF and ELSE lines are part and parcel of one overall logic test. In fact, the two SAY lines are equally part of this logic test. In addition to the IF instruction, the DO and SELECT instructions automatically generate more than one line of code.

A statement, then, is the basic unit of code in a REXX program. Unless a statement begins with an IF, DO, or SELECT instruction, a statement and clause are identical. When a statement begins with an IF, DO, or SELECT instruction, that statement can extend across multiple lines and thus include multiple clauses. Note that in this case a statement can contain other statements inside it. The following:

```
IF X = 7 THEN
    SAY "X Is 7"
ELSE
    SAY "X Is Not 7"
```

contains two SAY statements (and clauses) embedded inside it. My terminology is somewhat different than Cowlishaw used in *The REXX Language* and is therefore somewhat different from books based on that work. My terminology is much closer to what Daney used in *Programming in REXX*, but again not exactly. I mention this in case you read either of these books (both are excellent) so you can be aware of the differences. Happily, except for explaining how REXX works, terminology isn't a big deal. In fact, once you finish this chapter, this terminology won't be a concern for you at all.

File

The entire REXX program must be contained in a single file, unlike some languages like C and C++ that allow you to break a large program down into logical components and store each component in a separate file. That isn't to say that one REXX program can't call another REXX program or procedure stored in a separate file; it can. It just means that these two files are treated as separate programs, where one is calling another and (perhaps) passing some information to it and (perhaps) receiving some information from it rather than being two pieces of the same program.

More on Clauses

As you saw previously in this chapter, a clause normally ends at the end of the line. In addition to the end of the line, three other things will terminate a clause:

- A semicolon.
- The keywords THEN, ELSE, or OTHERWISE, when used appropriately.
- A colon when used as the second token.

Several conditions will cause a clause to span more than one line, so let's look at this issue in more depth.

A comment begins with the /* characters and end with the */ characters, without regard to ends of lines. Thus, both of the following are valid comments:

```
/* This is a comment */
/*
This
is
also
a
comment
*/
```

Comments can also be nested, so the following is a valid comment:

```
/* This Is A /*Comment*/ Inside A Comment */
```

Suppose you had the following section of code:

```
X = X + 1           /* Increment Counter */
SAY "X Is" X        /* Display Value     */
```

and you wanted to temporarily "turn off" the code. You don't want to remove it since you might want to use it later. The easiest way to do this is to "comment out" the code, as follows:

```
/*
X = X + 1           /* Increment Counter */
SAY "X Is" X        /* Display Value     */
*/
```

Even though this results in a nested comment, it's an acceptable way to temporarily turn off the code. This is typically done during debugging. Once the code is operational, you can turn this section back on by removing the extra comment markers.

Nested comments must have matched pairs of beginning and ending comment markers. That is, the entire comment must have the same number of beginning and ending markers. The following comments are both invalid:

```
/* This Is */ An */ Invalid Comment /*
/* This Is Also /* An /* Invalid */ Comment */
```

The first comment has two ending comment markers after An and only one beginning comment marker, so the number of ending markers exceeds the number of beginning markers. The second comment has three beginning markers and only two ending markers.

Many REXX clauses can end up being very long. While the OS/2 Enhanced Editor has no problem working with long lines, they can be hard to read and debug since you can't see the entire line on the screen at once. REXX solves this problem by allowing you to end a line with a comma. When the line is tokenized, the comma and line return are replaced with a single space and so the two lines are recombined. Thus, the instruction:

```
SAY "Ronny",
    "Richardson",
    "Wrote This Book"
```

would display the text Ronny Richardson Wrote This Book all on one line even though the instruction is spread out over three lines.

There are three important items about using the comma for line continuation. First, a string enclosed in quotation marks must all be on one line, so the following two instructions:

```
Message = "You Have Made,
           A Mistake"
Message = "You Have Made",
           "Another Mistake"
```

are both invalid because they split a string definition across two lines. The fact that the first splits the quotation marks and the second doesn't make any difference.

Second, as will be discussed in detail in chapter 7, two strings can be combined using the string concatenation operator ¦¦. So the instruction:

```
Message = "You Have Made "¦¦"A Mistake"
```

would be a valid instruction. The instruction:

```
Message = "You Have Made ",
          ¦¦"A Mistake"
```

is also valid since you're splitting the concatenation operation and not the string definition operation.

Third, you must be careful when using a comma to split a line in the middle of a call for a function or procedure. Assuming you had a function called LocateCursor that required a row and column number and then positioned the cursor at that screen position. When run on a single line, you might call this function with the instruction:

```
CALL LocateCursor 12,20
```

If you were to split this into two lines using the instruction:

```
CALL LocateCursor 12,
  20
```

it would be invalid because the single comma functions as the line separator and it and the line feed are replaced by a space. To split the line in this fashion, you must have one comma for the line-split character and a second comma to separate the function arguments, as follows:

```
CALL LocateCursor 12,,
  20
```

Of course, this isn't good programming practice.

Statement Tokenization

Before discussing tokenization, I need to explain the way REXX classifies characters. Characters fall into one of four categories:

Symbol characters. These are characters like A–Z that you can use in a variable name. The first character must be A–Z, a–z, an exclamation point, question mark, or underscore. REXX translates lowercase letters to uppercase before using them. The rest of the variable name can also use a numeral, 0–9. Periods can also be used in a variable name, but have a special meaning and should be avoided until you're familiar with the rules for forming compound variables. (This is discussed in detail in chapter 5.)

Operational characters. These are characters, like the plus and minus sign, that indicate mathematical operations, and logical characters like the greater-than sign.

Punctuation characters. These are characters, like the comma and semicolon, that indicate REXX punctuation.

Invalid characters. If a character is not one of the previous three categories, then it's an invalid character and will generate an error message.

When REXX tokenizes a statement, it performs the following:

- All leading spaces are stripped off the statement.
- If the first character is a symbol character, then the line begins with either a symbol or number. Every character up to the first nonsymbol character is combined together with any letters converted to uppercase.
- If the first character is an operator character, then the line begins with a REXX operation. Spaces around the operator are removed and every character up to the first nonoperator character is combined into a single operator.
- If the first character is a special character, then it's treated as a token—as special characters are always treated. Spaces around the special character are removed, except for a space preceding an open parenthesis or after a close parenthesis.

- Comments are removed. They can occur in the middle of multicharacter operators (a bad idea), but a comment marks the end of a token so they shouldn't be used inside variable names, character strings, and the like.

- A single or double quotation marks the beginning of a string literal. Either quotation mark is acceptable. Any character (except the type of quotation mark used to begin the string) is allowable inside quotation marks. If the same quotation mark used to start the string literal is needed inside it, use that mark twice. For example:

```
SAY 'Don''t Do That!'
```

A nondoubled quotation mark of the same type that was used to start a string literal is used to terminate the string literal. A *b* or *x* immediately following a string literal causes the string literal to be treated as either binary or hexadecimal.

- A few special cases, such as scientific notation of numbers, are handled on an ad hoc basis.

Based on these rules, there are seven types of tokens that REXX recognizes:

Binary numbers.   These are numbers expressed in base two. They're made up of zeros and ones. When storing a binary value to a variable, the ending quotation mark must be immediately followed by the letter *b*. Blanks can be used inside the string to make it more readable. Except for the first character set, the characters must be grouped in sets of four when spaces are used.

Character string literals.   These are series of any characters enclosed in single or double quotation marks.

Hexadecimal numbers.   These are numbers expressed in base sixteen. They're made up of the characters 0–9 and A–F. Capitalization of the letters doesn't matter. When storing a hexadecimal value to a variable, the ending quotation mark must be immediately followed by the letter *x*. Blanks can be used inside the string to make it more readable. Except for the first character, the characters must be grouped in pairs when spaces are used.

Numbers.   Numbers are special strings that contain only an optional plus or negative sign, 0–9, one period and zero, or one exponential suffix (e) followed by a plus or negative sign and one or more digits.

Operators.   These are one or more operational characters.

Symbols.   A symbol is a stream of one or more symbol characters. If it's the first token it might be a command word, but it isn't required. If it isn't the first token it might still be a command word, like THEN, that isn't required to be at the beginning of a clause. If it isn't a command word, then it's either a system command or a variable name.

Syntax symbols. These are symbols, like the colon in a label name and the semi-colon, that are treated as tokens by themselves.

Given all the above information, you're now ready to see how REXX pulls together tokens into clauses:

Label. If the first token is a symbol and the second is a colon, then the clause is a label.

Assignment. If the first token is a symbol and the second is an equal sign, then the clause is an assignment clause.

Keyword (command word) instruction. If the first token is a symbol that's a REXX command word, then the clause is a REXX instruction.

Command. If the clause isn't a label, assignment, or keyword instruction, then it's a command that REXX passes to OS/2 for processing.

REXX programs run faster the second time! After tokenizing the program, REXX stores the tokenized version in the OS/2 extended attributes. It does this without modifying the original ASCII version. Then when you run the program again, the tokenized version is loaded and run rather than the ASCII version. Once a REXX program has been executed once, this saves the time required for the tokenization process.

You can see this by creating a small REXX program and using the DIR command before and after running it. If you're using the high-performance file system (HPFS), then the size of the extended attributes will show up automatically as the second size number. If you have a file-allocation table (FAT) system, then you must use a /N after the DIR command to see the extended attributes. Figure 2.1 shows the DIR command for the program TYPING.CMD. The first time is on an HPFS system. Here you see the file itself is 3,929 bytes and the extended attributes are 6,979 bytes. The second DIR command is on a FAT system without the /N switch and it shows only the size of the file.

Summary

- The most basic unit of a REXX program is a token. REXX has four different types of tokens: literal strings, operators, symbols, and special characters.

- A command word (also called a keyword) is a special token, a word REXX reserves to itself and doesn't allow you to use. This restriction applies only to the first token in a clause. REXX allows you to use keywords as variable names in assignment statements.

- When several clauses are combined together they form a complete REXX instruction, called a clause. There are four types of clauses: labels, assignments, instructions, and OS/2 commands. There are four things that can end a clause: the end of the line unless it ends with a comma, a semicolon, the keyword THEN when following an IF or WHEN instruction, and a colon when it's the second token and therefore identifies a label.

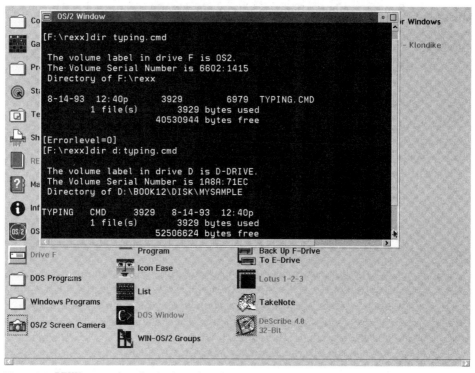

Figure 2.1 REXX stores the tokenized version of a program in extended attributes. This is shown automatically with the DIR command on an HPFS system and the /N switch on a FAT system.

- Sometimes it takes several clauses combined together to form a complete instruction. This complete instruction is called a statement. A statement is the basic unit of code in a REXX program. Unless a statement begins with an IF, DO, or SELECT instruction, a statement and clause are identical. When a statement begins with an IF, DO, or SELECT instruction, that statement can extend across multiple lines and thus include multiple clauses.

- An entire REXX program must be contained in a single file, unlike some languages, like C and C++, that allow you to break a large program down into logical components and store each component in a separate file.

- While a REXX program can call other REXX programs as subroutines or procedures, the interaction between the original and calling program is fairly limited.

- A clause can cover more than one line when it's a comment and the comment covers multiple lines or when the statement ends in a comma.

- Characters fall into one of four categories: symbol characters, operating characters, punctuation characters, and invalid characters.

- When REXX tokenizes a statement, it performs the following steps: it strips off leading spaces, combines leading symbol characters into a symbol or number, combines leading operator characters into operators, treats each leading special character as a separate token, removes comments, treats text inside quotation marks as string literals, and treats a few special cases on an ad hoc basis.

- There are seven types of tokens that REXX recognizes: binary numbers, character string literals, hexadecimal numbers, numbers, operators, symbols, and syntax symbols. REXX creates four different types of statements: labels, assignments, keyword instructions, and commands for the operating system.

- The first time a new or modified REXX program is run, REXX stores the tokenized version in the extended attributes so it can load and run the program faster the next time.

3

Writing Simple Programs

You've seen how to write programs using the Enhanced Editor, how to install those programs on your desktop and run them either from the desktop or from the command line, and even the internal workings of REXX regarding how it tokenizes programs. Now it's time to write some code. This chapter presents a brief introduction to REXX. Other chapters will expand on the concepts presented here.

REXX can display information on the screen much like a batch file; however, REXX uses the SAY instruction instead of the ECHO command. If the information isn't inside quotation marks, it's converted to all uppercase so you'll usually want to surround your messages with quotation marks. So a simple REXX program using comments and the SAY instruction would be:

```
/* NAME:    REXX-1.CMD */
/* PURPOSE: Demonstration REXX Program */
/* VERSION: 1.00 */
/* DATE:    June 11, 1993 */

SAY Hello Reader
Say I Am A New REXX Program
```

Since neither line is surrounded by quotation marks, both lines would be displayed in all uppercase.

Variables and Branching

In a batch file, the only variable you have access to are environmental variables. REXX can create its own variables by assigning a value to a variable name. From then on, that variable name is replaced with the contents of the variable. The following example will make that clearer:

```
/* NAME:    REXX-2.CMD */
/* PURPOSE: Demonstration REXX Program */
/* VERSION: 1.00 */
/* DATE:    June 11, 1993 */

READER="Ronny"
SAY Hello Reader
Say I Am A New REXX Program
```

In this program, `Reader` is now a variable name, so the first line it displays will be `HELLO Ronny`. (Since `Ronny` is in quotation marks when created, it isn't converted to uppercase.)

REXX variables aren't limited to strings; they can also contain numbers. Unlike many languages, there's no difference in REXX between a string and numeric variable. In working with numeric variables, REXX can perform the normal mathematical operations of addition, subtraction, multiplication, and division. The results can be either stored to a variable or printed with the SAY instruction. The following example illustrates that:

```
/* NAME:    REXX-3.CMD */
/* PURPOSE: Demonstration REXX Program */
/* VERSION: 1.00 */
/* DATE:    June 11, 1993 */

First=12
Second=14
SAY "Sum Is" First + Second
Times=First*Second
Say "Product Is" Times
```

Like a batch file, REXX programs generally flow from top to bottom in a straight line. They also have two instructions to alter program flow, EXIT and SIGNAL.

The EXIT instruction causes a REXX program to immediately terminate and return control to the operating system. With a batch file, you specify a label named *preceded* by a colon, e.g., :TOP, and you can jump to that label with a GOTO TOP command. In REXX, you mark a label with a name *followed* by a colon, e.g., TOP:, and you can jump to that label with a SIGNAL instruction, e.g., SIGNAL TOP.

The SIGNAL instruction terminates all loops, so you shouldn't use it just to jump around the program the way you would in a batch file. Its normal use is to jump to a special section when an error occurs.

One way to get input from the user is with the PULL instruction. The PULL instruction takes everything the user enters until pressing Return and stores it in a variable. The following program illustrates that:

```
/* NAME:    REXX-4.CMD */
/* PURPOSE: Demonstration REXX Program */
/* VERSION: 1.00 */
/* DATE:    June 11, 1993 */

SAY "Enter Your First Name"
PULL First
SAY "Enter Your Last Name"
```

```
PULL Last
Say "Hello" First Last
```

The PULL instruction can easily handle more than one variable, so the previous program could be shortened to the following:

```
/* NAME:    REXX-5.CMD */
/* PURPOSE: Demonstration REXX Program */
/* VERSION: 1.00 */
/* DATE:    June 11, 1993 */

SAY "Enter Your Name"
PULL First Last
Say "Hello" First Last
```

Each variable after the PULL instruction is assigned one word of the response. If the number of words exceeds the number of variables, all the extra words are assigned to the last variable. If there aren't enough words for all the variables, the extra variables aren't created.

Logic Testing and Looping

REXX supports logic testing with both IF/THEN and IF/THEN/ELSE statements. The following program illustrates logic testing:

```
/* NAME:    REXX-6.CMD */
/* PURPOSE: Demonstration REXX Program */
/* VERSION: 1.00 */
/* DATE:    June 11, 1993 */

SAY "Enter Two Numbers"
PULL One Two
Total=One+Two
IF Total > 20 THEN SAY "Total Over 20"
    ELSE SAY "Total Less Than Or Equal To 20"
```

This program will prompt the user for two numbers. Once it has the two numbers, it totals them and prints different messages if the total is either over 20 or less than or equal to 20. Note that the program lacks any error checking to force the user to enter numbers. It also doesn't try to check the numbers before attempting to add them.

REXX uses DO WHILE and DO UNTIL to loop until specific conditions are met. They work very similarly, only the DO WHILE loop requires the condition to exist first and the DO UNTIL doesn't. For example, the following program is an arithmetic test that prompts the user for two numbers and then keeps prompting for the sum until the right number is entered:

```
/* NAME:    REXX-7.CMD */
/* PURPOSE: Demonstration REXX Program */
/* VERSION: 1.00 */
/* DATE:    June 11, 1993 */

SAY "Enter Two Numbers"
PULL First Second
Answer=First+Second
Respond=0
```

```
DO UNTIL Respond = Answer
   SAY "What Is" First "+" Second
   PULL Respond
END
```

The DO UNTIL Respond = Answer line could be replaced with a DO WHILE Respond <> Answer line since Respond has a value before the loop begins. There's also a LEAVE instruction that causes REXX to immediately exit a loop. This arithmetic test could be rewritten as follows to give the user an option to "give up:"

```
/* NAME:    REXX-8.CMD */
/* PURPOSE: Demonstration REXX Program */
/* VERSION: 1.00 */
/* DATE:    June 11, 1993 */

SAY "Enter Two Numbers"
PULL First Second
Answer=First+Second
Respond=0
DO UNTIL Respond = Answer
   SAY "What Is" First "+" Second
   PULL Respond
   IF Respond=STOP THEN LEAVE
END
```

Since the PULL instruction converts the response to uppercase, no conversion is needed before performing the IF test on the response variable.

If you need to loop through an instruction or series of instructions a specific number of times, a DO instruction followed by a number does just that, as the following program illustrates:

```
/* NAME:    REXX-9.CMD */
/* PURPOSE: Demonstration REXX Program */
/* VERSION: 1.00 */
/* DATE:    June 11, 1993 */

DO 100
   SAY "Counting To 100"
END
```

If you need to know the line number, then you can modify the DO loop to include a variable to contain the loop number, as this program shows:

```
/* NAME:    REXX-10.CMD */
/* PURPOSE: Demonstration REXX Program */
/* VERSION: 1.00 */
/* DATE:    June 11, 1993 */

DO I - 1 TO 100
   SAY "Counting To 100. On Line" I
END
```

Subroutines

A REXX subroutine is a small section of code designed to be reused. With REXX, the subroutine must be stored as part of the main file. It starts with the subroutine name followed by a colon and ends with a RETURN instruction. The following program illustrates this:

```
/* NAME:     REXX-11.CMD */
/* PURPOSE: Demonstration REXX Program */
/* VERSION: 1.00 */
/* DATE:     June 11, 1993 */

CALL Setup
CALL Problem
EXIT

SETUP:
   SAY "Enter Two Numbers"
   PULL First Second
   Answer=First+Second
   Respond=0
RETURN

PROBLEM:
   DO UNTIL Respond = Answer
      SAY "What Is" First "+" Second
      PULL Respond
   END
RETURN
```

Notice the EXIT instruction before the beginning of the subroutines. Since REXX processes files from beginning to end unless told otherwise, after it finished running the programs it would run the subroutines again without the EXIT.

You can pass parameters to a subroutine by placing the parameters after the subroutine name. Multiple parameters must be separated with commas. The following program illustrates this:

```
/* NAME:     REXX-12.CMD */
/* PURPOSE: Demonstration REXX Program */
/* VERSION: 1.00 */
/* DATE:     June 11, 1993 */

CALL Count 50, "Ronny"
EXIT

COUNT:
   Count = Arg(1)
   Name  = Arg(2)
   SAY "Hello" Name "Counting To" Count
   DO I = 1 To Count
      SAY "Line Number" I "Of" Count
   END
RETURN
```

The Arg function (short for *argument*) is used to transfer the information passed to the subroutine to variables.

Summary

This chapter has presented a very brief introduction to REXX programming. The concepts you've seen in this chapter will be expanded on for the remainder of this book.

Interactive REXX

OS/2 includes two tools for interactive work: REXXTRY.CMD and PMREXX.EXE. REXXTRY.CMD is itself a REXX program that lets you interactively enter REXX instructions. Each command line is executed as soon as it's entered. PMREXX.EXE is a Presentation Manager shell for REXX. This chapter looks at both programs.

REXXTRY.CMD

If you want to learn BASIC under DOS, one way to do that is to enter QBASIC at the command line. That loads the BASIC interrupter into memory and allows you to enter commands interactively. You can enter a command and immediately see its results without having to create a program file and then run the program. While REXX doesn't offer that ability directly, it accomplishes the same thing with the program REXXTRY.CMD.

Enter the command REXXTRY from the command line and you'll see a screen much like the one in Figure 4.1. Here, you enter REXX instructions one at a time. REXXTRY.CMD feeds those instructions to REXX and displays the results, as shown in Figure 4.1. As this figure also shows, variables you create are remembered so you can reference them again. REXXTRY.CMD has a number of special instructions that make it even more useful:

=. Repeats the last instruction.

?. Takes you to the REXX help system. This is the same REXX help system you can access from the desktop.

CALL Show. Shows a list of variables provided by REXXTRY.CMD and their current value.

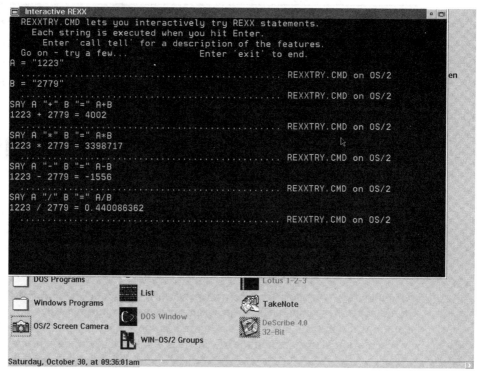

Figure 4.1 REXXTRY.CMD lets you enter REXX commands interactively.

CALL Tell. Shows a REXXTRY.CMD summary screen.

EXIT. Exits the REXXTRY.CMD program.

SAVE='file'. Saves each instruction to the file specified in the instruction. Instructions are appended to the end rather than overwriting the file, so you can turn this on and off at will in order to save particular instructions. Note that this doesn't automatically create a REXX program since REXX programs must have a comment at the top. Of course, comments can be entered into REXXTRY.CMD.

SAVE=". Turns off saving instructions to a file. However, the Save=" instruction is written to the file.

Since REXXTRY.CMD executes each line as you enter it, you might think that you can't enter multiple-line instructions, such as loops. This is true, but there's a way around it. If you wanted to enter the instructions:

```
FOR I = 1 TO 15
   SAY "Loop Number" I
END
```

REXXTRY.CMD would respond with an error message after you entered the first line. That's because REXXTRY.CMD treats each line as though it were independent.

However, you can rewrite this line to take up a single line by separating the clauses with a semicolon:

```
FOR I = 1 TO 15; SAY "Loop Number I"; END
```

and REXXTRY.CMD will happily accept it, as Figure 4.2 shows. REXXTRY.CMD also offers no way to recall prior commands, other than the command that was just executed, which can be replayed with the equal sign or recalled with the up arrow. This can be very frustrating when you have several long instructions you're experimenting with. Luckily, there's a way around this problem too. The REXX instruction INTERPRET executes an instruction stored inside a variable. So the instruction:

```
A = "SAY 'Value Of Var1:' Var1; SAY 'Value Of Var2:' Var2"
```

would store an instruction to express the values of Var1 and Var2 on separate lines to the variable A. After that, the instruction:

```
INTERPRET A
```

would evaluate the contents of variable A and execute that instruction. This gives you a way to save and recall frequently used instructions in REXXTRY.CMD. Figure 4.3

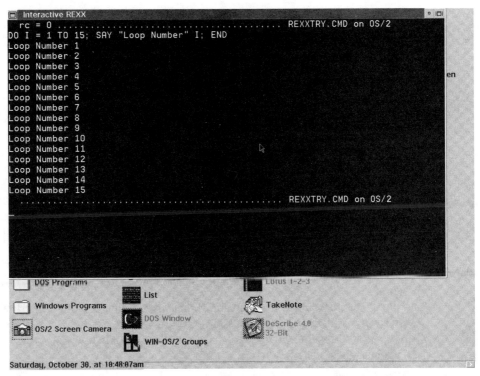

Figure 4.2 REXXTRY.CMD lets you enter loops and other items requiring multiple lines at one time, as long as all the items are entered on one line and are separated by semicolons.

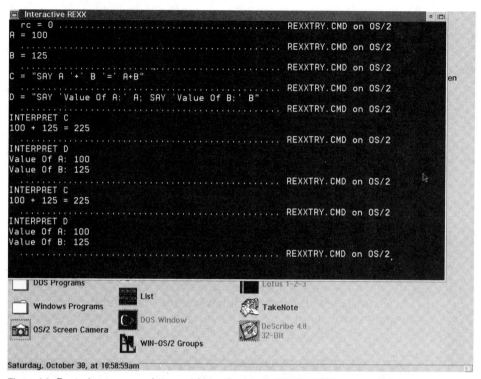

Figure 4.3 By storing a command to a variable and using the INTERPRET command, you can reuse commands in REXXTRY.CMD.

shows an example of this in action. Notice how easily the last two instructions are repeated.

Look back at the instructions stored inside variable A. Notice the use of double quotation marks around the entire instruction and the single quotation marks at all the points where REXX expects quotation marks. (Of course, the use of single and double quotation marks could be reversed.) In this case the quotation marks around the entire instruction are required; otherwise, the semicolon in the middle would be treated as the end of the assignment instruction. While quotation marks around the entire instruction never hurt, they aren't always required.

At first, you might also think you could save complex instructions to a file by using the instruction:

```
SAVE = "File"
```

to direct the instructions to a file and then later call that program file. However, that won't work. External subroutines have access to only the variables passed to them on the instruction line, so the external subroutine wouldn't be able to access the data to execute most instructions.

PMREXX.EXE

PMREXX.EXE is a windowed Presentation Manager application. It lets you view the output of your REXX programs. PMREXX.EXE adds a scrollable output window to your REXX programs that stores all the output during a session. Output text can easily be selected and copied (or cut) into the paste buffer for use in other applications. There's also a window for entering input if the REXX program requests any. This is shown in Figure 4.4.

To run PMREXX.EXE, enter its name on the command line followed by the name of the REXX program to run. If you want to turn tracing on, add a /T before the name of the REXX program to run. If the REXX program requires any parameters on the command line, enter them after the program name.

PMREXX.EXE is such a nice environment that I reconfigured my desktop to always run REXXTRY.CMD inside PMREXX.EXE. A major advantage of running REXXTRY.CMD inside PMREXX.EXE is that it makes reusing instructions extremely easy. Just scroll back to the point where the instruction was last used, use the mouse cursor to highlight it, and select Copy from focus window from the Edit menu. That places the instruction in the paste buffer. Then click on the input menu and select

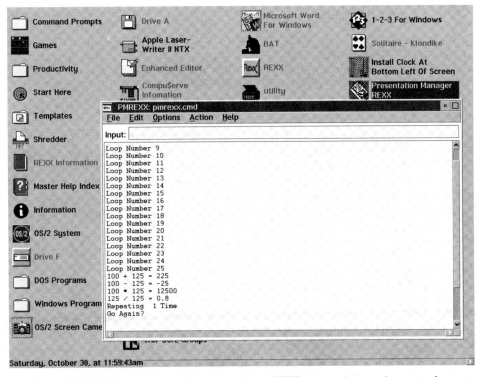

Figure 4.4 PMREXX.EXE lets you see the output of your REXX program in an environment where you can scroll back and see all the prior output.

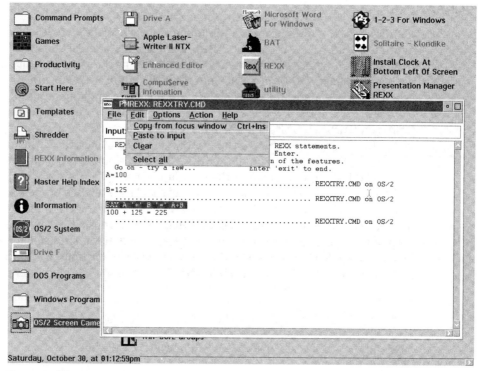

Figure 4.5 When running REXXTRY.CMD inside PMREXX.EXE, it's easy to reuse old commands by cutting them out of the output window and pasting them into the input window. After pasting them, you can edit them before reusing them.

Paste to input from the Edit menu, which will place a copy of the instruction in the input window. You can press Return to use it as is or edit it first if you need to make changes to it. All this is shown in Figure 4.5.

You'll really see the power of PMREXX.EXE when you have to debug a REXX program. With an errant program loaded into PMREXX.EXE, you can scroll around the output until you think you see the problem. By entering REXX instructions, as allowed in trace mode, you can display the contents of variables and examine what your program is doing. The ability to cut out old instructions and reuse them is particularly handy while debugging a program. All this is shown in Figure 4.6. The one drawback to debugging in PMREXX.EXE is there's no way to alter a program and have those changes immediately take effect in PMREXX.EXE. To have changes to your program take effect, you must close PMREXX.EXE and restart it, loading the modified program, since PMREXX.EXE lacks a way to load a new program while running.

PMREXX.EXE creates a Presentation Manager environment. None of the keyboard, cursor, and screen RexxUtil functions will work since the session doesn't have a keyboard or screen attached to it. That means that programs using functions like SysGetKey won't run properly under PMREXX.EXE.

Summary

The REXXTRY.CMD program lets you interactively enter REXX instructions one at a time and observe the results. By saving complex instructions to a variable, you can later reuse them as many times as required using the INTERPRET instruction.

PMREXX.EXE gives you a Presentation Manager shell for running REXX programs, where output is directed to a scrollable window and input is entered in a second window. This shell is an excellent way to run REXXTRY.CMD and any REXX program in debugging mode.

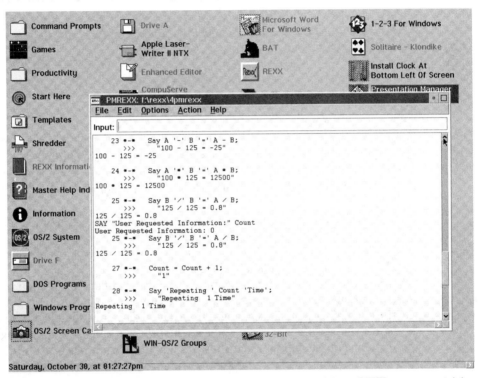

Figure 4.6 The real power of PMREXX.EXE shows through when you debug a REXX program containing an error.

5

Introduction to Variables

Forget about computers for a moment and think about using a mailbox at the post office. The first thing you have to do is go to the post office and tell them you want to rent a mailbox. Once you've rented your mailbox, the post office will store your mail in the box. Of course, the mail must have the proper address on it to make it to your box.

Once you have your mailbox, picking up your mail is easy. Instead of going to the post office and asking for your mail, you just ask for the contents of, say, box 57 to automatically get your mail. If you quit using the mailbox but let your friend use it, if he asks for the contents of box 57, he'll get his mail.

Variables are the computer programming equivalent of mailboxes. You use them to store data that's likely to change from run to run or even within the same run, just like the contents of a mailbox changes from day to day. For example, you might write a program that asks the user her name so the program can use it in messages. Since the name might change for each run, you need to have a place to store the name each time the program is run and a way to refer to the name once it's in storage. Variables do just that.

Creating Variables

Many languages require you to declare a variable before you can use it. REXX isn't like that. To create a new variable, all you have to do is assign a value to a new variable name.

Assigning Values to Variables

The basic method of assigning a value to a variable is with the instruction:

variable = value

where *variable* is the name of the variable to create and *value* is the value to assign to it. The value can be a number, a character string, an equation, or a function. For example, all of the following assignments would be valid:

```
Var1 = 123
Var2 = "This Is A String Variable"
Var3 = MAX(1, -99, 48, 72.5)
Var4 = (1+2+3)/6
```

Once the information is stored in the variable, it's available for the rest of the time the program is running. However, once the program terminates, the contents of the variable is lost. Given that, you might wonder why it wouldn't be a good idea to just "hardwire" the value into the program. Hardwiring means using the actual value rather than a variable. For example, you might create an error message with the instruction:

```
ErrorMessage = "You Pressed An Invalid Key"
```

and later display that error message with the instruction:

```
SAY ErrorMessage
```

However, the instruction:

```
SAY "You Pressed An Invalid Key"
```

works equally as well and doesn't require the creation of a variable. While this sounds easier at first, there are a number of advantages of using variables:

- If the user is going to provide the data while the program's running then there's no way to hardwire it into the program, so you must use a variable.
- If the program is going to read data from the computer while the program's running (for example, the time) then there's no way to hardwire the value into the program, so you must use a variable.
- If the program is going to read the data from a disk file then there's no way to hardwire the values into the program, so you must use a variable.
- Certain instructions, like a DO loop, require the creation of a loop-counter variable.
- When manipulating data with equations and functions, the resulting code can be much simpler and easier to visualize if you use variables when the data is lengthy.
- If the same message is going to be displayed more than once, storing it in a variable means the program has only one copy of that message. That saves storage space and allows you to update the message in one central location.

A string inside quotation marks is treated as a constant by REXX and isn't modified by the code unless you issue an instruction specifically to modify the contents. For example, the instructions:

```
SAY This is a label
```

```
SAY "This is a label"
```

will both display the phrase This is a label. However, since the first instruction doesn't have the phrase inside quotation marks, REXX will convert it to all upper-case before displaying it. The second phrase is inside quotation marks, so REXX will display the phrase exactly as typed. Strings must be defined on a single physical line. For example:

```
Message = "This Is A Label"
```

would be valid since the entire definition is on a single physical line. The instruction:

```
Message = "This Is,
A Label"
```

wouldn't be valid. While the comma is a valid line-continuation character, strings must be defined on a single line. You couldn't make this two-line assignment valid by adding extra quotation marks:

```
Message = "This Is",
"A Label"
```

since this still spreads the assignment over two lines. Any string with no characters is called a *null string*. Such a string is of zero length.

Assigning hexadecimal values to variables

Hexadecimal, or hex for short, is a method of counting in base 16, where the letters A–F are used to represent the extra digits. So the digits 0–33 would be 0, 1, 2, 3, 4, 5, 6, 7, 8, 9, A, B, C, D, E, F, 10, 11, 12, 13, 14, 15, 16, 17, 18, 19, 1A, 1B, 1C, 1D, 1E, 1F, 20, 21. Characters can have an ASCII value of 0 to 255, so they have a hex value of 0 to FF. The characters in *Ronny* have ASCII values of 82, 111, 110, 110, and 121 respectively. These numbers have hex values of 52, 6F, 6E, 6E, and 79 respectively.

REXX allows you to create variables by specifying hex values in the place of the characters. When variables are specified in this fashion, the closing quotation mark for the string must be immediately followed by the letter *x*, in either case, to tell REXX the variable is in hexadecimal. So the instructions:

```
Variable = "Ronny"
Variable = '52 6F 6E 6E 79"x
```

are identical and both create a variable containing the value Ronny. That is, the use of hexadecimal numbers controls only the form the data takes before being stored under the variable name, not the form it takes in storage. This is shown in Figure 5.1.

The space between the hex characters was added for readability and isn't required, as you can also see in Figure 5.1. When spaces are used, they must be used between the characters and aren't allowed at the beginning or end of the string. The

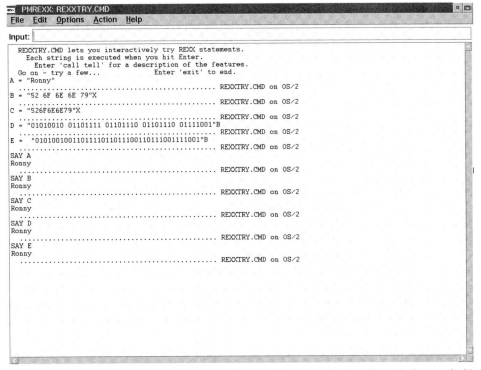

Figure 5.1 No matter if a variable is created using the actual characters, the hexadecimal values, or the binary values, the contents of that variable are the same.

capitalization of the letters used as part of the hex numbers is also not important. It can be all uppercase, all lowercase, or mixed.

Note that all hex characters, except the little-used first 16 characters 0–F, contain two digits. If a series of hex characters contains an odd number of characters, then REXX adds a zero to the left position in the string. As a general rule, you're much better off always specifying hex values with two digits even when they aren't required. For example, the string containing two characters each with the ASCII value of 15 can be written as FF in hex. Since this is a valid two-digit hex number (ASCII 255), REXX would create a variable containing that single character. To store the original, you would have to use 0F0F.

Assigning binary values to variables

Binary is a method of counting in base 2. Since binary has only two digits, only 0 and 1 are used. To count from 0 to 16 in binary, you would have 0, 01, 10, 11, 100, 101, 110, 111, 1000, 1001, 1010, 1011, 1100, 1101, 1110, 1111, and 10000. Characters can have an ASCII value of 0 to 255, so they have a binary value of 0 to 11111111. The characters in *Ronny* have ASCII values of 82, 111, 110, 110, and 121 respectively. These numbers have binary values of 01010010, 01101111, 01101110, 01101110, and 01111001 respectively.

REXX allows you to create string variables by specifying binary values in the place of the characters. When variables are specified in this fashion, the closing quotation mark for the string must be immediately followed by the letter *b* to tell REXX the variable is in binary, So the instructions:

```
Variable = "Ronny"
Variable = "01010010 01101111 01101110 01101110 01111001"b
```

are identical and both create a variable containing the value RONNY. That is, the use of binary numbers controls only the form the data takes before being stored under the variable name, not the form it takes in storage. You can see this in Figure 5.1.

The space between the binary characters was added for readability and isn't required. When spaces are used, they must be used between the characters and aren't allowed at the beginning or end of the string. They're also allowed in the middle of a character to split the eight characters into two groups of four characters. This grouping in fours is a carryover from other systems. Four binary digits are easily converted to a hexadecimal digit, so the custom of grouping them into fours continues.

REXX allows a shortcut in entering binary numbers that causes a lot of confusion and saves only a small amount of time. When the first, and only the first, binary character begins with four zeros, you can drop them. For example, both of the following instructions will display the heart-shaped symbol on the screen:

```
SAY "00000011"b
SAY "0011"b
```

While not documented in the REXX manual, you can also drop all the leading zeros off the first character and enter this instruction as:

```
SAY "11"b
```

There is, however, a problem with this shortcut. If you try to print two of these heart-shaped symbols using the instruction:

```
SAY "00110011"b
```

you'll get the number three instead. Try making it:

```
SAY "0011 0011"b
```

and you'll still get the number three. To print two heart-shaped symbols, you must use either of these instructions:

```
SAY "00000011 00000011"b
SAY "0011 00000011"b
```

Figure 5.2 shows this. The moral is that it's easier just to skip the "shortcut" of shortening the first character to four digits when it starts with four zeros and enter all binary characters using the full eight digits.

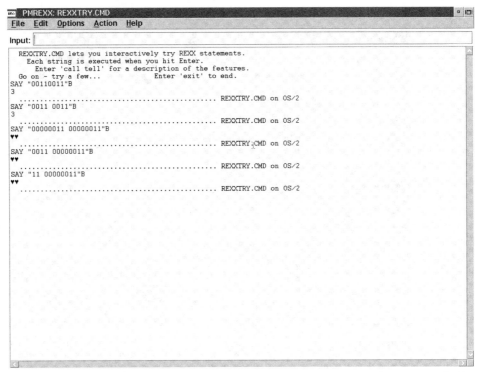

Figure 5.2 You must be careful when entering binary numbers if you plan on using less than all eight digits for the first character.

Getting Information from the Command Line

In batch files, the most common way of providing the batch file with information is entering it on the command line. While it's less common with REXX programs due to their ability to ask the user for information, it's still an important way of getting data into a variable. After all, if a program is always going to ask you for your name when it starts running, isn't it much easier to enter that on the command line when you start the program than it is to wait for the program to ask you?

Of course, if you're starting a REXX program from the desktop you aren't using a command line, so you do not have the opportunity to enter information on a command line. However, you can tell OS/2 to ask you for the information and feed it to the REXX program as though it were entered on the command line. You can do this from the Program page of the Settings dialog box. On this Program page, enter the path to the REXX program and its name. You can also enter parameters to pass to the program.

If the parameters will be the same each time, just enter them in the Parameters box on the Settings page. If the parameters will be different each time, you need OS/2 to prompt you for them. To do this, enter square brackets in the Parameter box with a message inside them (see Figure 5.3). After this, each time you start this program OS/2 will pop up a dialog box displaying the message you selected requesting the command line parameters (see Figure 5.4).

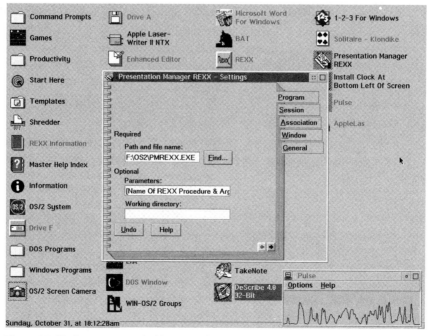

Figure 5.3 Placing a message inside square brackets in the Parameters box of the Program page of the Settings notebook causes OS/2 to prompt you for command-line parameters before running the program.

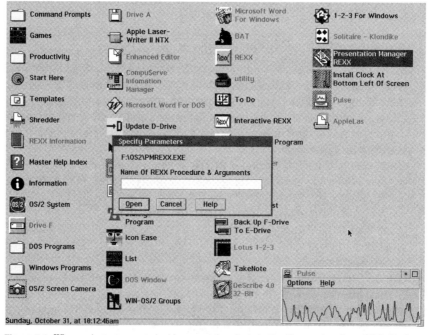

Figure 5.4 When using a message inside square brackets in the Parameters box, OS/2 displays a dialog box asking you to specify the parameters with which to run the program.

Just entering the data on the command line, however, is not enough. You need a way to get the data off the command line and into REXX. The ARG function, short for argument, is used to bring the argument string, or information about it, into the REXX program. The syntax is:

```
ARG([n][,E¦O])
```

where n is the number of the argument to check, and E¦O is an instruction. E is short for exists and checks to see if the specified argument exists. O is short for omitted and checks to see if the specified argument was omitted.

The function ARG( ) returns the number of arguments entered, and the function ARG(1) returns the first argument. Of course, ARG(2) returns the second argument, ARG(3) the third, and so on. If the argument requested doesn't exist, the null string is returned.

REXX handles arguments differently depending on how you enter them, and you need to be aware of this. When the arguments are coming from the command line, REXX treats everything as one argument. There's a program called ARG.CMD on the disk to let you experiment with arguments and if you start it with the instruction:

```
ARG One, Two, "Three" Four
```

ARG will treat everything after the program name as a single argument. The ARG ( ) function will return 1 and the ARG(1) function will return One, Two, "Three" Four.

However, when used in a subroutine, the ARG function treats the comma as a divider between arguments. If you were to call ARG.CMD from another program using the same command as above, One, Two and "Three" Four would each be treated as a separate argument. The "Three" and Four aren't treated as separate arguments because they aren't separated by a comma. The program CALLARG.CMD on the disk that comes with this book does just this. Remember when running CALLARG.CMD that ARG.CMD must be in the current subdirectory or in your path. Figure 5.5 shows running ARG.CMD from the command line and calling it using the CALLARG.CMD program.

To help clarify the ARG function, several examples follow. Assuming a REXX program, called EXAMPLE.CMD, was started with command line:

```
EXAMPLE One, Two, "Three"
```

then these functions would return the following values:

ARG( )	1
ARG(1)	One, Two, "Three"
ARG(2)	" " or a null string
ARG(1,"E")	1
ARG(1,"o")	0

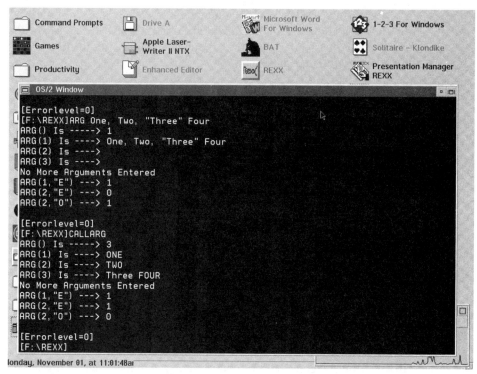

Figure 5.5 ARG.CMD returns different arguments when passed exactly the same parameters, depending if it's run from the command line or called by another program, CALLARG.CMD in this example.

If a subroutine called EXAMPLE was called with the same command, then these functions would return the following values:

ARG( )	3
ARG(1)	One
ARG(2)	Two
ARG(1,"E")	1
ARG(1,"o")	0

Note that the number returned by ARG( ) is the largest number n, so `Arg(n,"e")` would return a value of one. Additionally, when used inside of a program—as opposed to inside a subroutine—ARG( ) can return only a zero or one, unless that program is called by another program.

Taking Information from Another Variable

To set one variable equal to the contents of another, the syntax is:

```
Var1 = Var2
```

This completely replaces the contents of Var1 with the contents of Var2. At this point, both Var1 and Var2 contain the same information.

With a lot of languages, you must be careful that Var1 and Var2 are the same type of variable. If Var1 contains string data and Var2 contains numeric data, many languages would generate an error message if you tried to set Var1 equal to Var2. REXX doesn't have this limitation, as shown in Figure 5.6.

Asking the User for Data

Asking the user for data is probably the most common way of getting data into a variable. For example, the disk that comes with this book contains a "to-do" program called TODO.CMD. The REXX code for TODO.CMD is explained in detail in appendix A. When you start TODO.CMD, it reads your existing to-do list from the disk file. The program then simply waits for you to tell it what to do. You can scroll forwards and backwards, add new items, edit existing items, erase existing items you no longer want to accomplish, mark existing items as done, or print or save the data file. Once you select your course of action, the program will store your selection in a variable to test on it to figure out what you want to do.

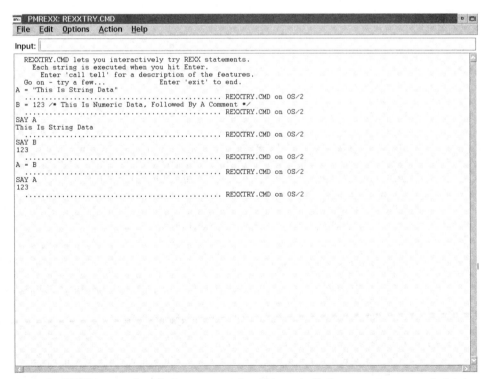

Figure 5.6 REXX is very relaxed in its treatment of variables and will allow you to store numeric data in a variable that originally contained string data. In fact, REXX places no restrictions at all on how data is exchanged between variables.

If you decide to enter new items, the program will prompt you for priorities and descriptions until you tell it you're finished entering new items. Each entry is stored in two variables, one for the priority and another for the text. If you decide to erase items or mark them as finished, the variables containing those items will be deleted. The only difference is that done items are written to a data file first along with the date and time before the variable is deleted, while the variables containing erased items are just deleted.

There are two basic ways to ask the user for data, and TODO.CMD uses them both. Use the first, and most common method, when you want the user to enter more than one character. This is the method used by TODO.CMD to get the descriptions of the to-do items. Use the second method when you want the user to enter a single character without having to press Return after that character. TODO.CMD uses this when it asks the user to select a menu option and when it enters priorities of the to-do items. It's also typically used when the user has to answer a yes or no question. I'll explain both methods in a moment.

REXX was designed as a mainframe language well before graphical user interfaces were developed, and it's still in use on mainframes and minicomputers. As such, REXX is orientated towards streams of characters as input from the user and output to the user. These streams of characters may be accessed either character by character or line by line.

Of course, it's limiting to discuss the user only as the input and output device. REXX also receives input from files and serial input devices and it sends outputs to printers, the display, serial devices, and networks. However, much of the interaction of the computer with these devices is very similar to that between the computer and the user.

A character input stream is either a serial character stream coming from the user or one that has the characteristics of a stream coming from the user. For example, data being read from a disk file doesn't come directly from the user, but it has the same characteristics as if it were coming from the user. Some streams, like disk files, are static and don't have characters added to them, at least until you save more data. Other streams, like data entered by the user, has characters added to the end of the stream. The CharIn function reads input character strings character by character, while the LineIn function reads them line by line. The PULL and PARSE PULL instructions read the default character string line by line.

Getting multiple characters from the user

The PARSE instruction is the main method of getting a multiple-character response from the user. The syntax is:

```
PARSE [Upper] [instruction] [template]
```

where Upper is an optional instruction to convert the input to all uppercase. Without this instruction, no case translation will take place. And *instruction* can be one of several subinstructions:

Arg. An instruction to parse the arguments passed to the program, subroutine, or function according to the rules of the Arg function.

LineIn. An instruction to read the next line and parse it. Note that this is a shorter version of the instruction:

```
PARSE VALUE LINEIN() WITH [template]
```

The LineIn instruction is generally used only when direct access to the character input stream is necessary. The PULL or PARSE PULL instructions are generally used for interactions with the user.

PULL. An instruction to pull the next string from the input queue and parse it. This is generally the method used to get data from the user.

SOURCE. An instruction to obtain a string representation of the source of the programming being executed. This string won't change while the program is executing.

VALUE [*expression*] WITH. An instruction to evaluate the expression given and parse the results.

VAR *variable*. An instruction to parse the variable.

VERSION. An instruction to return information about the language. Under OS/2 2.1, it returns REXXSAA 4.00 08 Jul 1992.

Template is a list of symbols separated by blanks and/or patterns.

Chapter 12 contains more information about the PARSE instruction. For now, all you should be concerned with is its ability to get information from the user and store it in a variable. The PULL instruction is a shortcut version of the PARSE UPPER PULL instruction. Its syntax is:

```
PULL [template]
```

where *template* is a list of symbols separated by blanks or patterns. Characters obtained using the PULL instruction by itself are always converted to uppercase. Chapter 12 contains more information about the PULL instruction.

The instruction TODO.CMD uses to get a new to-do description from the user is:

```
PARSE PULL Todo.Count
```

where Todo.Count is the name of the variable that contain the data the user enters. TODO.CMD uses the LineIn function to read to-do items from the disk file when it starts. The instruction to do that is:

```
Todo.Count = LineIn(InFile)
```

where Todo.Count is the name of the variable that stores the description and InFile is the name of the file containing the to-do descriptions. The program contains a loop that reads each description into a separate variable.

Getting a single character from the user

There are a number of occasions when you'll want the user to enter a single letter. The most common occasion is in response to a question like "Do you really want to do this (Y/N)?" Single-character responses are also very useful for selecting items from a list or menu. When you know ahead of time that a single character is all that's required, then there's no point in forcing the user to press Return after entering that character.

The SysGetKey function avoids having the user press Return. It accepts a single character from the user. The syntax is:

```
key = SysGetKey([option])
```

where *key* is the variable to contain the keystroke and *option* is either Echo, to display the keystroke to the screen (the default), or NoEcho, to skip displaying the character to the screen. The instruction used by TODO.CMD for the user to select a menu option is:

```
character = SysGetKey(NoEcho)
```

This instruction performs a series of logic tests on the value in *character* to figure out what the user selected.

Performing a Mathematical Calculation

Another way to get data into a variable is to perform a mathematical calculation and store the results in a variable. This is covered in chapter 9.

Performing a String Manipulation

Another way to get data into a variable is to perform string manipulation and store the results in a variable. This is covered in chapter 8.

Variable Arrays

Let's go back to the mailbox example for a moment. I teach at a small liberal arts college with about 45 faculty members. Our mailboxes have our names on them and they're in alphabetical order. As new faculty members are hired and existing faculty members leave, the boxes are rearranged to maintain the alphabetical order. That works in a small setting. This is how we've worked with variables so far. Each variable has a name that your program uses to access the contents of that variable. However, imagine the confusion that would result if a large post office in New York City tried to handle their mailboxes in this fashion!

Instead, they arrange their mailboxes in a two-dimensional array and assign each mailbox a number. When John Smith rents a new mailbox, they don't have to rearrange all the mailboxes to keep them in alphabetical order and they don't have to worry about duplicate names; they just assign him an empty mailbox and reference it by its number. Since the names don't have to be in any order, John Smith might end up with mailbox number 10135 and John Adams might have mailbox number 10134 right beside him.

So far, the data handling you've looked at has dealt with small amounts of data, and using a name for each variable has worked well. Now you need to see how to deal with larger amounts of data, data so massive that a name for each variable no longer works. For example, TODO.CMD allows you to enter as many to-do items as will fit in memory. The programming logic required to keep them straight would be massive if each item had its own name. Fortunately, programmers developed arrays to deal with this problem in much the same fashion as the post office deals with large numbers of mailboxes.

In a typical programming language, the first thing you do is declare the array (which is like a table). This both creates the variable and tells the language how many rows and columns it contains. (Arrays can contain just one column, effectively making them a one-dimensional array.) Once created, the size of this array variable is typically static. For the purposes of this example, let's assume a 4×4 array, VAR. Typically, you address the individual cells in this variable by giving the row and column address, so the instruction:

```
VAR(2,3) = 123
```

would store the value of 123 into the cell on the second row and third column. Note that languages vary and some list the column number first. Also, some languages begin numbering the rows and columns at zero rather than one.

In REXX, array variables are called either *stem variables* or *compound variables*. Using this notation, variables without a period are called *simple variables*. Stem variables are more powerful than most versions of array variables. As you might expect, stem variables don't have to be declared first; you simply begin using them as you would any other REXX variable. Since you don't declare the variable first, its size isn't static. That is, the variable can grow to contain as many cells as memory permits. REXX stem variables have other advantages over array variables, but first I need to explain the syntax of how to use them.

The parts of a stem variable are separated by a period, which is the only valid use of a period in a variable name. The part of the variable name before the period is a "standard" variable name, called the *stem*, and must follow all the normal rules for naming variables. A stem variable is divided into two or more segments by one or more periods. Daney calls these segments *nodes* and I'll continue to use that notation, so the stem of the stem variable is the first node.

The name for everything after the stem is the *tail*. The names for these remaining nodes of a stem variable don't have to follow standard variable naming rules. They can be numbers, names, or the names of variables. When these nodes are variable names, the value of the variable used for a node name is first evaluated, as illustrated in Figure 5.7. For more examples, see TODO.CMD and PC-1.CMD on the disk that comes with this book.

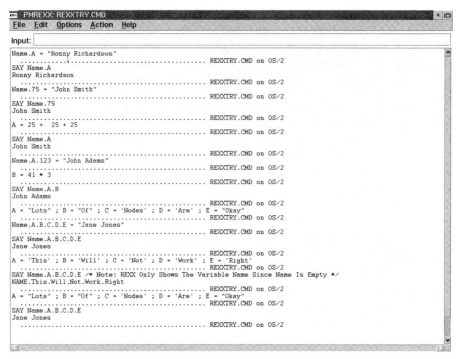

Figure 5.7 Stem variables allow for a lot of naming flexibility.

REXX allows very complex names for stem variables. For example, Data.Firm. Ratio.Quick.1993.Q1 would be a valid name for a variable containing data on several firms where the data includes accounting data by quarter for several years and where part of the accounting data is financial ratios.

You can think of the data variable as having five dimensions. The first dimension breaks it down into different firms. For each firm, the second dimension breaks the data down into different financial data, perhaps including sales, size, and ratio data. Since there are different measures of sales, size, and ratios, the next dimension breaks these down into categories. The sales value might have dimensions for cash, credit, and total. The size value might have dimensions for total asset size and number of employees, and the ratio value might have dimensions for each of over a dozen ratios. After that, it has dimensions for several years and four quarters per year.

If you think of Data.Firm.Ratio.Quick.1993.Q1 as an array, then it takes five dimensions (Data is its name and so not a dimension) to store all the data. Of course, no one knows how to construct a five-dimensional matrix. REXX first evaluates the tail of the variable and then internally treats the variable as Data.Tail. REXX then searches for the Data variable (the stem), then under the stem it searches for the tail. If it finds the Stem.Tail combination, it returns the value; otherwise, REXX treats it like any other variable without a value.

The program SPELLING.CMD on the disk that comes with this book stores the spelling word in a series of stem variables: Spelling.1, Spelling.2, and so on. If your program is going to loop through these, you need a variable to store the number of values the variable has to use as the stopping point for the loop. By convention, REXX programmers use the .0 version of the variable for this. So Spelling.0 stores the number of stem variables used in the program.

REXX stem variables have important advantages over traditional array variables. First, as mentioned previously, REXX doesn't require you to declare the size of the array before you use it. That means the array can grow to be as large as you need it, as long as you don't run out of memory.

Second, REXX doesn't require you to allocate memory for every possible cell. For example, assume you want to store the annual population of America from 1901 to 1994 in an array variable. This would require 94 cells. Further, assume you haven't been able to find the data for 1920–1930. In languages like BASIC, you would still have to create a 94 cell array to have space for all the data, and those cells would take up memory even if they had no data in them. In REXX, you can store values for Pop.1901 to Pop.1919 and Pop.1931 to Pop.1994 without creating and using space for Pop.1920 to Pop.1930 until that data becomes available.

Third, REXX allows the tail to be a meaningful value. In the last example, in a language like BASIC, you would probably have something like POP(01) to POP(94) and have to translate 94 into 1994. If you had data on both America and Canada, you'd have to have variables like POP(1,01) to POP(2,94), while in REXX you'd have variables like Pop.Canada.1901 to Pop.USA.1994. This makes keeping the program straight much easier. It also makes the programs themselves much shorter and easier to write and debug since you don't have the program to translate 01 to 1901 or POP(1,01) to Canada and POP(2,01) to the USA.

Summary

Variables are the computerized version of mailboxes, a place to store and retrieve information. You've seen how to create variables, name them, store data to a variable, and retrieve data once it's stored in a variable.

REXX programs can get information from the command line and use that information inside the program using the Arg function. That way, the program can behave differently depending on the information supplied to it by the user when it's started. Since many REXX programs are started from the desktop and not the command line, you can have OS/2 prompt you for information when you start a program and feed it to the program as though you had entered that information on the command line.

REXX treats arguments differently depending on whether they come from the command line or from another REXX program. When they come from the command line, everything is treated as one argument. When they come from another REXX program, each comma starts a new argument.

The most common way for a program to get data is to ask the user for data. There are two methods to do that: the SysGetKey, when you want only one character, and the PARSE and PULL instructions, when you want more data. Other devices, such as disk files, can be treated as though the data were coming from the user.

Stem variables share a common name yet store multiple pieces on numbers. You can name these variables and use them in programs.

6

Communicating with the User

Almost every program needs to communicate with the user. Some possible uses of that communication are:

- Ask the user for information.
- Ask the user what to do.
- Display information for the user.
- Warn the user of some unusual condition.
- Display an error message.
- Display help.

REXX offers a wealth of ways to communicate with the user.

Basic Communication

The standard way for a REXX program to communicate with the user is through a series of SAY instructions, like this:

```
SAY "This Is A Sample REXX Program"
SAY "It Displays A Series Of Text Lines On The Screen"
SAY "It Does Nothing Else"
```

Each SAY instruction displays the text that follows the instruction. If the text is inside quotation marks, it is displayed as written. If it's just text and isn't inside quotation marks, it's converted to uppercase before it's displayed. If it's a variable name and isn't inside quotation marks, its name is replaced by the contents of the variable and those contents are displayed. After displaying the text, the SAY instruction moves the cursor to the left of the next line. Once the text reaches the end of the screen, everything scrolls up one line and the text at the top of the screen scrolls off the top. You can see this by running the SHOWSAY.CMD program that comes with this book. You can also see the SAY instruction in action in Figure 6.1

In a batch file, you have to use all sorts of tricks to print a blank line because, if you issue an ECHO command by itself, OS/2 will think you're asking for the status of command echoing and display either an ECHO is off or ECHO is on message. The SAY instruction doesn't have this limitation, so issuing the instruction by itself will display a blank line.

Advanced Communication

The REXX SAY instruction isn't very powerful. In fact, it's a lot like the ECHO command in batch files. It displays text and not much more. However, REXX has some external functions that can really improve your communications with the user.

Positioning the cursor

One drawback to the SAY instruction is that it simply displays text on the next available line. If the program is just displaying information, that's fine. SHOWSAY.CMD works fine because it doesn't have to position the cursor. However, many programs

Figure 6.1 The SAY command displays information on the screen. That information can be text, the contents of variables, or the results of calculations.

need that ability. Error messages are much more visible in the middle of the screen. Complex screens are much easier to draw when you can move the cursor around and place different information in different spots.

REXX itself lacks the ability to position the cursor. However, the external function SysCurPos can both position the cursor and report on its position. The syntax is:

```
CALL SysCurPos row, column
```

where *row* and *column* are the screen coordinates to position the cursor at. A full-screen OS/2 session has 24 rows numbered 0–23 and 80 columns numbered 0–79. POSITION.CMD shows this in detail. The normal use of SysCurPos is to position the cursor on the screen prior to displaying a message with the SAY instruction. For example:

```
CALL SysCurPos 12,25
SAY "The File You Requested Does Not Exist!"
```

However, this doesn't have to be the case. Since SysCurPos simply positions the cursor, any OS/2 program that displays text on the screen will begin displaying text at that cursor position, so SysCurPos can be used to reposition the cursor before running an OS/2 utility or any other program where you want the text to go to a specific location.

If you're running a REXX program in a window, that window represents a virtual window on a full screen. A call to SysCurPos with a row number near 23 can position the cursor below the point that's being displayed in the virtual window, while a call to SysCurPos with a column number near 79 can position the cursor to the right of the point that's being displayed in the virtual window.

SysCurPos can also query the cursor to find out its current position. The code to do that is:

```
PARSE VALUE SysCurPos() WITH row column
SAY "Cursor Position Is" Row ||", " column
```

Of course, these values can be saved and used later if you need to return the cursor to a specific location on the screen. The program INTERACT.CMD makes extensive use of the SysCurPos function to move the cursor around the display of the variable that's currently being edited. INTERACT.CMD is explained in detail in appendix A.

Pausing a program

In a batch file, you use the PAUSE command to stop the batch file until the user presses a key. That gives the user time to read the screen or think about a decision. While REXX doesn't have a pause command, it does have everything you need in order to implement one. As discussed in chapter 5, the SysGetKey accepts a single keystroke from the user without the user having to press Return. Thus, a PAUSE command can be simulated with the two instructions:

```
SAY "Press Any Key To Continue..."
Character = SysGetKey(NoEcho)
```

Of course, you must load SysGetKey before you can use it. Using a PAUSE command in your programs can be even easier. The disk that comes with this book includes PAUSE.CMD. This is a program that uses the previous instructions to function as a PAUSE command. To use it, just add the instruction:

```
CALL PAUSE
```

to any program where you want to use a PAUSE command. Of course, PAUSE.CMD must either be in the current subdirectory or in your path. If you want PAUSE.CMD to clear the screen once the user presses a key, then call it with the instruction:

```
CALL PAUSE CLS
```

and it will clear the screen after the user presses a key. This is useful when your program is displaying several screens of information for the user to read.

One problem with pausing the program with the SysGetKey function is that the program waits forever for the user to press a key. If you would prefer for the program to resume execution after a period of time even if the user hasn't pressed a key, then SysGetKey isn't the best option. REXX lacks a function that returns control to the program when the user presses a key, like SysGetKey, and waits only a limited time for the user. The closest available function is the SysSleep function. This pauses the program for the specified number of seconds and then returns control to the program. It will continue to pause even if the user presses a key. The syntax is:

```
CALL SysSleep seconds
```

where *seconds* is the number of seconds to wait. The seconds must be specified in whole numbers. The program SLEEP.CMD that comes with this book automates the process. Just issue the instruction:

```
CALL SLEEP seconds
```

where *seconds* is the number of seconds to wait, and it will pause the program for you. SLEEP.CMD checks to make sure a number is entered.

Clearing the screen

When you're communicating with the user, you frequently need to clear the screen after displaying information so you can display more information. Many times, this takes place after you've paused the execution of the program for the user to read the first screen of information. If you use PAUSE.CMD, you can have it clear the screen, as discussed previously. Otherwise, the SysCls external function will clear the screen for you. The syntax is:

```
CALL SysCls
```

Nonvisual Communication

All of the communication I've talked about so far is visual communication. You now know how to put text on the screen at any location, pause the program, and clear the screen. However, visual communication isn't always enough. When visuals alone aren't enough to call attention to the program, then the next step is to beep the speaker. That is particularly important in a REXX program. If the program is running in the background, the user might not see your error messages, but the speaker will sound even when the REXX program isn't visible. With a batch file, you can do that with ECHO ^G. That also works with the SAY instruction as long as the ^Gs are inside quotation marks. Each ^G beeps the speaker once.

REXX also has a function, naturally called Beep, to sound the speaker. The syntax is:

```
CALL Beep frequency, duration
```

where *frequency* is the frequency to sound the bell at in hertz and *duration* is the length, in milliseconds, to sound the speaker. I've found that 1000, 500 works very well for drawing attention to error messages. You can also use the Beep function for entertainment, as BEEPS.CMD illustrates.

Summary

The basic way a REXX program communicates with the user is by displaying text on the screen. The REXX instruction to do this is the SAY instruction. The SAY instruction can display text, numbers, or the contents of variables.

The external REXX function SysCurPos allows you to position the cursor at a specific location on the screen. SysCurPos can also query the cursor's current position and return that data to the program. The SysGetKey external function and PAUSE.CMD utility program give you two ways to pause the execution of a REXX program until the user presses a key. The SysSleep external function allows you to stop program execution for a specified number of seconds. The SysCls external function clears the screen and the Beep function sounds the speaker.

Including Non-REXX Commands

A batch file is nothing more than a series of commands for OS/2 held together with a few specialized batch subcommands. It's less the ease of learning to write batch files that makes them so popular than how easy it is to issue OS/2 commands via a batch file. As you'll see, it's just as easy to issue these commands via a REXX program. Additionally, a REXX program can be much more powerful than a batch file. Batch subcommands include the following:

CALL. This lets one batch file run another and regain control when the second terminates. This is how batch files execute subroutines.

CHOICE. This is a command available only in DOS 6 that lets the batch file prompt the user for a single character and return that character to the batch file via the errorlevel.

ECHO. This command displays text on the screen.

Errorlevel. Technically, the errorlevel is not a command. Rather, it's a one-byte location in memory that programs can use to communicate with batch files by storing a number 0–255 in the location. A batch file can then test this number using an IF ERRORLEVEL test.

FOR. This loops through a list of items one at a time and performs a single command for each item in the list.

GOTO. This jumps to another part of the batch file to continue processing.

IF. This performs logic testing and executes a single command when the test is true. The results of the test can be reversed with the NOT modifier.

PAUSE. This pauses the batch file until the user presses a key.

REM. This adds documentation to the batch file. The REM command must be the first thing on the line, and nothing after the REM command is executed.

SHIFT. This brings in another replaceable parameter.

Of course, there are a number of specialized products to extend the batch language. If you're interested in learning more about batch files, then please see my book *OS/2 Batch Files to Go*, also available from Windcrest/McGraw-Hill.

As you can see, the batch language isn't very powerful. However, it has three advantages: it's available on every machine, it's easy to learn, and it's very easy to issue OS/2 commands and run OS/2 programs using a batch file. As you'll see in this chapter, REXX makes it just as easy to issue OS/2 commands and to run OS/2 programs. In fact, REXX can do more than a batch file. In addition, REXX can duplicate all the batch subcommands and offer a full suite of its own instructions. REXX is harder to learn than batch files and you must select to install it, but these are the only areas where batch files have any advantage over REXX programs.

Running Batch Commands in REXX

REXX has the ability to perform every batch subcommand in a REXX program. This section will look at the batch subcommands one at a time, but first it's important to note that REXX can issue commands to the operating system (which I'll discuss in more detail later). The point is that if you really need to issue a batch subcommand, then a REXX program can issue it for you. For example, BAT-FOR.CMD displays all the .CMD files in the current subdirectory by issuing a FOR command to OS/2.

CALL batch subcommand

The CALL command is used by one batch file to execute a second batch file and then regain control when that second batch file terminates. Given the power of REXX, it's unlikely that a REXX program would need to call on a batch file. Nevertheless, the syntax is:

```
CALL batch [parameters]
```

where *batch* is the name of the batch file to call and *parameters* is the list of replaceable parameters to pass to the batch file. Since CALL is a REXX keyword, the command must be placed inside quotation marks to execute properly.

CHOICE batch subcommand

The CHOICE command was added to DOS 6 to give a batch file a way to get a single keystroke from the user via the errorlevel. While it doesn't use the errorlevel, the SysGetKey external function gives REXX programs a much more powerful way to get a single keystroke from the user and store it to a variable. The SysGetKey function was discussed in detail in chapter 5.

ECHO batch subcommand

The ECHO command is used in batch files to display text on the screen. The SAY instruction does the same thing, only more powerfully, in REXX programs. The SAY instruction was discussed in detail in chapter 6.

The errorlevel

While a nice place for batch files, the environment is a very inhospitable place for programs to store information to communicate with each other. Each program is provided with a copy of the environment when it's first loaded. When a program reads from or writes to the environment, it's dealing with its copy of the environment and not with the original. When the program terminates, its copy of the environment—along with all the changes the program made to it—are destroyed.

The errorlevel value was provided to overcome this problem. Under DOS, the error level is a single byte of memory, so it can contain only a single character. Under OS/2, it's a 16-bit signed integer, so the smallest errorlevel value is $-32,768$ (-2^{15}) and the largest number is $32,767$ ($2^{15}-1$).

When a program terminates, it can store a number in the errorlevel to indicate its status at termination. When programs use the errorlevel, they usually set it to zero for a successful execution and to higher values to indicate different types of errors.

The errorlevel isn't stored in the environment, so changes made to it aren't lost when a program terminates. Unlike the environment, there's only one copy of the errorlevel for each session, and every program in that session changes the same one. Separate sessions have their own errorlevels. The errorlevel doesn't change unless a program changes it, you start another program, you reboot, or you close the session, so you can perform multiple tests on it. Unlike DOS, OS/2 resets the errorlevel for some internal commands. That way, internal commands like DIR can return their own errorlevels. The errorlevel is automatically reset to zero each time you start a new program, so each time a program runs the prior errorlevel value is lost.

You don't need the errorlevel when running programs from the command line since you'll see any error messages. However, a batch file wouldn't "see" an error message, so the errorlevel gives you a way to respond to errors during a batch file.

When a program started by a REXX program returns an errorlevel, that errorlevel value is available to the REXX program in the RC variables that REXX creates and maintains automatically. That way, all the logic testing power of REXX is available to work with errorlevels.

When a REXX program terminates, it usually terminates normally, that is, without error. Therefore, the errorlevel is zero. If you need for the program to terminate and retain the last errorlevel value of the programs it was running, then add the instruction EXIT RC as the last instruction in the program. You can see this in the program RC.CMD that comes with this book. It forces an errorlevel value by running the XCOPY command to copy a file that doesn't exist (ZZZZZZZZ.999) to the A: drive. This causes XCOPY to return an errorlevel value and RC.CMD reports that value.

FOR batch subcommand

A FOR loop in a batch file has two functions: to process a list of files and to process a list of items. The syntax is:

```
FOR %%J IN (set) DO command
```

where *set* is the list of items or files to process and *command* is the command to execute for each item in the list. For example, the command:

```
FOR %%J IN (A*.CMD B*.CMD) DO COPY %%J A:
```

would copy all the REXX programs and batch files beginning with A or B to the A: drive, while the command:

```
FOR %%J IN (RONNY.TXT A.TXT READ.MD) DO DEL %%J
```

would delete RONNY.TXT, A.TXT, and READ.ME. Each of these two functions is easy to simulate in REXX. The SysFileTree function allows you to process a wildcard specification and get a list of files matching that specification. The code to do this is:

```
CALL SysFileTree "*.*", 'Matching', 'FO'
DO J = 1 TO Matching.0
   SAY Matching.j "Is #" J "In List To Process"
END
```

The first line calls SysFileTree and passes it the file specification *.* to look for. Of course, any other file specification could be passed to it and this could be a variable taken from the command line. The `'Matching'` tells the program to store the matching filenames in this stem variable, with `Matching.0` containing the count of files stored to the variable. The F tells it to search for only files and the O tells it to report back only the full path to the file and not the size and other directory information.

The second function of processing a list is even easier. You simply create a variable containing a list of items and loop through it using the PARSE instruction to strip off one word at a time until the list is empty. The code to do that is:

```
DO WHILE Input \=  ""
  PARSE VAR Input Item Input
  SAY "Would Execute FOR Command Here",
      "Based On" Item "From List Of Items"
END
```

Of course, the Input variable could be created by reading the command line with the Arg function. Both of these uses of the FOR command are shown in FOR-LOOP.CMD. Looping through a series of files can also be seen in the LISTCALL.CMD file.

GOTO batch subcommand

The GOTO command is used in a batch file to jump from one location in the batch file to another and continue processing. It's needed much more in a batch file than a REXX program because batch files normally allow you to perform only one command after a true IF test, so that one command is usually a command to jump to a special section to process several commands. (Note that OS/2 batch files can process multiple commands after a single IF test, but this feature isn't widely used because it isn't supported by DOS.) Since REXX programs can process many instructions after an IF test using the DO/END instructions, a GOTO command is rarely needed in a REXX program. If it is, the SIGNAL instruction functions similarly to the GOTO instruction in a batch file.

IF batch subcommand

In a batch file, the IF test has three purposes: to test the errorlevel, to see if two strings are identical, and to see if a file exists. The test to see if two strings are equal is simply the following:

```
IF string1 = string2 THEN command
```

where *string1* and *string2* are the strings to test and *command* is the command to execute if they're equal. If you need to execute multiple commands, then use DO as the command and every instruction until the next END will be executed only when the IF test is true.

A common problem in batch files is string capitalization. If you can't be sure of the capitalization of either of the two strings to test, then you must perform multiple IF tests to test all reasonable values or use a utility like CAPITAL.CMD to convert the strings to the same case outside of the batch file. Fortunately, REXX has the string-handling abilities of the PARSE UPPER VAR instruction so this isn't a problem. This is illustrated by the program SHOWCAP.CMD. It asks you for the same string twice with different capitalization and then converts both strings to uppercase before making the comparison.

PAUSE batch subcommand

REXX doesn't offer a PAUSE command directly, but the SysGetKey function waits on the user to press a single key without pressing Return. By preceding this function with a message to "Press any key to continue . . . ." the PAUSE command can be simulated in REXX. PAUSE.CMD does just this, and other programs can use it rather than reinventing the PAUSE command with CALL PAUSE.

The advantage of using the SysGetKey function in PAUSE.CMD is that you can edit the message as you see fit. You can even modify PAUSE.CMD to take its message as an argument so it uses different messages for different occasions. If you simply want to pause the REXX program and you're satisfied with the way OS/2 handles this, you can insert a @PAUSE command in your REXX program to access the OS/2 shell PAUSE command. This is demonstrated in the OS2PAUSE.CMD program that comes with this book.

REM batch subcommand

The REM command must be the first command on a line, and causes a batch file to ignore the remainder of the line. (Note that this isn't completely true since piping isn't ignored, but that is a rare complication.) While REXX doesn't have a REM command, any line started with a /* is ignored until a closing */ occurs. This takes place even if the comment spans multiple lines.

SHIFT batch subcommand

Batch files accept replaceable parameters from the command line, where each replaceable parameter is generally separated by a space. If you start a batch file with the command:

```
BATCH One Two Three
```

then One is the first replaceable parameter and is referred to as %1, Two is the second replaceable parameter and is referred to as %2, and so on. (The name of the batch file is %0.) The SHIFT command discards the contents of %0, moves the contents of %1 down to %0, the contents of %2 down to %1, and so on. The SHIFT command is needed because batch files are limited to working with %0 through %9.

REXX programs can read command line parameters using the Arg function and can treat these as individual replaceable parameters, as BATSHIFT.CMD shows. Since REXX has the ability to address an unlimited number of replaceable parameters, a SHIFT command is not needed. The variables, however, could be moved down using REXX assignment instructions if that were really required, again as BATSHIFT.CMD shows.

Running External Programs

So you see, REXX programs can perform all of the batch subcommands, many times doing better than batch files themselves. The ability to simulate batch subcommands combined with the power of the REXX language makes REXX a great batch language.

The only thing yet to cover is running external programs. For example, if you want your batch file to run your DeScribe word processor, you might include the following two commands:

```
CD\DESCRIBE
DESCRIBE
```

Neither of these are batch subcommands. Rather, the first is an OS/2 internal command to change subdirectories and the second runs the external program DESCRIBE.EXE.

Any line that REXX doesn't recognize is automatically assumed to be a system command and is passed to OS/2 for execution. However, this isn't as straightforward as it first appears. Take the two lines from the previous DeScribe batch file.

The second line is DESCRIBE, and this line creates no problem at all. When REXX reaches this line, it passes it to OS/2 and if DESCRIBE.EXE is in the current subdirectory or in the path then DeScribe loads and executes. When it terminates, the REXX program regains control. However, the first line is CD\DESCRIBE and it creates a problem. Due to the \ symbol (which REXX uses as the NOT operator), REXX tries to treat this as an expression, with the variables CD and DESCRIBE operated on by the \ operator, so REXX returns an error. You would have a similar problem if you tried to issue the command FOR %%J IN (*.*) DO COPY %%J A: with REXX, only this time the FOR is a command word so the command wouldn't get passed to OS/2.

The solution to both problems is the same. When you know a command is to be passed to the operating system, then enclose the command inside quotation marks and REXX will just pass it on to OS/2 without checking it. Thus, the program becomes:

```
"CD\DESCRIBE"
"DESCRIBE"
```

You can also see this in the program BAT-FOR.CMD that comes with this book. There are, however, times when you'll want to avoid putting an entire command inside quotation marks. For example, you might want to start DeScribe and specify the name of a file to load on the command line. Assuming the REXX program reads the name of the file to edit from the command line using the Arg function and stores it in the variable named File, you might think you could start DeScribe and load this file into memory with the command:

```
"DESCRIBE File"
```

inside the REXX program. However, REXX won't alter anything inside the quotation marks so DeScribe will try to load a file called FILE rather than loading the filename stored inside the File variable. To change this, make sure that any variable or information you want REXX to interpret be outside the quotation marks. In this example, the command would be:

```
"DESCRIBE" File
```

and you can see this in the REXX program DESCRIBE.CMD. To illustrate the difference with another example, suppose a REXX program had the line:

```
Message = "This Was Executed From A REXX Program"
```

followed with the command:

```
"ECHO Message"
```

When a command is used in this fashion the variable is inside quotation marks, so the entire line is passed to OS/2 as a command. Change it to:

```
"ECHO" Message
```

and the command passed to OS/2 becomes ECHO This Was Executed From A REXX Program. For more examples, see the program REXXECHO.CMD that comes with this book. Of course, this means you must be careful how you use quotation marks when you're constructing commands for REXX to send to the operating system.

Summary

REXX offers all the power of OS/2 batch files and much, much more. Like a batch file, a REXX program can easily issue commands to the operating system. Given all the power of REXX and its natural ability to issue system commands, REXX can handle all your batch file needs.

8

Working with Strings

A string is simply a series of characters, optionally enclosed inside either single or double quotation marks. For example:

```
SAY "This is a label"
SAY 'This is also a label'
```

The quotation marks are used to mark the boundaries of the string for REXX. They aren't printed. If the string is being stored to a variable, the quotation marks aren't stored as part of the variable.

Strings don't have to be enclosed inside quotation marks. For example, the following code is completely valid even though neither string is contained inside quotation marks:

```
SAY This Is A Label
Name = Ronny Richardson
```

There are, however, two drawbacks to using strings without quotation marks. First, all strings created or used in this fashion are converted to all uppercase. Second, and more seriously, REXX checks each word in the string to see if it's a variable. If it is, that variable name is replaced with the contents of the variable. That can cause very unexpected results. For example, the code:

```
Label = "Avery 5160"
SAY This Is A Label
```

will display THIS IS A Avery 5160, not THIS IS A LABEL. In general, it's best to avoid using strings without surrounding them with quotation marks. This is particularly true with large programs, where it's easy for an innocent word to be used as a variable name then overlooked when writing prompts.

You can put one type of quotation marks inside a string if you then surround the string with the other type of quotation mark. For example, to place a piece of dialog inside double quotation marks, simply place the entire string within single quotation marks, as follows:

```
Variable = 'Sally said, "I do not believe you."'
```

This phrase also illustrates a slight problem that's easily avoided. If Sally had wanted to say "I don't" rather than "I do not," then you would have needed to embed the apostrophe inside single quotation marks. The solution is to replace the apostrophe with two apostrophes, which REXX will then display as a single apostrophe. So to display the phrase with "I don't," you would have to do the following:

```
Variable = 'Sally said, "I don''t believe you."'
```

Variable Typing

Many languages differentiate between string variables and numeric variables. Most languages don't allow you to store numbers to string variables and then perform mathematical operations on them. They do this because it makes it easier on the compiler to know in advance what type of information the variable is to contain. The process of telling the compiler what type of data a variable will contain is called *typing*.

While variable typing makes the compiler's job easier, it's harder on the programmer than just using variables as needed. REXX makes the programmer's job easier by not requiring variable typing. In fact, it's not even allowed since all variables are stored as strings. While all variables are stored as strings, mathematical operations can be performed on those variables containing numbers. For example, the following code:

```
One = "1"
Two = "2"
SAY One + Two
```

would display the answer 3 that you expect. To do this in another language, you would have to use a function to take the contents of the string variables and store it in a numeric variable. REXX makes it easy by avoiding all that. Of course, the variables must contain numbers. For example, the following code:

```
One = "One"
Two = "Two"
SAY One + Two
```

wouldn't work since the string variables don't contain any numbers that REXX can identify. When it tries to execute the third line, REXX will display a "Bad arithmetic conversion" error message, showing that it's handling the string-to-numeric conversion automatically. This is illustrated by Figure 8.1.

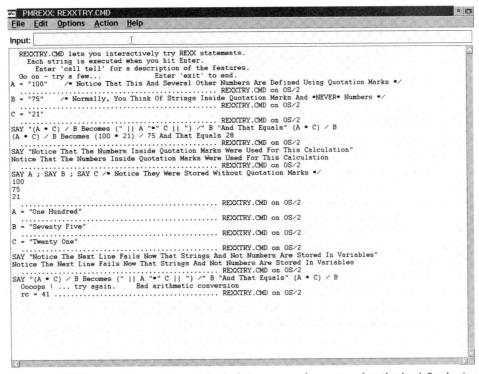

Figure 8.1 REXX can perform mathematical calculations on numbers, even when they're defined using quotation marks. However, non-numeric variables can't be used in calculations.

String Definition

A string inside quotation marks is treated as a constant by REXX and isn't modified by the code unless you issue an instruction specifically to modify the contents. For example, the instructions:

```
SAY This is a label
SAY "This is a label"
```

would both display the phrase `This is a label`. However, since the first instruction doesn't have the phrase inside quotation marks, REXX converts it to all uppercase before displaying it. The second phrase is inside quotation marks, so REXX displays the phrase exactly as typed. Strings must be assigned to variables on a single physical line. For example:

```
Message = "This Is A Label"
```

would be valid since the entire assignment is on a single physical line. The instruction:

```
Message = "This Is,
A Label"
```

wouldn't be valid. While the comma is a valid line-continuation character, strings must be assigned on a single line. Any string with no characters is called a *null string*. Such a string would have zero length. Using binary and hexadecimal notation to create string variables is discussed in detail back in chapter 5. Please refer back to this if you have any questions.

String Concatenation

String concatenation is combining two or more strings together to form a single string. The simplest way to concatenate strings is to use the strings with a space in between them. For example, the code:

```
First = "Ronny"
Last  = "Richardson"
Name  = First Last
```

would create a single variable called Name containing Ronny Richardson. No matter how many spaces there are between the variable names First and Last on the third line, REXX would store only a single variable between their contents when creating the variable Name. This same method can be used to print multiple variables on the same line. For example, the code:

```
First =  "Ronny"
Last  =  "Richardson"
Gender = "Male"
SAY First Last "Is A" Gender
```

would display the single line Ronny Richardson Is A Male. Note that REXX adds a space before Is and after A even though there isn't one in the code. That's because strings are always separated by a space in a concatenation unless you force REXX to do otherwise.

The method you use to force REXX to concatenate without a space depends on how the strings are being used. If the strings are all inside quotation marks, or if strings inside quotation marks and string variables alternate, then you can simply place them side by side. For example, in this code the first name is defined with a trailing space, so another space isn't needed between it and the last name:

```
First = "Ronny "
Name  = First"Richardson"
```

This approach is most useful when displaying the results of calculations, as this code illustrates in displaying the percent sign:

```
Bottom = 80
Top    = 16
SAY Top "Is" (Top * Bottom) / 100"% Of" Bottom
```

Since there's no space between the ending of the calculations and the percent sign, REXX will print the percent sign directly next to the number. Since there's a space between the variable name Top and Is, and between the string % Of and the variable name Bottom, REXX will display spaces between these.

When you need to concatenate two variables, you cannot simply place them together. If you try code like:

```
First = "Ronny "
Last  = "Richardson"
SAY FirstLast
```

REXX doesn't know that the last line contains two variable names. When you have a situation like this, where it isn't clear to REXX what to do, you can use the symbol ¦¦ to specify concatenation of two variables. So the last line would be replaced with:

```
SAY First¦¦Last
```

When the ¦¦ is used, spacing around it doesn't matter, so the line could be replaced with:

```
SAY First ¦¦ Last
```

for improved readability. The ¦¦ operator is sometimes required when REXX syntax would otherwise be ambiguous. For example, REXX would interpret the following instruction naturally as string concatenation:

```
SAY "ABC"Y+3
```

However, if you change the instruction to:

```
SAY "ABC"(Y+3)
```

then it's ambiguous because REXX expects ABC to be an internal function and returns a "Routine not found" error message. The instruction must be rewritten with the ¦¦ operator as:

```
SAY "ABC"¦¦(Y+3)
```

Additionally, the instruction:

```
SAY "ABCD"x
```

would normally be interpreted by REXX as an instruction to display a hexadecimal string. If you intended to display ABCDX (since a string not inside quotation marks is converted to uppercase) or ABCD with the value of the variable x directly beside, you must change the instruction to:

```
SAY "ABCD"¦¦X
```

You have to be a little more careful about concatenation when you're concatenating across lines. For example, the instruction:

```
SAY "Ronny",
    "Richardson"
```

would display Ronny Richardson all on one line because the comma and line feed are replaced by a space, as described in chapter 2, and the instruction is identical to:

```
SAY "Ronny" "Richardson"
```

However, if the instruction were:

```
SAY "Ronny"||,
    "Richardson"
```

The operation being split, then, is the concatenation and this instruction would be identical to:

```
SAY "Ronny"||"Richardson"
```

and would display RonnyRichardson on the screen. If you want to see string concatenation in action, run the program CONCATE.CMD on the disk that comes with this book. This program creates several variables and then concatenates them in different fashions. String concatenation is also used to display menus in TODO.CMD, CONCATE.CMD, and TODO.CMD, which are included on the disk that comes with this book. The code is explained line by line in appendix A.

Additional String Power with Functions

REXX includes a number of built-in functions that greatly expand its power to work with strings. They give you the power to strip off words, change capitalization, add and remove spaces, and much more. These are explained in detail in chapter 11. The following is a brief summary of these string-related functions:

Abbrev. This function compares an abbreviation to the full word. If the characters in the abbreviation match the starting characters in the full word, it returns a one. It returns a zero otherwise.

Arg. This function returns the arguments passed to a program or subroutine and information about those arguments.

B2X. This function converts a binary string to an equivalent hexadecimal string.

Center. This function pads enough spaces on both sides of a string so that it's centered within a string of the specified width. It can also be spelled Centre.

CharIn. This function is used to read characters from the input stream.

CharOut. This function is used to write characters to the output stream.

Chars. This function reads the number of characters remaining in the input stream. For a persistent stream, it counts the number of characters beginning with the current read position.

Compare. This function checks strings to see if they're the same.

Copies. This function returns multiple copies of a single string.

C2D. This function takes a character string and returns the decimal value of the binary representation (encoding) on the character string.

C2X. This function takes a character string and converts it to its hexadecimal representation.

DataType. This function is used to check what type of data is contained in a variable or string before using that data. That way you can avoid errors caused by the wrong type of data.

Date. This function returns the date in a variety of formats suitable for messages or database applications.

DelStr. This function deletes characters from a string.

DelWord. This function deletes words from a character string, where a word is defined as a string of characters surrounded by spaces unless it occurs at the beginning or end of the string, and then only if it has a space on one side.

Insert. This function is used to place one string inside another string.

LastPos. This function looks for one string (source) inside another string (target) and returns the position of the source string inside the target string.

Left. This function is used to obtain a specified number of characters out of a character string, beginning at the left-most character and moving to the right a specified number of positions.

Length. This function returns the length of a given character string.

Overlay. This function inserts one string (source) into a second string (target).

Pos. This function is used to find the location of a string (source) inside a second string (target).

Reverse. This function reverses the order of a character string.

Right. This function is used to obtain a specified number of characters out of a character string, beginning at the right-most character and moving to the left a specified number of positions.

Strip. This function removes a lead, trailing, or both characters from a character string. The character to be removed is usually a space for a character string or zero for a number.

SubStr. This function is used to return a portion of a character string.

SubWord. This function is used to return a word or words from a character string.

Translate. This function is used to convert a character string into another string using a translation table.

Value. This function is used to read and alter the contents of REXX variables and OS/2 environmental variables.

Verify. This function is used to test a character string to see if it has all its characters contained in a second string.

Word. This function returns a single word from a character string.

WordIndex. This function returns the starting character position for a specified word.

WordLength. This function returns the length of a word.

WordPos. This function is used to specify the starting position of a specific word.

Words. This function returns the number of words in a character string.

X2B. This function is used to convert hexadecimal strings to binary strings.

X2C. This function is used to convert hexadecimal strings to character strings.

X2D. This function is used to convert hexadecimal strings to decimal strings.

Summary

This chapter has presented an introduction to working with string data. The techniques introduced in this chapter, combined with the built-in functions REXX has for working with strings, gives REXX the power to perform very complex string manipulations.

Working with Numbers

As you've already seen, REXX is very flexible in its treatment of numbers, even allowing you to define numbers with quotation marks around them and then use them as numbers. In fact, the following sequence is completely valid:

```
A = "123"
B = 456
SAY A+B
```

Not only is it valid, but it will yield the correct result of 579. To REXX, a number is just a character string with the following characteristics:

- It can contain one or more digits, 0–9.
- It can contain zero or one decimal point.
- The decimal point can be at the start, in the middle, or at the end of the numbers.
- It can have leading or trailing spaces, but no spaces in the middle.
- It cannot contain commas.
- It can have either a leading plus or minus sign.
- A leading sign can have leading or trailing spaces.
- It can contain a single *e* denoting exponential notation.
- The letter *e* cannot have a leading or trailing space.
- The letter *e* can be followed by a plus or minus sign, without leading or trailing spaces.
- The letter *e* and the optional sign must be followed by a whole number. (The number 1.2E3 is exponential notation for 1.2 times three tens, or 1200. The number 1.2E–3 is exponential notation for 1.2 divided by three tens, or .0012.)

Any time you write down the rules of mathematics or a computer language dealing with mathematics, they tend to sound complex. These are no exception. However, don't get overly concerned about the rules. All they really say is that REXX thinks of numbers the way you do, except that commas aren't allowed. So if it looks like a valid way to write a number to you, chances are very high that it will be acceptable to REXX as well.

Display Rounding

Since numbers are stored as strings, their format isn't changed. That is, if you create a variable with the instruction:

```
A = 4.0000
```

and later display that variable, you'll see 4.0000 and not 4. This display precision is maintained for all operations except division and raising to a power. For these operations, all trailing zeros are removed. When performing operations on numbers with different numbers of decimal points, the number with the longest is used for display. For example, 4.0*2.000 equals 8.000.

The fact that extra zeros are stripped off the answer when performing division yields a quick way of stripping off all the extra zeros for display purposes. Simply divide by one. Dividing by one doesn't change the answer but the division operation forces REXX to remove the extra zeros, so 4.000/1 would display as 4. You can also use a similar method to control the number of extra zeros that are added. For example, to force the display of two decimal places, first divide by one (4.000/1) to remove the extra zeros, then multiple by 1.00 to add two decimal points. So (4.000/1)*1.00 would display two decimal points. Of course, this works only when the answer has extra trailing decimal points. Using the same method on 1.23444 wouldn't change its display since it has no trailing zeros to remove. Later on, you'll see how to affect these types of numbers.

Precision

Before I explain the types of mathematics REXX can perform, you need to understand how it performs those calculations internally.

What is the value of the calculation 1/3? What if I told you that it depends? In REXX, as in most computer languages, the answer really does depend. Specifically, it depends on the amount of precision you tell REXX to use in computing the answer. Precision is the amount of accuracy REXX uses in computing answers. Tell REXX to use only one digit of precision (its minimum) and 1/3 will equal 0.3. Tell it to use 15 digits and the answer will be 0.333333333333333. The default level of precision is nine. The instruction to change the level of precision is:

```
NUMERIC DIGITS [value]
```

where value is the number of digits to retain in calculations. The minimum value is one, the default is nine, and it will accept values far in excess of any you're likely to need. In fact, a value of 100,000 is acceptable. The maximum value is limited only by memory. To see this, run the BIGNUM.CMD program that comes with this book. Be warned, BIGNUM.CMD produces very large numbers that can take a long time to display on slower computers.

All calculations are affected when you change precision, so be careful when setting it too low or loop counters might not calculate properly. You can see this by running the PRECISE.CMD program that comes with this book.

Exponential Notation

Exponential notation is a method of writing very large or very small numbers. Numbers are written like 1.2e+3. The sign following the *e* represents the operation used to convert the first number. An addition sign means to multiply by tens and a negative sign to divide by tens. An addition sign can be dropped, so 1.2e+3 is the same as 1.2e3. The number after the *e* represents the number of tens used in the conversion, so 1.2e3 represents 1200 and 1.2e–3 represents .0012.

REXX accepts two forms of exponential notation: scientific and engineering. Scientific is the default and you can switch between them with the instructions:

```
NUMERIC FORM SCIENTIFIC
NUMERIC FORM ENGINEERING
```

In scientific notation, the power of ten is adjusted until the number on the left of the e is a single digit greater than negative ten and less than ten. In engineering notation, the same adjustment is made, only the exponent must be a multiple of three. As a result, the number to the left of the *e* must be only larger than –1000 and less than +1000. In other words, the integer portion of this number ranges from –999 to +999.

Whole Numbers

Some operations in REXX require whole numbers. A whole number is an integer, which is a number that can be expressed without a decimal point. REXX also requires that the number be small enough to be written without using exponential notation. This is controlled by the NUMERIC DIGITS setting. If the setting is nine, then the largest possible whole number is 999,999,999 since any integer larger than that must be rounded and expressed in exponential notation. REXX requires whole numbers for the following:

- Positional patterns in parsing templates.
- The right side of the power (**) operator.
- Some components of the DO instruction.
- The numbers used after the NUMERIC DIGITS and NUMERIC FUZZ instructions.
- Any number used in the trace setting in the TRACE instruction.

Mathematical Operations

REXX can perform the following mathematical operations:

+. This adds two numbers together. For example, 2+2 is 4 and 456+234 is 690.

−. This subtracts the second number from the first number. For example, 2–2 is zero and 456–234 is 222.

*. This multiplies two numbers together. For example, 2*2 is 4 and 456*234 is 106,704.

/. This divides the second number into the first number. For example, 2/2 is one and 456/234 is 1.9487179.

. This raises the first number to the power of the second number. For example, 22 is 4, 2**3 is 8, and 456**234 is 1.57678755E622, a number with 622 digits. REXX can raise a number to only a whole number power, so 4**.5 would be an invalid way to compute the square root of four.

%. This divides the second number into the first number, but returns only the integer portion of the answer. For example, 2%2 is 1 and 456%234 is also 1. It's important when performing this operation that the precision be set high enough. For example, the operation 9999999999%9 results in the answer 1111111111, which has ten digits. With the default value for NUMERIC DIGITS of nine, there isn't enough precision to display the results and the operation will fail. A similar problem can present itself with the remainder operation that follows.

//. This divides the second number into the first number, but returns only the remainder. For example, 2//2 is 0 and 456//234 is 222. You can see more examples in Figure 9.1.

Mathematical Precedence

What is the value of the expression 4–2*6? If you evaluate the 4–2 first to get 2 and then multiply by 6, you have 12. If you evaluate 2*6 first to get 12 and then evaluate 4–12, you get –8. Which is right?

Happily, the answer isn't "it depends!" Rather, the answer is –8. In REXX, expressions are evaluated from left to right. However, this is modified by two things: parentheses and operator precedence. The parentheses rule is easy; everything inside parentheses is evaluated first. If there's more than one operation inside the parentheses, it's evaluated from left to right and operator precedence applies.

The operators, in order of highest to lowest priority, are as follows:

- Prefix operators (+, –, and \\)
- Power operator (**)

- Multiplication and division (*, /, %, and //)

- Addition and subtraction (+ and –)

- Concatenation (blank, ¦¦, and abuttal)

- Comparative operators (=, ==, >, >>, and so on)

- And (&)

- Or and exclusive or (¦ and &&)

Run the PRECEDE.CMD that comes with this book to see examples of REXX precedence in operation. Generally, you won't encounter any difficulty with these precedences since they are, for the most part, the same ones you'll find in algebra and other programming languages. There's one difference and one condition you need to be aware of, however.

First the difference. REXX gives the prefix the highest priority. Thus the expression $-4**2$ is treated as $(-4)**2$ or $(-4)^2$ and is equal to 16. Some other languages treat $-4**2$ as $0-4**2$ and perform the $4**2$ first to get 16 and then evaluate $0-16$ to get -16.

Second, the condition you need to be aware of. REXX evaluates all expressions left to right, so $2**3**4$ is treated as $(2**3)**4$, which equals 4,096. Some other languages treat this as $2**(3**4)$ and return 2.4179e24.

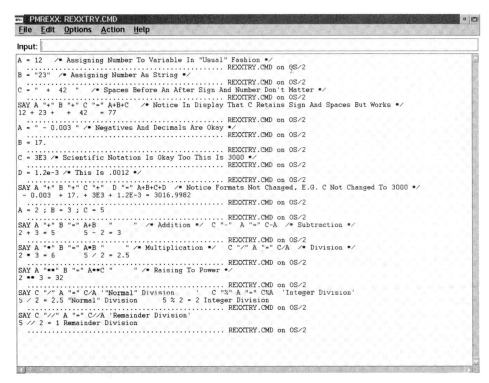

Figure 9.1 REXX can perform seven different types of mathematical operations.

Fuzziness

All of the comparative operators discussed in the next chapter can be used to compare two numbers; however, the strict comparisons (like == and <<) should not be used. With a strict comparison operator, leading and trailing spaces and zeros are significant. So 4, with a leading and trailing space, and 4.00 aren't "strictly" equal to one another.

Is 4.99998 equal to 4.99999? Is 4.999991 equal to 4.99999? The answer is, again, that it depends. The logic test = compares to see if two items equal each other, and is explained in more detail in the next chapter. However, for numbers the comparison:

```
A = B
```

is identical to the comparison:

```
(A - B) = 0
```

For all the logical operators discussed in the next chapter, it's the difference between two numbers, when subtracted under the REXX rules of subtraction, that determines the value of the comparison.

The comparison of two numbers is also controlled by something called the "fuzz value," which is controlled by the instruction NUMERIC FUZZ. Its function is to temporarily reduce the setting for NUMERIC DIGITS for the comparison. If the precision is set to nine digits and the fuzz value is one, then logical comparisons are made as though the setting was 9–1, or 8. The higher the fuzz value, the more easily numbers match. See Figure 9.2.

The minimum value for NUMERIC FUZZ is zero, meaning that no rounding is done before a comparison. The maximum value is one less than the value of NUMERIC DIGITS, so there's only one significant digit in the comparison. REXX won't allow you to change either the settings of NUMERIC FUZZ or NUMERIC DIGITS if that change would cause NUMERIC FUZZ to equal or exceed the value of NUMERIC DIGITS. For example, the following would be invalid:

```
NUMERIC DIGITS 100
NUMERIC FUZZ    99
/* Calculations Here */
NUMERIC DIGITS 9; NUMERIC FUZZ 1
```

It isn't allowed because the last line first tries to change NUMERIC DIGITS to 9 while NUMERIC FUZZ remains at 99 and so exceeds the value of NUMERIC DIGITS. Swapping the order of the last line would correct the problem.

Errors

Two types of errors are possible when working with numbers in REXX: overflow/underflow and insufficient storage. Overflow/underflow occurs when the number being calculated exceeds REXX's ability to display it. For example, 1/0 is infinity, which REXX cannot display, resulting in an overflow/underflow error. A number that's too large or small to display given the current value of NUMERIC DIGITS will generate

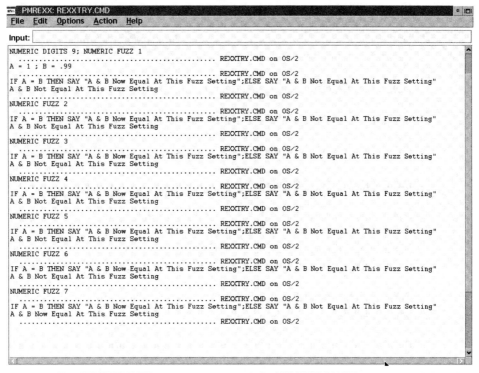

Figure 9.2 The NUMERIC FUZZ setting, in concert with the NUMERIC DIGITS setting, controls how close numbers must be in a logical comparison before the comparison is true.

this problem, but the language will handle it automatically by converting it to exponential notation.

An insufficient storage error occurs when there isn't enough memory to store the results of a calculation. This is considered a terminating error.

Additional Mathematical Power with Functions

REXX includes a number of built-in functions that greatly expand its power to perform mathematical calculations. They give you the power to compute absolute values, find maximum and minimum values, and much more. These are explained in detail in chapter 11. The following is a brief summary of these mathematical-related functions.

Abs. This function returns the absolute value of a number. Zero and positive numbers are unaffected. Negative numbers are converted to positive numbers.

B2X. This function converts a binary string to an equivalent hexadecimal string.

DataType. This function is used to check what type of data is contained in a variable or string before using that data. That way you can avoid errors caused by the wrong type of data.

Digits. This function returns the current setting of NUMERIC DIGITS.

D2C. This function returns a character string that's the binary representation of the decimal number supplied to the function.

D2X. This function converts a decimal number to a hexadecimal number.

Format. This controls the format of how numbers are displayed.

Fuzz. This function returns the current setting of NUMERIC FUZZ.

Max. This function finds the largest number in a sequence of numbers.

Min. This function finds the smallest number in a sequence of numbers.

Sign. This function returns a –1 if the number is below zero, a 0 if the number equals zero, and +1 if the number is above zero.

Strip. While primarily a character string-manipulation function, this function can be used to remove leading and trailing zeros from numbers.

SubStr. While primarily a character string-manipulation function, this function can be used to return digits from inside a number.

Trunc. This function is used to round numbers to a specific number of decimal points.

Value. This function is used to read and alter the contents of REXX variables and OS/2 environmental variables.

X2B. This function is used to convert hexadecimal strings to binary strings.

X2C. This function is used to convert hexadecimal strings to character strings.

X2D. This function is used to convert hexadecimal strings to decimal strings.

Summary

This chapter has discussed the important aspects of working with numbers in a REXX program.

Logic Testing and Looping

For most programs, logic testing is essential. Basically, logic testing allows a program to select between two or more alternatives depending on the conditions that exist at the time the program is executed. Without this ability, each program would execute exactly the same way each time it ran, regardless of the conditions that existed or the information entered by the user.

IF

The basic logic testing statement is the IF test. Its syntax is:

```
IF expression[;] THEN[;] instruction [ELSE[;] instruction2]
```

where *expression* is a logical statement that evaluates to either true or false, *instruction* is the instruction to be executed when *expression* is true, and *instruction2* is the instruction to be executed when *expression* is false.

Before looking at the IF statement in any more detail, I first need to explain logical statements in more detail.

Logical Statements

A logical statement is a statement that compares two terms and can be evaluated by REXX as either true or false. When the statement is true REXX returns a value of one, and when it's false REXX returns a value of zero.

Logical statements can be made up of two different types of operators: normal and strict. A *normal comparison* pads strings to equal length and strips off leading and trailing spaces from strings and numbers and zeros from numbers. A *strict comparison* doesn't allow padding of character strings, nor leading or trailing spaces or zeros to be stripped off.

Once each side of the comparison is determined when both of the terms are numeric, the logical comparison is made based on the rules of algebra. When either of the terms is a string, REXX performs a character-by-character test of the term using the ASCII value. When one string is shorter than the other, the shorter string is padded with null characters (ASCII value of zero) to make it the same length as the longer string. The normal comparative operators are:

Equal (=). Is the first term equal to the second term? For a numeric test, the numbers must be the same, to the defined precision. For a string test, all the characters must be the same, including capitalization, and the strings must be of equal length.

Test	Returns
SAY 1 = 1.01	0
SAY "abc" = "abc "	1
SAY " abc" = "abc"	1
SAY 2 = 2	1
SAY "abc" = "a"	0
SAY "a" = "abc"	0

Not equal (¬=, \=, <>, ><). The ¬ and \ operators stand for a logical NOT. It changes a true to a false and a false to a true. The ¬ symbol isn't on a standard PC keyboard; you can generate it only by entering its ASCII value of 170. For that reason, most programmers simply use the \ symbol, which is on the PC keyboard. The <> and >< are two additional ways of specifying not equals.

Test	Returns
SAY 1 \= 1.01	1
SAY "abc" \= "abc "	0
SAY " abc" ¬= "abc"	0
SAY 2 ¬= 2	0
SAY "abc" <> "a"	1
SAY "a" >< "abc"	1

Greater than (>). For a number, this operator compares to see if the first number is larger than the second number. For a string, it compares to see if the ASCII value of the first character in the left string that's different from the same position character in the right string has a higher ASCII value.

Test	Returns
SAY 1 > 1.01	0
SAY "abc" > "abc "	0
SAY " abc" > "abc"	0
SAY 2 > 2	0
SAY "abc" > "a"	1
SAY "a" > "abc"	0

Less than (<). For a number, this operator compares to see if the first number is smaller than the second number. For a string, it compares to see if the ASCII value of the first character in the left string that's different from the same position character in the right string has a lower ASCII value. At first, you might be tempted to say that < is the same as \>, but this isn't the case since, with two equal strings, neither are greater than or less than the other.

Test	Returns
SAY 1 < 1.01	1
SAY "abc" < "abc "	0
SAY " abc" < "abc"	0
SAY 2 < 2	0
SAY "abc" < "a"	0
SAY "a" < "abc"	1

Greater than or equal to (>=, ¬<, \<). For a number, this operator compares to see if the first number is larger than or equal to the second number. For a string, it compares to see if the ASCII value of the first character in the left string that's different from the same position character in the right string has a higher ASCII value. Unlike >, it returns a true if all the characters are the same.

Test	Returns
SAY 1 >= 1.01	0
SAY "abc" >= "abc "	1
SAY " abc" ¬< "abc"	1
SAY 2 ¬< 2	1
SAY "abc" \< "a"	1
SAY "a" \< "abc"	0

Less than or equal to (<=, ¬>, \>). For a number, this operator compares to see if the first number is smaller than or equal to the second number. For a string, it compares to see if the ASCII value of the first character in the left string that's different from the same position character in the right string has a lower ASCII value. Unlike <, it returns a true if all the characters are the same.

Test	Returns
SAY 1 <= 1.01	1
SAY "abc" <= "abc "	1
SAY " abc" ¬> "abc"	1
SAY 2 ¬> 2	1
SAY "abc" \> "a"	0
SAY "a" \> "abc"	1

The strict comparative operators are:

Strictly equal (==). This operator specifies that the first term is equal to the second term. For a numeric test, the numbers must be the same. For a string test, all the characters must be the same, including capitalization, and the strings must be of equal length.

Test	Returns
SAY 1 == 1.01	0
SAY "abc" == "abc "	0
SAY " abc" == "abc"	0
SAY 2 == 2	1
SAY "abc" == "a"	0
SAY "a" == "abc"	0

Strictly not equal (¬==, \==). This operator is the opposite of ==.

Test	Returns
SAY 1 \== 1.01	1
SAY "abc" \== "abc "	1
SAY " abc" ¬== "abc"	1
SAY 2 ¬== 2	0
SAY "abc" \== "a"	1
SAY "a" \== "abc"	1

Strictly greater than (>>). For a number or string, this operator compares to see if the ASCII value of the first character in the left string that's different from the same position character in the right string has a higher ASCII value.

Test	Returns
SAY 3 >> 04	1
SAY 1 >> 1.01	0
SAY "abc" >> "abc "	0
SAY " abc" >> "abc"	0
SAY 2 >> 2	0
SAY "abc" >> "a"	1
SAY "a" >> "abc"	0

Strictly less than (<<). For a number or string, this operator compares to see if the ASCII value of the first character in the left string that's different from the same position character in the right string has a lower ASCII value.

Test	Returns
SAY 1 << 1.01	1
SAY "abc" << "abc "	1
SAY " abc" << "abc"	1
SAY 2 << 2	0
SAY "abc" << "a"	0
SAY "a" << "abc"	1

Strictly greater than or equal to (>>=, ¬<<, \<<). For a number or string, this opera-tor compares to see if the ASCII value of the first character in the left string that's different from the same position character in the right string has a higher ASCII value.

Test	Returns
SAY 1 >>= 1.01	0
SAY "abc" >>= "abc "	0
SAY " abc" ¬<< "abc"	0
SAY 2 ¬<< 2	1
SAY "abc" \<< "a"	1
SAY "a" \<< "abc"	0

Strictly less than or equal to (<<=, ¬>>, \>>). For a number or string, this opera-tor compares to see if the ASCII value of the first character in the left string that's different from the same position character in the right string has a lower ASCII value.

Test	Returns
SAY 1 <<= 1.01	1
SAY "abc" <<= "abc "	1
SAY " abc" ¬>> "abc"	1
SAY 2 ¬>> 2	1
SAY "abc" \>> "a"	0
SAY "a" \>> "abc"	1

There are four Boolean logical operators. They are:

Logical not (¬, \). As you've already seen, this operator reverses a statement. If the statement evaluates to true, it changes it to false. If the statement evaluates to false, it changes it to true.

Logical and (&). This operator returns a true only if the statements on both sides are true.

Test	Returns
SAY 1=1 & 2=2	1
SAY 1=1 & 2=3	0

Inclusive or (¦). This operator returns a true if a statement on either side is true.

Test	Returns
SAY 1=1 ¦ 2=2	1
SAY 1=1 ¦ 2=3	1

Exclusive or (&&). This returns a true if exactly one statement on either side is true.

Test	Returns
SAY 1=1 && 2=2	0
SAY 1=1 && 2=3	1

Another Look at the IF Statement

Recall that the syntax for an IF statement is:

```
IF expression[;] THEN[;] instruction [ELSE[;] instruction2]
```

where *instruction* is the instruction to execute if *expression* is true and *instruction2* is the instruction to execute if *expression* is false. After covering the logical operators, it should now be clear that when *expression* is true it has a value of one, and when it's false it has a value of zero. This evaluation of *expression* is based on the logical operators previously discussed.

Multiple instructions

The syntax of the IF statement might look to be fairly restrictive at first. In a batch file you execute one instruction after a true IF statement, so you usually end up using a GOTO command to jump to a separate section to have multiple commands. REXX doesn't force you to do that. You can use a DO block to insert multiple instructions into an IF statement. The syntax is:

```
DO
   instruction1
   instruction2
   instructionlast
END
```

where all the instructions to execute are listed between the DO and END statements. Thus, the IF statement could be rewritten as:

```
IF expression THEN
   DO
      instruction1
      instruction2
      instructionlast
   END
ELSE
   DO
      instruction1
      instruction2
      instructionlast
   END
```

As an example, the following code shows the section of code in LOGIC.CMD that checks to see if the user has requested command-line help. Except for the message it displays, it's identical to the help section for most of the programs that come with this book. Note that it uses two instructions as part of the IF statement and one of them is an EXIT instruction.

```
HelpCheck = ARG(1)
  IF HelpCheck = "/?" THEN
    DO
      SAY "Illustrate Logical Comparisons"
      EXIT
    END
```

Multiple IF tests

REXX allows you to have one IF statement as the instruction inside another. This is called an *embedded IF statement*. For example, the program MULTI-IF.CMD asks the user to enter one of four words: One, Two, Three, or Four. It then uses an embedded IF statement to display the value entered by the user. The code to do this is:

```
IF Word = "ONE" THEN SAY "You Entered One"
  ELSE IF Word = "TWO" THEN SAY "You Entered Two"
    ELSE IF Word = "THREE" THEN SAY "You Entered Three"
      ELSE IF Word = "FOUR" THEN SAY "You Entered Four"
        ELSE SAY "You Did Not Follow Instructions!"
```

As you'll see next, there's often a better way to test on multiple values than using embedded IF statements.

Multiple IF statements using the SELECT statement

The SELECT statement can replace embedded IF statements when you have a program select one option from a list. The syntax is:

```
SELECT
  WHEN condition1 THEN instruction1
  WHEN condition2 THEN instruction2
  WHEN conditionlast THEN instructionlast
  OTHERWISE instruction
END
```

where the conditions are the logical expressions of the possible outcomes and the instructions are the instructions to execute when the specific condition is true. Note that a DO/END block is allowed to execute multiple instructions. The SELECT code used in MULTI-IF.CMD to repeat the test on the user's input is:

```
SELECT
  WHEN Word = "ONE"    THEN SAY "You Entered One"
  WHEN Word = "TWO"    THEN SAY "You Entered Two"
  WHEN Word = "THREE"  THEN SAY "You Entered Three"
  WHEN Word = "FOUR"   THEN SAY "You Entered Four"
  OTHERWISE SAY "You Did Not Follow Instructions!"
END
```

TODO.CMD uses a SELECT instruction to decide what action to take when the user makes a selection from the main menu. In TODO.CMD, each SELECT instruction calls up a subroutine. A DO/END block works well when you have a couple of instructions to execute for each option. When you have more instructions than that, collecting them into a subroutine is a better approach.

Looping

Looping is repeating the same sequence of instructions more than once. Why might you want to repeat the same code more than once?

I have a REXX program that makes a backup copy of all my .CMD programs by going through a loop once for each file. It checks to see if the file has been modified and, if so, calls XCOPY to copy it to the A: drive and reset the archive bit.

TODO.CMD functions as a massive loop. The main loop displays the text on the screen, displays the menu, and then waits. When the user makes any selection, it goes off and executes that selection. After that, for any selection except EXIT, it uses the same code as before to redisplay the text on the screen and the menu. In other words, it stays in a constant loop.

A password program might loop through a routine to get a password from the user three times before locking the user out. A disk-testing program might loop through its code once for each hard disk you have, as might a backup program. SPELLING.CMD loops through a series of instructions for each spelling word it asks you. MATHTEST.CMD also loops through a series of instructions for each math problem it gives the user. The DO instruction forms the basis of most looping in a REXX program. We will look at each configuration of the DO instruction in detail.

DO/END block

As described previously, instructions like IF and WHEN expect a single instruction after them. To include multiple instructions, make the first instruction a DO instruction. Follow that with all the instructions you need executed, and then terminate them with an END instruction. The basic syntax is:

```
IF condition THEN
  DO
    instruction1
    instruction2
    instructionlast
  END
```

where *condition* is a standard IF condition and the instructions are the sequence of instructions you want executed when *condition* is true. You can see more of this in DO-1.CMD.

Looping a fixed number of times

Sometimes your looping needs are fairly simple. You want to display a message a fixed number of times or you want to give the user a certain number of attempts to enter the proper password. The DO instruction has the ability to do this. The syntax is:

```
DO number
  instruction1
  instruction2
  instructionlast
END
```

where *number* is the number of times to repeat the loop. It must be a positive whole number. The instructions are the sequence of instructions to execute each time the loop is executed. You can see this in DO-2.CMD, which executes a loop and displays a single line of text 20 times.

Counting the loops

The DO *number*/END loop has two main drawbacks. First, the loop number isn't available to the program. That is, the program might be on the 12th loop but that number isn't available to the program. Second, you can't control the starting point, ending point, and incrementing amount of the loop. The DO instruction, however, can do all this. The syntax is:

```
DO I = startnum TO endnum BY increment
  instruction1
  instruction2
  instructionlast
End
```

where I in the name of the variable to store the loop counter value. Any legal variable name is acceptable. *Startnum* is the first value to assign to I. If *startnum* is being read from another variable, it's possible for its value to exceed the value of *endnum*. When that happens, the loop simply isn't executed. No error condition is raised.

Endnum is the last value to use. The first time I reaches or exceeds this value, the loop stops. This checking is performed before the loop starts, so:

```
DO I = 1 TO 5 BY 3
  SAY I
END
```

would loop through once with a value of 1 and a second time with a value of 4 (1+3), but would stop before the loop with the value of 7 (4+3), because it exceeds 5.

Increment is the amount to increase the loop-counter variable by each time it goes through the loop. There's no requirement that *increment* be positive. In fact, the following loop is completely valid:

```
DO I = 10 TO 1 BY -1
  SAY I
END
```

If no value is specified for *increment*, its default value is one. The instructions are the sequence of instructions to process each time the program goes through the loop.

This is an important concept, so let's look at a couple of examples. The program DO-3.CMD contains three examples. The first one is as follows:

```
DO I = 1 TO 12 BY 3
   SAY "First Loop Number:" I
END
```

This loop uses the loop-counter variable I. Its beginning value is 1 and its ending value is 12. One is less than 12 and the loop counter is positive, so the loop will be executed at least once. The first time through the loop, I has a value of 1. The increment is 3, so the next time through I has a value of 4 (1+3). The next time it's 7 (4+3), and the next time it's 10 (7+3). The loop isn't executed again because 10+3=13 and that exceeds the ending value of 12. You can see this in Figure 10.1. The next DO loop is very similar:

```
DO LoopCounter = 1 TO 8 BY 3
   SAY "Second Loop Number:" LoopCounter
END
```

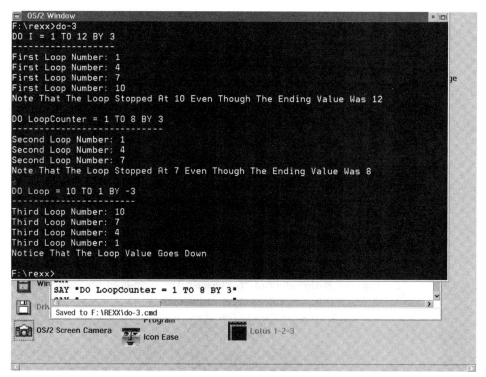

Figure 10.1 Using the DO I = *start* TO *end* BY *increment* format, you have a great deal of control over how the DO command performs its loops.

This time the loop-counter variable is named LoopCounter. Its initial value is 1, then 4, and then 7. This terminates the loop. You can see this in Figure 10.1. The final example from DO-3.CMD uses a negative increment:

```
DO Loop = 10 TO 1 BY -3
  SAY "Third Loop Number:" Loop
END
```

The initial value for the loop-counter variable Loop is 10, and the ending value is 1. However, the increment is negative so the loop is executed. The first value for Loop is 10, the next is 7 (10–3), the next is 4 (7–3), and the last is 1 (4–1).

Leaving the loop early

Occasionally, you might need to leave a loop early, for example, if you give the user three chances to enter the password correctly and he gets it right the first time. You don't want to ask two more times! Or if your backup program is trying to copy all your modified programs to the A: drive, but it finds the disk is full.

REXX gives you two different ways to leave a loop early. The first method is the LEAVE instruction. When this instruction is executed, it immediately causes the program to jump to the statement directly following the END instruction for the current loop. It's most useful to exit a loop when a specific condition has been met. As a general rule, the LEAVE instruction is issued after an IF test on a certain condition. For example, PASSWORD.CMD loops through five times asking the user for a password. If the user enters the correct password (Ronny), then it uses the LEAVE instruction to exit the loop. The code to do this is:

```
DO I = 1 TO 5
  PARSE PULL Word .
  IF Word = "Ronny" THEN LEAVE
  IF I = 5 THEN
    DO
      SAY "Correct Password Not Entered"
      SAY "Exiting Program"
      EXIT
    END
END
SAY "Correct Password Entered"
SAY "Rest Of Program Would Be Here"
```

Notice how PASSWORD.CMD tests the loop-counter variable to see if it has reached five yet. This is one example of where the program needs access to the value of the loop-counter variable. The program then uses this information to exit the program after the fifth attempt. If it didn't do this, after the fifth execution the loop would be done and the program would continue even if the user hadn't entered a valid password. You can see another example of the LEAVE instruction in DO-4.CMD.

The second way to leave a DO loop is with the FOR subinstruction. The syntax is:

```
DO I = startnum TO endnum BY increment FOR exitnum
  instruction1
```

```
    instruction2
    instructionlast
END
```

where *exitnum* is the maximum number of times to repeat the loop. It must be a whole number. All the other terms have the same use as discussed previously. The *exitnum* sets a maximum number of loops to execute, but it doesn't otherwise affect the number of loops to execute. In the following example:

```
DO I = 1 TO 20 BY 1 FOR 50
  SAY I
END
```

the loop will execute 20 times, which is less than the maximum of 50 specified by *exitnum*, so it has no impact on this loop. However, in the following example:

```
DO I = 1 TO 20 BY 1 FOR 5
  SAY I
END
```

the loop is supposed to execute 20 times, but the value of *exitnum* is five so the loop will execute only five times. You can see more examples of the FOR subinstruction in DO-4.CMD.

In an OS/2 batch file, you can jump to anywhere in the batch file by first placing a label in the batch file and then using a GOTO command (the "brute force" way). For example:

```
@ECHO OFF
GOTO SKIP
ECHO This Line Is Never Executed
:SKIP
```

REXX programs have a similar instruction, called SIGNAL. Labels are written with the colon at the end and don't have the eight-character limitation of batch file label names. Otherwise, the syntax is very similar. A REXX version of the previous batch file would look like this:

```
SIGNAL SKIP
SAY "This Line Is Never Executed"
SKIP:
```

However, the SIGNAL instruction has a major limitation that makes it generally unappealing both for exiting loops and for transferring control within a REXX program. The SIGNAL instruction cancels all DO loops, all IF tests, and all SELECT tests. When I first started writing REXX programs, I tried to write a program similar to the following segment from DO-7.CMD:

```
DO I = 1 TO 10
  SAY "Loop Number:" I
  IF I > 5 THEN SIGNAL SKIP
  SAY "This Line Only Executed For I <= 5"
```

```
      SKIP:
   END
```

where I tried to skip around inside a loop using the SIGNAL instruction. While the program stays within the DO loop area, the loop is canceled and the program will abort the first time it encounters an END instruction. You can see this in Figure 10.2.

The moral is twofold. First, there's usually a better approach to altering program flow than using the SIGNAL instruction. Second, when you do need to use the SIGNAL instruction, be very careful.

Looping forever

If you want a loop to continue forever, the DO instruction has a option for that. The syntax is:

```
DO FOREVER
   instructions
END
```

A DO FOREVER loop might be used in a program like TODO.CMD, to continually loop through a menu where the user selects a menu option and one of the options

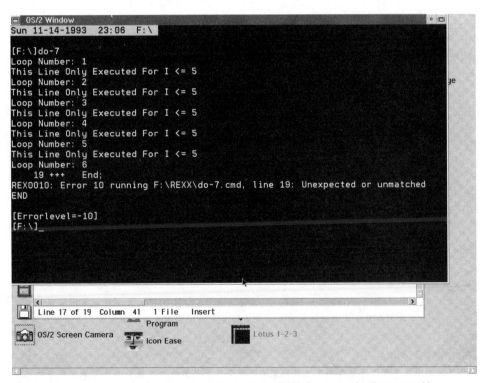

Figure 10.2 Trying to jump around inside a DO loop with a SIGNAL command will cause problems.

uses the EXIT instruction to leave the program. It might also be used to loop until some condition is met, at which point the program will leave the loop with a LEAVE instruction. You can see the DO FOREVER instruction in DO-5.CMD.

Looping until a condition is met

With the LEAVE instruction, you can test for the existence of a specific condition and then exit the program when that condition is met. You can also specify that condition on the DO instruction line using the UNTIL subinstruction. The syntax is:

```
DO I = startnum TO endnum BY increment UNTIL condition
  instruction1
  instruction2
  instructionlast
End
```

where *condition* is the condition that causes the loop to terminate. For example:

```
DO I = 1 TO 10 BY 2 UNTIL I > 5
  SAY I
END
```

will stop on the loop when I equals 7 because that is the first time it's greater than five. You can see another example in DO-6.CMD. For this example, you need to know that RANDOM(100) generates a random whole number between zero and 100.

Altering the loop counter

Occasionally, you need to process most of the values in a list but perhaps skip one or two, for example, if you want to execute a DO I = 1 TO 20 loop but need to skip the value of 15. The ITERATE instruction does just this. When REXX encounters the ITERATE instruction, it increments the loop counter by its increment value and jumps over all the remaining code down to the END statement. In other words, all the remaining code in the loop is skipped for that pass. For example, this code from DO-8.CMD:

```
DO Loop = 1 TO 20
  IF Loop =  5 THEN ITERATE
  IF Loop = 10 THEN ITERATE
  IF Loop = 15 THEN ITERATE
  IF Loop = 20 THEN ITERATE
  SAY "Currently On Loop Number" Loop
END
```

will skip loop values of 5, 10, 15, and 20 so the display created by the SAY instruction will display values of only 1–4, 6–9, 11–14, and 16–19.

Nesting DO loops

A DO loop is nested when you put one DO loop inside another DO loop. For example, DO-9.CMD uses the following code to count from 0,000 to 9,999 on the screen:

```
DO Thousand = 0 TO 9
  DO Hundred = 0 TO 9
    DO Ten = 0 TO 9
      DO One = 0 TO 9
        SAY Thousand ¦¦ "," ¦¦ Hundred ¦¦ Ten ¦¦ One
      End
    END
  END
END
```

The Thousand loop has three DO loops nested inside it, the Hundred loop has two, and the Ten loop has one.

In this setup, the Thousand loop begins with a value of zero. The next line starts the Hundred loop with a value of zero. The next line begins the Ten loop with a value of zero. The next line begins the One loop with a value of zero. Since the next two lines are inside the One loop, it loops through 10 times, with values 0–9. After that, the program passes the first END instruction and reaches the second END instruction.

That causes the value of the Ten loop to be increased by one. Now the program does everything inside the Ten loop again, which means running through the One loop again. Once the Ten loop has been gone through 10 times, the Hundred loop is gone through again, which means running through the Ten loop again, which means running through the One loop 10 times per Ten loop. The result is that the One loop is executed 10,000 times, the Ten loop is executed 1,000 times, the Hundred loop is executed 100 times, and the Thousand loop is executed 10 times.

In fact, the nested DO loops work exactly like the mechanical dials on your car's odometer. The first dial has to make a complete circle before it moves the next dial one digit. That dial has to make a complete circle before it moves the next dial one digit, and so on.

DO-9.CMD is great for understanding nested loops. It has four DO loops running together, so three of them are nested. It also has a visual display that shows the current value for each DO loop as well as the total number of times it has executed so far.

As you might expect, with a lot of nested DO loops it can become hard to keep them straight. REXX is supposed to help by allowing you to specify the name of the loop-counter variable after the END instruction and REXX will check and make sure that the right DO loop is being terminated. This is illustrated in the code from DO-11.CMD:

```
DO I = 1 TO 10
  DO J = 1 TO I
    SAY I ¦¦ "," ¦¦ J
  END I
END J
```

This code contains an error because the loops are closed in the wrong order. The J loop is the inside loop and must be closed first. However, this feature hasn't been implemented as of OS/2 2.1, so this code will run fine.

More on altering loops

In the last two sections, I've explained the ITERATE instruction, which is used for incrementing loop-counter variables, and nest DO loops for including one or more DO loops inside another DO loop. After these discussions, however, it's necessary to revisit the ITERATE instruction. Consider the following code:

```
DO I = 1 TO 5
  DO J = 1 TO 4
    IF J = 3 THEN ITERATE
    SAY I || "," || J
  END
END
```

As written, this program will display 1,1; 1,2; 1,4; 2,1; 2,2; 2,4; 3,1; 3,2; 3,4; 4,1; 4,2; 4,4; 5,1; 5,2; and 5,4. The ITERATE instruction allows you to name the loop to be incremented after the instruction, and the loop so named doesn't have to be the innermost loop in which the ITERATE instruction is located. For example, the following code uses the ITERATE instruction to increment the outer loop:

```
DO I = 1 TO 5
  DO J = 1 TO 4
    IF J = 3 THEN ITERATE I
    SAY I || "," || J
  END
END
```

When specified in this fashion, the name after the ITERATE must exactly match the name of the loop-counter variable to increment, except that the capitalization doesn't have to match.

When an outer loop is incremented with the ITERATE instruction, all its nested loops are canceled, so this code would display 1,1; 1,2; 2,1; 2,2; 3,1; 3,2; 4,1; 4,2; 5,1; and 5,2. You can see both of these code segments in operation in DO-10.CMD.

Summary

This chapter has discussed logic testing with the IF and SELECT instructions, and looping with the DO instruction.

11

Built-in Functions

REXX has a wealth of built-in functions for manipulating data. These are the functions that are available on every implementation of REXX across all platforms. These built-in or internal functions are discussed in this chapter. OS/2 REXX also has a wealth of external functions that give it even more power. These external functions are discussed in the next chapter. Before I explain the individual functions, a few notes are in order:

- A set of parentheses is always required after a function name, even if the function doesn't have any arguments.

- Many functions can be called in two different ways: using a variable and using the CALL instruction. For example, the CLS.CMD external REXX function can be executed with either of the following instructions:

```
Result = CLS()
CALL CLS
```

Many internal and RexxUtil external functions can be executed both ways. When a function is executed using the CALL instruction, the function parameters are listed after the name and separated with commas, but they aren't enclosed inside parentheses.

- The opening parenthesis must come immediately after the function name, without any space between the name and the parenthesis.

- If a function requires a numeric argument, that argument is rounded according to the setting of NUMERIC DIGITS before being supplied to the function. It's also checked for validity before being supplied to the function.

- Internally, functions work with the settings NUMERIC DIGITS 9 and NUMERIC FUZZ 0, regardless of the external setting.

- When a function returns a numeric value, that value must be compatible with the current NUMERIC DIGITS setting.

- When a function requires a string, a null string is always acceptable.

- When a function requires a length, it must be a non-negative whole number.

- When a number is used as the starting point in a string, it must be a positive whole number.

- When the last argument is optional, a comma can be added to the end of the argument list to indicate that the last argument has been omitted.

- When a pad argument is specified, it must be exactly one character long.

- When an option is selected by a character, capitalization is not important.

Before you look at the individual functions, I need to explain how the syntax for these functions is presented.

Syntax

On the syntax lines in this book, a word in all capital letters indicates a keyword. Words in mixed case, like SysCurPos, indicate a function. I've used mixed case for functions because some of them have very long names, like SysWaitNamedPipe, where the different parts of the name mean something. Using mixed capitalization makes those parts more visible, and the function easier to recognize. However, many functions—especially internal function—have only one word in their name, like Translate or Time. Variable information or input expected by functions are shown in lowercase italic. These names simply describe the type of information that should appear. When a variable or input is optional, its name is enclosed inside square brackets. With this in mind, let's look at the individual functions.

Application Programming Interface Functions

It's easy to extend the REXX language using external functions. These external functions can be written in REXX, like the CLS.CMD and PAUSE.CMD programs included with this book, or in another language like C++.

Using an external function written in REXX is easy. You simply locate the .CMD file in a subdirectory in your path and then access the program. If the program performs a function but doesn't need to return a value, then simply call the program. For example, CLS.CMD clears the screen and PAUSE.CMD pauses the screen until a key is pressed. Since neither return a value to the program that calls it, you run them with the instructions:

```
CALL CLS
CALL PAUSE
```

PAUSE.CMD takes an optional argument, CLS, and clears the screen after a key is pressed if it receives that argument. To pass one or more arguments when calling an external REXX program in this fashion, simply list them after the name of the function. If there's more than one, they must be separated with commas. For example:

```
CALL PAUSE CLS
```

would run PAUSE.CMD and pass it a CLS argument. When the external REXX function needs to return information, like COMMAS.CMD or FACTORAL.CMD, then you simply use it like any other function. For example, the COMMAS.CMD function takes a single number without commas and inserts commas in the integer portion of the number. If it's passed a second argument with the value of *decimal*, then it also inserts commas in the decimal portion of the number. The syntax for calling COMMAS.CMD is:

```
formatted = COMMAS(number[,"decimal"])
```

just like any internal REXX function. Of course, *number* is the number to be formatted by the function.

The external function FACTORAL.CMD computes the factorial of an integer, 0 through 92. A factorial (written as *n!*) is the product of every integer between one and the number a factorial is being computed for. So 3! is 3*2*1 or 6, and 10! is 10*9*8*7*6*5*4*3*2*1 or 3,628,800. As you can see, the numbers get large very fast, which is the reason the maximum value REXX can find a factorial of is 92. (Note that 0! is defined to be 1.) The syntax for calling FACTORAL.CMD is:

```
answer = FACTORAL(number)
```

where *number* is the number to compute the factorial of. Regardless of the method used, calling an external REXX program is similar to calling an internal routine. However, the external function has an implicit procedure instruction since all of the variables from the calling program are always hidden. Also, the state of internal values, such as the numeric setting, starts at the default rather than using the value from the calling program. Finally, the EXIT instruction can be used in an external function without terminating the calling program.

External functions can also be written in other languages, like C++ or Pascal. However, the techniques for doing so are beyond the scope of this book. My purpose here is to discuss how to use those functions once they've been written and debugged.

REXX offers something most other languages lack: an interface that allows communications to and from other languages and applications. This is called an *application programming interface* (API). In fact, any OS/2 program with the appropriate interface can use REXX as its own macro or script language.

You can also use other programming languages to program extensions to the REXX language in the form of external functions. REXX offers three functions for managing external functions. These are documented in the following sections and summarized in Table 11.1.

TABLE 11.1 Application Program Interface Functions

Function	Summary
RxFuncAdd	Registers external functions.
RxFuncDrop	Drops external functions.
RxFuncQuery	Checks to see if an external function has already been loaded.
RxQuery	Works with external data queues.
SysDropFuncs	This function drops all the RexxUtil external functions.

RxFuncAdd

Before REXX can access an external function, that external function must be "registered" with the REXX interpreter. RxFuncAdd (REXX Function Add) is the function that registers external functions. Its syntax is:

```
RxFuncAdd(name,module,procedure)
```

where *name* is the name of the external function, *module* is the name of the external module containing the external function, and *procedure* is the name of the entry point for the external function. Once an external function has been added to by a REXX program, it's available to REXX in all sessions.

RxFuncDrop

RxFuncDrop (REXX Function Drop) lets your program drop an external function that was added with the RxFuncAdd function. The syntax is:

```
RxFuncDrop(name)
```

where *name* is the name of the function to drop.

RxFuncQuery

RxFuncQuery (REXX Function Query) lets your program check to see if a function has already been loaded. The syntax is:

```
RxFuncQuery(name)
```

where *name* is the name of the function to check on. The program SHOWRX.CMD that comes with this book shows using each of these three functions to work in external functions.

RxQuery

There is a fourth API function for working with external data queues, called RxQueue.

Function search order

I've just finished explaining how to register external functions with the REXX interpreter, so now's a good time to discuss the search order REXX uses to find functions. A REXX program can have three different types of functions:

Internal labels. These are the functions you write into your program, like the FACTORIAL function inside FACTORAL.CMD.

Internal functions. These are functions, like ARG( ), that are built into the language.

External functions. These are external REXX programs, like PAUSE.CMD, or functions written in other languages and attached to REXX.

Normally, REXX searches for internal labels first, internal functions second, and external functions last. If the name of the function is enclosed in quotation marks, internal labels aren't checked, so only internal functions and external functions are checked—in that order. This lets you give an internal label function the same name as an internal function and still bypass it for the internal function as required.

One important note is in order. All internal functions and many external functions have their names in all uppercase. While capitalization normally doesn't matter, when you're putting the name of a function inside quotation marks, its capitalization must match the capitalization used for the function. So all calls to internal functions inside quotation marks must be in all uppercase.

Bitwise Functions

Bitwise functions perform a logical comparison of the individual binary bits making up two strings. Bitwise functions are a very specialized type of function and most REXX readers can safely skip all three of them. They can be useful in very specialized applications, like a simple form of data encryption and translating database formats. They're documented in the following sections and summarized in Table 11.2.

BitAnd

BitAnd is a way of comparing the binary equilavents of two strings on a bit-by-bit basis. The syntax is:

```
BitAnd(string1,string2[,pad])
```

TABLE 11.2 Bitwise Functions

Function	Summary
BitAnd	Returns a one when the bit from each of the two strings is a one, and a zero otherwise.
BitOr	Returns a one when the bit from either of the two strings is one, and a zero otherwise.
BixXOr	Returns a one when the bit from the two strings are different and a zero when they are the same.

where *string1* is the first string to be compared, *string2* is the second string to be compared, and *pad* is the padding to use when one of the strings is shorter than the other. If no pad is provided, when one string is exhausted the unprocessed portion of the longer string is appended to results. When a pad is provided, the shorter string is padded so its length is equal to the longer string.

To understand the operation of BitAnd, it's necessary to remember that each character can be represented, in binary form, as a series of zeros and ones. Once the string is represented in this form, you can stack them on top of each other, like this:

```
0010
0011
```

Once arranged in this fashion, the BitAnd function returns a one (logical true) if and only if both of the bits are the same and if they're a logical true (one). In other words, BitAnd places a one below each column that has two ones in it, and a zero below all other columns. In the example, this would return:

```
0010
0011
----
0010
```

For a slightly longer example, consider the character strings X and Q. The BitAnd function would look like this:

```
01011000
01010001
--------
01010000
```

and thus return a 01010000 in binary, which represents a P string. For more examples, run the BITAND.CMD program that comes with this book. It will prompt you for two characters and then display the ASCII and binary versions of those characters along with the ASCII and binary versions of the results of the BitAnd function.

While all of these examples plus the operation of BITAND.CMD involve using BitAnd on single characters, it works just as well on longer strings. After all, a longer string is nothing more than a yet longer binary string.

BitOr

BitOr is a second way of comparing the binary equilavents of two strings on a bit-by-bit basis. The syntax is:

```
BitOr(string1,string2[,pad])
```

where *string1* is the first string to be compared, *string2* is the second string to be compared, and *pad* is the padding to use when one of the strings is shorter than the other. If no pad is provided, when one string is exhausted the unprocessed portion of the longer string is appended to results. When a pad is provided, the shorter string is padded so its length is equal to the longer string.

To understand the operation of BitOr, it's necessary to remember that each character can be represented, in binary form, as a series of zeros and ones. Once the string is represented in this form, you can stack them on top of each other, like this:

```
0010
0011
```

Once arranged in this fashion, the BitOr function returns a one (logical true) if either character is a logical true (one). In other words, BitOr places a one below each column that has a one in it and a zero below all columns containing only zeros. In the example, this would return:

```
0010
0011
----
0011
```

For a slightly longer example, consider the character strings X and Q. The BitOr function would look like this:

```
01011000
01010001
--------
01011001
```

and so return a 01011001 in binary, which represents a Y string. For more examples, run the BITOR.CMD program that comes with this book. It will prompt you for two characters, then display the ASCII and binary versions of those characters along with the ASCII and binary versions of the results of the BitOr function. Like BitAnd, BitOr can also work on longer strings.

BitXOr

BitXOr is a third way of comparing the binary equilavents of two strings on a bit-by-bit basis. The syntax is:

```
BitXOr(string1,string2[,pad])
```

where *string1* is the first string to be compared, *string2* is the second string to be compared, and *pad* is the padding to use when one of the strings is shorter than the other. If no pad is provided, when one string is exhausted the unprocessed portion of the longer string is appended to results. When a pad is provided, the shorter string is padded so its length is equal to the longer string.

To understand the operation of BitXOr, it's necessary to remember that each character can be represented, in binary form, as a series of zeros and ones. Once the string is represented in this form, you can stack them on top of each other, like this:

```
0010
0011
```

Once arranged in this fashion, the BitXOr function returns a one (logical true) if and only if the two digits are different. In other words, BitXOr places a one below each column that has a single zero and a single one, and a zero below all other columns. In the example, this would return:

```
0010
0011
----
0001
```

For a slightly longer example, consider the character strings X and Q. The BitAnd function would look like this:

```
01011000
01010001
--------
00001001
```

and thus return a 00001001 in binary, which represents a tab. For more examples, run the BITXOR.CMD program that comes with this book, which will prompt you for two characters and then display the ASCII and binary versions of those characters along with the ASCII and binary versions of the results of the BitXOr function. Like BitAnd and BitOr, BitXOr can work with longer strings.

Exception Handling

Exception handling (also called error handling) is the ability of a program to respond to unexpected conditions. This is discussed in detail in chapter 16. The exception-handling internal functions are discussed in the following sections and summarized in Table 11.3.

TABLE 11.3 Exception-Handling Functions

Function	Summary
ErrorText	Returns the REXX error message associated with a given error number.
SourceLine	Displays lines of the currently active program.
Trace	Returns the trace setting and, optionally, changes it.

Condition

REXX traps for six conditions: error, failure, halt, no value, not ready, and syntax. The Condition function returns information about the currently trapped condition. The syntax is:

```
Condition[option]
```

where *option* is one of the following:

C. This returns the name of the currently trapped condition.

D. This returns a description of the currently trapped condition. If no description is available, a null string is returned.

I. This returns the name of the keyword that was being executed when the condition was raised.

S. This returns the state of the currently trapped condition.

If no condition is currently trapped, then each option will return a null string.

ErrorText

The ErrorText function returns the REXX error message associated with an error number. The syntax is:

```
ErrorText(number)
```

where *number* is a whole number zero through 99. If there's no text associated with that number, a null string is returned. The program ERRORTXT.CMD that comes with this book displays the text for all the valid error numbers.

SourceLine

The SourceLine function displays lines of the currently active program. The syntax is:

```
SourceLine([n])
```

when *n* is the line to display. If *n* isn't specified, the last line is displayed. If no lines are available, a zero is returned. For examples, run the SOURCE.CMD program that comes with this book.

Trace

The Trace function returns the trace setting that's in effect and optionally changes it. The syntax is:

```
Trace([setting])
```

If *setting* is supplied, it's used to change the trace setting. See the Trace keyword in chapter 13 for more details.

File Management

REXX has several functions for working with files. These functions allow you to open files, read data from files, write data to files, and close files. Those functions are documented in the following sections and summarized in Table 11.4.

TABLE 11.4 File-Management Functions

Function	Summary
CharIn	Reads one or more characters from a character input stream.
Chars	Returns the total number of characters remaining in the character input stream.
CharOut	Writes one or more characters to the character output stream.
LineIn	Reads data from the character input stream one line at a time.
LineOut	Writes data to the character output stream one line at a time.
Lines	Returns a one if any data remains after the read/write position and a zero otherwise.
Stream	Proves many of the file-management functions of these other functions. However, it is being phased out and it is suggested that you not use it.

CharIn

The CharIn function reads one or more characters from a character input stream. The character input stream can be either a file or the keyboard. The keyboard is the default. The syntax of the instruction is:

```
CharIn(stream[,start][,length])
```

where *stream* is the name of the character stream to use (when no name is given, the keyboard is used), *start* is the first position to read, and *length* is the number of characters to read (the default is one).

When reading characters from the keyboard, CharIn simply reads the specified number of characters. The keyboard is called a *transient stream*. Keep in mind that some characters, like the Return and cursor-movement keys, are treated by REXX as consisting of two characters rather than one. Any additional keystrokes the user pressed that aren't used by the CharIn function are left in the keyboard buffer for later use. For that reason, the CharIn is usually not the best method of reading keystrokes from the keyboard. The CharIn function is more useful for reading other transient streams, such as a serial port or data collection port.

If there are fewer characters available than specified by the *length* argument, then program execution will halt until enough characters become available to satisfy the *length* argument. However, if it's impossible for that many characters to become available due to an error or other problem, the NotReady condition will be raised and CharIn will return with fewer characters than specified.

The CharIn function can also be used to read characters from a file. When used in this fashion, the file is called a *persistent stream*. For each different persistent stream used by the CharIn, it maintains a cursor position. That position is the default for the next read using an instruction like CharIn and LineIn, and write using an instruction like CharOut and LineOut. When a read is completed, the cursor position is increased by the number of characters that were read. Standard REXX calls for CharIn to maintain a different read and write position in a persistent stream. OS/2 REXX doesn't support this. Rather, it maintains a single cursor position for each file.

Rather than using the default cursor position, you can specify a new start position by specifying the *start* argument. When a *start* argument is specified, the cursor position maintained by REXX is reset to the new *start* position plus the number of characters that was read. When specifying a *start* read position, it must be a positive number and within the bounds of the stream being read. It should also not be specified for a transient stream.

Chars

Chars returns the total number of characters remaining in the character input stream. This count includes any line separation characters. For a persistent stream, the measurement is made from the current read position. The syntax is:

```
Chars([name])
```

where *name* is the name of the stream to read. You can leave it blank to read the default stream. The program CHARS.CMD that comes with this book uses this function to read the number of characters in your C:\CONFIG.SYS and C:\AUTOEXEC.BAT files.

CharOut

Like the CharIn function, the CharOut function is used on one or more characters at a time. The character output stream can be either a file or the screen. The screen is the default. The syntax of the instruction is:

```
CharOut(stream[,string,start])
```

where *stream* is the name of the character stream to use (when no name is given, the screen is used), *string* is the set of characters to output, and *start* is the first position to write to.

The main use of CharOut is to write one of more characters to a file. It can also write characters to the Com ports and the screen. In fact, the screen is the default when no stream is named. However, the SAY instruction is generally much better at displaying information on the screen.

Let's look at several examples using the CharOut function. First, assume you have a text file called MYFILE.TXT containing the following text. So you can follow the examples more easily, I've added character-count markers below the text:

```
now is the time for all good men to vote.
  ¦    ¦    ¦    ¦    ¦    ¦    ¦    ¦  ¦
  5   10   15   20   25   30   35   40 45
```

The instruction CHAROUT("MYFILE.TXT","Now",1) would write the string Now on top of the existing string starting at position 1, and the file would look like this:

```
Now is the time for all good men to vote.
  ¦    ¦    ¦    ¦    ¦    ¦    ¦    ¦  ¦
  5   10   15   20   25   30   35   40 45
```

with the cursor positioned over the first space character. The instruction CHAROUT ("MYFILE.TXT","people to vote.",30) would write the string people to vote. on top of the text starting at position 30, and the file would look like this:

```
Now is the time for all good people to vote.
    ¦     ¦     ¦     ¦     ¦     ¦     ¦     ¦     ¦
    5    10    15    20    25    30    35    40    45
```

Had you tried to overwrite men with people like this, CHAROUT("MYFILE.TXT", "people",30), then the file would look like this:

```
Now is the time for all good people vote.
    ¦     ¦     ¦     ¦     ¦     ¦     ¦     ¦   ¦
    5    10    15    20    25    30    35    40  45
```

The CharOut function is always in overwrite mode. Since the people string is longer than the men string, additional text was overwritten. You must always be very careful when using the CharOut function to be sure you don't inadvertently overwrite text you want to keep.

CharOut has another very important function. The instruction CALL CHAROUT (*file*) closes the file. Files should always be closed when you're finished reading from and writing to them to reduce the chances of the file being damaged.

For persistent streams, the CharOut function maintains its cursor position in each stream. Like the CharIn function, the read and write cursor position is always the same. The initial write position is the end of the file, so new text is appended to the end of the file.

When a program calls CharOut to output text, the execution of that program stops until the CharOut function is finished. If it becomes impossible for all the characters to be written to the output stream, the NotReady condition is raised and CharOut has a return value equal to the number of characters remaining to be written to the output stream.

If you would like to see examples of the CharOut function in action, the CHAR OUT.CMD program that comes with this book has several examples. It creates a temporary file called JUNK.@@!, which it erases when it finishes. However, if this file exists when you start CHAROUT.CMD, it will refuse to run in order to protect your data.

LineIn

The LineIn function reads data from a data file one line at a time. REXX maintains a read and write position in a file. Under OS/2, these two are always the same. The LineIn function begins reading from this read/write position and reads the remainder of the line. Therefore, if the read/write position is in the middle of a line, less than a full line of data will be returned by the LineIn function. The syntax is:

```
LineIn([name][,line][,count])
```

where *name* is the name of the stream to read from. If the name is omitted, LineIn reads from the default input stream. *Line* is the number of the line to begin reading from. Under OS/2, the only valid value for *line* is a one to reset the read/write position to the start of the file. *Count* is the number of lines to return from the stream. The only valid values are zero (no lines returned) or one (one line returned). Some examples follow:

```
LineIn()                        ---Returns---> One Line From
                                               Default Stream
LineIn(LINEIN.CMD)      ------------> One Line From File
LineIn(LINEIN.CMD,1,0) ------------> Opens File, No Read
                                               If Already Open
                                               Resets To Start
LineIn(LINEIN.CMD,,0)                    Opens File, No Read
```

For more examples, run the LINEIN.CMD program that comes with the book. Additionally, the TODO.CMD program that comes with this book uses LineIn to read its data from a data file.

The LineIn function returns a value of zero or one that can be used to check on its success. A zero means no line was read while a one means that one line was read. If you're planning for a program to have a dialog with the user, the PARSE PULL keyword is a better approach. This is discussed in chapter 13.

LineOut

The LineOut function writes data to a data file one line at a time. REXX maintains a read and write position in a file. Under OS/2, these two are always the same. The LineOut function begins writing from this read/write position and writes the remainder of the line. A new line isn't generated until the end of the write, so when LineOut begin writing in the middle of the line its text will be appended onto that line. The syntax is:

```
LineOut([name][,string][,line])
```

where *name* is the name of the output stream to write to. If this is omitted, the string is written to the default stream. *String* is the character string to write to. LineOut automatically adds a carriage return after the string. If *string* is a null string, a new line is generated in the file but no data is written. *Line* is the line number to write to. One is the only acceptable value for *line* and this resets the read/write pointer to the beginning of the file.

LineOut returns the number of lines remaining to be written when it terminates. A value of zero means the write was successful and none if the character string remains to be written. A value of one means that some or all of the data was not successfully written to the stream. Some examples follow:

```
A = LineOut(,"To Screen")   ---Results---> Writes String
                                           To Screen
A = LineOut(MyFile,"ABC")   ------------> Writes String
                                           To File
CALL LineOut(MyFile,"XYZ")  ------------> Writes String
                                           To File
CALL LineOut(MyFile)        ------------> Closes File
```

For more examples, run the LINEOUT.CMD program that comes with this book.

Lines

The Lines function returns a one if any data remains after the read/write position and a zero if no data remains. In effect, it reports whether or not a read by CharIn or LineIn will work. The syntax is:

```
Lines([name])
```

where *name* is the name of the stream to read. It can be left blank to read the default stream. Note that this is different under OS/2 than under standard REXX, where Lines returns the number of completed lines remaining in the data stream.

Stream

The Stream function provides many of the file- and stream-management functions that are provided by other functions, such as the CharIn function. The ANSI REXX committee is considering replacing this function with other instructions so you might want to avoid using it in your programs. The syntax for the Stream function is:

```
Stream(name, function[, instruction])
```

where *name* is the name of the stream to access or process and *function* is an instruction to Stream to tell it what to do. There are three possible values for *function*:

C (command). This performs an operation on the named stream. The command requires a subcommand to tell the Stream function what command to perform.

D (description). This returns the state of the named stream (just like the State subinstruction) and information about the ERROR and NOTREADY states.

S (state). This returns the state of the named stream.

When using the S value, one of four states is returned:

ERROR. The stream has been subjected to an improper operation. This could happen during input or output, or when using the Stream function.

NOTREADY. The stream is in a condition where input or output conditions would raise the NOTREADY condition. For example, the read/write pointer is positioned at the end of the stream and thus nothing can be read.

READY. The stream is ready for input or output operations.

UNKNOWN. The state of the stream is unknown. This usually means that the stream is a file and it hasn't yet been opened.

The available values for *instruction* are:

OPEN. Opens the named stream for reading and writing.

OPEN WRITE. Opens the named stream for writing.

OPEN READ. Opens the named stream for reading.

CLOSE. Closes the named stream.

SEEK offset. Moves the read/write position a given number of characters (the offset) within a persistent stream. Of course, the stream must be opened first. The offset can be expressed in one of four ways:

=#. Specifies the offset from the start of the stream. This is the default if a number is provided without a prefix.

<#. Specifies the offset from the end of the stream.

+#. Specifies the offset forwards from the current read/write position.

–#. Specifies the offset backwards from the current read/write position.

QUERY EXISTS. Returns the full path to the stream or a null string if it doesn't exist.

QUERY SIZE. Returns the size of a persistent stream in bytes.

QUERY DATETIME. Returns the date and time of a stream.

Format-Conversion Functions

Format-conversion functions are used to convert a string from one format to another. This modified form can be displayed, can be stored under another variable, or can replace the original form. These are documented in the following sections and summarized in Table 11.5.

TABLE 11.5 Format-Conversion Functions

Function	Summary
B2X	Converts a binary string into an equivalent hexadecimal string.
C2D	Converts a character string into the decimal value of the binary representation of the character string.
C2X	Converts a character string into its hexadecimal representation.
D2C	Converts a decimal number into a binary representation.
D2X	Converts a decimal number into a hexadecimal number.
X2B	Converts a hexadecimal string into a binary string.
X2C	Converts a hexadecimal string into a character string.
X2D	Converts a hexadecimal string into a decimal string.

B2X

The B2X function converts a binary string (0 or 1) into an equivalent hexadecimal string (0–9 or A–F). See the sections in chapter 5 on defining binary and hexadecimal strings. The syntax is:

```
B2X(binarystring)
```

where *binarystring* is a binary string made up of zeros and ones. The value returned by B2X uses uppercase letters and doesn't contain any spaces. Some examples follow:

```
B2X('01010010')                                     Returns '52'
B2X('01111001')                                     ------> '79'
B2X('01010010 01101111 01101110 01101110 01111001') ------> '526F6E6E79'
```

If you want to experiment more, the STRCONVT.CMD program that comes with this book makes a number of string conversions. B2X can be combined with other format conversion functions in order to convert binary strings into other formats.

C2D

The C2D function is a function that not many REXX programmers will need. It takes a character string and returns the decimal value of the binary representation (encoding) on the character string. Its syntax is:

```
C2D(string[,n])
```

where *string* is the character string to convert and n is an optional length. When n is specified, *string* is taken as a signed number expressed in n characters. If the leftmost character is zero, the number is taken as positive. Otherwise, the number is taken as a negative number in two's complement form. If n is zero, C2D returns a zero.

For example, the string "FF81"x converts to 65409. Since hexadecimal numbers can take on 16 different values, the conversion is:

```
(15*16³)+(15*16²)+(8*16¹)+(1*16⁰)=65409
```

Three notes are in order. First, recall that the hexadecimal number F has a value of 15. Second, since this is a bit-by-bit conversion, the rightmost digit is raised to the zero power, the next to the first, and so on. Third, recall from high school math that any number raised to the zero power (except zero) equals one.

The conversion for the string Ronny is different. Since this is an ASCII string, the ASCII values are 82, 111, 110, 110, and 121. Since there are 256 different possible ASCII values, the equation becomes:

```
(82*256⁴)+(111*256³)+(110*256²)+(110*256¹)+(121*256⁰)
```

If you enter the instruction:

```
SAY C2D("Ronny")
```

into REXX, chances are you'll get an error message. That's because the answer is 354056826489 and this number exceeds the default setting (9) of NUMERIC DIGITS. For that reason, you have to be careful about your NUMERIC DIGITS setting when converting large strings.

As I said previously, C2D is not normally used by most REXX programmers. However, it does have one very useful function. If you enter a single ASCII digit, the conversion becomes $(\#*256^0)$ and, since the 256^0 portion equals one, the function will return the ASCII value of the character. For example, the instruction:

```
SAY C2D("R")
```

will return 82, the ASCII value of R. Of course, this works for only a single character at a time.

In two's complement form, the negative form of a number is formed by taking the positive binary representation of that number and changing all the ones and zeros in that number to zeros and ones, respectively, and then adding one to the number. Two's complement form leads to the simplest approach for adding and subtracting signed numbers. Also, in two's complement form you have only one zero, not a +0 and a –0. Last and least, you get one more negative number than positive. For four bits (0000–1111), for example, you get all the numbers from –8 to +7.

C2X

The C2X function takes a character string and converts it to its hexadecimal representation. Since each ASCII character takes two hexadecimal characters, the resulting string will be twice as long as the input string. The syntax is:

```
C2X(string)
```

where *string* is the character string to be converted. Some examples are:

```
SAY C2X('abc')        ---Returns--->    414243
SAY C2X('a')          ------------->    41
SAY C2X('b')          ------------->    42
SAY C2X('c')          ------------->    43
```

For more examples, run the STRCONVT.CMD program that comes with this book.

D2C

The D2C function returns a character string that's the binary representation of the decimal number supplied to the function. The syntax is:

```
D2C[number[,n])
```

where *number* is a non-negative whole number if *n* is not specified. If *n* is specified, it represents the length of the final string. Most readers won't use this function.

D2X

The D2X function converts a decimal number to a hexadecimal number. The resulting hexadecimal number uses all uppercase letters and doesn't contain any spaces. Unless a length is specified, the leading zeros are removed. This is called an *unpacked number*. The syntax is:

```
D2X(number[,n])
```

where *number* is a non-negative whole number (unless *n* is specified) and *n* is the optional length of the number to return. If the resulting number is shorter than *n*, it's padded with zeros. If it's too long, it's truncated on the left. Some examples are:

```
D2X(10)        ---Returns---> 'A'
D2X(10,5)      -------------> '0000A'
D2X(256)       -------------> '100'
D2X(-256,8)    -------------> 'FFFFFF00'
```

For more examples, run the D2X.CMD program that comes with this book.

X2B

The X2B function converts hexadecimal strings to binary strings. The syntax is:

```
X2B(hexstring)
```

where *hexstring* is the character string to convert. Some examples follow:

```
SAY X2B('FF')     ---Returns---> 11111111
SAY X2B(AB)       -------------> 10101011
SAY X2B(23)       -------------> 00100011
SAY X2B('48')     -------------> 01001000
```

For more examples, run the STRCONVT.CMD program that comes with this book.

X2C

The X2C function converts hexadecimal strings to character strings. The syntax is:

```
X2C(hexstring)
```

where *hexstring* is the character string to convert. Some examples follow:

```
SAY X2C(4869)          ---Returns---> Hi
SAY X2C(52 6F 6E 6E 79) -------------> Ronny
SAY X2C(4F532F32)      -------------> OS/2
SAY X2C(52 45 58 58)   -------------> REXX
```

For more examples, run the STRCONVT.CMD program that comes with this book.

X2D

The X2D function converts hexadecimal strings to decimal strings. The syntax is:

```
X2D(hexstring)
```

where *hexstring* is the character string to convert. Since the numbers can be fairly large, you need to make sure your NUMERIC DIGITS setting is high enough. Some examples follow:

```
SAY X2C(4869)        ---Returns---> 18537
SAY X2C(526F6E6E79) -------------> 354056826489
SAY X2C(4F532F32)   -------------> 1330851634
SAY X2C(52455858)   -------------> 1380276310
```

For more examples, run the STRCONVT.CMD program that comes with this book.

Mathematical Functions

Mathematical functions are those functions designed to perform numeric manipulations of numbers or variables. Those functions are documented in the following sections and in Table 11.6.

TABLE 11.6 Mathematical Functions

Function	Summary
Abs	Returns the absolute value of a number.
Max	Returns the largest value in a set of numbers.
Min	Returns the smallest value in a set of numbers.
Digits	Returns the current setting of NUMERIC DIGITS.
Form	Returns the current setting of NUMERIC FORM.
Format	Controls how many places are used before and after the decimal point when displaying a number.
Fuzz	Returns the current setting of NUMERIC FUZZ.
Random	Generates a random number.
Sign	Returns the sign of a number.
Trunc	Rounds a number to a specified number of decimal points.

Abs

The Abs function computes the absolute value of a number. If the number is zero or larger than zero, this has no effect on the number. If the number is less than zero, this converts it to a positive number. The syntax is:

```
Abs(number)
```

where *number* is the number to be converted. Some examples are:

```
Abs('-1')           ---Returns--->           1
Abs('1')            ------------->           1
Abs('+1')           ------------->           1
Abs('12.345')       ------------->           12.345
```

For more examples, run the program MATH.CMD that comes with this book.

Max

The Max function computes the largest number in a sequence of numbers. The largest number is the number closest to positive infinity. The syntax is:

```
Max(num1,num2,...,numlast)
```

where *num1* through *numlast* are the numbers to use in finding the maximum. Some examples are:

```
Max(-1,-99,1)           ---Returns--->   1
Max(1,-500)             ------------->   1
Max(1,.001,1e-3)        ------------->   1
Max(12.345,-500,1,3,5)  ------------->   12.345
```

For more examples, run the program MATH.CMD that comes with this book.

Min

The Min function computes the smallest number in a sequence of numbers. The smallest number is the number closest to negative infinity. The syntax is:

```
Min(num1,num2,...,numlast)
```

where *num1* through *numlast* are the numbers to use in finding the minimum. Some examples are:

```
Min(-1,-99,1)           ---Returns--->   -99
Min(1,-500)             ------------->   -500
Min(1,.001,1e-3)        ------------->   .001
Min(12.345,-500,1,3,5)  ------------->   -500
```

For more examples, run the program MATH.CMD that comes with this book.

Digits

The Digits function returns the current setting of NUMERIC DIGITS. The syntax is:

```
Digits()
```

Form

The Form function returns the current setting of NUMERIC FORM. The syntax is:

```
Form()
```

Format

The Format function controls the formatting of numbers for display. When used with standard (not exponential) format numbers, the syntax is:

```
Format(number[,before][,after])
```

where *number* is the number to format and *before* is the number of spaces to have before the decimal point. If the number is too short, extra spaces are added. If the number is too long for the specified length, the function returns an error. *After* is the number of spaces to have after the decimal point. If the number is too short, extra zeros are added. If the number is too long, it's rounded to the specified length. Some examples of the Format function follow:

```
Format(123.45,4,4)    ---Returns---> ' 123.4500'
Format(123.45,4,1)    ------------> ' 123.5'
Format(123.45,3,1)    ------------> '123.5'
```

For more examples, run the program FORMAT.CMD that comes with this book. One excellent use of the Format function is in formatting numbers to a consistent length to make sure they line up on the display. The D2X.CMD program that comes with this book does that for some of its numbers. When dealing with exponential notation, the syntax is:

```
Format(number[,before][,after][,expp][,expt])
```

where *number*, *before*, and *after* have the same meaning as defined previously, and *expp* sets the number of digits to use for the exponent part (the part after the e). If the NUMERIC FORM is set to Engineering, this will need to be set in three-digit increments. *Expt* sets the trigger number of decimal points for using exponential notation. When the number of places needed for the integer portion of the number exceeds *expt* or the number of places needed for the decimal portion of the number exceeds twice *expt*, exponential notation is used.

The default setting for *expt* is the setting for NUMERIC DIGITS. If zero is used for *expt*, exponential notation is always used, except when the exponent is zero. Some examples of the Format function follow:

```
Format(123.45,4,4,3,2)    ---Returns---> '  1.2345E+002'
Format(4400.444,4,1,1,2)  ------------> '   4.4E+3'
Format(4400.444,6,1,1,1)  ------------> '   4.4E+3'
```

For more examples, run the program FORMAT.CMD that comes with this book.

Fuzz

The Form function returns the current setting of NUMERIC FUZZ. The syntax is:

```
Fuzz()
```

Random

The Random function generates a pseudorandom non-negative whole number. The numbers are called "pseudorandom" because they aren't actually random, rather they're generated by a mathematical algorithm. However, the algorithm is complex enough that the numbers behave as though they were random numbers, and they'll pass a "chi-squared goodness of fit" test for randomness. The Random function has two different syntaxes. The simplest is:

```
Random(max)
```

which will generate a random number between zero and *max*. If not specified, the default value for *max* is 999. The second form for the syntax is:

```
Random([min][,max][,seed])
```

where *min* is the minimum value for the random number (the default is zero), *max* is the maximum value for the random number (the default is 999 and the maximum allowable value is 100,000), and *seed* is an optional starting point for the mathematical algorithm. This allows a particular sequence of random numbers to be repeated since the numbers following a seed will always be identical. If a seed isn't supplied one is computed internally using the date and time, so it's different each time the program is run.

The Random function is used in the program D2X.CMD that comes with this book. Additionally, the program RANDOM.CMD that comes with this book will generate a series of ten random numbers using a seed and will then regenerate the same series by using the same seed.

Sign

The Sign function returns a –1 if the number is below zero, a 0 if the number equals zero, and a +1 if the number is above zero. The syntax is:

```
Sign(number)
```

where *number* is the number to check. Some examples follow:

```
Sign( 2)   ---Returns--->    1
Sign(-2)   ------------->   -1
Sign(-4)   ------------->   -1
Sign(0)    ------------->    0
```

For more examples, run the SIGN.CMD program that comes with this book.

Trunc

The Trunc function rounds a number to a specific number of decimal points. The syntax is:

```
Trunc(number[,n])
```

where *number* is the number to round and *n* is the number of decimal points to use. If *n* is not specified, zero is used. Some examples follow:

```
Trunc(143.116)    ---Returns---> 143
Trunc(143.116,1) ------------> 143.1
Trunc(143.116,2) ------------> 143.11
Trunc(143.116,3) ------------> 143.116
Trunc(143.116,4) ------------> 143.1160
```

For more examples, run the TRUNC.CMD program that comes with this book.

Miscellaneous Functions

Miscellaneous functions are those functions that don't fit into one of the other categories. They're documented in the following chapters and summarized in Table 11.7.

TABLE 11.7 Miscellaneous Functions

Function	Summary
Address	Returns the name of the environment to which the REXX commands are currently being submitted.
Beep	Beeps the speaker.
Date	Returns the date in a number of different formats.
DataType	Returns the type of data stored in a variable.
Queued	Returns the number of lines remaining in the external data queue.
Symbol	Returns the state of a named symbol. Usually used to check on the status of a variable.
Time	Returns the time in a number of different formats.
Value	Reads and alters the contents of REXX variables as well as OS/2 environmental variables.
Xrange	Returns all the characters between two characters.

Address

The Address function returns the name of the environment to which the REXX instructions are currently being submitted. Most of the time, this will be CMD. The syntax is:

```
Address()
```

Beep

The Beep function sounds the speaker. The syntax is:

```
Beep(frequency,duration)
```

where *frequency* is the frequency of the sound to play in hertz from 37 to 32,767, and *duration* is the time in milliseconds to play the note. It can be a number 1 to 60,000 milliseconds. The program BEEPS.CMD that comes with this book uses the Beep function to play scales on the computer.

Date

The Date function returns a string containing either the date or information about the date. The syntax is:

```
Date([option])
```

If no *option* is specified, the Date function returns a date in the form dd mmm yyyy. The possible values for *option* are:

B. This returns the number of days that have passed since January 1, 0001 using the current Gregorian calendar.

D. This returns the number of days that have passed so far this year, including today.

E. This returns the date in European format, dd/mm/yy.

M. This returns the name of the current month with proper capitalization.

N. This returns the date in the normal format, dd-mmm-yyyy.

O. This returns the date in the format yy/mm/dd. Since the date goes from most significant to least significant, this is suitable for sorting.

S. This returns the date in the standard format, yyyymmdd, which is, again, suitable for sorting.

U. This returns the date in the U.S. format mm/dd/yy.

W. This returns the day of the week in proper capitalization.

If you run DATES.CMD, it will show you all these formats. Sample output from DATES.CMD is:

```
The Date Is.............................................. 19 Nov 1993
There Have Been This Many Days Since January 1, 0001..... 727885
The Day Of The Week Is................................... Friday
```

```
The Number Of Days So Far In This Year (Today Included).. 323
The Date In European Format Is........................... 19/11/93
The Month Is............................................. November
The Date In 'Normal' Format Is.......................... 19 Nov 1993
The Date In An Order Suitable For Sorting Is............. 93/11/19
The Date In 'Standard' Format Is........................ 19931119
The Date In 'USA' Format Is............................. 11/19/93
The Day Of The Week Is.................................. Friday
```

When a clause makes a call to the Date or Time function, REXX locks in the value for the remainder of the clause. That makes sure that multiple calls to these functions within a single clause receive the same value.

DataType

The DataType function determines the type of data stored in a variable. Its typical use is to evaluate data supplied by the user or other unreliable source. The syntax is:

```
DataType(string[,type])
```

where *string* is the variable or data string to evaluate and *type* is an optional data type to test for. If you don't specify a type to test for, DataType will return NUM if the data is a number that can be added to zero without generating a syntax error; otherwise, it will return CHAR. The values available for *type* are:

A (alphanumeric). Returns a one if the string contains only characters A–Z, a–z, and 0–9; otherwise, it returns a zero.

B (binary). Returns a one if the string contains only zeros and ones; otherwise, it returns a zero.

L (lowercase). Returns a one if the string contains only characters a–z; otherwise, it returns a zero.

M (mixed case). Returns a one if the string contains only characters a–z and A–Z; otherwise, it returns a zero.

N (number). Returns a one if the string contains a number that can be added to zero without generating an error; otherwise, it returns a zero.

S (symbol). Returns a one if the string contains only characters that are valid in REXX symbols; otherwise, it returns a zero.

U (uppercase). Returns a one if the string contains only characters A–Z; otherwise, it returns a zero.

W (whole number). Returns a one if the string contains a whole number; otherwise, it returns a zero.

X (hexadecimal number). Returns a one if the string contains a valid hexadecimal number; otherwise, it returns a zero.

If your program needs to get a certain type of information from the user, for example a number, then it makes a lot of sense to check out that data with the DataType function before using it. If the user enters 1o (lowercase letter el, uppercase letter oh) for the number ten, as you do on some typewriters, and you try to use that as a number, your program might crash. A quick check with the DataType function can avoid that problem. The program DATATYPE.CMD shows the DataType function in action.

Queued

The Queued function returns the number of lines remaining in the external data queue. The syntax is:

```
Queued()
```

Symbol

The Symbol function returns the state of a named symbol. The syntax is:

```
Symbol(name)
```

where *name* is the name of a symbol to check. Symbol returns the following values:

BAD. The named symbol isn't a valid REXX symbol.

VAR. The named symbol is a REXX variable that has been assigned a value.

LIT. The named symbol is a REXX literal.

Some examples follow:

```
A = 100
B = "IBM OS/2 REXX"
Symbol(A)     ---Returns---> LIT
Symbol("A") -------------> VAR
Symbol(B)   -------------> BAD
Symbol("B") -------------> VAR
Symbol("2") -------------> LIT
Symbol("+") -------------> BAD
```

For more examples, run the SYMBOL.CMD program that comes with this book. The Symbol function evaluates the contents of the name passed to it if it's a variable, so the following code:

```
Ronny = "123"
A = "Ronny"
SAY Symbol(A)
```

would return a value of VAR. The A on the last line would be evaluated to its value of Ronny, which is a currently assigned variable. Normally, *name* is specified as a literal string or computed from an expression to prevent substitution of its value before being passed to the function. Remember, REXX evaluates the line before passing it to the subroutine.

Time

The Time function displays the time in different formats, and can be used to time operations. The syntax is:

```
Time([option])
```

and by default it returns the time in the form hh:mm:ss in 24-hour format, for example 14:33:22. *Option* has the following possible values:

C (civil). Returns the time in the form hh:mmxx, where the hours are in 12-hour format and the minutes are followed immediately by an am or pm. The hour doesn't have a leading zero, and the minute is the current minute rather than being rounded.

E (elapsed). The first time this option is used, it starts the elapsed time clock. After that, each time it's used it returns the time that has elapsed since its first use in the format ss.uu, showing the number of seconds and microseconds.

H (hour). Shows the hours since midnight in the format hh. It shows no leading zero, except when zero hours have elapsed since midnight.

L (long). Returns the time in the form hh:mm:ss.uuuuuu, where u is microseconds. The microsecond portion is always six digits.

M (minutes). Returns the number of minutes since midnight. To display the number of minutes since the top of the hour, use TIME("M")//60.

N (normal). Returns the time in the format hh:mm:ss using a 24-hour clock. Hours, minutes, and seconds are always two digits and there's no rounding. This is the default mode.

R (reset). Returns the time since the elapsed clock counter was started, just like E, only this also resets the elapsed clock counter to zero.

S (seconds). Returns the number of seconds since midnight in the form sssss, but without any leading zeros except for a result of zero. To find the number of seconds since the top of the minute, use the formula TIME(S)-(TIME(M)*60).

Examples of each format follows:

```
Time()       ---Returns---> 16:48:31
Time("C")    ------------> 4:48pm
Time("E")    ------------> 07000000
Time("H")    ------------> 16
Time("L")    ------------> 16:48:31.940000
Time("M")    ------------> 1008
Time("N")    ------------> 16:48:31
Time("R")    ------------> 13000000
Time("S")    ------------> 60511
```

To recreate these examples, run THETIME.CMD program that comes with the book. Of course, your times will vary depending on the time of day you run the program.

Value

The Value function reads and alters the contents of REXX variables and OS/2 environmental variables. The syntax is:

```
Value(name[,newvalue][,selector])
```

where *name* is the name of the variable to work with. When working with REXX variables, *name* must be a valid REXX variable name. This isn't the case for OS/2 environmental variables, which use a slightly different naming convention. (For example, 222 is a valid name for an environmental variable.)

Newvalue is an optional new value to assign to that variable. When assigning new values to OS/2 environmental variables, those assignments are only for the current session and are lost when the REXX program terminates.

Leaving *selector* blank accesses REXX variables. Using the value OS2ENVIRONMENT or a variable that evaluates to this accesses OS/2 environmental variables. Some examples follow:

```
A = "A Variable"
Value("A","New A Value")  ---Returns---> A Variable
Value("A")                ------------> New A Value
Env = "OS2ENVIRONMENT"
Value("KEYS",,Env)        ------------> ON
Value("IOPL",,Env)        ------------> YES
Value("COMSPEC",,Env)     ------------> F:\OS2\CMD.EXE
```

For more examples, run the VALUE.CMD program that comes with this book.

XRange

The XRange function returns all the characters between two characters. The syntax is:

```
XRange([first][,last])
```

where *first* is the first character to return (the default is '00'x) and *last* is the last character to return (the default is 'FF'x). If *first* is larger than *last*, the character string will wrap from 'FF'x to '00'x. *First* and *last* must be single characters.

Some examples follow:

```
XRange("A","Z")   ----Returns---->  ABCDEFGHIJKLMNOPQRSTUVWXYZ
XRange(1,9)       --------------->  123456789
XRange("a","c")   --------------->  abc
XRange("X","d")   --------------->  XYZ[\]^_`abcd
```

For more examples, run the XRANGE.CMD program that comes with this book.

String Functions

As you might expect, since variables in REXX are always string variables, REXX has a wealth of string functions. Each of these functions is documented in the following sections and summarized in Table 11.8.

TABLE 11.8 String Functions

Function	Summary
Abbrev	Checks to see if an abbreviation matches a longer string.
Arg	Stores data passed to a REXX program into variables and returns information about the data being passed to the program.
Center Centre	Pads a character string with spaces so the text is centered inside a longer string.
Compare	Compares two strings to see if they are identical.
Copies	Makes copies of a character string.
DelStr	Deletes characters from a string.
DelWord	Deletes words from a character string.
Insert	Inserts one character string inside another character string.
LastPos	Returns the position of one character string inside another character string.
Left	Returns a specified number of characters from the left side of a character string.
Length	Returns the length of a character string.
Overlay	Inserts one character string inside another character string.
Pos	Returns the location of one character string inside another character string.
Right	Returns a specified number of characters from the right side of a character string.
Space	Removes spaces before and after a character string, and makes sure the words inside a character string have the same number of spaces between them.
Strip	Removes leading, trailing, or both leading and trailing characters from a character string.
SubStr	Returns a portion of a character string.
SubWord	Returns a word or words from a character string.
Translate	Converts one character string into another character string using a translation table.
Verify	Tests a character string to see if it has all its characters contained in a second string.
Word	Returns a single word from a character string.
WordIndex	Returns the starting character position for a specified word.

TABLE 11.8 (Continued)

Function	Summary
WordLength	Returns the length of a specified word inside a longer character string.
WordPos	Returns the starting position of a specified word inside a longer character string.
Words	Returns the number of words in a character string.

Abbrev

The Abbrev function sees if an abbreviation matches a longer string. You might use this when getting information from the user. This would allow experienced users to enter abbreviated instructions and inexperienced users the full instruction. The syntax is:

```
Abbrev(longstring,abbreviation[,length])
```

where *longstring* is the string that contains the long version of the string, *abbreviation* is the shorter string you're checking to see if it's an abbreviation of the string stored under *longstring*, and *length* optionally specifies a minimum length for *abbreviation*. When not specified, its default is the length of the string.

The Abbrev function returns a one when *abbreviation* matches the first characters in *longstring* and, if *length* is specified, *abbreviation* is at least that long. Otherwise, it returns a zero. This is illustrated by ABBREV.CMD. Its output is:

```
Abbrev("Ronny Richardson","Ronny")   --Returns--> 1
Abbrev("Ronny Richardson","Ron")     -----------> 1
Abbrev("Ronny Richardson","ronny")   -----------> 0
("ronny" Not Capitalized)
Abbrev("Ronny Richardson","Ron",5)   -----------> 0
("Ron" Is Not Five Characters Long)
Abbrev("Exit","Ex")                  -----------> 1
```

A null string used as the *abbreviation* will always match *longstring* when the default *length* is used or when *length* is zero. This allows you to specify a default keyword that's always selected when the *abbreviation* doesn't match any other *longstring*. For more examples, run the ABBREV.CMD program that comes with this book.

Arg

When you start a REXX program, you can pass information to that program by entering the information on the command line after the name of the program or after the name of a subroutine inside a REXX program. For example, with a password program you might enter the password on the command line after the name of the program. The Arg function brings the argument string, or information about it, into the REXX program. The syntax is:

```
Arg([number][,E¦O])
```

where *number* is the number of the argument to check and E¦O is an instruction. E is short for Exists and checks to see if the specified argument exists. O is short for Omitted and checks to see if the specified argument was omitted.

The function ARG( ) returns the number of arguments entered, and the function ARG(1) returns the first argument. Of course, ARG(2) returns the second argument, ARG(3) the third, and so on. If the argument requested doesn't exist, the null string is returned.

REXX handles arguments differently depending on how you enter them. When the arguments are coming from the command line, REXX treats everything as one argument. There's a program called ARG.CMD on the disk to let you experiment with arguments, and if you start it with the command:

```
ARG One,Two,"Three"Four
```

ARG will treat everything after the program name as a single argument. The ARG( ) function will return 1 and the ARG(1) function will return One,Two,"Three"Four.

However, when used in a subroutine, the Arg function treats each argument separately. If you were to call ARG.CMD from another program using the same command, One, Two, and "Three"Four would each be treated as a separate argument. The "Three" and Four aren't treated as separate arguments because they aren't separated by a comma. The program CALLARG.CMD that comes with this book does just this. Remember, when running CALLARG.CMD, that ARG.CMD must be in the current subdirectory or in your path.

To help clarify the Arg function, several examples follow. Assuming a REXX program called EXAMPLE.CMD was started with the command line:

```
EXAMPLE One,Two,"Three"
```

then these functions return the values indicated:

```
Arg()       ---Returns---> 1
Arg(1)      -------------> One,Two,"Three"
Arg(2)      -------------> "" or a null string
Arg(1,"E")  -------------> 1
Arg(1,"O")  -------------> 0
```

If a subroutine called EXAMPLE is called with the same command, then these functions return the values indicated:

```
Arg()       -----Returns-----> 3
Arg(1)      ----------------> One
Arg(2)      ----------------> Two
Arg(1,"E")  ----------------> 1
Arg(1,"O")  ----------------> 0
```

Note that number returned by ARG( ) is the largest number n, so that ARG(n,"e") would return a value of one. Additionally, when used inside of a program—as opposed to inside a subroutine—ARG( ) can return only a zero or one.

Center/Centre

The Center function centers text. The syntax for the function is:

```
Center(string,width[,pad])
```

where *string* is the character string to center, *width* is the width of the character string to center the string in, and *pad* is the optional character to pad the extra space on the left and right. If no pad character is specified, the space is used.

If the string is narrower than the width variable, it's padded in equal amounts on the left and right with either the pad character or a space if none is specified. If the string is too wide, an equal amount is trimmed from both sides. If an odd number of characters must be added or deleted, the right side of the string has one extra character added or deleted. Some examples follow:

```
Center("Ronny",9)                 ---Returns--->  "  Ronny  "
Center("Ronny",8,"-")             ------------->  "-Ronny--"
Center("Ronny Richardson,10)      ------------->  "ny Richard"
Center("Ronny Richardson,10,"-")  ------------->  "ny Richard"
```

The Center function is used in the STRCONVT.CMD program that comes with this book. This function can be called Center or Centre, to accommodate both the American and British spellings.

Compare

The Compare function compares two strings. If the two strings are identical, it returns a zero; otherwise, it returns the position where they first differ. Capitalization is significant, so Ronny doesn't match ronny. The syntax is:

```
Compare(string1,string2[,pad])
```

where *string1* is the first string to compare, *string2* is the second string to compare, and *pad* is a single optional pad character to use. When one string is shorter than the other, enough pad characters are added to the end of the shorter string to make its length equal to the longer string. Several examples follow:

```
Compare("Ronny","ronny")       ---Returns--->  1
Compare("Ronny","Ron","n")     ------------->  5
Compare("Ronny","Ronny","y")   ------------->  0
```

For more examples, see the COMPARE.CMD program that comes with this book.

Copies

The Copies function make zero or more copies of a string. The syntax is:

```
Copies(string,n)
```

where *string* is the string to make a copy of and n is the number of copies to make. N must be a whole non-negative number. Using zero for n will return a null string. Several examples follow:

```
Copies("X",0)        ---Returns--->         " "
Copies("X",1)        ------------->         "X"
Copies("XY",4)       ------------->    "XYXYXYXY"
```

For more examples, run the COPIES.CMD program that comes with this book.

DelStr

The DelStr function deletes characters from a string. The syntax is:

```
DelStr(string,n[,length])
```

where *string* is the original string from which the characters are removed, n is the starting position to begin deleting characters (this must be a whole number, and if it exceeds the length of the string the string is unmodified), and *length* is the optional length of characters to delete. If no length is specified, all the characters from the nth position to the end of the string are deleted. Some examples follow:

```
DelStr("Ronny",4)          ---Returns--->      "Ron"
DelStr("ABC123XYZ",4,3)    ------------->    "ABCXYZ"
DelStr("ABC123XYZ",7)      ------------->    "ABC123"
DelStr("Ronny",15)         ------------->     "Ronny"
```

For more examples, run the DELSTR.CMD program that comes with this book.

DelWord

The DelWord removes words from a character string, where a word is defined as a string of characters surrounded by spaces, unless it occurs at the beginning or end of the string and then it only has a space on one side. The syntax is:

```
DelWord(string,n[,length])
```

where *string* is the character string to remove words from, n is the number of the first word to remove, and *length* is the number of words to remove. If no length is specified, the remainder of the string is deleted. Some examples follow:

```
String = "Ronny Richardson Wrote This"
DelWord(String,3)      ---Returns---> "Ronny Richardson"
DelWord(String,1,2)    ------------->  "Wrote This"
DelWord(String,1)      ------------->  " "
```

For more examples, run the program DELWORD.CMD that comes with this book.

Insert

The Insert function places one string inside another string. The syntax is:

```
Insert(insert,target[,n][,length][,pad])
```

where *insert* is the string that is to be inserted inside the other string, *target* is the string that is to have another string inserted into it, and *n* is the position in the existing target string to insert the insert string after. If no value is specified, the new string is inserted at the beginning of the target string, e.g., n=0.

Length is the length of the insert string. The default value for *length* is the actual length of the insert string. If the Length value specified is shorter that the insert string, enough characters are removed from the right of the insert string to make its length match the length value. If the length value exceeds the length of the insert string, the insert string is padded with spaces on its right side to make its length match the specified length value.

Pad is the pad character to use if needed. If no pad character is specified, the space is used. Some examples follow:

```
Insert("Wor","Hello ld!",6)       ---Returns---> Hello World!
Insert("/","OS2",2)               -------------> OS/2
Insert("Hello","World!",0,6," ")  -------------> Hello World!
```

For more examples, run the INSERT.CMD program that comes with this book.

LastPos

The LastPos function looks for one string (source) inside another string (target) and returns the position of the source string inside the target string. The syntax is:

```
LastPos(source, target[, start])
```

where *source* is the string that you're looking for, *target* is the string that you're searching to see where the source string occurs, and *start* is the starting position of the search. The default is at the end of the string.

This is a case-sensitive search that begins at the right end of the string (or at the starting position specified by *start*) and works to the left. Since the search is right to left, any characters to the right of the starting position are ignored. If no match is found, a zero is returned. Some examples follow:

```
Now Is The Time For All Good Men To Come To The Aid Of Their Country
----:----:----:----:----:----:----:----:----:----:----:----:----:----
    5   10   15   20   25   30   35   40   45   50   55   60   65

LastPos("The",String)        ---Returns---> 56
LastPos("The",String,40)     -------------> 8
LastPos("y",String)          -------------> 68
LastPos(" ",String)          -------------> 61
```

For more examples, run the LASTPOS.CMD program that comes with this book.

Left

The Left function obtains a specified number of characters out of a character string, beginning at the leftmost character and moving to the right a specified number of positions. The syntax is:

```
Left(string, length[,pad])
```

where *string* is the character string to remove the characters from, *length* is the number of characters to return, and *pad* is the character to finish filling the return string with if the specified length is longer that the string. Some examples follow:

```
LEFT("IBM OS/2 REXX",1," ")   --Returns--> 'I'
LEFT("IBM OS/2 REXX",2," ")   ----------> 'IB'
LEFT("IBM OS/2 REXX",3," ")   ----------> 'IBM'
LEFT("IBM OS/2 REXX",15," ")  ----------> 'IBM OS/2 REXX  '
LEFT("IBM OS/2 REXX",16," ")  ----------> 'IBM OS/2 REXX   '
```

For more examples, run the LEFT.CMD program that comes with this book.

Length

The Length function returns the length of a given character string. The syntax is:

```
Length(string)
```

where *string* is the character string to find the length of. Some examples follow:

```
Length("Ronny")            ---Returns---> 5
Length("IBM OS/2")         -------------> 8
Length("IBM OS/2 REXX")    -------------> 13
```

For more examples, run the LENGTH.CMD program that comes with this book.

Overlay

The Overlay function inserts one string (source) into a second string (target). The syntax is:

```
Overlay(source, target[,n][,length][,pad])
```

where *source* is the character string to be inserted into the target string, *target* is the character string to have the source character string inserted into it, and *n* is the starting position inside *target* to begin inserting *source*. If *n* isn't specified, the beginning of the string is used.

Length is the amount of the source character string to use. If *length* exceeds the length of the source character string, then the source character string is padded with the pad character if it was specified and the space if no pad was specified. If *length* is less than the length of the source character string, the rightmost part of the source is truncated so its length equals the specified length.

Pad is the single character to use for padding when the length specified as the length of the source character string exceeds its actual length. Some examples follow:

```
Overlay("efg","ABCDEFGHI",5,3)      ---Returns---> ABCDefgHI
Overlay("efg","ABCDEFGHI",5,4," ")  ------------> ABCDefg I
Overlay("cde","ABCDEFGHI",3,3)      ------------> ABCdeFGHI
Overlay("cde","ABCDEFGHI",3,6,"-")  ------------> ABcde---I
```

For more examples, run the OVERLAY.CMD program that comes with this book.

Pos

The Pos function finds the location of a string (source) inside a second string (target). The syntax is:

```
Pos(source,target[,start])
```

where *source* is the character string to look for inside the target string, *target* is the character string in which to look for the source string, and *start* is the optional starting position. Normally, Pos starts with the first (leftmost) character in the target string and searches to the end (rightmost) character. When *start* is specified, it relocates the starting position and must be equal to or less than the length of the target string. Some examples follow:

```
Now Is The Time For All Good Men To Come To The Aid Of Their Country
----¦----¦----¦----¦----¦----¦----¦----¦----¦----¦----¦----¦----¦----
    5   10   15   20   25   30   35   40   45   50   55   60   65
```

```
Pos("The",String)      ---Returns---> 8
Pos("The",String,25)   ------------> 45
Pos("Women",String)    ------------> 0
Pos("Aid",String)      ------------> 49
```

For more examples, run the POS.CMD program that comes with this book.

Right

The Right function obtains a specified number of characters out of a character string, beginning at the rightmost character and moving to the left a specified number of positions. The syntax is:

```
Right(string,length[,pad])
```

where *string* is the character string to remove the characters from, *length* is the number of characters to return, and *pad* is the character to finish filling the return string with if the specified length is longer that the string. Some examples follow:

```
Right("IBM OS/2 REXX",1," ")  --Returns--> 'I'
Right("IBM OS/2 REXX",2," ")  ----------> 'IB'
```

```
Right("IBM OS/2 REXX",3," ")  -----------> 'IBM'
Right("IBM OS/2 REXX",13," ") -----------> 'IBM OS/2 REXX'
Right("IBM OS/2 REXX",14," ") -----------> 'IBM OS/2 REXX '
Right("IBM OS/2 REXX",15," ") -----------> 'IBM OS/2 REXX  '
```

For more examples, run the RIGHT.CMD program that comes with this book.

Space

The Space function removes the spaces before and after a character string and makes sure that the words within the character string have the same number of spaces (or pad characters) between them. The syntax is:

```
Space(string[,n][,pad])
```

where *string* is the character string to process. All spaces at the beginning and end of the character string are removed. Sets of spaces inside the character string are replaced with *n* spaces (or pad characters). *N* is the number of spaces (or pad characters) to add between each word. The default is one. *Pad* is the pad character to use. If no pad character is specified, the space is used. Some examples follow:

```
Space("Abc   Def  Ghi   ")        --Returns--> 'Abc Def Ghi'
Space("Abc   Def  Ghi   ",2)      -----------> 'Abc  Def  Ghi'
Space("  Abc Def Ghi    ",3)      -----------> 'Abc   Def   Ghi'
Space("  Abc Def Ghi    ",1,"-")  -----------> 'Abc-Def-Ghi'
```

For more examples, run the SPACE.CMD program that comes with this book.

Strip

The Strip function removes leading, trailing, or both leading and trailing characters from a character string. For a character string, this character is usually a space and, for a number, this character is usually a zero. The syntax is:

```
Strip(string[,option][,character])
```

where *string* is the character string or number to process, *option* is the subinstruction to the function, and *character* is the single character to remove. The default is a space. Note that this character is removed from only the ends of the character string. If this same character is found inside the character string, those occurrences are unaffected. Options for *option* follow:

B (both). Removes both the leading and trailing characters. This is the default if no option is specified.

L (leading). Removes only the leading characters.

T (trailing). Removes only the trailing characters.

Some examples follow:

```
Strip("   IBM OS/2 REXX   ")            --Return--> 'IBM OS/2 REXX'
Strip("   IBM OS/2 REXX   ","L")        ----------> 'IBM OS/2 REXX   '
Strip("   IBM OS/2 REXX   ","T")        ---------->  '   IBM OS/2 REXX'
Strip("---IBM OS/2 REXX--","B","-")     ----------> 'IBM OS/2 REXX'
Strip(000123.456000,,"0")               ----------> '123.456'
```

For more examples, run the STRIP.CMD program that comes with this book.

SubStr

The SubStr function returns a portion of a character string. The syntax is:

```
SubStr(string,begin[,length][,pad])
```

where *string* is the character string to be processed, *begin* is the first character in the string character string to return, and *length* is the number of characters to return from the string character. The default if no length is specified is to return all the remaining characters. If *length* exceeds the number of characters remaining in the character string, the pad character or a space is used to pad the returned string.

Pad is the character to pad the returned string if more characters are requested than the string character string can supply. The default is the space. Some examples follow:

```
String = "IBM OS/2 REXX"
SubStr(String,5)            --Returns--> OS/2 REXX
SubStr(String,5,4)          ----------> OS/2
SubStr(String,1,3)          ----------> IBM
SubStr(String,10,10,"-")    ----------> REXX------
SubStr(String,5,20)         ----------> OS/2 REXX              '
```

For more examples, run the SUBSTR.CMD program that comes with this book.

SubWord

The SubWord function returns a word or words from a character string. The syntax is:

```
SubWord(string,word[,number])
```

where *string* is the character string to return the words from, *word* is the number of the first word to return, and *number* is the number of words to return. The default is the rest of the words in the character string. Some examples follow:

```
String = Now Is The Time For All Good Men To Come To The Aid
         --- -- --- ---- --- --- ---- --- -- ---- -- --- ---
          1   2   3    4    5   6    7    8   9  10  11  12  13

SubWord(String,1,4)    ---Returns---> Now Is The Time
SubWord(String,7,2)    ------------> Good Men
SubWord(String,4,1)    ------------> Time
```

For more examples, run the SUBWORD.CMD program that comes with this book.

Translate

The Translate function converts one character string into another character string using a translation table. The syntax is:

```
Translate(string[,outtable][,intable][,pad])
```

where *string* is the string to convert, *outtable* is the output table, *intable* is the input table, and *pad* is the single character used to pad *outtable* if it isn't as long as *intable*. Consider the following example:

```
Translate("REXX","1234567890","abcRdEfgXz")
```

The first thing the Translate function does is match the input table (*intable*) and output table (*outtable*), like this:

```
InTable:   abcRdEfgXz
OutTable:  1234567890
```

Now, for each character in the input string, it searches through *intable* for the first match. Once it finds the match, it drops down to *outtable* in the same position and reads that character. That is the character the input character is translated to. This is repeated for each character. If a match isn't found in the input table, the character isn't translated. For REXX, the first character is R. That is found in the input table and corresponds to the 4 in the output table, so R is translated to 4. The E is translated to a 6 and the Xs are translated to 9s. Some more examples follow:

```
Translate("Abc")                        ---Returns---> ABC
Translate(12345,54321,12345)                    ---> 54321
Translate("ABC","1234567890","ABCDEFGHIJ") ---> 123
Translate(1234,"ABCDEFG","1234567")         ---> ABCD
```

For more examples, run the CHANGE.CMD program that comes with this book. The Translate function can convert data formats and also encrypt simple data files.

Verify

The Verify function tests a character string to see if it has all its characters contained in a second string. The syntax is:

```
Verify(string,checkstring[,option][,start])
```

where *string* is the character string to have its characters checked, *checkstring* is the character string that functions as a master list to check against, and *option* is either M (match), which causes the first matching character position to be returned or N (no match, the default), which causes the first nonmatching character position to be returned. With M, a zero is returned if there isn't a match and, with N, a zero is returned if they all match. *Start* is the starting point in *string* to begin searching. Some examples follow:

```
Verify("Abc","ABCDEFGHIJKLMNOPQRSTUVWXYZ")        -Returns-> 2
Verify("REXX","ABCDEFGHIJKLMNOPQRSTUVWXYZ")       ---------> 0
Verify("OS/2","ABCDEFGHIJKLMNOPQRSTUVWXYZ")       ---------> 3
Verify("OS/2","ABCDEFGHIJKLMNOPQRSTUVWXYZ",,4) ---------> 4
Verify("OS/2","ABCDEFGHIJKLMNOPQRSTUVWXYZ",N)  ---------> 3
Verify("OS/2","ABCDEFGHIJKLMNOPQRSTUVWXYZ",M)  ---------> 1
```

For more examples, run the VERIFIED.CMD program that comes with this book.

Word

The Word function returns a single word from a character string. The syntax is:

```
Word(string,number)
```

where *string* is the character string to use and *number* is the number of the word to return. If there are fewer than *number* words, a null string is returned. Several examples follow where the variable *string* contains "Now Is The Time For All Good Men To Come To The Aid Of Their Country":

```
Word(String,1)    ---Returns---> 'Now'
Word(String,2)    ------------> 'Is'
Word(String,3)    ------------> 'The'
Word(String,4)    ------------> 'Time'
Word(String,5)    ------------> 'For'
```

For more examples, run the WORDS.CMD program that comes with this book.

WordIndex

The WordIndex function returns the starting character position for a specified word. The syntax is:

```
WordIndex(string,number)
```

where *string* is the character string to process and *number* is the number of the word to search for. If there are fewer than *number* words, zero is returned. Some examples follow where the variable *string* contains "Now Is The Time For All Good Men To Come To The Aid Of Their Country":

```
WordIndex(String,1)    -----Returns    > 1
WordIndex(String,2)    -----------    > 5
WordIndex(String,3)    -----------    > 8
WordIndex(String,4)    -----------    > 12
WordIndex(String,5)    -----------    > 17
```

For more examples, run the WORDS.CMD program that comes with this book.

WordLength

The WordLength function returns the length of a word. The syntax is:

```
WordLength(string,position)
```

where *string* is the character string in which to search for a word and *position* is the number of the word to measure. Some examples follow where the variable *string* contains "Now Is The Time For All Good Men To Come To The Aid Of Their Country":

```
WordLength(String,1)      ---Returns---> 3
WordLength(String,2)      ------------> 2
WordLength(String,3)      ------------> 3
WordLength(String,4)      ------------> 4
WordLength(String,5)      ------------> 3
```

For more examples, run the WORDS.CMD program that comes with this book.

WordPos

The WordPos function specifies the starting position of a specific word. The syntax is:

```
WordPos(phrase,string[,start])
```

where *phrase* is the word or words to look for in the character string, *string* is the character string in which to search for *phrase*, and *start* is the optional starting point from which to begin the search. If *start* isn't specified, the search begins at the first word in *string*. Some examples follow where the variable *string* contains "Now Is The Time For All Good Men To Come To The Aid Of Their Country":

```
WordPos("Now",String)       ---Returns---> 1
WordPos("Is",String)        ------------> 2
WordPos("IS",String)        ------------> 0
WordPos("The",String)       ------------> 3
WordPos("The",String,4)     ------------> 12
```

For more examples, run the WORDS.CMD program that comes with this book.

Words

The Words function returns the number of words in a character string. The syntax is:

```
Words(string)
```

where *string* is the character string to check. Some examples follow:

```
Words("Now Is The Time")          ---Results---> 4
Words("IBM OS/2 REXX")            ------------> 3
Words("No Time Like The Present") ------------> 5
Words("Ronny Richardson")         ------------> 2
```

For more examples, run the WORDS.CMD program that comes with this book.

12

External Functions

As you saw in the last chapter, REXX functions are divided into built-in functions, which work across all implementation of REXX, and external functions, which are platform-specific. The last chapter covered built-in functions. This chapter will cover the OS/2-specific, or external, REXX functions. External REXX functions are stored in RexxUtil, a dynamic link library, or DLL. These functions deal primarily with the OS/2 system, user input/output, screen input/output, and .INI files.

Function Review

Before looking at the external functions, let's review a few notes on functions in general from the last chapter:

- A set of parentheses is always required after a function name when the function is called using a variable, even if the function doesn't need any arguments.

- The opening parenthesis must come immediately after the function name, without any space between the name and parenthesis.

- If a function requires a numeric argument, that argument is rounded according to the setting of NUMERIC DIGITS before being supplied to the function. It's also checked for validity before being supplied to the function.

- Internally, functions work with the settings NUMERIC DIGITS 9 and NUMERIC FUZZ 0, regardless of the external setting.

- When a function returns a numeric value, that value must be compatible with the current NUMERIC DIGITS setting.

- When a function requires a string, a null string is always acceptable.

- When a function requires a length, it must be a non-negative whole number.

- When a number is used as the starting point in a string, it must be a positive whole number.

- When the last argument is optional, you can add a comma to the end of the argument list to indicate that last argument has been omitted.

- When a pad argument is specified, it must be exactly one character long.

- When an option is selected by a character, capitalization isn't important.

With that in mind, let's look at the external functions:

Application Programming Interface Function Review

As you saw in the last chapter, it's easy to extend the REXX language using external functions. These external functions can be written in REXX, like the CLS.CMD and PAUSE.CMD programs included with this book, or in another language like C++. This section will review the internal REXX functions used to manage the external REXX functions.

External functions can be written in languages like C++ or Pascal, but the techniques for doing so are beyond the scope of this book. My purpose here is to discuss how to use those functions once they've been written and debugged.

REXX offers something most other languages lack: an interface that allows communications to and from other languages and applications, called an *application programming interface* (API). In fact, any OS/2 program with the appropriate interface can use REXX as its own macro or script language.

You can also use other programming languages to program extensions to the REXX language in the form of external functions. REXX offers four functions for managing external functions. These are documented in the following sections and summarized in Table 11.1, back in chapter 11.

RxFuncAdd

Before REXX can access an external function, that external function must be "registered" with the REXX interpreter. RxFuncAdd (REXX Function Add) is the function that registers external functions. Its syntax is:

```
RxFuncAdd(name, module, procedure)
```

where *name* is the name of the external function, *module* is the name of the external module containing the external function, and *procedure* is the name of the entry point for the external function.

Once an external function has been added to by a REXX program, it's available to REXX in all sessions until the function is dropped by a REXX session or until OS/2 is rebooted. If you use a lot of external functions, it can be cumbersome to load them one at a time. The following two lines of code will automatically load every one of the external functions:

```
CALL RxFuncAdd 'SysLoadFuncs', 'RexxUtil', 'SysLoadFuncs'
CALL SysLoadFuncs
```

Once these functions are loaded, they're usable by all OS/2 sessions. It doesn't hurt to have another session attempt to load them again and you probably want each program you write that will use these functions to load them because you can never depend on another program to load them before your program. Since they take up only a little memory, the best approach is usually to have each REXX program that needs external functions load them all.

RxFuncDrop

RxFuncDrop (short for REXX Function Drop) lets your program drop an external function that was added with the RxFuncAdd function. The syntax is:

```
RxFuncDrop(name)
```

where *name* is the name of the function to drop.

RxFuncQuery

RxFuncQuery (short for REXX Function Query) lets your program check to see if a function has already been loaded. The syntax is:

```
RxFuncQuery(name)
```

where *name* is the name of the function to check on. The program SHOWRX.CMD that comes with this book shows using each of these three functions to work in external functions.

SysDropFuncs

The SysDropFuncs external function drops all the RexxUtil functions. After this, they aren't available in any session. The syntax is:

```
CALL SysDropFuncs
```

Function Search Oorder

Since I've just finished discussing how to register external functions with the REXX interpreter, now is a good time to talk about the search order REXX uses to find functions. A REXX program can have three different types of functions:

Internal labels.   These are the functions you write into your program, like the FACTORIAL function inside FACTORAL.CMD.

Internal functions.   These are functions like ARG( ) that are built into the language.

External functions.   These are external REXX programs, like PAUSE.CMD, or functions written in other languages and attached to REXX.

Normally, REXX searches for internal labels first, internal functions second, and external functions last. If the name of the function is enclosed in quotation marks, internal labels aren't checked, so only internal functions and external functions are checked—in that order. This lets you give an internal label function the same name as an internal function and still bypass it for the internal function as required.

One important note is in order. All internal functions and many external functions have their names in all uppercase. While capitalization normally doesn't matter, when you put the name of a function inside quotation marks its capitalization must match the capitalization used for the function. So all calls to internal functions inside quotation marks must be in all uppercase.

Controlling the Screen

Some of the external functions extend your program's ability to control the screen. These functions are discussed in the following sections and summarized in Table 12.1.

TABLE 12.1 Screen Functions

Function	Summary
RxMessageBox	Display a message box on the screen with a title, message, icon, and one or more buttons. Must run under PMREXX.
SysCls	Clears the screen.
SysCurPos	Positions the cursor and reports its current position.
SysTextScreenRead	Reads text from the screen and stores it in a variable.
SysTextScreenSize	Returns the size of the current screen.
SysGetMessage	Returns National Language Support messages.
SysIni	Allows limited editing of initialization variables.
SysOS2Ver	Returns the OS/2 version number.
SysWaitNamedPipe	Performs a timed wait on a named pipe.

RxMessageBox

The RxMessageBox function displays a message box on the screen with one or more buttons, a message and title, and a single icon that the user selects. Once the user clicks on a button, a number corresponding to that button is returned to the program. This function was designed to run only under PMREXX. The syntax is:

```
variable = RxMessageBox(text[,title][,button][,icon])
```

where *text* is left-justified text to display inside the message box, *title* is the centered title to display at the top of the message box (the default title is Error if you don't specify a title), and *button* is the type of button to display. The options are:

Ok. Display a single button labeled OK. This is the default button if none is selected.

OkCancel. Display two buttons, labeled OK and Cancel.

Cancel. Display a single button labeled Cancel.

Enter. Display a single button labeled Enter.

EnterCancel. Display two buttons labeled Enter and Cancel.

RetryCancel. Display two buttons labeled Retry and Cancel.

AbortRetryIgnore. Display three buttons labeled Abort, Retry, and Ignore.

YesNo. Display two buttons labeled Yes and No.

YesNoCancel. Display three buttons labeled Yes, No, and Cancel.

Icon is the type of icon to display as part of the message box. The available icon styles are Asterisk, Error, Exclamation, Hand, Information, None (the default), Query, Question, and Warning. *Variable* contains a numeric value corresponding to the button selected by the user. The possible values are:

1. The Ok key was pressed.

2. The Cancel key was pressed.

3. The Abort key was pressed.

4. The Retry key was pressed.

5. The Ignore key was pressed.

6. The Yes key was pressed.

7. The No key was pressed.

8. The Enter key was pressed.

Of course, none of the button style keywords display all eight possible buttons, so any use of the function will return only a subset of all these possible values. You can see the RxMessageBox function in operation by running the MESSAGE.CMD program that comes with this book. MESSAGE.CMD is shown running in Figure 12.1.

SysCls

The SysCls function clears the screen. The syntax is:

```
CALL SysCls
```

Figure 12.1 The RxMessageBox RexxUtil function lets you place dialog boxes on the screen where the user can select from different options. This function requires that the program be running under PM REXX.EXE.

The TODO.CMD program that comes with this book uses the SysCls function to clear the screen.

SysCurPos

The SysCurPos function positions the cursor at a particular row and column on the screen and reports on the current position of the cursor. The syntax is:

```
position = SysCurPos([row, column])
```

where *row* is the row to position the cursor on (the top row is row number zero), *column* is the column to position the cursor on (the leftmost column is column zero), and *position* is the variable to store the results in. The instructions to display the cursor position are:

```
PARSE VALUE SysCurPos() WITH row column
SAY "Cursor Position Is: row = " row "column =" column
```

The MATHTEST.CMD and POSITION.CMD programs that come with this book use the SysCurPos function to position the cursor, and the SHOW-POS.CMD program that comes with this book uses it to report the position of the cursor.

SysTextScreenRead

The SysTextScreenRead function allows you to save some or all of the screen contents to a variable. This has two useful functions. First, you can read data off the screen that might be written there by another program. Second, you can save the screen when a program starts and later restore the screen when the program terminates. The syntax is:

```
variable = SysReadScreen(row,column[,length])
```

where *row* is the row to start reading on (the default is row zero), *column* is the column to start reading on (the default is column zero), and *length* is the number of characters to read (the default is to read to the end of the screen). When combined with the row and column defaults, the default is to read the entire screen.

Variable is the name of the variable to store the screen contents to. If the read spans more than one line, *variable* contains carriage returns and line feeds at the end of each line. That way, a simple SAY instruction can be used to display its contents.

Only the contents of the screen is saved; the color information is lost. The SCREEN.CMD program that comes with this book shows this function in action.

SysTextScreenSize

The SysTextScreenSize function reads in the size of the current screen. The syntax is:

```
Result = SysTextScreenSize()
```

where Result is the name of the variable to store the data to. The normal way to issue the instruction would be:

```
PARSE VALUE SysTextScreenSize() WITH row column
```

where *row* and *column* contain separate values indicating their respective values. This function won't tell you the size of an OS/2 window since OS/2 treats this as a virtual window on a 25×80 screen and will return 25×80 to this function. The SCREEN.CMD program that comes with this book shows the function in action.

Dealing with Objects

Underlying the workplace shell is something called the System Object Model, or SOM for short. SOM is very similar to the Apple Macintosh Apple Events Object Model, or AEOM. A class defines the behavior, graphical appearance, and information content used to represent something that exists in the real world. An object is a working copy of the thing defined by that object's class. For example, a folder (specifically WPFolder in OS/2's workplace shell) is a class for which there are many copies (one for each directory), but each folder behaves and is visually depicted in a consistent manner. The following are three classes that REXX can work with. They are:

WPFolder. This class is for folder objects. The object ID (if there is one) for these items is generally a WP_ followed by the name of the folder, with everything inside angle brackets. So <WP_DESKTOP> is the desktop, <WP_GAMES> is the games folder, <WP_PROMPTS> is the command prompts folder, and <WP_DRIVES> is the disk drive folder.

WPProgram. This class is for program objects. The object ID for these items is generally a WP_ followed by the name of the program. One of the object properties is the name of the program file, so the name might not match the name of the .EXE or .COM program. For example, the chess program is OS2CHESS.EXE, but the object ID is <WP_CHESS>. <WP_EPM> is the Enhanced Editor, <WP_MOUSE> represents the mouse settings, and <WP_SPOOL> is the print spooler.

WPShadow. This class is for folder and program shadow objects. Working with objects allows REXX to shift some of the burden of working with these items off to OS/2 rather than dealing with it all by itself. Note that these functions work only in OS/2 2.1, or OS/2 2.0 with the REXX20 patch or service pack installed. For more information on objects, see chapters 7 and 8 of the *OS/2 2.1 Application Design Guide* (S10G-6260). Object functions are documented in the following sections and summarized in Table 12.2.

TABLE 12.2 Object Functions

Function	Summary
SysCreateObject	Creates a new object in a class.
SysDeregisterObjectClass	Removes an object class definition from the system.
SysDestroyObject	Removes an existing Workplace Shell object.
SysQueryClassList	Returns a listing of all registered object classes.
SysRegisterObjectClass	Registers a new object class.
SysSetObjectData	Changes the setting of an object.

SysCreateObject

To create a new object in a class, use the SysCreateObject external function. For example, an installation program might create a new folder and then add its icons to that folder. The syntax is:

```
variable = SysCreateObject(classname,title,location[,setup][,option])
```

where *classname* is the name of the object's class, *title* is the object's title, and *location* is the object's location. This can be specified as an object ID, such as <WP_DESKTOP>, to put it on the desktop, or as a path, such as C:\OS2.

Setup is a string of options to pass to the OS/2 WinCreateObject function, and *option* specifies the action to take if the object already exists. Available options are Fail, which will cause the instruction to fail, Replace, which will cause the instruction to delete the existing object and replace it, and Update, which will cause the instruction to update the settings for the existing object. Only the first letter of the option is significant.

Variable is the variable to store the return code in. A zero means the object wasn't created and a one means it was successfully created.

The OBJECT.CMD program that comes with this book uses the SysCreateObject external function to create a new folder called REXX Example on the desktop, and then a shadow of folder, also on the desktop.

SysDeregisterObjectClass

To remove an object class definition from the system, use the SysDeregisterObject-Class function. The syntax is:

```
variable = SysDeregisterObjectClass(classname)
```

where *classname* is the name of the object class to deregister, and *variable* is the variable to store the return code in. A zero means the object class wasn't deregistered and a one means it was successfully deregistered.

SysDestroyObject

You can remove an existing workplace shell object with the SysDestroyObject function. The syntax is:

```
variable = SysDestroyObject(name)
```

where *name* is the name of the object to destroy, which can be an object ID or a fully specified filename, and *variable* is the variable to store the return code in. A zero means the object class wasn't destroyed and a one means it was successfully destroyed.

The OBJECT.CMD program that comes with this book uses SysDestroyObject to destroy a desktop folder after creating that folder. Destroying the folder automatically destroys the attached shadow of that folder.

SysQueryClassList

To get a listing of all the registered object classes, use the SysQueryClassList function. The syntax is:

```
CALL SysQueryClassList stem
```

where *stem*, in the form of a variable in quotation marks, is the name of a stem variable to store the information to. Variable.0 will contain the count. To display the items, use the following code:

```
CALL SysQueryClassList "List."
DO I = 1 TO List.0
  SAY "Class" I "Is:" List. I
END
```

The CLASSES.CMD program that comes with this book does just this.

SysRegisterObjectClass

Once a new object class has been created, you must register it before you can use it. This is done with the SysRegisterObjectClass function. The syntax is:

```
variable = SysRegisterObjectClass(classname,module)
```

where *classname* is the name of the new object class, *module* is the name of the module containing the external function, and *variable* is the variable to store the return code in. A zero means the object class wasn't registered and a one means it was successfully registered. If the new object includes a template, that template is placed in the Templates folder so users can access it.

SysSetObjectData

Once an object has been created, you can change its settings with the SysSetObjectData function. The syntax is:

```
variable = SysSetObjectData(name,setup)
```

where *name* is the name of the object ID or file path, *setup* is a string of options to pass to the OS/2 WinCreateObject function, and *variable* is the variable to store the return code in. A zero means the object wasn't created and a one means it was successfully created.

Disk and File Management

There are a number of external functions for working with the disk, its structure, and its files. These functions are documented in the following sections and summarized in Table 12.3.

TABLE 12.3 Disk and File-Management Functions

Function	Summary
SysDriveInfo	Returns information about a drive.
SysDriveMap	Returns information about the available drives.
SysFileDelete	Deletes a file.
SysFileTree	Returns all the files on a drive matching a wildcard specification.
SysFileSearch	Returns all the lines in a file containing the specified text.
SysMkDir	Creates a subdirectory.
SysRmDir	Removes an empty subdirectory.
SysSearchPath	Searches for a file along a specified path.
Sys TempFileName	Returns an unused filename for use as a temporary file.

SysDriveInfo

The SysDriveInfo function obtains information about a drive. It returns the letter of the drive checked, its amount of free space, its total amount of space, and its volume label. The syntax is:

```
info = SysDriveInfo(drive)
```

where *info* is the variable to contain the drive information and *drive* is the drive to check. The code to use this information is as follows:

```
PARSE VALUE SysDriveInfo(drive) WITH drive,free,totalsize,label
```

The CHKDRIVE.CMD program that comes with this book uses the SysDriveInfo external function and this code to display information about the drive specified. The information is displayed much more quickly than when using the DIR or CHKDSK commands. The syntax is:

```
CHKDRIVE drive
```

where *drive* is the drive to check. It also checks for a valid drive using the SysDriveMap function. You can enter the names of drives with or without the colon and in either upper- or lowercase. If no drive is specified, the C: drive is checked. CHKDRIVE.CMD uses COMMAS.CMD, so this program must either be in the current subdirectory or in your path.

SysDriveMap

The SysDriveMap function displays all the available drives. The syntax is:

```
map = SysDriveMap([drive][,option])
```

where *drive* is the first drive to check. The drive must be stated with a colon after the drive letter. If no drive is specified, the C: drive is used as a starting point. This avoids the slowdown associated with accessing the floppy drives. *Option* is the instruction option for the function to run. The available instruction options are:

USED.   This displays all drives that are accessible or in use. This is the default if no option is specified.

FREE.   This displays the drive letters that aren't assigned.

LOCAL.   This reports all local drives that are accessible or in use.

REMOTE.   This displays all remote drives that are accessible or in use.

DETACHED.   This displays all detached LAN resources drives.

Map is the name of the variable to contain the results of the function. The MAP.CMD program that comes with this book will issue a full report on your system using this function. The CHKDRIVE.CMD program that comes with this book uses the Sys-DriveMap function to obtain a list of accessible drives. It then restricts the user to checking these drives. This shows a good way to approach error checking to make sure the user enters a valid drive specification.

SysFileDelete

The SysFileDelete function deletes a file. The syntax is:

```
variable = SysFileDelete(file)
```

where *file* is the file to delete and *variable* is the variable to store the return code. SysFileDelete doesn't support wildcards. The return codes are:

0. The file was deleted.

2. The file wasn't found.

3. The path wasn't found.

5. Access was denied.

26. OS/2 can't read the specified disk.

32. There was a sharing violation.

36. The sharing buffer was exceeded.

87. The function was passed an invalid parameter.

206. The filename exceeds the range.

The FILES.CMD program that comes with this book uses the SysFileDelete function to delete a file.

SysFileSearch

The SysFileSearch function searches through a file and finds all the lines in that file containing the specified text. The syntax is:

```
CALL SysFileSearch(text,file,stem[,options])
```

where *text* is the character string to search for, *file* is the full filename of the file to search (wildcard specifications aren't supported), and *stem* is the name of the stem variable to store the results to. The results being stored are the lines in the file that contain the character string being searched for. Stem.0 will contain the number of matching lines.

Options contains optional parameters. Only two parameters are supported: C to make the search case-sensitive (the default is to ignore case) and N to add a line number to the report generated by SysFileSearch. The FILES.CMD program that comes with this book uses SysFileSearch to search through your C:\CONFIG.SYS file and report on all the lines containing the SET command.

While SysFileSearch doesn't support wildcards, it's fairly easy to add wildcard support. The SysFileTree function, following, searches for all the files matching a file specification and stores their name in a stem variable. It can be used first to generate a list of files to process and then SysFileSearch can process each file. The FF2.CMD program that comes with this book does this to allow you to search for all the files matching a given file specification and containing the specified text. The operation of FF2.CMD is explained in appendix A. SysFileSearch returns three different return codes. They are:

0. The function was successful.

2. There wasn't enough memory to complete its operation.

3. The function encountered an error opening a file.

SysFileTree

The SysFileTree function finds all the files on a hard disk matching a particular wildcard description and places their description into a stem variable for additional processing. The syntax is:

```
variable = SysFileTree(filespec,stem[,options][,targetattrib][,newattrib])
```

where *filespec* is the specification of the file to look for (wildcards are allowed), *stem* is the name of the stem variable to store the results in (Stem.0 will contain the number of matching files), and *options* contains any logical combination of the following options:

B. Search for both files and subdirectories. This is the default.

D. Search for only subdirectories.

F. Search for only files.

O. Report only matching, fully qualified filenames. The default is to include the date, time, size, and attributes in the report.

S. Scan the subdirectories recursively. This is not the default.

T. Return the time field in the form hh/mm and the date field in the form yy/mm/dd.

Targetattrib is the attributes a file must have in order to be considered a match. An attribute can be either + for set, – for clear, or * for either. The attributes in the mask are positionally dependent and must be in the order of archive, directory, hidden, read-only, and system. The default is *****. For example, +**** will find all the files that have been modified since the last backup and ***+* will find all the read-only files.

Newattrib specifies the new attributes the matching files are to have. The mask is in the same order as the targetattrib mask; * means the attribute isn't changed, + means it's set, and – means it's cleared.

Two notes are in order. First, you can't change the directory attribute—that is, you can't change a file to a directory or a directory to a file. Second, the attributes shown in the report are the new attributes.

Two return codes are provided by SysFileTree. A zero means it executed properly, while a two means it encountered an error. The FF.CMD program that comes with this book uses the file specification you enter on the command line to find all matching files below the current subdirectory on the current hard drive. This is an excellent tool for finding a particular file.

SysMkDir

The SysMkDir function creates a subdirectory. The syntax is:

```
variable = SysMkDir(subdirectory)
```

where *subdirectory* is the name of the subdirectory to create and *variable* is the name of the variable to contain the return codes. The return codes are:

0. The subdirectory was successfully created.

2. The file wasn't found.

3. The path wasn't found.

5. Access was denied.

26. OS/2 can't read the specified disk.

87. The function was passed an invalid parameter.

108. The specified drive is locked.

206. The filename exceeds the range.

SysRmDir

The SysRmDir function removes an empty subdirectory. The syntax is:

```
variable = SysRmDir(subdirectory)
```

where *subdirectory* is the name of the subdirectory to remove and *variable* is the name of the variable to contain the return codes. SysRmDir won't remove the current subdirectory or any subdirectory still containing files. The return codes are:

0.   The subdirectory was successfully removed.

2.   The subdirectory wasn't found.

3.   The path wasn't found.

5.   Access was denied.

16.   An attempt was made to remove the current subdirectory.

26.   OS/2 can't read the specified disk.

87.   The function was passed an invalid parameter.

108.   The specified drive is locked.

206.   The filename exceeds the range.

SysSearchPath

The SysSearchPath function searches a path looking for a file. The syntax is:

```
filespec = SysSearchPath(path, filename)
```

where *path* is the name of an environmental variable, such as PATH or DPATH, that resembles a path statement. The name must be in all uppercase to match the way OS/2 stores environmental names. *Filename* is the name of the file to search for along the path. Wildcards aren't supported, although they could be added, as described previously, using the SysFileTree function. *Filespec* is the variable to contain the fully qualified filename.

The WHICH.CMD program that comes with this book uses the SysSearchPath function to find a program along the path. To use WHICH.CMD, enter the name of the program on the command line without the extension. It will search for .EXE, .COM, .CMD, and .BAT files and report the first occurrence.

SysTempFileName

Occasionally, a program will need to create a temporary file the way FILES.CMD creates and then deletes the JUNK.@@! file. If the program has the filename hardwired into it the way FILES.CMD does, then it needs to deal with the problem of the temporary file already existing (error checking). A better approach is to let the program figure out a unique temporary filename when it runs. The SysTempFileName does just that. The syntax is:

```
file = SysTempFileName(template[,filter])
```

where *template* describes the general form of the temporary filename. It's a combination of characters and single-character wildcards. For example, TEMP????.TMP and C:\TEMP\TODAY.??? would both be valid. The more wildcard characters each name has, the better SysTempFileName will work.

Filter is the single-character wildcard character. The default is a question mark. Each filter character will be replaced with a number at run time. This number is selected at random, so sequentially generated filenames won't have sequential numbers. *File* is the name of the variable to store the resulting filename in.

Extended Attributes

Extended attributes is an area on the disk where a program can store information about a file or subdirectory. For example, REXX stores a tokenized version of a .CMD program in the extended attributes the first time it executes the program. The extended attributes are stored in a separate location and aren't part of the file itself. Extended attributes are limited to 64K in size. The functions that work with extended attributes are discussed in the following sections and summarized in Table 12.4.

TABLE 12.4 Extended Attribute Functions

Function	Summary
SysGetEA	Reads a named extended attribute.
SysPutEA	Writes extended attribute information to a file.

SysGetEA

The SysGetEA function reads a named extended attribute for a file. The syntax is:

```
Result = SysGetEA(file,name,variable)
```

where *file* is the name of the file to read the extended attribute, *name* is the name of the extended attribute to read, *variable* is the name of the variable to store the extended attribute information in, and Result is the name of the variable to store the results of the function. A zero indicates that the function was successful.

The EA.CMD program that comes with the book will read the extended attribute data for the XCOPY.CMD program that comes with OS/2. XCOPY.CMD must be installed in the \OS2 subdirectory and EA.CMD must be run from the same drive.

SysPutEA

The SysPutEA function writes extended attribute information to a file. The syntax is:

```
Result = SysPutEA(file,name,value)
```

where *file* is the name of the file to which the extended attribute will refer, *name* is the name of the extended attribute, *value* is the new value for the extended attribute, and Result is the variable to store the results of calling the function. A zero means the extended attribute was successfully written to a file; otherwise, Result will contain an OS/2 return code.

Miscellaneous Functions

The functions that don't fit into any other category are documented in the following sections summarized in Table 12.5.

TABLE 12.5 Miscellaneous Functions

Function	Summary
SysSetIcon	Matches an icon file to a file.
SysSleep	Pauses the computer for a specified number of seconds.
SysGetKey	Returns a single keystroke pressed by the user.
SysGetMessage	Returns National Language Support messages.
SysIni	Allows limited editing of initialization variables.
SysOS2Ver	Returns the OS/2 version number.
SysWaitNamedPipe	Performs a timed wait on a named pipe.

SysGetKey

The SysGetKey function gets a single keystroke from the user. The syntax is:

```
key = SysGetKey([option])
```

where *option* is either ECHO to display the keystroke to the screen (the default), or NOECHO to stop the keystroke from being echoed to the screen, and *key* is the ASCII code of the keystroke that was pressed. SysGetKey will wait until a keystroke is pressed. The character doesn't have to be followed by the Enter key.

You must be careful when using SysGetKey to get cursor movement keystrokes from the user or in situations where the user might accidently press a cursor-movement key. These keystrokes actually send two keystrokes to SysGetKey. For example, the Home key sends 0,71 and the left arrow sends 0,75. When the first keystroke read by SysGetKey has a value of zero, there's a second keystroke waiting in the keyboard buffer that must also be read by SysGetKey.

The KEYVALUE.CMD program that comes with this book can help you find out what number(s) are returned by SysGetKey for any keystroke. To use it, just run it from the command line or desktop. It will prompt you for the keystroke to check. Once you press that keystroke, it reports the number(s) SysGetKey sees. For extended keystrokes, it reports both numbers. So it will continue in an endless loop asking you for keystrokes to process, allowing you to rapidly check a lot of numbers. Press the Enter key to stop it.

SysGetMessage

OS/2 and its applications can provide National Language Support (NLS) using message files. Message files contain character strings and associated numbers. Any application can reference the text by the associated number. These messages can be accessed by REXX using the SysGetMessage function. The syntax is:

```
message = SysGetMessage(number[,file][,str1]...[,str9)
```

where *number* is the number of the message to return and *file* is the message file to search. The default file is OSO001.MSG. Message files are searched in C:\, the current subdirectory, and the DPATH.

Str# are insertion text variables. Messages can have points where text passed to it is inserted, much like a batch file can insert %1 into messages. *Str#* provides a way to pass this text to the message. Up to nine phrases can be passed. *Message* is the returned message.

SysIni

SysIni allows limited editing of initialization (.INI) files. Six modes are available and each mode has its own syntax. Mode one is to set a single key value. Mode two is to query a single key value. Mode three is to delete a single key. Mode four is to delete an application and all associated keys. Mode five is to query the names of all keys associated with a particular application. Mode six is to query the names of all applications. The syntax for these six modes is:

```
Mode 1: Result = SysIni([inifile],app,key,value)
Mode 2: Result = SysIni([inifile],app,key)
Mode 3: Result = SysIni([inifile],app,key,"DELETE:")
Mode 4: Result = SysIni([inifile],app,["DELETE:"])
Mode 5: Result = SysIni([inifile],app,"ALL:","stem")
Mode 6: Result = SysIni([inifile],"ALL:","stem")
```

where *inifile* is the name of the .INI file to work with. The default is C:\OS2\OS2.INI and this can also be specified as USER. The system file is C:\OS2\OS2SYS.INI, which can also be specified as SYSTEM. Using BOTH will search both files.

App is the name of the application or other meaningful value to use to store keywords to, *key* is the name of the keyword that will hold the data, *value* is the value to store, and *stem* is the name of the stem variable to store data to when the results exceed being stored in a single variable.

Result contains the results of the function call. For a successful invocation, this will be a null string for successful setting and deleting invocation. For successful querying, it will be equal to the value of the specified application keyword. The string ERROR will be returned if an error occurs.

SysOS2Ver

The SysOS2Ver function returns the OS/2 version number in the form #.##. The syntax is:

```
variable = SysOS2Ver()
```

where *variable* is the name of the variable to store the version number.

SysSetIcon

The SysSetIcon function attaches an icon file to a file. The syntax is:

```
Result = SysSetIcon(file,iconfile)
```

where *file* is the name of the file for which the icon file is set, *iconfile* is the name of the icon file, and Result is the name of the variable to store the results. A one indicates the icon file was successfully set and a zero indicates it wasn't set.

SysSleep

The SysSleep function pauses the computer for a specified number of seconds. The syntax is:

```
CALL SysSleep (seconds)
```

where *seconds* is the number of seconds to pause the computer. The BEEPS.CMD program that comes with this book uses SysSleep to pause the computer between playing up and down the scales. The two spelling programs (SPELLING.CMD and SPELDISK.CMD) both use SysSleep to show new spelling words to the user for a specified time period before erasing the screen.

SysWaitNamedPipe

The SysWaitNamedPipe performs a timed wait on a named pipe. The syntax is:

```
Result = SysWaitNamedPipe(name[,timeout])
```

where *name* is the named pipe (this must be of the form \PIPE*pipename*), *timeout* is the number of microseconds to wait on the pipe (A value of –1 causes REXX to wait on the pipe until it's free), and Result is the name of the variable to store the return code. The return codes are:

0. The named pipe isn't busy.

2. The named pipe wasn't found.

231. The function timed out before the pipe became available.

Summary

Table 12.6 summarizes all the external RexxUtil functions.

TABLE 12.6 External RexxUtil Functions

Function	Summary
RxMessageBox	Displays a message box on the screen with a title, message, icon, and one or more buttons. Must run under PMREXX.
SysCls	Clears the screen.
SysCreateObject	Creates a new object in a class.
SysCurPos	Positions the cursor and reports its current position.
SysDeregisterObjectClass	Removes an object class definition from the system.
SysDestroyObject	Removes an existing Workplace Shell object.
SysDriveInfo	Returns information about a drive.
SysDriveMap	Returns information about the available drives.
SysDropFuncs	This function drops all the RexxUtil external functions.
SysFileDelete	Deletes a file.
SysFileSearch	Returns all the lines in a file containing the specified text.
SysFileTree	Returns all the files on a drive matching a wildcard specification.
SysGetEA	Reads a named extended attribute.
SysGetKey	Returns a single keystroke pressed by the user.
SysGetMessage	Returns National Language Support messages.
SysIni	Allows limited editing of initialization variables.
SysMkDir	Creates a subdirectory.
SysOS2Ver	Returns the OS/2 version number.
SysPutEA	Writes extended attribute information to a file.
SysQueryClassList	Returns a listing of all registered object classes.
SysRegisterObjectClass	Registers a new object class.
SysRmDir	Removes an empty subdirectory.
SysSearchPath	Searches for a file along a specified path.
SysSetIcon	Matches an icon file to a file.
SysSetObjectData	Changes the setting of an object.
SysSleep	Pauses the computer for a specified number of seconds.
SysTempFileName	Returns an unused filename for use as a temporary file.
SysTextScreenRead	Reads text from the screen and stores it in a variable.
SysTextScreenSize	Returns the size of the current screen.
SysWaitNamedPipe	Performs a timed wait on a named pipe.

13

Keyword Instructions

A keyword instruction is composed of one or more clauses where the first word of the first clause is a keyword. That keyword tells REXX what instruction to execute for that clause. Some keywords, like DO, can have nested keyword instructions. Others, like IF and WHEN, require additional keywords to complete their construction.

You can add spaces before a keyword to improve readability, and REXX will ignore these. Generally, one space is required after a keyword to separate it from the next portion of the instruction. Again, you can add more spaces for readability and REXX will ignore them. In a few cases, like this one:

```
DO WHILE"Yes"=Error
```

a space isn't needed after a keyword. However, it's generally a good idea to include at least one space, even when it is not needed, to improve readability.

ADDRESS

A command is a character string that's sent to an external environment for additional processing. Normally, commands are sent to the external environment (generally OS/2) fairly automatically by REXX. Any expression REXX doesn't recognize is assumed to be a command. An expression is any clause that begins with a word that isn't a REXX keyword. (For more information on clauses, refer back to chapter 2.) For example, all of the following would be passed on to the operating system for processing:

```
DIR
ECHO Good Morning!
CHKDSK
DISKCOPY A: B:
```

Occasionally, a command that's intended for the external environment can be pre-processed by REXX. For example, if Message were a valid REXX variable containing the character string "Good Morning!" then the line:

```
ECHO Message
```

would have the variable preprocessed by REXX and the command passed to OS/2 would be:

```
ECHO Good Morning!
```

You can avoid this preprocessing by enclosing the part of the command you don't want processed in quotation marks. So the command:

```
ECHO "Message"
```

would display Message on the screen. Sometimes the REXX preprocessing gets in the way and forces you to use quotation marks. If you used the following command:

```
XCOPY A:\*.* C:\*.* /S
```

you would get an "Invalid expression" error message. The /S is seen as a division operation and S isn't a variable, so division is impossible. Plus, the \ character is the NOT operator and the expression that follows isn't a logical operation it can operate on. The solution is to enclose part or all of the command inside quotation marks. Either of the following would work:

```
"XCOPY A:\*.* C:\*.* /S"
XCOPY "A:\*.* C:\*.* /S"
```

Unless you have a variable you need evaluated in the expression, it's usually best to enclose the entire statement inside quotation marks. That gives a very strong visual statement that commands are being sent to the environment.

The ADDRESS instruction changes the command environment that receives these commands. Its syntax is:

```
ADDRESS [environment] [expression]
```

or

```
ADDRESS [value] expression
```

where *environment* is the new environment to receive the commands and *expression* is a command to send to that environment. This is a temporary change to the environment receiving the command that's in effect for only this instruction.

If the instruction is executed without an expression, then a new environment for receiving commands is selected and this change is permanent, staying in effect until it's overwritten by another instruction. This allows programs to register themselves as an environment and then use REXX as a macro language where they can receive the commands from the REXX program. The prior environment is saved. If the ADDRESS instruction is given by itself, control toggles back to the prior environment.

ARG

The ARG instruction retrieves the arguments passed to a program, much like the internal Arg( ) function. Its syntax is:

```
ARG [template]
```

where *template* is a list of variables separated by blanks and patterns. Templates are discussed in detail as part of the discussion of the PARSE instruction later in this chapter.

All arguments retrieved using the ARG instruction are converted to uppercase. You can avoid this by using the PARSE ARG instruction, also discussed later. The ARG instruction doesn't destroy the data it processes from the command line, so you can issue the instruction repeatedly to generate the same command-line data in different fashions.

You can see this in ARG-CMD.CMD, where the ARG( ) function is first used to bring in the first command-line argument to see if it's a /? and the user is requesting help. Next, the ARG instruction reads the entire command line into one variable for display purposes. Finally, the ARG instruction is used with a template to read each word into a separate variable. ARG-CMD.CMD stores the first ten words into variables, using the period (.) template to discard the remaining words. The tenth variable is not displayed. Rather, it's used as a test to see if more than nine words were entered.

There's no limit on the length or number of arguments that the ARG instruction can process, other than the limits OS/2 places on the command line and REXX places on line length. There's also no limit on the number of times these arguments can be accessed with the ARG, PARSE, and PULL instructions.

CALL

The main use for the CALL instruction is to invoke an internal subroutine or procedure, a built-in or external function, or an external routine. (For ease of reference, I'll refer to all of these as routines.) When used in this fashion, the syntax is:

```
CALL name [firstargument][,remainingarguments]
```

where *name* is the name of the routine call and the arguments are any arguments to be passed to the routine. Note that there isn't a comma between the name of the routine to call and the first argument. A particular argument can have more than one word in it since the arguments are separated with commas.

Arguments used with the CALL instruction

Look at the CALL-1.CMD program that comes with this book. It passes four routines to a subroutine. This subroutine simply displays these four arguments. The first argument it passes is 1+2+3. The mathematics are performed by REXX before passing the argument to the subroutine, so it receives 6 as the first argument. The second argument is String. This is a variable that contains This Is A String and it's the contents of this variable that get passed to the subroutine. The third argument is Max(1,2,3) and again REXX performs the mathematics and passes a 3 to the subroutine. The final argument is Now Is The Time To Learn REXX. Even though this contains seven words, there's no comma, so it's treated as one argument.

REXX handles arguments differently depending on how you enter them. When the arguments are coming from the command line, REXX treats everything as one argument. However, when used in a subroutine being executed via the CALL instruction, the Arg function treats the comma as a divider between arguments. This was explained in more detail back in chapter 5.

Calling functions

Back in chapter 11, you saw that the external function Max could be used to find the largest number using an instruction like:

```
Result = Max(1,2,3)
```

Of course, not all functions need to report results back like the Max function. For example, the instruction:

```
Result = SysSleep(10)
```

will pause the program for ten seconds using the external SysSleep function, but doesn't need to return any results back to the program. In either case, the function can also be executed using the CALL instruction. When executed in this fashion, the function doesn't use parentheses and only space separates the name of the function from the first argument. These two instructions could be replaced with:

```
CALL Max 1,2,3
CALL SysSleep 10
```

When a function like Max is executed in this fashion and it needs to returns its results, it returns this in a variable called Result that it creates automatically. If you experiment a little, you'll find that the instruction:

```
CALL Abs(-1)
```

works fine. You might be tempted to think that the CALL instruction can be used with functional notation and try another instruction like:

```
CALL Max(1,2,3)
```

but this version won't work. REXX doesn't treat them differently nor does it allow functional notation when using the CALL instruction with the Abs function. REXX allows you to surround any number with parentheses to make sure that the sign is properly associated with the number. In the first example, Abs is passed a single number in parentheses. Since it causes no confusion to REXX, the space between the name of the function and the opening parenthesis can be used or eliminated. The Max function could be provided numbers in parentheses in the form:

```
CALL MAX(1),(2),(3)
```

and it would work as expected.

Executing internal and external routines

You can use the CALL instruction to execute a special section of code inside a subroutine or a stand-alone REXX program.

Exception handling

The instructions CALL ON and CALL OFF are part of the REXX exception-handling routines, discussed in chapter 17.

Search order

When REXX encounters a CALL instruction, it first checks to see if the name represents a subroutine inside the current program, and if so it executes that subroutine. You can bypass this step by enclosing the name of the subroutine in quotation marks. That allows you to give an internal subroutine the name of an internal function and still access both. You access the subroutine by using its name and the internal function by using the name inside quotation marks.

If the name isn't a subroutine or if it's enclosed inside quotation marks, REXX next checks for a built-in function like Max or Min. If it isn't a built-in function, it finally checks to see if it's an external function, like SysCls or a stand-alone REXX program.

DO

The DO instruction groups a series of instructions together and optionally executes them either a specified number of times or until some condition is met. The syntax to group a series of instructions together is:

```
DO
  instruction1
  instruction2
  instructionlast
END
```

where *instruction1* through *instructionlast* are listed between the DO and END keyword. Of course, they can be listed on a single line as well and separated by semicolons. REXX uses the DO WHILE and DO UNTIL instructions to loop until specific conditions are met. The syntax for the DO WHILE instruction is:

```
DO WHILE expression
   instructions
END
```

where *expression* is a REXX expression that evaluates to either zero or one, and *instructions* is the list of instructions to execute until *expression* evaluates to one. The syntax for the DO UNTIL instruction is:

```
DO UNTIL expression
   instructions
END
```

The DO WHILE and DO UNTIL instructions work very similarly, only the DO WHILE loop requires the condition to exist first and the DO UNTIL doesn't. The syntax to loop a specific number of times is:

```
DO number
   instruction1
   instruction2
   instructionlast
END
```

where *number* is the number of times to repeat the loop. It must be a whole nonnegative number. If the number is zero, the loop is not executed. The syntax, when you need access to the loop-counter variable and want to control the starting and ending points and increment amount, is:

```
DO I = start TO end BY increment
   instruction1
   instruction2
   instructionlast
End
```

where I is the name of the variable to store the loop counter value. Any legal variable name is acceptable. *Start* is the first value to assign to I. If *start* is being read from another variable, it's possible that its value exceeds the value of *end*. When that happens, the loop simply is not executed. No error condition is raised. *End* is the last value to use. The first time I reaches or exceeds this value, the loop stops. This checking is performed before the loop starts, so:

```
DO I = 1 TO 5 BY 3
   SAY I
END
```

would loop through once with a value of 1 and a second time with a value of 4 (1+3), but would stop before the loop with the value of 7 (4+3) because that exceeds 5. *In-*

crement is the amount to increase the loop-counter variable by each time it goes through the loop. There's no requirement that the increment be positive. In fact, the following loop is completely valid:

```
DO I = 10 TO 1 BY -1
  SAY I
END
```

If no value is specified for *increment*, its default value is one. For more detailed information on the DO instruction, refer back to chapter 10.

DROP

The DROP instruction unassigns a variable. The syntax is:

```
DROP variablelist
```

where *variablelist* is the list of variables to drop, separated by spaces. If a single name is used and is enclosed with parentheses, then that name is used as the name of a variable containing a list of variables to drop. That list must have variable names separated by spaces with no parentheses and no leading or trailing spaces. It isn't an error to drop variables that don't exist or to drop the same variable more than once. Of course, there's no reason to do either. Once a variable has been dropped, REXX acts as though it never existed. For example, the instructions:

```
MyVariable = "A String Variable"
DROP MyVariable
SAY MyVariable
```

would simply display the name of the variable since it doesn't exist. The DROP instruction can be seen in the TODO.CMD and LISTIT.CMD programs that come with this book.

EXIT

The EXIT instruction unconditionally terminates a program and optionally returns a character string or number to the caller. The syntax is:

```
EXIT [expression]
```

where *expression* is the string or number to return to the caller. If *expression* is made up of a mathematical expression and/or REXX variables, then those are evaluated and the result is what is returned.

If the program was called by OS/2, then *expression* must be a whole number. The smallest number that can be returned is $-32,768$ (-2^{15}), and the largest number is $32,767$ $(2^{15}-1)$. (In other words, it must be a 16-bit signed integer.) This number is stored in the errorlevel and can be tested with the batch file IF ERROR LEVEL subcommand.

If the program was called by another REXX program, then any information—character string or number—can be returned to the calling program. If the program is called like a function, for example:

```
variable = program
```

then the information is returned to the program and stored under the variable used in the expression. If the program is called using the CALL instruction, then the information is returned and stored in the variable Result, created automatically by REXX. The YESORNO.CMD program that comes with this book uses the EXIT program to return the ASCII value of the keystroke it received from the user.

IF

The basic logic testing statement is the IF test. Its syntax is:

```
IF expression[;] THEN[;] instruction1 [ELSE[;] instruction2]
```

where *expression* is a logical statement that evaluates to either true or false, *instruction1* is the instruction to be executed when *expression* is true, and *instruction2* is the instruction to be executed when *expression* is false. The IF instruction is discussed in detail in chapter 10.

INTERPRET

The INTERPRET instruction evaluates the contents of an expression and then executes that expression as though it were an expression that had been written into the program. This allows the instructions to be determined at run-time. The syntax is:

```
INTERPRET expression
```

where *expression* is the expression to evaluate. Any instruction is allowed, but multiple-line instructions like DO and SELECT must be completed in the expression. Labels aren't permitted in the expression. The COMPUTE.CMD program that comes with this book uses the INTERPRET instruction to evaluate the mathematical expression entered on the command line to display the results. Additionally, the REXXTRY.CMD program that comes with OS/2 uses INTERPRET to execute user instructions.

ITERATE

The ITERATE instruction alters a DO loop's flow of control. When the ITERATE instruction is executed, control immediately passes to the END instruction for the current DO loop and the loop-counter variable is incremented. The syntax is:

```
ITERATE [name]
```

where *name* is the name of the loop-counter variable to increment. The ITERATE instruction is discussed in detail in chapter 10.

LEAVE

The LEAVE instruction also alters a DO loop's flow of control. When the LEAVE instruction is executed, control immediately passes to the instruction following the END instruction for the current DO loop and the loop is terminated. The syntax is:

```
LEAVE [name]
```

where *name* is the name of the loop-counter variable of the loop to LEAVE. The LEAVE instruction is discussed in detail in chapter 10.

NOP

The NOP instruction is a dummy instruction that has no impact other than serving as a place holder. Consider the sample program:

```
SELECT
   WHEN Input < 0 THEN SAY "Negative Not Allowed"
   WHEN Input = 0 THEN ; /* Try To Do Nothing */
   WHEN Input > 0 THEN SAY "Number Okay"
END
```

the program simply wants to not do anything when the Input variable is zero, but the extra semicolon won't work. It would be treated as a null clause so the THEN keyword would be directly followed by a WHEN keyword, resulting in a syntax error. This could be replaced by the following:

```
SELECT
   WHEN Input < 0 THEN SAY "Negative Not Allowed"
   WHEN Input = 0 THEN NOP
   WHEN Input > 0 THEN SAY "Number Okay"
END
```

to achieve the desired results. While this example program isn't good programming form and could be rewritten to not need the NOP as a place holder, there are times when it's very convenient to have a place-holder instruction that isn't executed.

NUMERIC

The NUMERIC instruction controls how mathematical operations are carried out and displayed. It's used to control three different settings: DIGITS, FORM, and FUZZ. The DIGITS setting controls how many significant digits are used for calculations. The default is nine and the syntax to change it is:

```
NUMERIC DIGITS expression
```

where *expression* is a non-negative whole number or mathematical expression that evaluates to one. It must also be larger than the current FUZZ setting. Very large numbers are supported, with a corresponding increase in memory usage and slowdown of calculations. Smaller settings (six and below) are useful only in very unusual settings and should be used with extreme caution since the DIGITS setting affects the precision of all calculations, including the calculation of loop-counter variables. The current setting can be returned with the Digits internal function.

REXX accepts two forms of exponential notation: scientific and engineering. These are explained in detail in chapter 9. NUMERIC FORM is used to control which is used. The syntax is:

```
NUMERIC FORM SCIENTIFIC
NUMERIC FORM ENGINEERING
NUMERIC FORM VALUE expression
```

The FORM is set directly by either the SCIENTIFIC or ENGINEERING keywords or by *expression*, where it must be an expression that evaluates to either of these keywords. The default is SCIENTIFIC.

REXX has the option of ignoring a certain number of trailing digits in making numeric comparisons. The number of digits ignored is controlled by the NUMERIC FUZZ setting. This is explained in detail in chapter 9. The syntax is:

```
NUMERIC FUZZ expression
```

where *expression* is a non-negative whole number of an expression that evaluates to one. The number must be smaller than the setting for NUMERIC DIGITS and the default is zero.

OPTIONS

The OPTIONS instruction passes special parameters to the language processor. The syntax is:

```
OPTIONS expression
```

where *expression* is one of the following parameters that are, under OS/2, recognized by the language processor:

ETMODE. Allows literal strings to contain double-byte character-set (DBCS) characters.

NOETMODE. Disallows using DBCS characters (the default).

EXMODE. Specifies that DBCS data in mixed strings is handled on a logical-character basis.

NOEXMODE. Specifies that data in strings be handled on a byte basis (the default).

PARSE

Parsing is the breaking down of a character string into two or more substrings. Typically, the character string being processed is the character string that was passed to the program from the command line when the program was run from OS/2 or to another REXX program when the program was being run as a subroutine. The PARSE instruction is the main method of parsing variables. The syntax is:

```
PARSE [upper] [instruction] [template]
```

where *upper* is an optional instruction to convert the input to all uppercase (without this instruction, no case translation takes place) and *instruction* is one of several subinstructions. They are:

ARG.   An instruction to parse the arguments passed to the program, subroutine, or function according to the rules of the Arg function.

LINEIN.   An instruction to read the next line and parse it. Note that this is a shorter version of the instruction:

```
PARSE VALUE LINEIN() WITH [template]
```

The LINEIN instruction is generally used only when direct access to the character input stream is necessary. If a line isn't available, the program will pause until a line is completed. The PULL or PARSE PULL instructions are generally used to interact with the user.

PULL.   An instruction to pull the next string from the input queue and parse it. This is generally the method used to get data from the user.

SOURCE.   An instruction to obtain a string representation of the source of the program being executed. This string won't change while the program is executing.

VALUE [*expression*] WITH.   An instruction to evaluate the expression given and parse the results. In this context, WITH is a reserved word used to mark the end of the expression.

VAR *variable*.   An instruction to parse the variable.

VERSION.   An instruction to return information about the language. Under OS/2 2.1, it returns REXXSAA 4.00 08 Jul 1992.

Template is a list of symbols separated by blanks or patterns. This is discussed in more detail later. In order to understand the PARSE instruction, it's important to understand the parsing template.

Parsing template

The parsing template gives directions on how to parse a character string and which symbols are stored in which variables. A string can be parsed by words, characters, or position.

Perhaps the most common form of parsing is by word. Recall that a word is a portion of a character string with a space on both sides. The first word in a character string might have only a space after it, while the last word in a character string might have only a space before it. For some of these examples, I'll be parsing the phrase "Now Is The Time To Learn REXX" stored to the variable String. It contains seven words. Five of them, `Is` through `Learn`, have a space on both sides while two of them, `Now` and `REXX`, have only a space on one side.

When parsing by word, a list of variables is used as the template and each word goes into the corresponding variables. The first word goes into the first variable, the second word goes into the second variable, and so on. If there are more variables than words, the extra variables remain undefined. If there are more words than variables, all the remaining words are stored to the last variable in the list.

While the words go into the variables, their leading and trailing spaces do not. However, when multiple words are stored to the last variable, the space between words is maintained.

A period can be substituted for any variable name. The word or words that would normally be stored to the variable being replaced by the period are ignored. For example, the instruction:

```
PARSE VALUE String WITH Var1 Var2 ... Var7
```

would store `Now` to Var1, `Is` to Var2 and `REXX` to Var7. Since `The Time To Learn` have periods in place of variable names for their position, they're ignored. The instruction:

```
PARSE VALUE String WITH Var1 Var2
```

would store `Now` to Var1 and `Is` to Var2, and ignore everything else since a period is used in place of the last variable and everything remaining would normally be stored to this variable. Examples of all of this can be seen in the SHOWTEMP.CMD program that comes with this book.

A second way to parse a character string is to use specific characters inside the string. For example, the default method for displaying time with the Time function is 19:16:03. You know already that the numbers before the first colon represent the hour, the numbers after the first and before the second colon represent the minutes, and the numbers after the second colon represents seconds. This can be parsed using the instruction:

```
PARSE VALUE Time() WITH hour ":" minute ":" second
```

This will work no matter how many numbers are used to display the hours, minutes, and seconds, just as long as they're separated by a colon. Since the colons are used as part of the template, they aren't stored to either variable. As a second example, the Date(O) function displays the date in the form yy/mm/dd, and this can be parsed with the instruction:

```
PARSE VALUE DATE(O) WITH year "/" month "/" day
```

Of course, if you wanted only the month, you could use a period in the template and replace it with:

```
PARSE VALUE DATE(O) WITH . "/" month "/" .
```

Additionally, you can use variables to store portions of the template. When you do this, REXX needs a way to separate variables to contain data from the PARSE instruction from variables that store character strings for the template. Do this by surrounding the variables that store character strings for the template with parentheses. If the variable Slash contained a slash, you could replace the instruction with:

```
PARSE VALUE Date(O) WITH . (Slash) month (Slash) .
```

and obtain the same results. However, the period cannot be replaced with a variable. The third method of parsing is by position. Look back at the original string:

```
Now Is The Time To Learn REXX
----|----|----|----|----|----|
    5   10   15   20   25   30
```

The spaces are at positions 4, 7, 11, 16, 19, and 25. With positional parsing, each variable is separated by a number to indicate where that variable ends. Thus, the variable could be parsed with the instruction:

```
PARSE VALUE String WITH Var1 4 Var2 7 Var3 11,
Var4 16 Var5 19 Var6 25 Var7
```

However, this introduces a problem because the spaces aren't ignored. So each variable except Var1 contains a leading space. However, you can avoid that problem. The full syntax calls for two numbers between variables, the first being the ending point of the variable on the left and the second being the beginning point for the variable on the right. When only one number is used, the same value is used for both. However, in the example, you can specify both and skip the spaces. The instruction becomes:

```
PARSE VALUE String WITH Var1 4 5 Var2 7 8 Var3,
11 12 Var4 16 17 Var5 19 20 Var6 25 26 Var7
```

Normally, positional parsing parses data that has a fixed format rather than trying to parse words in this fashion. For example, the default display for the Date function is in the form 26 Nov 1993. One way to just get the year is with the instruction:

```
PARSE VALUE Date() WITH 8 year
```

When using positional parsing, column numbers don't have to be expressed in absolute numbers. You can also express them in increments from the last position by preceding the number with a plus sign. For example, the Date(A) function displays the date in the form 19931126. One way to positionally parse it is with the instruction:

```
PARSE VALUE Date(A) WITH year 5 month 7 day
```

Rather than counting the column position, it can also be positionally parsed with the instruction:

```
PARSE VALUE Date(A) WITH year 5 month +2 day
```

The first column number must be specified as a starting point, but any others can be specified using offsets from that point, as the +2 does in this example. Negative numbers are allowed as offsets, but the results aren't intuitive and this is best avoided. Examples of all three forms of parsing can be seen by running the SHOWTEMP.CMD program that comes with this book.

PROCEDURE

The PROCEDURE instruction is used with internal subroutines to protect the existing variables by hiding them from the subroutine. Selected variables can be made available to the subroutine. The syntax is:

```
PROCEDURE [EXPOSE variables]
```

where *variables* are those variable to optionally be made available to the subroutine. Once a RETURN instruction is encountered, the original variables are restored (any changes made to exposed variables are retained) and all variables created in the subroutine are dropped.

PULL

The PULL instruction is a shortcut version of the PARSE UPPER PULL instruction. Its syntax is:

```
PULL [template]
```

where *template* is a list of symbols separated by blanks or patterns. Characters obtained using the PULL instruction are always converted to uppercase.

PUSH

The PUSH instruction places information into the external data queue. The syntax is:

```
PUSH [expression]
```

where *expression* is the line to place into the external data queue. It's added in LIFO (last in, first out) order. If *expression* isn't specified, a null string is placed into the queue.

QUEUE

The QUEUE instruction places information into the external data queue. The syntax is:

```
QUEUE [expression]
```

where *expression* is the line to place into the external data queue. It's added in FIFO (first in, first out) order. If *expression* isn't specified, a null string is placed into the queue.

RETURN

The RETURN instruction terminates a subroutine or function. The syntax is:

```
RETURN [expression]
```

where *expression* is the value to return to the calling program. If used at the end of a subroutine, *expression* is optional. When used at the end of a function, it's required.

SAY

The SAY instruction displays text or a blank line on the screen. The syntax is:

```
SAY [expression]
```

where *expression* is the text to display on the screen. When used by itself, the SAY instruction displays a blank line on the screen. The SAY instruction is explained in detail in chapter 6.

SELECT

The SELECT instruction picks (or selects) one option out of a list of options and executes the instructions associated with that option. The syntax is:

```
SELECT
  WHEN condition1 THEN instruction1
  WHEN condition2 THEN instruction2
  WHEN conditionlast THEN instructionlast
  OTHERWISE instructionotherwise
END
```

where the conditions are the logical expressions of the possible outcomes and the instructions are the instructions to execute when the specific condition is true. Note that a DO/END block is allowed in order to execute multiple instructions. The SELECT instruction is explained in detail in chapter 10.

SIGNAL

The SIGNAL instruction is used to alter the normal flow of the program. It's normally used to handle errors, which is discussed in detail in chapter 17. It can also be used as an unconditional GOTO command. The syntax for this is:

```
SIGNAL label
```

where *label* is the label to jump to. This instruction closes all active loops, which can cause problems, so this form of the instruction is best avoided. Using the SIGNAL instruction as a GOTO command is discussed in detail in chapter 10.

There is an alternative form for the SIGNAL Label instruction where the label is computed at runtime. Its syntax is:

```
SIGNAL VALUE expression
```

where *expression* is a REXX expression that evaluates to a valid REXX label. This can be used at the beginning of a program to jump to a particular point based on input from the user. However, you must use it with care since trying to jump to a label that doesn't exist will cause the program to abort with a "Label not found" error message.

TRACE

The TRACE instruction controls the execution of a REXX program for debugging. The syntax is:

```
TRACE [tracesetting]
TRACE [VALUE expression]
```

where *expression* evaluates to a valid TRACE setting (*tracesetting*).

Summary

While REXX has only a few keyword instructions, they're very powerful. These keyword instructions are summarized in Table 13.1.

TABLE 13.1 Keyword Instruction Summary

Keyword	Summary
ADDRESS	Changes the command environment that receives commands from REXX and sends commands to that environment.
ARG	Retrieves the arguments that are passed to a program from either the command line or another program. Works much like the Arg internal function.
CALL	Primarily used to invoke an internal subroutine or procedure, a built-in or external function, or an external routine. Also used as part of the REXX error-handling routines.
DO	Groups a series of instructions together, loops until a specific condition is met, loops a specific number of times, and loops from a starting point to an ending point by a specific increment.
DROP	Unassigns a variable. After that, REXX treats the variable as though it had never been created.
EXIT	Unconditionally terminates a program and optionally returns a character string or number to the caller.
INTERPRET	Evaluates the contents of an expression and then executes that expression as though it were an expression that had been written into the program.

TABLE 13.1 (Continued)

Keyword	Summary
ITERATE	Alters the flow of a DO loop by passing control to the END instruction and incrementing the loop counter.
LEAVE	Alters the flow of a DO loop by terminating the loop and passing control to the instruction following the END instruction.
NOP	A place-holding dummy instruction that does nothing other than holding a place.
NUMERIC	Controls how mathematical operations are carried out and displayed. Specifically controls the DIGITS, FORM, and FUZZY settings.
OPTIONS	Passes special parameters to the language processor.
PARSE	Processes a character string into one or more substrings.
PROCEDURE	In internal subroutines, it protects the existing variables by hiding them from the subroutine.
PULL	A shortcut version of the PARSE UPPER PULL instruction.
PUSH	Places information into the external data queue in LIFO order.
QUEUE	Places information into the external data queue in FIFO order.
RETURN	Terminates a subroutine or function and optionally returns information to the calling program.
SAY	Displays text or a blank line on the screen.
SELECT	Picks one option out of a list of options and execute the instructions associated with that option.
SIGNAL	Alters the normal flow of a program.
TRACE	Controls the execute of a program for debugging.

Internal Subroutines

A subroutine is a special block inside a program that functions very much like a stand-alone program. It has its own starting and ending points and, while it's running, the main program is suspended. When the subroutine is finished, control is passed back to the main program, which continues from the line after where it passed control to the subroutine. Figure 14.1 illustrates this.

Types of Subroutines

REXX supports two types of subroutines: internal and external. An internal subroutine is one that's completely self-contained within the main program. That is, both the program and subroutine are stored in one program file. An external subroutine is a separate program file that the main program calls when needed. Internal subroutines are able to meet most users' needs when using subroutines. For that reason, you'll rarely need to resort to external subroutines.

However, it sometimes makes a lot of sense to write an external subroutine. The PAUSE.CMD and CLS.CMD programs are perfect examples. These programs perform actions that many of your programs will need to perform and that don't need to receive or return much data to do their job. Therefore, it makes a lot of sense to write them once as stand-alone subroutines and call them from other programs as needed. External subroutines are discussed in detail in the next chapter.

Introduction to Internal Subroutines

An internal subroutine is a program within a program. It's generally devoted to performing tasks that need to be performed more than once. By using an internal subroutine, those tasks can be programmed just one time.

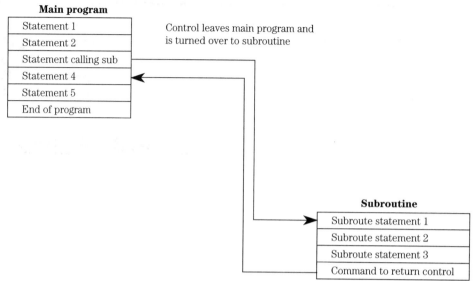

Figure 14.1 How a program calls a subroutine.

A simple example

Take a look back at SHOWTEMP.CMD from chapter 13. While running, it has to center a main title on the screen by padding it with spaces on four different occasions. I figured up each of these manually as I was writing the code. If I go back and edit the titles, then I have to recenter them. Since it repeats the same action four times, it makes sense to write this code once and reuse that code each time. This reusable code might look like this:

```
ToShow = Center(Title,79)
SAY ToShow
```

As long as the Title variable contains the title, you can reuse this code each time the program needs to center a title. This is a very simple subroutine and it's made even simpler because it doesn't need to return a value to the main program. All it needs to do is display text on the screen. Each subroutine needs two things. First, it needs a unique name. This goes on the first line of the subroutine and is followed immediately by a colon. It's a good idea to make the name meaningful but avoid using the names of any keywords or functions. This is allowed, but avoiding it makes your code easier to follow.

This subroutine is called CenterTitle. Each subroutine also needs a RETURN instruction. This is placed at the point in the subroutine where you want the subroutine to terminate and control to pass back to the main program. For many subroutines, this is the last line of the subroutine. The subroutine now looks like this:

```
CENTERTITLE:
  ToShow = Center(Title,79)
  SAY ToShow
RETURN
```

Notice that everything between the name of the subroutine and the RETURN instruction is indented. This isn't required, but it gives a good visual representation that the code is grouped together. Once you have the subroutine in the program, you need a way to execute it. That's the easy part. The CALL instruction, followed by the name of the subroutine, executes the subroutine.

Subroutines are almost always listed at the end of your program, one after another. However, this can present a problem. Consider the CALL-2.CMD program that comes with this book. Its operational code is as follows:

```
Title = "Now Is The Time"
CALL CenterTitle
Title = "For All Good Women"
Call CenterTitle
Title = "To Come To The Aid"
Call CenterTitle
Title = "Of Their Country"
Call CenterTitle
CENTERTITLE:
   ToShow = Center(Title,79)
   SAY ToShow
RETURN
```

When you run CALL-2.CMD, however, the last title is unexpectedly displayed twice on the screen (see Figure 14.2). The reason is simple. Once REXX reaches the last

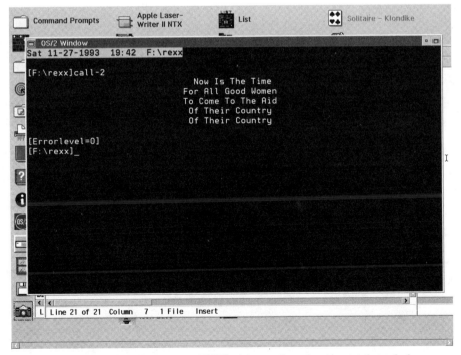

Figure 14.2 Without an EXIT instruction, REXX might run the subroutines at the end of your program when the program is done.

line of the program portion of the file, it continues processing lines and so executes the subroutine one last time, only this time as part of the program rather than as a subroutine. The reason that subroutines are placed at the end of a program is to avoid this problem. You do so by placing an EXIT instruction above the first subroutine. That way the subroutines can be executed only when they're called as subroutines.

The CALL-3.CMD program that comes with this book puts the simple subroutine you've worked on so far into practice. It's identical to SHOWTEMP.CMD except that the titles are stored to the Title variable and then the CenterTitle subroutine is called to center them and display them on the screen.

Improving the example

So far, you might not be impressed. After all, CALL-3.CMD has more lines in it than SHOWTEMP.CMD, so it isn't any shorter. However, once the CenterTitle subroutine is debugged, you can use it over and over without worrying about debugging new code. For the next change, let's move the underlining out of the main body of the program and do it once in the subroutine. While you're at it, you might was well skip the blank line under the title in the subroutine as well. The subroutine now looks like this:

```
CENTERTITLE:
  ToShow = Center(Title,79)
  SAY ToShow
  ToShow = Copies("=",79)
  SAY ToShow
  SAY
RETURN
```

You'll find this version in the CALL-4.CMD program that comes with this book.

Adding a second subroutine

So far, the program has only one subroutine and it hasn't really saved you a lot of time in writing the program since the tasks the subroutine performs are fairly simple. Now let's add a second subroutine and have it do something a little more complex. SHOWTEMP.CMP displays a number of instructions on the screen, underlines the instruction, and then executes that instruction. The first example is shown below:

```
PARSE VALUE String WITH Var.1 Var.2 Var.3 Var.4 Var.5 Var.6 Var.7
SAY "PARSE VALUE String WITH Var.1 Var.2 Var.3 Var.4 Var.5 Var.6 Var.7"
SAY "----------------------------------------------------------------"
```

The subroutine to do this is:

```
SHOWANDDO:
  SAY Instruction
  SAY Copies('-',Length(Instruction))
  SAY
  INTERPRET Instruction
RETURN
```

The CALL-5.CMD program that comes with this book uses these two subroutines to perform the same work of SHOWTEMP.CMD.

The example subroutines in CALL-5.CMD are fairly simple. The main program performs most of the work and calls a subroutine only to display a title or display and execute an instruction. In either case, the subroutine needs access to only one piece of information. The CenterTitle subroutine needs access to the title to center and the ShowAndDo subroutine needs access to the command to display and execute. The CenterTitle subroutine doesn't need to return any information to the main program. That isn't the case with the ShowAndDo subroutine, which must return the results of the command it executes to the main program. That often involves several variables.

As you'll see in the next chapter, variable management can be more difficult in external subroutines. However, it's easy with internal subroutines. Internal subroutines work with the same pool of variables as the main program. That means that any change to a variable in the subroutine is instantly reflected in the value of that variable seen by the main program.

This is why the ShowAndDo subroutine in CALL-5.CMD works. It has access to the variable Instruction that contains the instruction it's to execute. That execution creates as many as seven different variables containing results. Once those are created by the subroutine, they're instantly available to the main program as well, without the internal subroutine having to do anything to make that happen.

Internal Subroutine Advantages

CALL-5.CMD has two subroutines: ShowAndDo and CenterTitle. Adding internal subroutines to a program essentially adds new instructions to the REXX language that are available only inside that program. Internal subroutines have a number of important advantages:

Smaller code. While not the case in converting SHOWTEMP.CMD, with 101 lines, into CALL-5.CMD, with 105 lines, subroutines often result in shorter programs since the same code is used over and over rather than being included in the program in every spot it's needed.

Fewer bugs. Since the code contains less duplication of instruction, the chances of making a programming error (bug) are reduced.

Easier modifications. Since all of one type of action is controlled by one location in the program, it's much easier to modify the action. For example, if I decided to change the underlining below the instructions in the CALL-5.CMD program from a dash to an asterisk, I would have to make the change in only one location.

Consistency. The SHOWTEMP.CMD program is not a model of consistency. Sometimes the instructions to be executed have a dashed line directly below them and, in other cases, additional information is displayed before the dashed line. In the CALL-5.CMD program, all the instructions are displayed by one subroutine, so they're forced to be displayed consistently. As a general rule, users prefer consistent programs.

Goto with SIGNAL

You might recall from the discussion of the SIGNAL instruction in chapter 13 that using SIGNAL terminates all DO loops and similar structures. It continues to do that in a subroutine, but the impact of the SIGNAL instruction is localized within the subroutine. That is, using a SIGNAL instruction inside a subroutine terminates all the DO loops and similar structures within the subroutine but doesn't impact any active loops outside the subroutine. This is illustrated by the CALL-6.CMD program that comes with this book.

You can use the SIGNAL instruction to jump from a point within a subroutine to a label outside the subroutine. However, the results are very unpredictable, so you should avoid doing so.

Leaving a Subroutine

There are two ways to leave a subroutine: the RETURN and EXIT instructions. RETURN signals the logical end of the subroutine, which might be at the physical end of the subroutine. A subroutine can have as many RETURN instructions as it needs and it isn't required that any of them be at the physical end of the subroutine. An EXIT instruction terminates both the subroutine and main program, and returns you to either the desktop or command prompt depending on how the program was executed. As you'll see in the next chapter, this isn't the case with an external subroutine.

Occasionally, an internal subroutine needs to return a single number to the main program when it terminates. While you can accomplish this by creating a variable, there's another way. When followed by a number, the RETURN instruction makes that number available to the main program. You can see this with the CALL-7.CMD program that comes with this book. The subroutine simply returns a random number, as follows:

```
SUB:
  X = RANDOM(1,100)
RETURN x
```

The main program calls this subroutine using two different methods:

```
CALL Sub
SAY "Number Returned Is" Result
SAY "Second Number Returned Is" SUB()
```

The first time the subroutine is called, no specific action is taken to use the value being returned by the subroutine on the first line. However, REXX automatically saves the value to the Result variable, which is used on the second line to display the results of the first access of the subroutine. The second time, the subroutine is treated like an internal function and its value is displayed directly. Of course, neither of these methods would display a value if the subroutine didn't return a value.

Right now you might not see much use for this. After all, the subroutine stores its random number to the variable X. Since this variable is available to the main program, it could just use the variable whenever it needed the random number. Later, you'll see where these other two approaches to running the subroutine and using its results can be very useful.

Internal Subroutine Rules

- Internal subroutines are usually declared at the end of the script. Generally, the first subroutine is preceded by the EXIT instruction.

- One internal subroutine can call on another internal subroutine. An internal subroutine can even call itself, as the FACTORAL.CMD program that comes with this book does.

- The SIGNAL instruction is local inside an internal subroutine. That is, it doesn't terminate DO loops and similar structures outside the signal.

- You can use only the Exit or Return instructions to leave an internal subroutine. If the Return instruction is followed by a number or character string, that information is made available to the main program.

Saved Information

When a program calls an internal subroutine or function, the following data is automatically saved, and then restored when the subroutine terminates:

- The state of DO loops and other similar structures (discussed previously).

- NUMERIC settings (DIGITS, FUZZ, and FORM). This allows a subroutine to set the values for precision it needs without affecting the main program.

- The current and saved destination for commands, as controlled by the ADDRESS instruction.

- The condition traps used for debugging. These are discussed in chapter 18.

- The OPTION settings.

- Elapsed-time clock settings, so the subroutine can stop and restart the clock without affecting the main program. It also means that settings from within the subroutine aren't available to the main program.

- Trace settings. This allows you to turn off debugging in a subroutine once it's debugged without affecting debugging in the main program. This is discussed in detail in chapter 18.

In addition, when a subroutine is accessed, REXX creates a special variable called Sigl, which contains the number of the line that issued the CALL instruction. If the subroutine uses PROCEDURE, this variable must be exposed to be used. This variable is a debugging aid.

A More Realistic Example

Take a look at the TODO.CMD program that comes with this book. (It's explained in detail in appendix A.) This program makes extensive use of internal subroutines. Following is a brief description of each of the subroutines used in TODO.CMD:

Add. This subroutine is used to add new to-do items to the list.

Backwards. This subroutine decrements the counter that marks the starting point in the file at which the ShowScreen subroutine begins displaying the file, thus scrolling the data backwards.

Change. This subroutine makes corrections and modifications to existing to-do items. As changes are made, it calls the ShowScreen subroutine to redisplay the screen. Also note that it calls the external subroutine INTERACT.CMD as a function, passing it the text to be edited interactively and accepting its results back as the edited text. External subroutines will be discussed in the next chapter.

Delete. This subroutine is used to delete existing items from the list. Notice that it calls the ShowScreen subroutine to display the screen before asking the user which one to delete and, once the user has made a selection, it calls the KillIt subroutine to perform the actual deletion.

Display. This subroutine controls the screen display. It calls two other subroutines to help it: ShowScreen to display the screen and FigureOutMessage to figure out which menu items to display.

Exit. This subroutine is used to exit the program. Notice that it calls the Save subroutine to make sure the data is saved before exiting.

FigureOutMessage. The menu in TODO.CMD is an intelligent menu that displays only the available options. At the beginning of a file or when all the data fits on one screen, it won't give you the option of scrolling backwards. At the end of the file or when all the data fits on one screen, it won't give you the option of scrolling forwards. When there are no to-do items, it won't give you the option of deleting them, modifying them, or marking them as done. This subroutine figures all that out so only the appropriate menu items are displayed. Note that while the inappropriate menu options are not displayed, FigureOutMessage doesn't communicate with the menu selection portion of the program so the user can still select one of these inappropriate options.

FileIt. This subroutine writes a done to-do task, along with the current date and time, to a disk file.

Forwards. This subroutine increments the counter that marks the starting point in the file that the ShowScreen subroutine uses to begin displaying the file, thus scrolling the data forwards.

Print. This subroutine is used to print the data.

ReadData. This subroutine reads the data from a data file and stores it to variables. This subroutine is used only once each time the program is executed. However, for debugging purposes, it still makes sense to make it a subroutine rather than part of the program.

Save. This subroutine saves new data to the disk file. Notice that it calls the Sort subroutine first to make sure the data is sorted.

SetUp. This subroutine performs the initial configuration of the program. Like the ReadData subroutine, it's performed only once when the program starts.

ShowScreen. This subroutine displays the current screen of to-do items. This information changes as the user adds and deletes items and scrolls around in the file. This is the first subroutine in the file and is preceded by an EXIT instruction. In this case, it isn't necessary and is simply added for completeness. TODO.CMD stays in an endless loop and the only way out of that loop is to select the menu option to exit the program, and that issues an EXIT instruction. Therefore, TODO.CMD can never reach the end of the program part of the file and run the subroutines one last time before exiting.

Sort. This subroutine sorts the data into priority order and alphabetical order within priorities. When two items need to be swapped to be in order, it calls the Swap subroutine.

Swap. This subroutine is called by the Sort subroutine when it finds two items that need to be swapped to be in order. The Swap subroutine does the actual swapping.

TaskDone. This subroutine is used to mark a task as being finished. That task, along with the current date and time, are written to a done file and then the completed item is deleted from the to-do database. Notice that it calls on the ShowScreen subroutine to redisplay the screen. It also calls on the FileIt subroutine to actually write the done to-do task to a file.

As you can see, TODO.CMD makes extensive usage of subroutines. Were it not for these subroutines, TODO.CMD would be much longer due to all the repeated code, and would be much harder to debug.

If would also be much harder to write. Once I got the main menu working, I was able to work on one subroutine at a time to get that subroutine working and debugged, which is the main reason for the ad-hoc order of the subroutines. I added new ones to the bottom of the file and simply left them in that order. If I were planning extensive modifications in the future, I would go back and rearrange the subroutines into alphabetical order.

Variable Management in Internal Subroutines

Imagine writing a program even larger than TODO.CMD, with even more subroutines. One of the major problems you would face would be keeping all the variables straight. By default, all variables in a REXX program are global variables. That is, every internal subroutine can read and modify all the variables from the main program.

Even what seems like a fairly minor mistake can cause major problems for a program. Usually it's the minor problems that are so hard to find. For example, what if one of the loops you had currently active in your main program was a DO I = 1 TO 100 loop and, while nested three or four deep in a subroutine, you forgot about this and tried to use I as a loop counter for a loop in a subroutine? The CALL-8.CMD program that comes with this book simulates just such an error. The functional portion of the code is as follows:

```
DO I = 1 TO 10
  SAY "Value In Main Routine Is Now:" I
  CALL Sub
END
EXIT
SUB:
  DO I = 1 TO 5
    SAY "Value In Subroutine Is Now:" I
  END
RETURN
```

The first time through the main loop, I has a value of one. The subroutine is called where I loops through the values 1–5. When the END instruction is reached when I equals five, it's incremented to six before REXX decides the loop doesn't need to be repeated. It then goes to the next instruction, a RETURN, and control returns to the main program. The next line in the main program is the END instruction, where I (now six) is incremented to seven. Since this is less than ten, it goes through the loop again.

After displaying the message that I is currently seven, the subroutine is called and, again, I loops through 1–5 and returns to the main program with a value of six. It's incremented to seven and the process begins again. This will continue forever! (Press Ctrl–Break to stop it.)

As you can imagine, that would be a hard mistake to spot in a large program like TODO.CMD. It would be especially hard to spot if it didn't cause an endless loop but rather caused a minor problem like causing only part of the data to be sorted or some lines being missed on the printout.

Now imagine that several different people are working on the program. You're working on the main program while two other programmers are writing the subroutines. Now just keeping the names of the variables you're using straight becomes a significant administrative task.

Using local variables

Much of this administrative task of tracking variables could be eliminated if there was a way to make variables inside a subroutine local. A local variable is a variable that's active only within the subroutine and has no impact outside the subroutine. Since a local variable has no impact outside the subroutine, naming conflicts like the previous one could be avoided.

The PROCEDURE instruction is used in a subroutine to hide all the variables from the subroutine. Furthermore, when the subroutine terminates, all its variables are discarded and the original variables are restored. The CALL-9.CMD program that comes with this book is a modified version of the CALL-8.CMD program that uses the PROCEDURE instruction. Its operational code is as follows:

```
DO I = 1 TO 10
  SAY "Value In Main Routine Is Now:" I
  CALL Sub
```

```
END
EXIT
SUB:
  PROCEDURE
  DO I = 1 TO 5
    SAY "Value In Subroutine Is Now:" I
  END
RETURN
```

The subroutine now runs fine and produces no interference with the main program. When a PROCEDURE instruction is used in a subroutine, it must be the first instruction executed after the CALL instruction. That is, it must come on the line directly after the label that identifies the subroutine.

Mixing local and global variables

So far you've seen the two extremes. At one end, every variable is a global variable and can be modified by every subroutine. At the other end, every variable is a local variable that is protected from every subroutine except the one that creates it. Most of the time, neither of these alternatives is what you want.

You want to be able to work with a selected number of variables in a subroutine, while protecting other variables. The EXPOSE subinstruction for the PROCEDURE instruction does just that. The syntax is:

```
PROCEDURE EXPOSE variablelist
```

where *variablelist* is a list of variables to use with EXPOSE. These "exposed" variables then work like global variables while the remainder of the variables remain as local variables.

The variables in *variablelist* are exposed from left to right. The variables in the list should be separated by spaces and not commas. If you want to expose a stem variable, you can expose either the elements individually or all of them at once by exposing the stem, e.g., the name of the variable followed by a period and nothing more. It isn't an error to expose a variable more than once or a variable that doesn't exist. If a single variable is enclosed inside parentheses, then it's treated as a list of variables to expose. The variable is first exposed and then the list of variables it contains is exposed.

Once a variable is used with the EXPOSE subinstruction, it functions exactly like a global variable. Changes made to the variable in the subroutine are reflected to the contents of the variable back in the main program. You can see that the EXPOSE subinstruction makes selected variables global variables while keeping others as local variables in the CALL-10.CMD program included with this book. The operational code is:

```
DO I = 1 TO 10
  SAY "Value In Main Routine Is Now:" I
  FromMain = I
  CALL Sub
END
EXIT
SUB:
```

```
PROCEDURE EXPOSE FromMain
DO I = 1 TO 5
  SAY "Value In Subroutine Is Now:" I,
      "Value In Main Is Now:" FromMain
END
RETURN
```

The variable FromMain is used in both the main program and subroutine, so it's a global variable. The I variable isn't exposed, so the loop counters in both the main program and subroutine can use it without any interference.

It's necessary to store the contents of the I loop-counter variable in the main program to the FromMain variable before exposing it in order to keep the I loop-counter variable in the subroutine from conflicting with it. When working on large projects, it's a good idea to have an agreed-on list of variables that will be exposed and keep the rest as local variables. This minimizes the risk of having conflicts between the separate modules.

Local and global variables in nested subroutines

So far, I've discussed exposing variables as though the main program called only one subroutine at a time. However, you saw in the TODO.CMD program that it isn't uncommon for one subroutine to call another subroutine. This forms what's called a *nested subroutine*. The issue of exposing variables becomes more complex when dealing with nested subroutines.

When REXX first reaches a subroutine, all the variables available to that subroutine are global variables. The PROCEDURE instruction hides all the variables, with the EXPOSE subinstruction unhiding a selected few of those hidden variables. The EXPOSE subinstruction can unhide only the variables the subroutine would have had access to without the PROCEDURE instruction.

I'll review this based on the CALL-11.CMD program that comes with this book. The main routine takes the phrase "Now Is The Time For All Good Women To Come To The Aid Of Their Country" and stores the first word to the One variable, the second word to the Two variable, and so on until the last word is stored to the Sixteen variable. It then calls the subroutine Sub1 and exits. The subroutines are shown in the following (except for a few redundant SAY instructions):

```
EXIT
SUB1:
  PROCEDURE EXPOSE Two Four Six Eight Ten Twelve Fourteen Sixteen
  CALL Sub2
RETURN
SUB2:
  PROCEDURE EXPOSE One Two Three Four Five
  CALL Sub3
RETURN
SUB3:
  PROCEDURE EXPOSE One Two Three Four Five Six Seven Eight,
                  Nine Ten Eleven Twelve Thirteen Fourteen,
                  Fifteen Sixteen Seventeen Eighteen,
                  Nineteen Twenty
  SAY "One Is........" One
  SAY "Two Is........" Two
  SAY "Three Is......" Three
```

```
      SAY "Four Is......." Four
      /* The Rest Of The Variables Are Listed Similarly */
      SAY
      CALL PAUSE
RETURN
```

When the main program calls the subroutine Sub1, Sub1 has access to all the variables. It then hides them with the PROCEDURE instruction. After that, it exposes some of the variables (Two, Four, Six, Eight, Ten, Twelve, Fourteen, and Sixteen) with the EXPOSE subinstruction. The remaining variables (One, Three, Five, Seven, Nine, Eleven, Thirteen, and Fifteen) will remain hidden until Sub1 terminates. After this, Sub1 calls the subroutine Sub2.

Since Sub1 hasn't yet terminated, the variables One, Three, Five, Seven, Nine, Eleven, Thirteen, and Fifteen remain hidden, so Sub2 has access to only the variables Sub1 created (there are none) and those it exposed, namely Two, Four, Six, Eight, Ten, Twelve, Fourteen, and Sixteen. Sub2 hides all the variables with a PROCEDURE instruction and then tries to expose the variables One, Two, Three, Four, and Five. Since it has access to only two of these five (Two and Four), only two variables are exposed. The attempt to expose One, Three, and Five doesn't produce an error message as REXX doesn't consider it an error to try to expose variables you don't have access to.

After this, Sub2 calls the subroutine Sub3 and tries to expose all sixteen variables, along with four that haven't existed so far in the program: Seventeen, Eighteen, Nineteen, and Twenty. Since Sub2 passed Sub3 access to only Two and Four, these are the only variables it successfully exposes. When it goes to display the contents of the variables, the others are empty and display their name while these two display their contents.

Transferring data without global variables

When you need to supply a subroutine with several pieces of data to perform its operation but want to keep the subroutine variables isolated, then you need to take a different approach to getting the data to the subroutine. This approach allows the subroutine to transfer only one piece of information back to the calling program.

When you start a subroutine with a PROCEDURE instruction without an EXPOSE subinstruction, all the variables are local variables and the subroutine doesn't have access to any of the variables created by the main program. However, the PROCEDURE instruction doesn't affect arguments. Rather than just calling the subroutine, the main program can call the subroutine and pass it the information it needs in the form of arguments. The subroutine can then use the Arg internal function to strip off the arguments and store them to local variables for use in the subroutine. Subroutines that use only local variables, get all their data from arguments, and transfer information back to the main program are sometimes called user-defined functions. When used with an internal function, all the arguments up to the first comma go into Arg(1), everything between the first and second comma goes into Arg(2), and so on. The dividing commas and any spaces surrounding them are used as dividers and aren't stored to any argument.

This technique is shown in the CALL-12.CMD program that comes in this book. The main operational portion of the program is as follows:

```
Heading1     = "Solution To A Math Problem"
Heading2     = "==========================="
FirstNumber  = 12
SecondNumber = 15
Operation    = "+"
Answer       = Sub1(FirstNumber, SecondNumber, Operation)
SAY Heading1
SAY Heading2
SAY FirstNumber Operation SecondNumber "=" Answer
```

The program first creates the variables it needs and then calls the subroutine with the instruction:

```
Answer       = Sub1(FirstNumber, SecondNumber, Operation)
```

This instruction passes the subroutine the values stored in the FirstNumber, SecondNumber, and Operation variables, so the subroutine has access to them as arguments. However, if the subroutine has a PROCEDURE instruction, the variables aren't passed to the subroutine, so it cannot modify the original variables. The CALL instruction could have also been used for this purpose. The instruction would be:

```
CALL Sub1 FirstNumber, SecondNumber, Operation
```

and the results would automatically be stored in the variable named Result. The subroutine uses the Arg internal function to access these three values. The subroutine is as follows:

```
Sub1:
  PROCEDURE /* No Variables Retained
                No Conflict Possible   */
  X = Arg(1)
  Y = Arg(2)
  Todo = Arg(3)
  SELECT
    WHEN Todo = "+" THEN RETURN X + Y
    WHEN Todo = "-" THEN RETURN X - Y
    WHEN Todo = "*" THEN RETURN X * Y
    WHEN Todo = "/" THEN RETURN X / Y
  END
RETURN "Error"
```

(I've left out the portion of the subroutine where it shows it doesn't have access to the variables from the main program.) The first thing the subroutine does is read in the arguments and store them to variables with the instructions:

```
X = Arg(1)
Y = Arg(2)
Todo = Arg(3)
```

These values can now be accessed via the X, Y, and Todo variables. These are local variables that will be discarded once the subroutine terminates.

Once the subroutine is finished, it needs to pass back its results to the main program. It can't do that with a variable because all its variables are local variables and will be lost when the subroutine terminates. It does so by including the value to return after the RETURN instruction. In this example, the calculations themselves are used; however, the results could have been stored to a variable and the variable used after the RETURN instruction. While the contents of the variable are lost when the subroutine terminates, that doesn't happen until after the RETURN instruction, so the transfer would take place before the variable was discarded.

This is an excellent approach to gaining the maximum variable protection in your subroutines, but there's a significant drawback. While you can send as much data to the subroutine as you need to, only one number or character string is permitted after the RETURN instruction, so you're limited in the amount of data you can transfer back to the main program from the subroutine. This is exactly the same limitation you'll face with external subroutines in the next chapter.

Summary

A subroutine is a "mini program" that the main program can call to perform a specialized task. The main program is suspended while the subroutine runs. The main program resumes when the subroutine terminates. Subroutines can be stored either inside the main program or in a separate file. The former is called an internal subroutine and the latter is called an external subroutine.

Internal subroutines are generally listed at the end of a program and the first subroutine is generally preceded by a EXIT instruction to make sure program execution doesn't "bleed over" into the subroutines.

Internal subroutines work with the same variables as the main program. A change in the subroutine is reflected in the main program. Variables can be made local to the subroutine with the PROCEDURE instruction, and then selected variables can be made global again with the EXPOSE subinstruction.

Programs with internal subroutines are generally smaller, have fewer bugs, are easier to modify, and are more consistent. The SIGNAL instruction is local to a subroutine.

In a subroutine, the EXIT instruction terminates both a subroutine and the main program. The RETURN instruction terminates just the subroutine. When the RETURN instruction is followed by a number or character string, that data is returned to the main program.

The following states are saved when a subroutine starts and restored when the subroutine terminates: the state of DO loops and similar structures, NUMERIC settings, the current and saved destination for commands, condition traps, OPTION settings, elapsed-time clock settings, and trace settings.

A nested subroutine can expose only the variables it would have had access to without the PROCEDURE instruction. If the variable was hidden before reaching the nested subroutine, that subroutine cannot expose it. The PROCEDURE instruction doesn't affect arguments, so a subroutine with only local variables can still receive data from the main program via arguments. It can also return the signal number of a character string by specifying it after the RETURN instruction.

15

External Functions

External subroutines are subroutines that exist as separate files, as opposed to internal subroutines, which exist in the same file as the main program. You saw in the last chapter that internal subroutines can access all the variables of the main program or they can be restricted to accessing as few as you desire. They can return zero, one, or many pieces of data back to the main program.

External subroutines, on the other hand, are more limited. They can never access any of the variables of the program that called them. They can be passed as much data as is necessary, but it must be in the form of arguments, which must be in the same fixed format each time. External subroutines are also limited in that they can pass back only one piece of data, either a number or character string. Granted, a character string can be encoded to carry more than one piece of data to get around this limitation, but that can be complicated and messy.

Additionally, if you give a copy of your program to someone else to run, you must make sure you give them copies of all the external subroutines it accesses, something you don't have to worry about with internal subroutines. Just giving them the external subroutines isn't even enough; you must make sure they install them in a subdirectory in their path.

Given all this, why in the world would you ever elect to write an external subroutine over an internal subroutine?

Advantages of External Subroutines

External subroutines have two significant advantages over internal subroutines: accessibility and cohesion. Let's look at each of these.

Accessibility

Once you've written and debugged an external subroutine like PAUSE.CMD, it remains debugged and operational forever. Every time you write a program that needs to pause the screen, you can add a "CALL PAUSE" instruction to that program and know that the pause will be carried out perfectly. Now granted, you could add a @PAUSE command to do the same thing. However, PAUSE.CMD is just an example.

Would you feel as comfortable adding the commands to get a yes or no response from the user where the program continued prompting the user until a valid response was entered? It's still not a hard program to write, but it's more than one or two lines. And why bother when YESORNO.CMD will do it for you?

The point is that the more external subroutines you write, the easier your programming becomes because you have access to your own library of debugged external subroutines you can depend on to work right without testing. This is particularly important as you begin to write more complex programs.

The INTERACT.CMD program that comes with this book is an excellent example. I wrote it as an example for this book and it still needs some minor cleanup before I'd call it a fully ready-to-use external subroutine. However, TODO.CMD uses it very successfully right now as an external subroutine. INTERACT.CMD has over one hundred lines of code. Add support for a few more editing keys and the ability to take the screen position and string length as an argument and you have an external subroutine that any program needing interactive editing of a word or phrase could call on without further need of debugging. Imagine having dozens of longer external subroutines like this debugged and ready to use with any programming project!

Cohesion

Imagine trying to debug INTERACT.CMD as an internal subroutine, especially without a PROCEDURE instruction! Its size alone would make it difficult. Plus, you would have to worry about all the possible variable interactions.

When I started writing TODO.CMD, the code that's now INTERACT.CMD was going to be part of TODO.CMD as an internal subroutine. However, as it got longer and longer, it just became too difficult to write and debug. I split it off as an external subroutine and wrote a tiny program just to call INTERACT.CMD so I could test it without all the overhead of running TODO.CMD. Once INTERACT.CMD was finished, I was tempted to merge it back into TODO.CMD. However, by then TODO.CMD had grown to its present size of over three hundred lines so I decided to leave INTERACT.CMD as an external subroutine.

When Is an External Subroutine Desirable?

When might you want to use an external subroutine over an internal subroutine? Clearly, external subroutines are preferable only when:

- The amount of data the external subroutine needs to receive to operate is fairly limited since each piece of data must be passed to the external subroutine as an argument and must be decoded by the external subroutine using the Arg function.

- The data to be sent to the external subroutine must be fairly consistent in nature. Since you must code particular pieces of data into the first, second, third, and so on arguments, you need consistent data in order to develop a workable coding scheme.

- The data being returned by the external subroutine generally needs to be limited to zero or one number or character string. More are possible, but they must be coded into a single character string by the external subroutine and decoded by the main program receiving the data, so the advantages of using the external subroutine must overcome this encoding and decoding overhead.

The best candidates are subroutines that will either perform some function that you expect several different programs will take advantage of or be so long and complex that debugging it as part of a longer program would be difficult. PAUSE.CMD and CLS.CMD are examples of the former and INTERACT.CMD is an example of the latter.

Anatomy of an External Subroutine

An external subroutine is different from an internal subroutine in only two major aspects: how data comes into the program and how data goes out of the program. While an internal subroutine might receive its data in the form of variables, an external subroutine always receives its data in the form of arguments. Of course, both types of subroutines can also ask the user or poll the computer for additional data, such as the time or number of drives. An internal subroutine can pass its data back to the main program in the form of variables, but an external subroutine always passes back a single number or character string via the RETURN or EXIT instruction.

To demonstrate, let's construct a new external subroutine to handle pausing. This one, called SPAUSE.CMD, will be much more complex than PAUSE.CMD. Its syntax will be:

```
SPAUSE [Message, Row, Column, ClsBefore, ClsAfter]
```

where Message is the message to display while the program is pausing (the default message if none is entered will be "Press Any Key To Continue . . ."), Row is the row number to position the cursor on (if the row and column arguments are both left blank, the cursor will be left in its current position), and Column is the column number to position the cursor on. If the Row and Column arguments are both left blank, the cursor will be left in its current position.

ClsBefore is a flag to indicate if the screen should be cleared before displaying the Message and pausing the program. Valid inputs are Yes and No. Capitalization doesn't matter. You should clear the screen if the cursor is being positioned, but the routine won't enforce this.

ClsAfter is a flag to indicate if the screen should be cleared after the pausing and just before control is returned to the calling program. Valid inputs are Yes and No. Capitalization doesn't matter.

Getting the Input

As has already been stated, external subroutines get their input as arguments. The code to obtain the arguments is:

```
Message = Arg(1)
Row = Arg(2)
Column = Arg(3)
ClsBefore = Arg(4)
ClsAfter = Arg(5)
```

If you were designing SPAUSE.CMD as an internal subroutine, you could make sure, as you called on the internal subroutine, that you passed it the proper arguments. However, SPAUSE.CMD will go into the arsenal of external subroutines that you can use for years to come. It's possible that, at some point in time, you'll make a mistake and call SPAUSE.CMD with an invalid argument. Therefore, SPAUSE.CMD needs to protect itself against that.

As you'll see, the code SPAUSE.CMD uses to protect itself against invalid arguments ends up taking more lines of code than the SPAUSE.CMD routine itself. This is typical of external subroutines that receive a lot of data from the calling program, particularly when much of the data must be of a specific type. All of the arguments being received by SPAUSE.CMD, except the first one, must fit some criteria. The row coordinate must be a whole number 0–23, the column coordinate must be a whole number 0–79, and the two clear screen arguments must be Yes or No. All this takes a lot of checking. The resulting program is over 90 lines long and is explained in detail in appendix A.

As you look at the explanation of SPAUSE.CMD, note that this external subroutine itself uses five internal subroutines, two of which use the PROCEDURE instruction to protect some or all of the variables. Since an external subroutine is first of all a stand-alone program, this is allowed. Remember, the only major difference between an external subroutine and any other stand-alone program is the way it receives data and returns results to the calling program.

SPAUSE.CMD will work even as a stand-alone program, as you can see if you type its name at the command line. However, since SPAUSE.CMD uses Arg(1) through Arg(5) to receive its arguments rather than parsing the command line, it won't receive its arguments properly if you run it from the command line. All of the arguments will end up as part of Arg(1) and therefore as part of the message.

Calling the External Subroutine

There are two ways to call an external subroutine. The syntax for both is as follows, using the SPAUSE.CMD external subroutine as an example:

```
CALL SPAUSE Message,Row,Column,ClsBefore,ClsAfter
Var = SPAUSE(Message,Row,Column,ClsBefore,ClsAfter)
```

The first method can be used with any external subroutine. If it passes back results, those are automatically stored in the variable Result. With this method, there's a space between the name of the subroutine and the first argument. All subsequent arguments are separated with commas. The second method is identical to the method used to run an internal function. This method can be used only with an external function that returns a value.

The DOSPAUSE.CMD program that comes with this book runs SPAUSE.CMD four times using both methods and four different sets of arguments. After it finishes, it displays the results of those four runs. Its operational code is as follows:

```
Var1 = SPAUSE("First Run")
Var2 = SPAUSE("Second Run,0,0,Yes,Yes",0,0,Yes,Yes)
CALL SPAUSE "Third Run,10,30,Yes,No",10,30,Yes,No
Var3 = Result
CALL SPAUSE "Fourth Run,15,30,No,No",15,30,No,No
Var4 = Result
SAY "Results Are" Var1 Var2 Var3 Var4
```

Returning a Value

An external subroutine faces a minor disadvantage over a stand-alone program or internal subroutine. When it encounters a serious error, it can't just exit to the operating system with an EXIT instruction because the EXIT instruction in an external subroutine returns control to the calling program. For that reason, every external subroutine needs a way of returning an error message to the calling program.

Even though SPAUSE.CMD can run without returning a value, it returns a zero if it runs without a problem and a one if it encounters a problem. It also displays an error message and beeps the speaker. However, the calling program might erase or overwrite the error message. SPAUSE.CMD has to depend on the calling program to evaluate its return code and act accordingly.

Returning a string from an external subroutine is the same as returning a number, as STRINGBK.CMD shows. STRINGBK.CMD returns one of eleven different sayings depending on the argument that's passed to it. This string isn't displayed on the screen, so you can't run STRINGBK.CMD from the command line and see its results. Since the errorlevel can't handle a string, there's no way to determine the value returned by STRINGBK.CMD from the command line. However, the STRINGDO.CMD program that comes with this book will run STRINGBK.CMD twice and display the results. It then gives you the option of running it again. STRINGDO.CMD uses both methods of running an external subroutine:

```
Saying = STRINGBK(RANDOM(1,10))
SAY Saying
CALL STRINGBK RANDOM(1,10)
SAY Result
```

As you can see, except for not showing up in the errorlevel value when run from the command line, passing a string back from an external subroutine works the same as passing a number back.

Summary

An external subroutine is a subroutine that's stored in a separate file rather than being stored in the same file as the main program. External subroutines can access only arguments passed to it, not any of the variables from the main program. They can pass only a single number or character string back to the main program.

External subroutines have two significant advantages over internal subroutines: accessibility and cohesion. Once an external subroutine is debugged, any other program can use it without having to worry about errors. External subroutines are also an excellent way to handle large programming tasks.

In order to be a good candidate to be an external subroutine, a routine must need to receive a fairly limited set of data, the data it receives must be consistent in nature, and it needs to return either zero or one number or character string.

16

Using the External Data Queue

How would you like for one of your REXX programs to be able to communicate with another REXX program, even if that second program is running in a different session or running much later than the first program? If you answered yes to this question, then the REXX external data queue is the answer you're looking for.

The normal form of communications between a REXX program and the user is a stream of characters that can be acted on either a per-character or per-line basis. The normal form of communications between a REXX program and its external subroutine is a series of arguments going from the main program to the external subroutine and a single number or character string returning from the external subroutine to the calling program. The arguments are acted on in a per-argument fashion while the returning number or character string must be acted on all together. The external data queue is a line-based form of communication that differs from both of these methods.

Before OS/2 had REXX, it had several types of interprocess communications that C (and other languages) programs could use. One of these used a data structure the OS/2 folks called a *queue*. Meanwhile, before OS/2, REXX was on other systems, which also included a data structure called a queue. As it happens, the OS/2 queues behave differently than REXX queues, so they're two different things. If data is in an OS/2 queue, a REXX program can't touch it with any of the REXX queueing instructions like PULL—and vice versa.

There are application program interfaces (API) that all C programs can use to read and write to REXX queues, but IBM hasn't documented them. The personal REXX programs from Quercus Systems support the same APIs and have documentation on how other programs can interface with REXX queues.

Three Demonstrations

The following three demonstrations will illustrate the power of external data queues.

GETDATA.CMD and SENDATA.CMD

First, open two OS/2 command-line sessions. The easiest way to do this is to open one full-screen and one windowed session. Now in one of the sessions (it doesn't matter which), run GETDATA.CMD. Nothing will appear to happen. GETDATA.CMD is waiting for data to be placed in an external data queue. Now switch to the second window and run SENDATA.CMD. You'll see it run and display its progress on the screen. It will place 101 lines of data into an external data queue. Now switch back to the session running GETDATA.CMD and you'll see that it has read in and displayed 100 lines of data. The last line was a TERMINATE, which the program uses as a flag to indicate that no more data is coming.

GETDATA.CMD then SENDATA.CMD

Now, with only one command-line session open, run SENDATA.CMD. After it finishes, close the session. Now reopen that session or open a new session. Once you have a new session open, run GETDATA.CMD. You'll see that, even though the command-line session was closed, OS/2 maintained the data in the external data queue until another program was run to read it out of the queue. As long as you don't reboot or turn the computer off, it doesn't matter how long you wait between sessions.

SENDATA2.CMD

You might recall from chapter 15 that external subroutines can return only one number or one character string to the calling program. That isn't the case when the transfer is completed using an external data queue. SENDATA2.CMD calls an external subroutine. This external subroutine places 101 lines of data into an external data queue called RONNY2. Again, this is 100 lines of data plus the line TERMINATE to tell the program that no more data is coming. You can see this by running SENDATA2.CMD in a command-line session. When a calling program needs to send a lot of data to an external subroutine, it too might rely on the external data queue rather than trying to send it all as arguments.

In order to make sure the external subroutine is available, SENDATA2.CMD calls itself as an external subroutine. Logic at the top of the program handles the branching so SENDATA2.CMD can run both as a calling program and as an external subroutine. SENDATA2.CMD is explained in detail in appendix A.

Understanding External Data Queues

REXX actually works with three different types of queues: session queues, detached session queues, and external data queues. Since each of these works with data, a common generic term is *data queue*.

Session queue. This queue is created automatically for REXX by OS/2 when the REXX program first transfers data, say between the keyboard and the program. It's called SESSION and is managed by OS/2.

Detached session queue. A detached session queue is a special version of a session queue. OS/2 allows a program, batch file, or internal command to be run "detached" from its command processor by preceding its name with the OS/2 (not REXX) DE-TACH command. OS/2 automatically generates a unique name for this queue. OS/2 also manages this queue.

External data queue. An external data queue is a stream of characters that's stored by OS/2 external to any active REXX program. Since it's external to REXX, other programs can place characters into the stream or read characters from the stream. None of the characters in the external data queue have any special meaning to OS/2, other than the Return character marking the end of a line. REXX can read data from the external data queue only by using line-orientated instructions. Additionally, the external data queue is managed by REXX rather than by OS/2. Outside of REXX, the external data queue must be managed by whatever program accesses it.

Think of each external data queue as a section of pipe that contains data (like a water or plumbing pipe, not a command-line pipe). REXX programs have the ability to create new pipes, add data to existing pipes, and remove data from an existing pipe. As you'll see later, data can be added to either end of the pipe. When a REXX program accesses a pipe and reads data, that data is removed from the pipe.

Managing the External Data Queue

Management of an external data queue is up to the REXX program rather than OS/2. This section discusses the REXX tools for managing a queue.

Creating a new queue

The first thing you must do in managing any queue is create it. In order to create a queue, that queue must have a name. You have two options for generating a name: supply one yourself or let OS/2 pick a unique name. The RxQueue internal function is used in either case. The syntax for creating an external data queue with OS/2 supplying the name is:

```
QueueName = RxQueue("Create")
```

The function returns the queue name to be stored in the QueueName variable. Of course, any legal variable name may be used. To supply the name, the syntax is:

```
QueueName = RxQueue("Create",name)
```

where *name* is either a variable containing the queue name or a character string. If the queue named in *name* exists, OS/2 will create the queue but give it a unique system name just as though you hadn't supplied a queue name. That name is returned to the QueueName variable. For that reason, it's usually better to run Rx-Queue as a function returning a queue name and then use that returned name rather than using the CALL instruction, unless you can be very sure the queue doesn't already exist.

Additionally, only the first letter of the subinstruction, like Create, needs to be supplied and capitalization for the subinstruction and queue names doesn't matter. The Create subinstruction can be seen in the QUEUE-1.CMD program that comes with this book.

Making a queue active

Once a queue has been created, the next step is to make it the active queue. The syntax to do that is:

```
OldQueue = RxQueue("Set",name)
```

where *name* is the name of the queue to make active. The name of the previously active queue is returned so it can be saved as OldQueue to be made active again if required. The Set subinstruction can be seen in the QUEUE-1.CMD program that comes with this book.

Putting data into a queue

Once a queue is active, data can be written to it. Recall that an external data queue is line-orientated, so data can be added only one line at a time. REXX offers two instructions, PUSH and QUEUE, specifically for writing data to the currently active queue. Their syntax is:

```
PUSH expression
QUEUE expression
```

where *expression* is the line to be added to the queue. The PUSH instruction places the line at the head of the queue, in last-in-first-out (LIFO) order. The QUEUE instruction places the line at the tail of the queue, in first-in-first-out (FIFO) order. Both of these instructions can be seen in the QUEUE-1.CMD program that comes with this book.

Since the queue is a line-orientated data source, data can also be added with the internal LineOut function, using QUEUE: as the name of the output stream to write to. This can be seen in the SENDATA.CMD program that comes with this book. The LineOut function is discussed in detail in chapter 11.

Putting data into a queue from the command line

OS/2 offers the RXQUEUE.EXE filter to allow data to be added to the queue from the OS/2 command line. (To avoid confusing the RXQUEUE.EXE filter with the RxQueue internal function, I'll always refer to the filter as RXQUEUE.EXE.) RXQUEUE.EXE also proves that other programs can successfully write to a REXX queue. The syntax for using RXQUEUE.EXE is:

```
RXQUEUE.EXE [queuename] [/flag]
```

where *queuename* is the name of the queue to add the data to (if none is specified, the default queue is used), and *flag* is one of the three following optional arguments:

FIFO. This causes the data to be appended to the tail of the queue.

LIFO. This causes the data to be appended to the head of the queue.

CLEAR. This causes the queue to be cleared of all data.

Remember, these are OS/2 commands and not REXX commands. Of course, a REXX program can issue this command to the operating system, just like any other command. This can be seen in the QUEUE-2.CMD program that comes with the book.

Getting data from a queue

You can remove data from the queue using the standard PARSE and PULL instructions discussed in chapter 13. This can be seen in action in the QUEUE-2.CMD program that comes with this book. You can also remove data with the LineIn internal function, using QUEUE: as the name of the output stream to read from. The LineIn function was discussed in chapter 11 and can be seen in action in the GETDATA.CMD program that comes with this book. While you have the option of writing to the head or tail of the queue, data is always read from the head of the queue.

The PARSE and PULL (converts to uppercase) instructions are different from the LineIn internal function. PARSE and PULL will automatically switch over and read data from the keyboard (the standard input stream) when data in the external data queue is exhausted, while the LineIn function won't.

You can see this by running the QUEUE-4.CMD program that comes with this book. QUEUE-4.CMD places a first name and last name (Ronny and Richardson) into the external data queue and then calls QUEUE-3.CMD. QUEUE-3.CMD reads a first name, last name, and age using the PARSE PULL instruction. Since two lines have been placed into the queue, QUEUE-3.CMD will read the first and last name from this queue and then prompt the user for an age. (Even though the first and last name come from the queue, the request for information still shows since it's just a SAY instruction.) Once an age is entered, QUEUE-3.CMD displays the results and then terminates.

After QUEUE-3.CMD terminates and returns control to QUEUE-4.CMD, QUEUE-4.CMD again places a first and last name into the external data queue and then calls QUEUE-5.CMD as an external subroutine. QUEUE-5.CMD tries to read the first name, last name, and age using the LineIn internal function. Since only two lines are in the external data queue, the program will wait forever on the third call to the LineIn function. While the prompt shows (it's a SAY command), the LineIn function won't accept input from the keyboard. You must press Ctrl–Break to abort QUEUE-5.CMD.

You can use this to your advantage. If you write your REXX programs to get all their input using the PARSE or PULL instructions, then you can always call that program from another REXX program and supply it with all the inputs it wants by having the calling program place those inputs into the queue. You can even use the RXQUEUE.EXE filter to pipe responses in from the command line and then have the program run unattended, as shown in Figure 16.1.

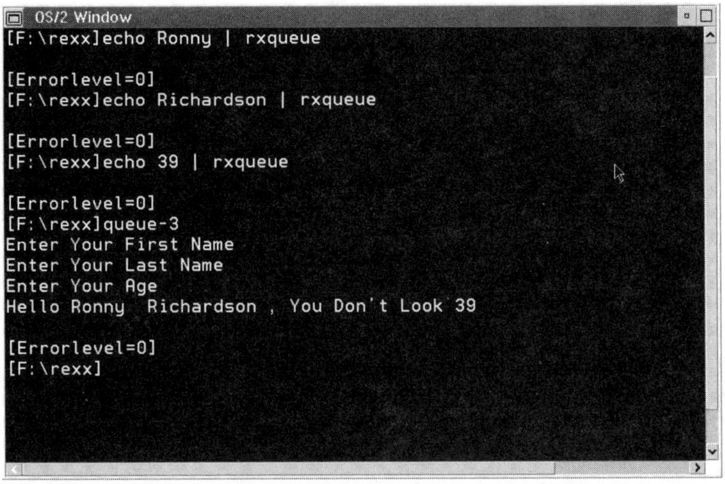

Figure 16.1 When data is read using the PARSE or PULL instructions, you can supply all the inputs to the queue by piping them to the RXQUEUE.EXE filter and then walk away while the program runs, and it will still get its inputs.

If you don't know the number of lines to expect, the Queued internal function returns the number of lines pending in the currently active queue. The program can read from the queue in a loop until the Queued function returns a zero, as QUEUE-2.CMD does, or the sending program can send a special line to mark the end of data, as SENDATA.CMD does, and the program reading from the queue can test for that special line, as GETDATA.CMD does. The second method works well when an external subroutine is using an external data queue to return data to the calling program.

Finding the active queue

If you need to find the name of the current queue, the syntax is:

```
ActiveQueue = RxQueue("Get")
```

where ActiveQueue is the variable to store the name of the currently active queue.

Deleting a queue

Once you've finished with a queue, you can delete it. The syntax is:

```
Code=RxQueue("Delete",name)
```

where *name* is the name of the queue to delete and Code is the variable to contain the return code. Possible values are:

0. The queue was successfully deleted.

5. An invalid queue name was supplied to the function.

9. The queue to be deleted doesn't exist.

10. The queue to be deleted is busy.

12. A memory error has occurred.

1000. An initialization error has occurred.

It isn't an error to delete the current queue. However, it will cause the program to not have an active queue, which will result in an error if any queue activity takes place. To avoid this, always make sure to either make another queue active after deleting the active queue or to replace an active queue with another queue before deleting it.

Avoiding Conflicts

An external data queue is never private. That is, other applications can also write data to the queue. This can be a particular problem when you write data to an existing queue and expect to read that data back from the queue. This works as you expect only when the queue is empty. When the queue contains data, you run the risk of reading in that data rather than the data your program is expecting.

You can, of course, avoid this by always creating your own queues. Another way to avoid the problem is to always place data at the head of the queue using the PUSH instruction. That way, if 50 lines of new data are added to the head of the queue and your program then reads 50 lines, it will get its own data, even if the queue contains existing data. Of course, if the order of the data is important, you must go through the extra step of writing it to the queue in reverse order.

Summary

The external data queue is a powerful method for REXX programs to communicate with each other, and for non-REXX programs to communicate with a REXX program. It's particularly useful for a large volume of communication between an external subroutine and calling program.

Exception Handling

For the first 16 chapters, I've discussed making your program work. For the next two chapters, I'm going to concentrate on showing you how to handle problems that keep your programs from running.

Programs suffer from two broad categories of problems: programming mistakes and exceptions. Programming mistakes—called bugs and problems—are created by the programmer. They might include logic errors, syntax errors, or other types of programming mistakes. Finding and dealing with these is discussed in the next chapter.

Problems outside the programmer's control are called errors or exceptions. For example, a user might press Ctrl–Break to halt a program, or a disk drive might not be ready to receive data. While the programmer can anticipate these and, perhaps, build logic into the program to deal with them, he cannot prevent them. The process of building logic into a program to deal with unexpected events (exceptions) is called *exception handling*, which is the subject of this chapter.

As you'll see, the REXX terminology for exceptions is *conditions*. Thus, I might have called this chapter *Condition handling* and changed every reference to exceptions in the chapter to conditions. I've chosen not to do that. In a global sense, *exception* better describes the events I discuss, so I've chosen to retain the term *exception handling*. When discussing REXX coding, I'll use the term *condition*, since it's the appropriate REXX term. Error handling, which has been mentioned earlier in the book, is a subset of exception handling that involves those exceptions that also happen to be errors.

What Is Exception Handling?

Normally, a program follows a predetermined pattern developed by the programmer. As an example, let's look at the following code from the CAPITAL.CMD program that comes with this book:

```
Word = ARG(1)
PARSE UPPER VAR Word OutWord Word
SAY OutWord
ENV = 'OS2ENVIRONMENT'
LastRC = VALUE('Return',OutWord,Env)
```

I've removed the comments and the section at the top that checks to see if the user requested help. Once the program reaches this point in the program, you know precisely what sequence of events will take place since there's no logic to jump to another location, select between different paths, or loop. Even if there was, if you knew the conditions in effect when the program was run, you could describe the exact sequence of lines that the program would progress through. Or could you?

If the user pressed Ctrl–Break, the program would abort. If you want the program to continue running in spite of a Ctrl–Break, then you need to build in logic to handle that. As a more realistic example, how would the TODO.CMD program that comes with this book behave if the disk were full when it tried to write its data file to disk? Since it has no special logic built in, it would end up creating a zero length file on the disk and then acting like the file had been saved. Wouldn't it be better if the program gave the user the option of saving the file to another drive? That is an example of exception handling.

Do You Always Need Exception Handling?

No! A great many programs never need exception handling. One of the big advantages of REXX is how easy it is to write a short program to accomplish some repetitive task. Many of these are run once, or at most a few times, and then discarded. Adding exception handling to these programs is more work than it's worth. Most times, the programmer will be right there to take care of any problems that arise.

Many more programs are written for personal use. I originally wrote TODO.CMD for my own use long before I started this book. Since I was the only one who was going to use it (back then), it never occurred to me to include exception handling. My system has a one-gigabyte hard drive, so I have lots of free space and I wasn't worried about running out. I would also know if I pressed Ctrl–Break or if the printer was out of paper. The point is that TODO.CMD was originally going to be run only by an experienced programmer who could handle any problem that arose, so exception handling wouldn't add any value to the program.

Now TODO.CMD is likely to be used by a large number of the readers of this book and perhaps passed on to family and co-workers. As its audience grows, the need for exception handling increases. For example, if you were to press Ctrl–Break at exactly the right time, all your data would be lost. It's tricky and your timing must be just right, but it can be done. TODO.BAK will still exist, so you'll have lost only the data since the last save. However, this is certainly no way for production software to behave! (As an excuse in my favor, TODO.CMD is intended as a programing example and not as production software.)

Types of Exceptions

REXX treats exceptions as though they were events generated by an unpredictable cause outside the program, which is in most cases true. In REXX nomenclature, these events are called *conditions*. REXX allows program instructions to take place out of sequence when one of these conditions arises. This out-of-sequence performance of the instructions is the mechanism you use to handle these conditions. REXX recognizes six different events as conditions:

Error. This condition is when a command to OS/2 returns control to REXX with some indication that it encountered an error. OS/2 usually indicates this condition with a return code. Not all events you'd consider an error will raise the error flag to REXX. For example, the REXX command COPY *.SYS A:, when executed with the A: drive open, won't generate an Error, Failure, or NotReady condition! This is a holdover from the DOS COPY command, which doesn't set an errorlevel value when it encounters a problem.

Failure. This condition is when a command to OS/2 returns control to REXX with some indication that it encountered a failure. The most common cause of a failure is issuing a nonexisting command to OS/2. Note that having exception handling for a Failure condition won't prevent the error message OS/2 normally displays when you try to run a command that doesn't exist since this is displayed before REXX regains control after the failure.

Halt. This condition occurs when the user presses Ctrl–Break or Ctrl–C to stop a program. This condition can be particularly important to plan for when a program has a lot of processing to perform and gives little or no screen indications that it's running. It's easy for the user to think the program has "locked up" and press Ctrl–Break to regain control.

NoValue. The NoValue condition is raised under certain circumstances when a variable that hasn't been initialized is used as though it contained a value. Dividing by an uninitialized variable using either an uninitialized variable with the PARSE or VAR instruction or uninitialized variable as a variable reference (the variable is enclosed in parentheses to indicate it contains a list of variables) with the DROP instruction or EXPOSE subinstruction will all raise the NoValue condition. Trying to display an uninitialized variable with the SAY instruction using either an uninitialized variable with the Value function or an uninitialized variable as the tail of a stem variable are all actions that won't raise the NoValue condition.

NotReady. The NotReady condition is raised by an input/output (I/O) action that fails. This can happen with the SAY and PARSE instructions or the LineIn and CharIn functions. NotReady is also raised by trying to read beyond the end of a file.

Syntax. The syntax condition is often raised when a program has a bug, or programming mistake. These are true syntax errors and are dealt with more fully in the next chapter. However, some syntax errors are truly exceptions, such as a variable containing character data rather than a number that was obtained from the user and then used in a calculation, or the program being unable to locate an external subroutine.

Types of Exception Handling

REXX programs have three different types of exception handling available: default, Type I, and Type II. (The notation of Type I and II condition handling is Daney's and not Cowlishaw's. Cowlishaw doesn't explicitly name them. I've followed Daney's notation in this chapter as it's cleaner than Cowlishaw's.)

Default exception handling

When a REXX program first starts, the program has no internal condition handlers turned on. In REXX terminology, conditions are said to be disabled. While these conditions can still happen, they're handled by REXX itself and not by the program. REXX ignores the Error, NotReady, and NoValue conditions. By default, REXX treats a Failure condition as an Error condition, which it ignores. The default handlers for Halt and Syntax immediately terminate the program, display a message, and return a return code to OS/2.

When exception handling is built into a program, it takes priority over the default exception handling built into REXX itself. Both Type I and Type II exception handling work very similarly, but there are differences. Following a discussion of these differences, I'll explain the general approach to using either type of condition handling.

Type I exception handling

Type I exception handling is invoked with the SIGNAL ON instruction. It has the following characteristics:

- It works for any of the six conditions.
- As soon as the first condition is encountered, that condition handler is disabled. It must be reinvoked to be used again.
- It automatically terminates all DO, IF, SELECT, and INTERPRET instructions. This is expected because it's the normal action of the SIGNAL instruction.
- It doesn't terminate active procedures.
- It's generally not possible to return to the point where the condition was raised.

Type II exception handling

Type II exception handling is invoked with the CALL ON instruction. It has the following characteristics:

- It works for only four of the six conditions: Error, Failure, Halt, and NotReady. It doesn't work with NoValue and Syntax.

- It isn't disabled when a condition is encountered. Rather, it's placed in a delayed state. If another condition is encountered, the first one is resolved, but the exact handling depends on the condition.

- It doesn't terminate DO, IF, SELECT, or INTERPRET instructions.

- It doesn't terminate active procedures.

- A RETURN instruction will return the program to the point where the condition occurred. This is expected because it's the normal action of the CALL instruction.

Enabling and Disabling Exception Handling

If a program were to try and test for every condition that could arise at every point it was possible for that condition to arise, even the simplest program would be overburdened with exception handling. The solution in REXX is to turn on exception handling and define what routine will handle each specific condition once. Then REXX will automatically jump to that routine any time a condition occurs.

The process of turning on exception handling is called *enabling*. Exception handling is enabled for a particular condition by either the SIGNAL ON or CALL ON instruction, followed by the name of the condition. Of course, CALL ON cannot be used with NoValue or Syntax. Thus, valid instructions are:

```
SIGNAL ON ERROR
SIGNAL ON FAILURE
SIGNAL ON HALT
SIGNAL ON NOTREADY
SIGNAL ON NOVALUE
SIGNAL ON SYNTAX
CALL ON ERROR
CALL ON FAILURE
CALL ON HALT
CALL ON NOTREADY
```

If you need to turn exception handling back off, just replace the ON subinstruction with an OFF subinstruction. This will return the handling to the default REXX exception handler previously discussed.

It's possible to turn on program based exception handling without adding a specific routine to process the exception. This isn't considered an error. However, if the condition is ever raised, the program will look for a label that doesn't exist, raising the Syntax condition. If Syntax exception is turned on, then that routine will handle the condition. Otherwise, the program will abort with a "Label not found" error message.

Defining Exception Handling

You define an exception handling routine by starting it with a label having the name of the condition, so valid labels are:

```
ERROR:
FAILURE:
```

```
HALT:
NOTREADY:
NOVALUE:
SYNTAX:
```

Only one label with each name is allowed. (Technically, you could have two or more; however, when REXX searches for a label it ignores all duplicates and uses only the first it encounters.) The full syntax of the expression is:

```
SIGNAL/CALL ON condition [NAME label]
```

where *condition* is the condition to trap and *label* is the optional label that starts the trapping routine. The default if *label* isn't specified is to make it the same as the name of the condition. Thus, while only one handler per condition can be active at any given time, it's easy to switch between exception-handling routines as needed.

It's valid to use an EXIT instruction to terminate the program inside an exception handler. When used with Type II exception handling, it's also valid to use a RETURN instruction to resume processing and the point the condition arose.

An internal subroutine inherits exception handling from the main program. The subroutine can make any changes it likes to the way conditions are handled, but once control returns to the calling program the original conditions are restored. This is identical to the way REXX handles other status information when using internal subroutines. This allows you to turn off exception handling in subroutines that you feel don't need it without affecting the main program. It also allows different subroutines to handle exceptions differently, again without affecting the main program.

Note that when REXX first encounters the condition, I refer to the condition as being *raised*. When the exception handling routine is invoked, I refer to the condition as being *trapped*.

EXCEPT-1.CMD

This is a demonstration program that counts to 10,000 using a DO instruction to simulate a "hung" program. (Unlike an actual hung program, this one displays a counter on the screen.) If the user presses Ctrl–Break, it raises the Halt condition, and the following code (without the line numbers) takes over to trap the condition:

```
 1 HALT:
 2    CALL CLS
 3    SAY "Currently On Loop #" || I "Of 10,000"
 4    SAY "Do You Really Want To Stop (Y/N)?"
 5    Character = SysGetKey(NoEcho)
 6    IF Character = "y" THEN EXIT I
 7    IF Character = "Y" THEN EXIT I
 8    CALL CLS
 9    CALL SysCurPos 18, 00
10    SAY "Try Pressing Ctrl-Break While The Programming Is Running"
11 RETURN
```

The following is a line-by-line explanation of this routine:

1. This is the label that causes the routine to be the one called when the Halt condition is first raised.

2. This calls an external subroutine to clear the screen.

3. This tells the user what was going on when he pressed Ctrl–Break.

4. This asks the user if he really wants to quit the program.

5. This gets a single keystroke response from the user.

6. If the user answers Y, that he really wants to quit, this line exits the program.

7. This line handles the uppercase response.

8. If the routine reaches this point, then the user elected to return to the program, so it clears the screen to remove the error message.

9. This line repositions the cursor.

10. This line replaces the message on the screen. Since the screen isn't redrawn within the loop, it must be restored prior to returning to the main routine. With a more complex screen, redrawing the entire screen inside the loop to avoid this problem would drastically slow down processing. However, having multiple screens the program might need to return to could make writing this subroutine much more complex.

11. This line returns control to the line in the program after the line where the condition was raised. This line works only because the exception handler was enabled with the CALL ON instruction rather than the SIGNAL ON instruction.

The result of running EXCEPT-1.CMD and pressing Ctrl–Break can be seen in Figure 17.1.

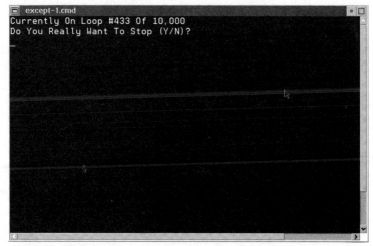

Figure 17.1 When the user presses Ctrl–Break, EXCEPT-1.CMD has a special routine that takes over to process that request to halt the program.

EXCEPT-2.CMD

This is a demonstration program that tries to write to the A: drive with the following code:

```
SIGNAL ON NOTREADY
TOP:
CALL LineOut "A:JUNK.TXT", "Erase This File"
SAY ".CMD Files Copied To A: Drive"
```

Only before it begins, it asks the user to make sure there isn't a diskette in the A: drive. That raises the NotReady condition. The code to handle the NotReady condition is as follows:

```
NOTREADY:
  SAY "Failure Writing To A: Drive"
  SAY "Would You Like To Try Again (Y/N)?"
  Character = SysGetKey(NoEcho)
  IF Character = "n" THEN EXIT I
  IF Character = "N" THEN EXIT I
  SIGNAL ON NOTREADY
  SAY "Trying Again"
  SAY
SIGNAL TOP
```

Like EXCEPT-1.CMD, this program asks the user if he wants to continue. Since the exception handling was enabled with the SIGNAL ON instruction, a RETURN instruction cannot be used to return control to the main program when the user elects to continue. In this example, another SIGNAL ON instruction is used to jump back to the main routine. As you'll see later, that isn't always possible.

As I mentioned earlier, Type I exception handling is disabled as soon as the first condition is raised. As a result, line seven in the previous routine turns it back on so it will be in effect as the program tries again. Since a Type I exception handler doesn't treat the code it runs as a subroutine, this remains in effect when the main program resumes.

EXCEPT-3.CMD

This is a demonstration program that raises the NoValue condition using the following instruction:

```
DROP (VarNotSet)
```

Since the variable VarNotSet is not initialized, the DROP instruction doesn't have a list of variables to drop and the NoValue condition is raised. The routine that deals with that is:

```
NOVALUE:
  SAY "The Variable On Line" Sigl "Does Not Have A Value"
  SAY "The Line Is:      '" || SourceLine(Sigl) || "'"
  SAY "The Program Is Aborting"
EXIT Sigl
```

This routine displays the line number where the error occurred (using the special Sigl variable) and the line containing the error (using the SourceLine internal function) and then exits. Since the EXIT instruction is followed by the Sigl variable, the number of the line containing the condition is returned as a return code.

Selecting Between Type I and II Exception Handlers

The Type I exception handler doesn't allow you to return to the location where the condition was raised, except in very simple programs. While it terminates all DO loops and similar structures, it doesn't terminate the active subroutine. When a condition is raised in a deeply nested subroutine, the lack of the ability to return to the location that raised the condition makes it very difficult to "back out of" the nested subroutine structure. This is particularly true in recursive subroutines.

Type I exception handlers are best used when the program displays information about the condition and then terminates, rather than giving the user an option of correcting the problem and then resuming. They can, however, be very useful in dealing with conditions that can be isolated to a particular subroutine, so the exception handler knows how to return to the subroutine that was active when the condition was raised and thus avoid the problems associated with backing out of the subroutine. In programs without much looping, they can also be effectively used at the top level of the program. Using a Type I exception handler across multiple subroutines and expecting the program to successfully resume running is problematical at best.

The Type II exception handler often has a delay between the time a condition is raised and the time it's trapped. This is because REXX specifies that the Type II exception handler traps the condition at the end of the current clause. During the gap between raising and trapping, the condition is said to be *pending*. This is the reason that Type II exception handlers cannot be used for the Syntax and NoValue conditions. Any clause containing one of these conditions is most likely too flawed to continue executing until the end of the clause is reached.

A subroutine called by the Type II exception handler must be terminated by a RETURN or EXIT instruction rather than a SIGNAL instruction. This is because the SIGNAL instruction doesn't terminate the subroutine, so control isn't properly passed back to the location where the condition was raised. There's no need to specify a value after the RETURN instruction since it's ignored. It isn't returned to the program and it isn't stored in the Result variable.

Other than not returning a value, a subroutine called by the Type II exception handler behaves like a "normal" subroutine. That is, any changes to the status of the program remain in effect only while the subroutine is running. Once it terminates, the status is returned to its state prior to calling the subroutine.

Like any subroutine, control returns to the calling program at the line after the line that called the subroutine—the line that raised the condition in this case. All DO loops and similar structures remain in effect. As a result, it's impossible for a Type II exception handler to return the point in the program where the instruction that raised the condition could be easily repeated. If the command needs to be reissued, the exception handler itself must take care of that.

Information Available to Exception Handlers

REXX has several internal functions that return information the exception handler can use to either display information for the user or to make a decision on how to proceed. The Condition function is used to return information about the currently trapped condition. The syntax is:

```
Condition[option]
```

where *option* is one of the following:

C. This returns the name of the currently trapped condition.

D. This returns a description of the currently trapped condition. If no description is available, a null string is returned.

I. This returns the name of the keyword that was being executed when the condition was trapped. This will either be CALL or SIGNAL.

S. This returns the state of the currently trapped condition.

If no condition is currently trapped, then each option will return a null string. Of course, the program would already know most of this information. The C returns the name of the trapped condition, but since each condition has its own handler, the program knows the name of the condition just by knowing which handler is running. The D returns a description of the trapped condition, but again by knowing which handler is running the program already knows this. The I returns either CALL or SIGNAL to indicate how the handler was enabled. Since most programs don't alternate between CALL and SIGNAL, the program already knows this as well. Finally, the S indicates the state of handling for the condition: ON, OFF, or DELAYED. Again, the program will usually know this.

The ErrorText function returns the REXX error message associated with an error number. The syntax is:

```
ErrorText(n)
```

where *n* is a whole number 0–99. If there's no text associated with that number, a null string is returned. ErrorText can be used to display a REXX error message for the user. The SourceLine internal function is used to display lines of the currently active program. The syntax is:

```
SourceLine([n])
```

when *n* is the line to display. Since the Sigl variable contains the line number of the line that raised the condition, the SourceLine internal function can be used to display this line to the user. It might also be possible to repeat the execution of this line using the INTERPRET instruction once whatever caused the condition has been corrected, if that's required. You can see the SourceLine function in action in the EXCEPT-3.CMD program that comes with this book.

Summary

Exception handling allows a programmer to be proactive and decide how to handle exceptional conditions before they arise. Some conditions, such as the user pressing Ctrl–Break or the program needing to know the path to another program, can be resolved and the program can continue. With other conditions, exception handling at least allows the program to shut down cleanly and display a meaningful error message for the user.

Chapter

18

Debugging

I hate debugging! No, I mean I really hate debugging! Trying to figure out how to write a program to attack a particular problem is fun, and writing the program itself is partially work but it's still very enjoyable. But figuring out why the program displays 17 when the correct result is clearly 19 (for example) is a pain. Now that you know how I feel about debugging, let's see how to debug REXX programs.

Few programming languages offer any sort of debugging facilities as part of the language, which makes REXX an exception since debugging tools are built in. Many languages offer external extensions that give the language very powerful debugging tools. REXX doesn't do that, however, so you're left with the limited features the language itself offers.

Introduction to Debugging

The basis of all debugging in REXX is the TRACE instruction. Its syntax is:

```
TRACE option
TRACE VALUE expression
```

where *option* is a TRACE mode and *expression* is an expression that evaluates to a valid TRACE mode.

The TRACE instruction is just another REXX instruction. It doesn't take effect until the program encounters it. It can be repeated as many times as necessary, so tracing can be turned on in a troublesome area and turned off otherwise. You might also want to turn it off before going into a loop that you know works to avoid getting a lot of output. Its value is saved across subroutines, like any other setting. That way, once a subroutine is debugged you can turn off tracing in that subroutine without affecting the TRACE settings outside the subroutine.

There are two different kinds of tracing: passive and interactive. In passive tracing, the program displays information on the screen as it operates but otherwise runs as though tracing wasn't in effect. In interactive tracing, the program pauses after most traced clauses to give the user time to enter REXX instructions.

Passive tracing

In passive tracing, the program displays various levels of information about its operation on the screen, but otherwise runs as though tracing wasn't in effect. The various information levels are:

O. This is the default mode, with tracing turned off.

A. This displays each clause as it executes.

R. This does everything the A mode does, plus displays the results of expressions.

I. This does everything the R mode does, plus displays all intermediate results.

These are options, or modes, for the TRACE instruction, so to see each clause as it executes, you would start your program with the:

```
TRACE A
```

command. Each of these options provides progressively more information. The I mode shows a great deal of information and is best left for those few clauses that you're having a great deal of difficulty with. The A mode shows very little information and isn't usually adequate for spotting errors. You'll end up using the R mode most often.

You can see passive tracing in action by running the TRACE-1.CMD program that comes with this book. It performs the following series of commands:

```
I = Max(1, 5, 9)
I = I ** 2
I = Min(I, 200, 475)
I = I / 3
I = I + 17
SAY I
```

three times, first with A tracing, then with R tracing, and finally with I tracing. The TRACE-2.CMD program that comes with this book performs these calculations once with the level of tracing specified on the command line. Figure 18.1 shows running TRACE-2.CMD in A tracing mode and then in R tracing mode. Figure 18.2 shows running TRACE-2.CMD in the I tracing mode.

While tracing is in the I mode, REXX displays a great deal of information about each clause. To help you keep it straight, REXX codes the various lines, shown in Figure. 18.2. The meaning of the codes is as follows:

>C>. This line displays the name of a compound variable after any variables in the name have been substituted for.

>F>. This line displays the results of a function call.

>L>. This line displays a literal value.

```
OS/2 Window
F:\>trace-2 a
    20 *-*   I = Max(1, 5, 9);
    21 *-*   I = I ** 2;
    22 *-*   I = Min(I, 200, 475);
    23 *-*   I = I / 3;
    24 *-*   I = I + 17;
    25 *-*   Say I;
44

F:\>trace-2 r
    20 *-*   I = Max(1, 5, 9);
       >>>     "9"
    21 *-*   I = I ** 2;
       >>>     "81"
    22 *-*   I = Min(I, 200, 475);
       >>>     "81"
    23 *-*   I = I / 3;
       >>>     "27"
    24 *-*   I = I + 17;
       >>>     "44"
    25 *-*   Say I;
       >>>     "44"
44

F:\>_
```

Figure 18.1 Running TRACE-2.CMD in the A and R tracing modes.

```
OS/2 Window
F:\>trace-2 i
    20 *-*   I = Max(1, 5, 9);
       >L>     "1"
       >L>     "5"
       >L>     "9"
       >F>     "9"
       >>>     "9"
    21 *-*   I = I ** 2;
       >V>     "9"
       >L>     "2"
       >O>     "81"
       >>>     "81"
    22 *-*   I = Min(I, 200, 475);
       >V>     "81"
       >L>     "200"
       >L>     "475"
       >F>     "81"
       >>>     "81"
    23 *-*   I = I / 3;
       >V>     "81"
       >L>     "3"
       >O>     "27"
       >>>     "27"
    24 *-*   I = I + 17;
       >V>     "27"
       >L>     "17"
       >O>     "44"
       >>>     "44"
    25 *-*   Say I;
       >V>     "44"
       >>>     "44"
44
```

Figure 18.2 Running TRACE-2.CMD in the I tracing mode.

>O>. This line displays the results of a binary operation.

>P>. This line displays the results of a prefix operation.

>V>. This line displays the value of a variable.

If the primary purpose of your REXX program is to interact with OS/2 and that interaction is causing you problems, there are three additional passive tracing modes that are useful. They are:

C. This traces all OS/2 commands.

E. This traces those OS/2 commands that end with an abnormal error code.

F. This traces those OS/2 commands that end in a Failure condition.

Interactive tracing

Passive tracing will spot simple bugs, but for down-and-dirty bugs where you have to really dig for the cause, passive tracing just won't do. For that, you need active tracing. The difference between the two is exactly what the names indicates. In passive tracing, you passively watch as REXX displays tracing information on the screen. With interactive tracing, you interact with your program to find out the exact information you need in order to figure out what's going on.

Interactive tracing has exactly the same modes as passive tracing. To activate one of the interactive tracing modes, you use the same code as you do for passive mode, only you precede it with a question mode. For example:

```
TRACE ?A
```

would interactively trace all clauses. REXX displays exactly the same information as it would under passive tracing, but then the difference shows up. After each traced clause in interactive mode, REXX displays its information and then pauses for you to enter REXX commands. At this point, your program functions much like REXXTRY.CMD and each REXX command you enter is immediately executed. Only there's a difference. Your commands are executed just as though they were the next command in your program. If your program has just stored a value of 107 to the variable Size and you issue the instruction SAY Size * 2, then REXX will display 214. Change its value to 110 and, when your program resumes, it will use 110 for Size rather than 107.

You can see this in Figure 18.3. This figure shows TRACE-2.CMD running in the ?R mode. After the first clause, the contents of the I variable is displayed with a SAY instruction. After the second clause, the result of a calculation is displayed, then an external subroutine is called and its results are displayed. After the third clause, the value of the I variable being used by the program is changed and then displayed. When the fourth clause executes, you can see that the new value for the I variable is used. After that clause, the value of the I variable is interactively changed again and you can see that new value is used by the fifth clause.

If you enter EXIT, the program is terminated. If you enter an equal sign, the last instruction is repeated, only using any new or altered values you've created during interactive tracing. For this reason, REXX doesn't pause after some clauses where it couldn't

```
trace-2.cmd
[F:\]trace-2 ?r
    20 *-*    I = Max(1, 5, 9);
       >>>       "9"
       +++    Interactive trace. "Trace Off" to end debug, ENTER to Continue.
SAY I
9

    21 *-*    I = I ** 2;
       >>>       "81"
SAY I**3
531441
CALL COMMAS I**3
SAY Result
531,441

    22 *-*    I = Min(I, 200, 475);
       >>>       "81"
I = 75
SAY I
75

    23 *-*    I = I / 3;
       >>>       "25"
I = 42

    24 *-*    I = I + 17;
       >>>       "59"

    25 *-*    Say I;
       >>>       "59"
59
```

Figure 18.3 During interactive tracing, you can enter commands and change program values once the tracing information on a clause has been displayed.

safely repeat them. These include the CALL, ELSE, END, EXIT, OTHERWISE, RE-TURN, SIGNAL, and THEN instructions. If you think you've found the problem or you want more details, you can use the TRACE instruction to alter the tracing mode.

You can also issue commands to OS/2 to examine files and environmental variables that REXX might be working with. Viewing the files can be tricky and is best done with caution since these files are already open under your REXX program.

If you're in the middle of a loop you're sure is working right and want to avoid tracing each execution of the loop, you can enter a TRACE *number* instruction, where *number* is a positive number and tracing will continue without pausing for the specified number of clauses. Make *number* a negative number and all tracing will be turned off for the specified number of clauses. Thus, a TRACE -10 instruction would turn off all tracing for the next ten clauses.

While a program is in interactive trace mode, TRACE instructions inside the program are ignored. However, there is a Trace internal function that both changes the trace mode and returns the current mode. It remains effective during interactive tracing and can alter the trace mode.

Summary

While debugging a buggy program is never fun, REXX at least offers you the tools you need to get the job done. Between passive and interactive tracing, you have access to all the information you need to make short work of program bugs.

Programs in the Book

ALLCAPS.CMD

REXX Commands	Explanation

`/* NAME:       ALLCAPS.CMD`
`   PURPOSE:    Convert File To`
`               All Uppercase`
`   VERSION:    1.00`
`   DATE:       August 7, 1993`
`   COPYRIGHT: 1994 McGraw Hill */`
	Documentation remarks.

`HelpCheck = ARG(1)`
`IF HelpCheck = "/?" THEN`
`  DO`
`    SAY "Takes A File Piped To It"`
`    SAY "And Converts To All"`
`    SAY "Uppercase"`
`    SAY "Sends Output To Screen"`
`    SAY "Or Elsewhere Via Pipes"`
`    EXIT`
`  END`
	Display a help screen and exit the batch file when the user requests help.

`ARG InFile OutFile`	Store the first argument passed into the variable InFile to be used as the input file and the second to OutFile to be used as the output file. Normally, it's used as a filter and information is piped to and from it, so these have a null value.

ALLCAPS.CMD, continued

REXX Commands	Explanation
`DO WHILE LINES(InFile)`	Loop through the following as long as the input file or information piped by the operating system has additional lines.
`  Line = LineIn(InFile)`	Read the next line using the built-in LineIn function.
`  PARSE UPPER VAR Line Line`	Convert to all upper-case.
`  CALL LineOut OutFile, Line`	Write out using the built-in LineOut function.
`END`	End of the DO WHILE loop.
`CALL LineOut OutFile`	Use the built-in LineOut function to close the output file.
`CALL LineOut InFile`	Use the built-in LineOut function to close the input file.

BACKCONF.CMD

REXX Command	Explanation

`/* NAME:    BACKCONF.CMD`
`   PURPOSE: Create a backup of`
`            the CONFIG.SYS file`
`            if it has changed.`
`            This code works best`
`            when automatically`
`            executed on a daily`
`            basis. There are OS/2`
`            program scheduling`
`            products on the`
`            market, such as Chron`
`            from Hilbert`
`            Computing, that will`
`            execute programs on a`
`            recurring basis.`
`   VERSION: 1.00`
`   DATE:    August 16, 1993 */`
	Documentation remarks.

`/* Copyright (c) 1993, Hilbert` `   Computing */`	Documentation remarks.

```if arg(1) = "/?" then```
 ```   call Syntax```
 ```if arg(1) = "-?" then```
 ```   call Syntax```
	If the user requested help, then jump to a routine to display help.

```BootDrive = "C:" /* Drive on``` ``` which OS/2 was installed */```	Store the drive that OS/2 boots off. Users using the dual boot option might need to change this.
```call LoadFunctions```	Jump to a routine to load the functions used by this program.

```call SysFileTree BootDrive'```
 ```   \CONFIG.SYS', 'Found',```
 ```   'F', '+****', '-****'```
	SysFileTree locates all files matching a given file specification and, optionally, having specified attributes. Here, it is used to find the CONFIG.SYS file when it has the archive bit turned on.

```if Found.0 then``` ``` do```	Each file SysFileTree found matching the file specification was stored in the Found.J stem variable, where J goes from 1 to the number found. In this case, only one could be found. The count is stored in Found.0. If that variable exists, SysFileTree found the CONFIG.SYS file, so do the following.

```FileExt = right(date("days")```
 ```   ,3,"0")   /* Julian date```
 ```   padded w/ 0's */```
	Compute a new extension for the backup CONFIG.SYS file using today's date.

```'copy' BootDrive'\CONFIG.SYS'``` ``` BootDrive'\CONFIG.'FileExt```	Copy the CONFIG.SYS file to the backup filename.
```attrib -A' BootDrive'\CONFIG.SYS'``` ``` /* Turn off the 'A' bit */```	Reset the archive bit on the CONFIG.SYS file.
```say 'CONFIG.SYS was backed up.'```	Tell the user what happened.
```end```	End of Do loop for the if Found.0 If test.
```else```	Else portion of if Found.0 test.

BACKCONF.CMD, continued

REXX Command	Explanation
`say 'CONFIG.SYS hasn't changed.'`	Tell the user what happened.
`return`	Exit the subroutine.
`LoadFunctions: procedure`	Procedure to load the functions required by this program.
```/** *** This will load the DLL for the Rexx system functions supplied *** with OS/2 v2.0 **/```	Documentation remarks.
`call RxFuncAdd 'SysLoadFuncs',` `    'RexxUtil', 'SysLoadFuncs'`	Load the SysLoadFuncs function.
`call SysLoadFuncs`	Call SysLoadFuncs to load all the OS/2 functions.
`return`	Exit the subroutine.
```Syntax: procedure /** *** Display the command syntax **/ say "Syntax: BACKCONF" say say "Purpose: This will check the archive attribute for the file. If it is " say " on, the program will make a copy." exit```	Display help information and program syntax when the user requests help and then exit the program.

CALL-5.CMD

REXX Commands	Explanation
```/* NAME: CALL-5.CMD PURPOSE: Shows Various Templating Methods Using One Subroutine VERSION: 1.00 DATE: November 27, 1993 COPYRIGHT: 1994 McGraw Hill */```	Documentation remarks.

```HelpCheck = ARG(1)```
  ```IF HelpCheck = "/?" THEN```
    ```DO```
      ```SAY "Shows Various```
          ```Templating Methods```
          ```Using One Subroutine"```
      ```EXIT```
    ```END```
	Display a help screen and exit when the user requests help.

```CALL RxFuncAdd 'SysLoadFuncs',``` ```'RexxUtil', 'SysLoadFuncs'```	Load the SysLoadFunc function from the Rexx Util dynamic link library using the RxFunc-Add command.
```CALL SysLoadFuncs```	Run the SysLoadFuncs function to load all the external functions in the RexxUtil DLL.

```String = "Now Is The Time To```
        ```Learn REXX"```
```Title = "Parsing By Word"```
	Create variables.

```CALL CenterTitle```	Run a subroutine to center the title on the screen and underline it.

```Instruction = "PARSE VALUE String```
      ```WITH Var.1 Var.2 Var.3```
      ```Var.4 Var.5 Var.6 Var.7"```
	Create a variable containing the instruction to be displayed and then executed by a subroutine.

```Call ShowAndDo```	Run the subroutine to display and execute the instruction.
```DO I = 1 TO 7``` ```SAY "Word #" || I "Is " Var.I```	Loop through and display all the variables.
```DROP Var.```	Drop the stem variable.

```Instruction = "PARSE VALUE```
```String```
      ```WITH Var.1 Var.2 Var.3```
      ```Var.4 Var.5"```
	Create a variable containing the instruction to be displayed and then executed by a subroutine.

```Call ShowAndDo```	Run the subroutine to display and execute the instruction.

```DO I = 1 TO 7```
  ```SAY "Word #" || I "Is " Var.I```
```END```
```SAY```
```SAY "Notice That Var.6 And Var.7```
    ```Now Undefined"```
	Loop through and display all the variables.

CALL-5.CMD, continued

REXX Commands	Explanation
`DROP Var.`	Drop the stem variable.
`CALL PAUSE` `CALL CLS`	Pause the program and then clear the screen using external subroutines.
`Title = "Parsing By Word"`	Create a title variable for use by the subroutine.
`CALL CenterTitle`	Run a subroutine to center the title on the screen and underline it.

`Instruction = "PARSE VALUE`
`String`
`        WITH Var.1 Var.2 . . .`
`        Var.6 Var.7"`
	Create a variable containing the instruction to be displayed and then executed by a subroutine.

`Call ShowAndDo` `SAY`	Run the subroutine to display and execute the instruction.

`DO I = 1 TO 7`
`  SAY "Word #" || I "Is " Var.I`
`END`
`SAY`
`SAY "Notice That Var.3 Var.4 And`
`    Var.5 Now Undefined"`
	Loop through and display the variables.

`CALL PAUSE` `CALL CLS`	Pause the program and then clear the screen using external subroutines.
`Title = "Parsing By Character"`	Create a title variable for use by the subroutine.
`CALL CenterTitle`	Run a subroutine to center the title on the screen and underline it.

`Instruction = 'PARSE VALUE`
`    Date(U) WITH Month "/" Day`
`    "/" Year'`
	Create a variable containing the instruction to be displayed and then executed by a subroutine.

`Call ShowAndDo`	Run the subroutine to display and execute the instruction.

`SAY "Day............." Day`
`SAY "Month..........." Month`
`SAY "Year............" Year`
`SAY`
	Display the variables.

`Instruction = 'PARSE VALUE`
`     Time(L) WITH Hour ":" Minute`
`     ":" Second "." Microsecond'`
	Create a variable containing the instruction to be displayed and then executed by a subroutine.

`Call ShowAndDo`	Run the subroutine to display and execute the instruction.

`SAY "Hour............" Hour`
`SAY "Minute.........." Minute`
`SAY "Second.........." Second`
`SAY "Microsecond....."`
` Microsecond`
	Display the variables.

`CALL PAUSE` `CALL CLS`	Pause the program and then clear the screen using external subroutines.
`Title = "Positional Parsing"`	Create a title variable for use by the subroutine.
`CALL CenterTitle`	Run a subroutine to center the title on the screen and underline it.

`Instruction = "PARSE VALUE`
` Date(U) WITH Month 3 4 Day 6 7`
` Year"`
	Create a variable containing the instruction to be displayed and then executed by a subroutine.

`Call ShowAndDo`	Run the subroutine to display and execute the instruction.

`SAY 'mm/dd/yy'`
`SAY '—|—|—'`
`SAY '   3  6'`
	Display information on the screen.

`SAY "Day............" Day`
`SAY "Month.........." Month`
`SAY "Year..........." Year`
`SAY`
	Display variables on the screen.

`Instruction = "PARSE VALUE`
` Time(L) WITH Hour 3 4 Minute 6 7`
` Second 9 10 Microsecond"`
	Create a variable containing the instruction to be displayed and then executed by a subroutine.

`Call ShowAndDo`	Run the subroutine to display and execute the instruction.

CALL-5.CMD, continued

REXX Commands	Explanation
SAY 'hh:mm:ss.uuuuuu' SAY '—|—|—|——' SAY ' 3 6 9'	Display information on the screen.
SAY "Hour........." Hour SAY "Minute........" Minute SAY "Second........" Second SAY "Microsecond...." Microsecond	Display the variables.
CALL PAUSE CALL CLS	Pause the program and then clear the screen using external subroutines.
EXIT	Exit the program.
CENTERTITLE:	Label marking the beginning of a subroutine to center the title on the screen and underline it.
ToShow = Center(Title,79)	Create a variable containing the Title variable, padded with spaces to where it centers on the screen.
SAY ToShow	Display this variable on the screen.
ToShow = Copies("=",79)	Store a line of 79 equal signs to a variable. (I did not use 80 because it causes the cursor to go down to the next line.)
SAY ToShow	Display the variable.
SAY	Display a blank line.
RETURN	Return to the main program.
SHOWANDDO:	Label marking the beginning of the subroutine to display and execute an instruction passed to it by the main program.
SAY Instruction	Display the instruction.
SAY Copies('-',Length (Instruction))	Underline the instruction with a dashed line the same length as the instruction.
SAY	Display a blank line.

REXX Commands	Explanation
`INTERPRET Instruction`	Use the INTERPRET instruction to execute the instruction.
`RETURN`	Exit the subroutine.

COMMAS.CMD

REXX Commands	Explanation

```/* NAME: COMMAS.CMD```
```   PURPOSE: Format A Number```
```   With Commas```
```   VERSION: 1.00```
```   DATE: October 18, 1993```
```   COPYRIGHT: 1994 McGraw Hill */```
	Documentation remarks.

```HelpCheck = ARG(1)```
```   IF HelpCheck = "/?" THEN```
```   DO```
```   SAY "Format A Number```
```   With Commas"```
```   EXIT```
```   END```
	Display a help screen and exit when the user requests help.

```Number = ARG(1)```	Bring the number passed to the program as an argument into a variable.
```Integer = TRUNC(Number,0)```	Store the integer portion to a variable.
```Decimal = Number - Integer```	Store the decimal remainder to a variable.
```Length = LENGTH(Integer)```	Compute the length of the integer portion.
```IF Length > 3 THEN DO```	If the length of the integer portion is three or less, then there is no need to insert commas, so do this for only longer numbers.
``` DO I = 3 TO 50 BY 4```	Loop through the digits locations to insert a comma. The loop steps four places due to the inserted comma.
``` IF Length > I THEN``` ``` DO```	If the integer is longer than the current value of the loop counter, then it needs another comma, so do the following.

COMMAS.CMD, continued

REXX Commands	Explanation

`Integer = SUBSTR(Integer,`
`1,Length-I)||","||`
`SUBSTR(Integer,`
`Length-(I-1),I)`
	When I equals three, it inserts the comma before the last three numbers. When it's seven, it inserts the comma before the last six numbers and one comma, and so on. This command uses the SubStr function to strip the integer variable into its component parts and recombine it with the comma.

`Length = Length + 1`	Now that a comma has been added, increase its length by one.
`END`	End of the loop to process the number.
`END`	End of the DO I = 3 TO 50 BY 4 loop.
`END`	End of the IF Length > 3 THEN DO section.
`Switch = ARG(2)` `PARSE UPPER VAR Switch`	Bring in the second argument and convert it to uppercase.
`IF Switch <> "DECIMAL" THEN` `RETURN Integer||"."||Decimal`	If the user did not request commas for the decimal portion, append a period and the decimal portion to the end of the integer and return that value.
`IF Decimal = 0 THEN` `RETURN Integer`	If there was no decimal part, return the integer.
`Length = LENGTH(Decimal)`	Compute the length of the decimal portion.
`Decimal = SUBSTR(Decimal,` `3,Length-2)`	Strip off the leading 0 and period.
`Length = Length -2`	Reduce the length to reflect the removed 0. portion.
`IF Length < 4 THEN RETURN` `Integer||"."||Decimal`	If the length is three or less, the decimal portion needs no comma, so return the finished number.

REXX Commands	Explanation
`DO I = 0 TO 50 BY 4`	Loop through the decimal portion. Since decimal commas are entered left to right, the program loops "backwards."
`  IF Length > I+3 THEN` `    DO`	If the length is long enough to need another comma, then do the following.

`      Decimal = SUBSTR(Decimal,1,`
`        I+3)||","||SUBSTR(Decimal,`
`          I+4,Length-(I+3))`
	Insert the comma in the middle of the series of numbers.

`      Length = Length + 1`	Increase the length.
`    END`	End of the If test.
`END`	End of the loop.
`RETURN Integer||"."||Decimal`	Return the number.

CONCATE.CMD

REXX Commands	Explanation

`/* Name:      CONCATE.CMD`
`   PURPOSE:   Show Concatenation`
`   VERSION:   1.00`
`   DATE:      October 3, 1993`
`   COPYRIGHT: 1994 McGraw Hill */`
	Documentation remarks.

`HelpCheck = ARG(1)`
`IF HelpCheck = "/?" THEN`
`  DO`
`    SAY "Program To Illustrate`
`        Concatenation"`
`    EXIT`
`  END`
`DROP HelpCheck`
	Display a help screen and exit the batch file when the user requests help.

`FirstNoSpace = "Ronny"`
`FirstSpace   = "Ronny "`
`Last         = "Richardson"`
`Number1      = "48"`
`Number2      = 54`
`Number3      = "4"`
	Define some strings to work with.

CONCATE.CMD, continued

REXX Command	Explanation

SAY "The Variables Are:"
SAY "FirstNoSpace........."
    '"'FirstNoSpace'"'
SAY "FirstSpace..........."
    '"'FirstSpace'"'
SAY "Last................"
    '"'Last'"'
SAY "Number1.............."
    '"'Number1'"'
SAY "Number2.............."
    '"'Number2'"'
SAY "Number3.............."
    '"'Number3'"'
	Display the variable names and their contents for the user.

SAY 'The Next Command Is: ' 'SAY
    Number1 "+" Number2 "+"
    Number3 "=" Number1+Number2+
    Number3'
	Tell the user what the next command will be.

SAY Number1 "+" Number2 "+"
    Number3 "=" Number1+Number2+
    Number3
	Execute that command.

SAY 'The Next Command Is: ' 'SAY
    Number1" + "Number2" +
    "Number3" = "Number1+Number2+
    Number3'
	Tell the user what the next command will be.

SAY Number1" + "Number2" +
    "Number3" = "Number1+Number2+
    Number3
	Execute that command.

SAY 'The Next Command Is: ' 'SAY
    Number1"+"Number2 "+"
    Number3"="Number1+
    Number2+Number3'
	Tell the user what the next command will be.

SAY Number1"+"Number2 "+"
    Number3"="Number1+Number2+
    Number3
	Execute that command.

SAY 'The Next Command Is: ' 'SAY FirstNoSpace||Last'	Tell the user what the next command will be.
SAY FirstNoSpace||Last	Execute that command.
SAY 'The Last Command Is: ' 'SAY FirstSpace||Last'	Tell the user what the next command will be.
SAY FirstSpace||Last	Execute that command.

DELBLANK.CMD

REXX Commands	Explanation
```/* NAME: DELBLANK.CMD PURPOSE: Filter Out Blank Line VERSION: 1.00 DATE: August 7, 1993 COPYRIGHT: 1994 McGraw Hill */```	Documentation remarks.
```HelpCheck = ARG(1) IF HelpCheck = "/?" THEN DO SAY "Takes A File Piped To It" SAY "And Strips Out Blank Line" SAY "Sends Output To Screen" SAY "Or Elsewhere Via Pipes" EXIT END```	Display a help screen and exit when the user requests help.
```ARG InFile OutFile```	This stores the first argument passed into the variable InFile to be used as the input file and the second to OutFile to be used as the output file. Normally, it's used as a filter and information is piped to and from it, so these have a null value.
```DO WHILE LINES(InFile)```	Loop through the following as long as the input file or information piped by the operating system has additional lines.
``` Line = LineIn(InFile)```	Read the next line using the built-in LineIn function.
``` IF Line <> '' THEN CALL LineOut OutFile, Line```	If this line is not blank, write out using the built-in LineOut function.
```END```	End of the DO WHILE loop.
```CALL LineOut OutFile```	Use the built-in LineOut function to close the output file.
```CALL LineOut InFile```	Use the built-in LineOut function to close the input file.

FACTORAL.CMD

REXX Commands	Explanation

`/* NAME:       FACTORAL.CMD`
`   PURPOSE:    Compute Factorials`
`   VERSION:    1.00`
`   DATE:       October 18, 1993`
`   COPYRIGHT: 1994 McGraw Hill */`
	Documentation remarks.

`HelpCheck = ARG(1)`
`  IF HelpCheck = "/?" THEN`
`     DO`
`        SAY "Computer Factorials"`
`        EXIT`
`     END`
	Display a help screen and exit when the user requests help.

`Number = ARG(1)`	Bring the number passed to the function as an argument into a variable.
`Integer = TRUNC(Number)`	Convert the number to an integer.

`IF Number > Integer THEN`
`   DO`
`      SAY "Factorials Only Apply`
`          To Integers"`
`      SAY Number "Is Not An`
`          Integer"`
`      RETURN -1`
`   END`
	If the original number is larger than the integer, then the function was not passed a whole number, so exit with an error message.

`IF Integer < 0 THEN`
`   DO`
`      SAY "Factorials Only Apply`
`          To Positive Numbers"`
`      SAY Number "Is Not Positive"`
`      RETURN -1`
`   END`
	If the integer is less than zero, a factorial is not defined, so exit with an error message.

`IF Integer > 92 THEN`
`   DO`
`      SAY "Only Numbers 92 Or Less`
`          Can Be Handled"`
`      SAY Number "Is Too Large"`
`      RETURN -1`
`   END`
	If the number is larger than 92, it's too large for REXX to handle, so exit with an error message.

`IF Integer = 0 THEN RETURN 1`	If the integer is zero, then the factorial is defined to be one. This is a definition that the formula cannot compute, so exit with the value.
`Result = FACTORIAL(Integer)`	Call an internal procedure to perform the actual calculations.

RETURN Result	Return the results.
FACTORIAL: PROCEDURE	Beginning of the internal procedure to calculate the actual factorial value.
N = ARG(1)	Store the argument passed to it in a variable.
IF N = 0 THEN RETURN 1	Return one if it is zero. Since the procedure calls itself repeatedly while decreasing the integer value, this is required even though a value for zero was returned above.
RETURN FACTORIAL(N-1) * N	Multiply the current value of N times a value returned by the procedure. This procedure will repeated call itself recursively until N equals zero.

FF2.CMD

REXX Commands	Explanation

/* NAME: FF2.CMD
   PURPOSE: Find All The Files
              Matching A Given
              Specification
              Containing
              Specified Text
   VERSION: 1.00
   DATE: November 10, 1993
   COPYRIGHT: 1994 McGraw Hill */
	Documentation remarks.

HelpCheck = ARG(1)
  IF HelpCheck = "/?" THEN
    DO
      SAY "Find All The Files
          Matching"
      SAY "A Given Specification"
      SAY "Containing Specified
         Text"
      EXIT
    END
	Display help information and exit when the user requests help.

Input = ARG(1)	Convert the first argument passed to the program into a variable.

FF2.CMD, continued

REXX Commands	Explanation

`IF Input = "" THEN`
`   DO`
`      SAY "No Wildcard`
`            Specification Entered"`
`      EXIT 99`
`   END`
	If this first input is missing, the user did not enter any information to search on, so display an error message and exit.

`PARSE UPPER VAR Input Wildcard` `   Text`	Since FF2.CMD is run as a stand-alone program, all the information passed to it on the command line comes in as the first argument. This line splits this first argument into the wildcard, which comes in as the first word, and the text to search for, which is everything else.

`IF Text = "" THEN`
`   DO`
`      SAY "No Text Entered To`
`            Search File"`
`      EXIT 98`
`   END`
	If the user did not enter any text to search for, display an error message and exit.

`CALL RxFuncAdd 'SysLoadFuncs',` `   'RexxUtil', 'SysLoadFuncs'`	Load the SysLoadFunc function from the RexxUtil dynamic link library using the RxFuncAdd command.
`CALL SysLoadFuncs`	Run the SysLoadFuncs function to load all the external functions in the RexxUtil DLL.
`CALL SysFileTree Wildcard,` `   'Matching', 'FSO'`	Run the SysFileTree external function to find all the files matching the wildcard specification. The function will return just the full path to the files and will search from the current subdirectory and below or, if one is specified, from the subdirectory specified as part of the wildcard and below.

REXX Commands	Explanation

IF Matching.0 = 0 THEN
  DO
    SAY "No Files Matching"
       Wildcard "Were Found"
    EXIT
  END
	If no files matched the wildcard specification, display an error message and exit.

DO I = 1 TO Matching.0	Loop through each file matching the wildcard specification.
CALL SysFileSearch Text, Matching.I, Found.	Call the SysFileSearch external function to search the file for the specified text.
IF Found.0 > 0 THEN DO	If the file contains matching text, then do the following.

SAY
    SAY "Lines In" Matching.I
      "Containing" "'"||
      Text||"'"
    SAY "———————————
      ————"
	Display the name of the file and the text that was searched for.

DO J = 1 TO Found.0
      SAY "   " Found.J
    END
	Loop through and display each line in the file that contains the text to search for.

END	End of the IF Found.0 > 0 DO section.
END	End of the DO I = 1 TO Matching.0 loop.

ISITANUM.CMD

REXX Commands	Explanation

/* NAME: ISITANUM.CMD
   PURPOSE: Checks To See If An
           Argument Passed
           To It Is A Number
   VERSION: 1.00
   DATE: November 7, 1993
   COPYRIGHT: 1994 McGraw Hill */
	Documentation remarks.

ISITANUM.CMD, continued

REXX Commands	Explanation

```HelpCheck = ARG(1)```
``` IF HelpCheck = "/?" THEN```
```   DO```
```   SAY "Checks To See If An```
```   Argument Passed"```
```   SAY "To It Is A Number"```
```   SAY```
```   SAY "Return Codes Are:"```
```   SAY```
```   SAY "0 More Than One Item```
```   Passed To Program"```
```   SAY " No Testing Performed```
```   On These Items"```
```   SAY "   Works On Only```
```   Single Items"```
```   SAY "1 Argument Is Not A```
```   , Number"```
```   SAY "2 Argument Is A Whole```
```   Number"```
```   SAY "3 Argument Is A Real```
```   Number"```
```   SAY "   But Not An Integer"```
```   SAY "4 An Unexpected Error```
```   Occurred"```
```   SAY```
```   EXIT```
```   END```
	Display a help screen and exit when the user requests help.

```CheckNumber = ARG(1)```	Store the first argument to a variable.
```NextNumber = ARG(2)```	Store the second argument to a variable.
```IF NextNumber <> "" THEN EXIT 0```	Unless the second variable is empty, ISITANUM.CMD was passed two arguments. When this happens, return the value of zero.
```IF DATATYPE(CheckNumber) <> "NUM"``` ``` THEN EXIT 1```	If the DataType function does not return a value of NUM then the argument was not a number, so return the value of one.
```Integer = TRUNC(CheckNumber)```	Store the integer portion of the number to another variable.

REXX Commands	Explanation
`IF Integer = CheckNumber THEN` `  EXIT 2`	If the integer portion of the number matches the number passed to the program, then the program received an integer, so return a two.
`IF Integer <> CheckNumber THEN` `  EXIT 3`	If the integer portion of the number does not match the number passed to the program, it was not an integer, so return a three.
`EXIT 4`	The program should never reach this point, but if it does, return a four.

LISTIT.CMD

REXX Commands	Explanation

`/* NAME:      LISTIT.CMD`
`   PURPOSE:   Display ASCII Files`
`   VERSION:   1.00`
`   DATE:      August 7, 1993`
`   COPYRIGHT: 1994 McGraw Hill */`
	Documentation remarks.

`HelpCheck = ARG(1)`
`IF HelpCheck = "/?" THEN`
`  DO`
`     SAY "Displays An ASCII File"`
`     SAY "One Screen At A Time"`
`     SAY "Syntax Is LISTIT file"`
`     SAY "Wildcards Are *NOT*"`
`     SAY "Supported"`
`     EXIT`
`  END`
	Display a help screen and exit when the user requests help.

`CALL RxFuncAdd 'SysCls',`
`   'RexxUtil', 'SysCls'`
`CALL RxFuncAdd 'SysGetKey',`
`   'RexxUtil', 'SysGetKey'`
	Load functions from the RexxUtil dynamic link library using the RxFuncAdd command.

`Count = 0`	The Count variable will be used to count the number of lines in the file. This is the number of lines to display and not the actual physical number of lines in the file.
`Start = 1`	The Start variable will be used to mark the first line to display.

LISTIT.CMD, continued

REXX Commands	Explanation
`ErrorMessage = " "`	This variable is initialized, so it will not display its name when displayed with no contents.
`ScreenLength = 18`	This defines how many lines of text to display. It must leave room for two lines of instructions and a blank line between the instructions and text. Users running LISTIT.CMD in a window will want to change this and the next setting.
`ScreenWidth  = 75`	This defines how many columns of text to display before wrapping the text to the next line. It must leave room for the line number, period, and space that are shown on the left side of the screen.
`/* ScreenLength Needs To Allow Room For Instructions At The Bottom Of The Screen. Users Running LISTIT.CMD In A Window Should Adjust ScreenWidth And ScreenLength Accordingly */`	Documentation remarks.
`/* Get Input File */`	Documentation remark.
`ARG InFile`	Read in the first argument and store it to a variable. This is used as a filename. No error checking is performed because if the filename is invalid, the routine that follows to read in the data will not find any data and will report an error.
`CALL SysCls`	Clear the screen.

`SAY "Reading File, Please Wait"`	Reading in a large file takes time, so tell the user the program is running.
`/* Read In File */`	Documentation remarks.
`DO WHILE LINES(InFile)`	Loop through the entire file.
`    Count = Count + 1`	Increase the line counter by one.
`    Line.Count = LineIn(InFile)`	Read in a line of text.
`    /* Check For Lines That` `       Wrap On Screen */`	Documentation remarks.
`    IF LENGTH(Line.Count) >` `       ScreenWidth THEN CALL LongLine`	If the line is longer than can be displayed, jump to a section to handle that problem.
`END`	End of the DO WHILE loop for reading in the text.
`CALL SysCls`	Clear the screen.
`/* Close Input File */` `CALL LineOut InFile`	Close the input file.
`/* Handle Short Files */`	Documentation remarks.

`IF Count = 0 THEN`
`    DO`
`       SAY "File Not Found Or Empty"`
`       SAY "Remember, Wildcards"`
`       SAY "Not Supported"`
`       EXIT 1`
`    END`
	If the Count variable was not incremented, then the routine above did not read in any text. Either the file was not found or the user entered a wildcard, which is not supported.

`IF Count < ScreenLength THEN` `       CALL ShortFile`	If the file is less than one screen full of information, display the file and exit.

LISTIT.CMD, continued

REXX Commands	Explanation
/* At This Point, File Has Been Read In And Contains More Than One Screen Of Information. The Variables To Be Used In The Remainder Of This Program Are: Count: File Length ErrorMessage: Tells The User About Error Line.Count The Data File ScreenLength: Used As A Loop Variable To Decide How Many Lines To Display Start: The Next Line To Display */	Documentation remarks.
DROP InFile ScreenWidth Temp	Drop the unused variables.
DO FOREVER	Continue looping until the user selects Exit from the menu.
CALL Display	Call the display subroutine.
Character = SysGetKey(NoEcho)	Get the user's menu selection. The menu is displayed by the Display subroutine.
SELECT	Perform logic testing on a series of possible values.
WHEN Character = "F" THEN CALL Forward WHEN Character = "f" THEN CALL Forward	If the user selects F in either case, call the Forward subroutine.
WHEN Character = "B" THEN CALL Backward WHEN Character = "b" THEN Call Backward	If the user selects B in either case, call the Backward subroutine.
WHEN Character = "E" THEN EXIT WHEN Character = "e" THEN EXIT	If the user selects E in either case, exit the program.

`    OTHERWISE ErrorMessage =` `        "Invalid Selection"`	If the logic testing reaches this point, the user selected something that is not valid. So create an error message.
`  END`	End of the SELECT testing.
`END`	End of the DO FOREVER loop.
`EXIT`	Exit the program. Since the only way out of the DO FOREVER loop is to select exit from the menu, the program never reaches this point. However, it is conventional to have an EXIT before the beginning of the subroutines, so it is included for completeness.
`DISPLAY:`	This routine displays one screen full of text, a menu option at the bottom, some information about the file, and an error message if any exists.
`  CALL SysCls`	Clear the screen.
`  /* Displays One Screen Of` `     Information */`	Documentation remarks.
`  DO I = Start To Min(Start +` `    ScreenLength,Count)`	Loop through one screen full of information, unless there is less than that much remaining.
`    SAY I ‖ "." Line.I`	Display a line number, period, and then the line. The ‖ prevents a space between the line number and period.
`  END`	End of the DO loop.

LISTIT.CMD, continued

REXX Commands	Explanation
SAY	Skip a line.

IF Start > 1 & Start +
   ScreenLength <= Count THEN
   SAY "F = Forwards B =
   Backwards E = Exit"
	If the user can move for-
	wards or backwards,
	display the appropriate
	message.

ELSE IF Start + ScreenLength
   > Count THEN
   SAY "B = Backwards
      E = Exit"
	If the user can move
	only backwards, display
	the appropriate message.

ELSE SAY "F = Forwards E = Exit"	If the user can move only forwards, display the appropriate message.

SAY "Starting Line Is"
   Start " File Length
   Is" Count
	Display the starting line
	number and the file
	length.

SAY ErrorMessage	Display an error mes- sage.
ErrorMessage = " "	Reset the error message. Rather than testing to see if an error message is pending, the routine always displays the vari- able and resets it. That way, an error message appears only once, after another routine has set it.
RETURN	Exit the subroutine.
FORWARD:	This subroutine incre- ments the counter, so the display moves forward.

IF Start + ScreenLength >
   Count THEN
   ErrorMessage = "At End
    Of File"
	If moving forward
	would exceed the file
	length, then selecting
	forward from the menu
	was an invalid choice, so
	create an error message.

ELSE Start = Start+ScreenLength	Increment the counter for the line number to start with.
RETURN	Exit the subroutine.
BACKWARD:	This subroutine decre- ments the counter, so the display moves back- ward.

`IF Start - ScreenLength< 1 THEN` `    ErrorMessage="At Top Of File"`	If moving backward would cause the display to start before the first line, then selecting backward from the menu was an invalid choice, so create an error message.
`    ELSE Start=Start-ScreenLength`	Decrement the counter for the line number to start with.
`RETURN`	Exit the subroutine.
`SHORTFILE:`	This routine is used to display the file and exit when it is less than one screen full of information. It behaves this way because no forwards or backwards scrolling is required.
`DO I = 1 TO Count`	Loop through the lines.
`    SAY I || "." Line.I`	Display a line number, period, and then the line. The || prevents a space between the line number and period.
`END`	End of the DO loop.
`EXIT`	Exit the program.
`RETURN`	The EXIT above this line causes the program to unconditionally terminate, so this command is used just for completeness.
`LONGLINE:`	This subroutine handles lines that are longer than can be displayed.
`    Temp = Line.Count`	Store the long line to a temporary variable.
`    Line.Count =` `        SUBSTR(Temp,1,ScreenWidth)`	Strip off one screen full of text and store it to the line variable.
`    Count = Count + 1`	Increase the line counter by one. Actions that follow will now add text to a new line.

LISTIT.CMD, continued

REXX Commands	Explanation
`Line.Count =` `    SUBSTR(Temp,ScreenWidth+1)`	Store all of the text not used above to a new line variable.

`IF LENGTH(Line.Count) >`
`ScreenWidth THEN CALL`
`LongLine`
	If the line is still too long, call this routine again recursively.

`RETURN`	Exit the subroutine.

MATHTEST.CMD

REXX Commands	Explanation

`/* NAME:      MATHTEST.CMD`
`   PURPOSE:   Math Test`
`   VERSION:   1.00`
`   Date:      August 8, 1993`
`   COPYRIGHT: 1994 McGraw Hill */`
	Documentation remarks.

`CALL RxFuncAdd 'SysCls',`
`    'RexxUtil', 'SysCls'`
`CALL RxFuncAdd 'SysGetKey',`
`    'RexxUtil', 'SysGetKey'`
	Load functions from the RexxUtil dynamic link library using the RxFuncAdd command.

`HelpCheck=ARG(1)`
`IF HelpCheck="/?" THEN`
`  DO`
`    SAY "Asks The User Math`
`    Questions"`
`    SAY "Checks The Answers"`
`    SAY "And Keeps Score"`
`    EXIT`
`  END`
	Display a help screen and exit the batch file when the user requests help.

`CALL SysCls`	Clear the screen.
`SELECT1:`	Label used by the SIGNAL command to loop back through this menu if the user makes an invalid selection.

`SAY`
`SAY "Select Test Type:"`
`SAY "1=Addition"`
`SAY "2=Subtraction"`
`SAY "3=Multiplication"`
`SAY "4=Division"`
`SAY "5=Mixed"`
	Display a menu.

`Character=SysGetKey(echo)`	Get a single keystroke from the user and use the echo option to display that keystroke.

| ```
SELECT
  WHEN Character="1" THEN Type=1
  WHEN Character="2" THEN Type=2
  WHEN Character="3" THEN Type=3
  WHEN Character="4" THEN Type=4
  WHEN Character="5" THEN Type=5
``` | If the user made a valid selection, then create a variable to store that value. |
| ```
  OTHERWISE SIGNAL SELECT1
``` | Otherwise the selection was invalid, so loop back through the menu. The SIGNAL command cancels all loops that can cause problems in the middle of a loop. However, that is what you want here. |
| ```
END
``` | End of the SELECT loop. |
| ```
SAY
SAY "Select Test Difficulty:"
SAY "1=Easy"
SAY "2=Moderate"
SAY "3=Hard (Default)"
``` | Display a second menu. This menu has a default value, so the SIGNAL command and its associated label are not needed. |
| ```
Character=SysGetKey(echo)
``` | Get a single keystroke from the user and use the echo option to display that keystroke. |
| ```
Maximum=20
``` | Create a default maximum for a number in the problems. This might be lowered by the logic tests below. |
| ```
SELECT
``` | Perform logic testing on a series of possible values. |
| ```
  WHEN Character="1"
      THEN Maximum=10
``` | If the user selected the easy option, lower the maximum number to ten. |
| ```
  WHEN Character="2"
      THEN Maximum=15
``` | If the user selected the moderate option, lower the maximum number to fifteen. |
| ```
  OTHERWISE SAY "Default Hard
      Setting Used"
``` | Otherwise, leave the default to the hard setting and tell the user. |
| ```
END
``` | End of the SELECT command. |
```

MATHTEST.CMD, continued

REXX Commands	Explanation

`Tried=-1`
`Right=0`
`Wrong=0`
	Initialize the scoring variables. Tried is started at minus one rather than zero because the problem where the user enters EXIT gets counted, so lowering the counter by one corrects this.

`DO  FOREVER`	Loop through and display problems until the user selects the exit option.
`  WhichTest=Type`	Store the type of problem flag to a temporary variable.
`  If  WhichTest=5 THEN` `      WhichTest=RANDOM(1,4)`	If the user selected mixed problems, then randomly select one of the four types of problems. A temporary variable is used to keep the problem flag from being overwritten on this line when its value is five.

`  SELECT`
`    WHEN WhichTest=1 THEN CALL ADD`
`    WHEN WhichTest=2 THEN CALL SUB`
`    WHEN WhichTest=3 THEN CALL MUL`
`    WHEN WhichTest=4 THEN CALL DIV`
`  END`
	Call a different subroutine depending on the type of problem requested. The subroutine will define the first and last numbers, the answer, and the operator so the same display and scoring commands can be used for all four.

`  CALL SysCls`	Clear the screen.
`  CALL SysCurPos 12,30`	Position the cursor.
`  SAY  First Operator Second "=?"`	Display the problem.

`  CALL SysCurPos 23,53`
`  SAY "Enter The Solution"`
`  CALL SysCurPos 24,47`
`  SAY "Enter 'QUIT' To`
`      Exit The Program"`
`  CALL SysCurPos 00,00`
	Display instructions.

`  UserAnswer=-99`	Initialize the user answer to an impossible result so the not equal loop below will start.

`Tried=Tried + 1`	Increase the number of problems attempted counter by one.
`DO WHILE UserAnswer <> Answer`	Loop through and get answers from the user until a correct answer is obtained.
`PARSE UPPER PULL UserAnswer`	Get an answer from the user.

`IF UserAnswer=""`
`    THEN CALL Shutdown`
`IF UserAnswer="QUIT"`
`    THEN CALL Shutdown`
`IF UserAnswer="EXIT"`
`    THEN CALL Shutdown`
	If the user elected to exit, then jump to the appropriate routine.

`IF UserAnswer=Answer`
`    THEN Right=Right + 1`
`    ELSE Wrong=Wrong + 1`
	Increase the correct or incorrect answer counter by one.

`END`	End of the DO WHILE loop.
`END`	End of the DO FOR-EVER loop.
`EXIT`	Exit the program. This line is never reached be-cause of the DO FOR-EVER loop, but you should always have an EXIT command before your subroutines.
`ADD:`	The addition subroutine.
`First=RANDOM(1,Maximum)` `Second=RANDOM(1,Maximum)`	Pick the first two num-bers.
`Answer  =First + Second`	Compute the answer. Doing so here allows the same display routine to be used for all opera-tions.
`Operator="+"`	Define the operator. Do-ing so here allows the same display routine to be used for all opera-tions.
`RETURN`	Exit the subroutine.
`SUB:`	The subtraction subrou-tine.
`Second=RANDOM(1,Maximum)`	Define the second num-ber.

MATHTEST.CMD, continued

REXX Commands	Explanation
`First=Second+RANDOM(1,Maximum)`	Define the first number as the second number plus a random number. That way, the answer is always positive.
`Answer  =First - Second`	Compute the answer.
`Operator="-"`	Define the operator.
`RETURN`	Exit the subroutine.
`MUL:`	The multiplication subroutine.
`First=RANDOM(1,Maximum)` `Second=RANDOM(1,Maximum)`	Define the first and second numbers.
`Answer=First * Second`	Define the answer.
`Operator="*"`	Define the operator.
`RETURN`	Exit the subroutine.
`DIV:`	The division subroutine.
`Second=RANDOM(1,Maximum)`	Define the second number.
`First=Second*RANDOM(1,Maximum)`	Define the first number as the second number times a random number. That way, the result of division is always a whole number.
`Answer  =First / Second`	Define the answer.
`Operator="/"`	Define the operator.
`RETURN`	Exit the subroutine.
`SHUTDOWN:`	The shut-down routine.

`SAY`
`SAY "Problems:`
`      " Tried`
`SAY "Incorrect Answers:`
`      " Wrong`
`SAY "Correct Answers:`
`      " Right`
`SAY "Total Responses:`
`      " Right + Wrong`
`SAY "Percentage Right`
`      " (Right / (Right +`
`        Wrong)) * 1.00`
`SAY "Goodbye"`
	Display the score.

`EXIT`	Exit the batch file.
`RETURN`	Exit the subroutine. Since this line above is an EXIT command, this line is included only for completeness.

MKCMD.CMD

REXX Commands	Explanation
| ```
/* NAME:       MkCmd.CMD
   PURPOSE:    Make a batch file
               from command-line
               parameters
   VERSION:    1.00
   DATE:       September 9, 1993
   COPYRIGHT:  1993, Hilbert
               Computing */
``` | Documentation remarks. |
| ```
parse arg Wildcard Before After
``` | Parse the command line arguments into three components. Since everything not used in Wildcard and Before goes into After, that is the only argument that can have multiple words. |
| ```
if Wildcard = "/?" then
   call Syntax
if Wildcard = "-?" then
   call Syntax
``` | If the user requested help, jump to a special section to display help. |
| ```
if Wildcard = '' then
   do
   say "You must specify a
       file wildcard."
   say
   call Syntax
   end
``` | If the user does not enter a wildcard, then display an error message and jump to the help section to display more information and exit the program. |
| ```
call LoadFunctions
``` | Jump to a routine to load the functions used by this program. |
| ```
call SysFileTree Wildcard,
     'Found', 'FSO'
``` | Call SysFileTree to find all the files matching the file specification. These will be stored in the stem variable Found. |
| ```
do j = 1 to Found.0
``` | Loop through each variable it finds. |
| ```
   say Before Found.j After
``` | Display the Before command, the full path to one file, and the After command(s). |

MKCMD.CMD, continued

REXX Commands	Explanation
`end`	End of the do j = 1 to Found.0 loop.
`exit`	Exit the program.
`LoadFunctions: procedure`	Procedure to load the functions required by this program.

`/**`
`***    This will load the DLL`
`       for the Rexx system`
`       functions supplied`
`***    with OS/2 v2.0`
`**/`
	Documentation remarks.

`call RxFuncAdd 'SysLoadFuncs',` `    'RexxUtil', 'SysLoadFuncs'`	Load the SysLoadFuncs function.
`call SysLoadFuncs`	Call SysLoadFuncs to load all the OS/2 functions.
`return`	Exit the subroutine.
`Syntax: procedure`	Procedure to display help.

`/**`
`*** Display command syntax`
`    and exit.`
`**/`
	Documentation remarks.

`say "Syntax:  MKCMD filespec`
`    [before [after]]"`
`say`
`say "Purpose: This will write`
`    a command file to the`
`    screen that is created by"`
`say "   combining the filespec`
`    with the string 'before'`
`    before the filespec"`
`say "   with the string`
`    'after' after the`
`    filespec."`
	Display help screen and syntax.

REXX Commands	Explanation
`say`	Display an example.
`say "Example: MKCMD * copy` `    a:\"`	
`say`	
`say "   will create output` `    such as:"`	
`say`	
`say "      copy` `    c:\rexx\pc.ipf a:\      "`	
`say "      copy` `    c:\rexx\pc.styles a:\   "`	
`say "      copy` `    c:\rexx\pc2.asc a:\     "`	
`say "      copy` `    c:\rexx\pc2.ipf a:\     "`	
`say "      copy` `    c:\rexx\rxsumry.cmd a:\ "`	
`say "      copy` `    c:\rexx\say.cmd a:\     "`	
`say "      copy` `    c:\rexx\space.cmd a:\   "`	
`say`	

`say "   It is assumed that the`
`    user will redirect the`
`    output to a file for "`
`say "   later execution."`
	Display more information.

`exit`	Exit the program.

PARSEOPT.CMD

REXX Commands	Explanation

`/* NAME:     PARSEOPT.CMD`
`   PURPOSE: Demonstrate a`
`            general-purpose`
`            routine that will`
`            parse the command`
`            line options for REXX`
`            programs and place`
`            the result in a stem`
`            variable.`
`   VERSION: 1.00`
`   DATE:    August 16, 1993 */`
	Documentation remarks.

`/* Copyright (c) 1993, Hilbert` `   Computing */`	Documentation remarks.

PARSEOPT.CMD, continued

REXX Commands	Explanation
`parse arg arguments`	Store the command-line arguments in the Arguments variable.
`call ParseOptions arguments`	Call the ParseOptions subroutine and pass it the Arguments variable.
`if Opt.Flag.SYNTAX = '+' then` `    call Syntax`	If the user requested help, then jump to a routine to display help.
`/* Display all of the flags */`	Documentation remarks.
`do i = 1 to words(Opt.Flag.List)`	Each flag is stored as a word in the stem variable Opt.Flag.List, so loop through all of them.
`    index = word(Opt.Flag.List, i)`	Store each word to a variable.
`    say '['index']'` `        ='Opt.Flag.index`	Display the word and the contents of that flag by using the stem variable keyed to that variable name.
`end`	End of the Do loop.
`/* Display all the parameters */`	Documentation remarks.
`do i = 1 to Opt.Parm.0`	Opt.Parm.0 stores the number of arguments, so loop through them.
`    say 'Positional parameter' i` `        'is:'Opt.Parm.i`	Display the information.
`end`	End of the Do loop.
`exit`	Exit the program.
`ParseOptions: procedure` `        expose Opt.`	Beginning of the ParseOptions procedure. Since this is a procedure, its variables are local variables. The expose Opt. command makes the Opt stem variable available to both the subroutine and the main routine.

```/**```
 ```***   This will parse the```
 ```   command-line options.```
 ```   Those parameters that```
 ```***   begin with a minus (-) or```
 ```   forward slash (/) are```
 ```   considered flags```
 ```***   and are placed in```
 ```   Opt.Flag.   The remaining```
 ```   options are placed```
 ```***   into Opt.parm.<x>.```
 ```***```
 ```***   NOTE: This code does not```
 ```   clear out the 'Opt.' stem```
 ```   variable since```
 ```***   the caller might```
 ```   want to establish defaults```
 ```   prior to calling```
 ```***   this code.```
 ```***```
 ```**/```
	Documentation remarks.

```parse arg arguments```	Store the command line arguments in the Arguments variable.
```Opt.Flag.List = ''```	Clear this variable.
```j = 0```	Set this variable equal to zero.
```do i = 1 to words(arguments)```	Loop through all the words passed to the program on the command line.
``` argument = word(arguments, i)```	Store the word to a variable.
``` FirstChar = left(argument, 1)```	Store the first character to a variable.

```   if ((FirstChar = '-') |```
 ```   (FirstChar = '/')) then```
 ```   do```
	If the first character is a - or / then this is a switch, so do the following.

```/* This is a flag. The value```
 ```   of the flag is the```
 ```   remainder of */```
 ```/* the string. If the```
 ```   remainder is the null```
 ```   string, then it   */```
 ```/* has an implicit value of```
 ```   '+' implying "on" or "true"```
 ```   */```
	Documentation remarks.

PARSEOPT.CMD, continued

REXX Commands	Explanation

`FlagName = substr(argument,`
`2, 1)    /* Second`
`character       */`
	Store the second character to a variable.

`FlagName=translate(FlagName)` `/* Convert to uppercase */`	Convert the second character to uppercase.

`/* If any of the flag names`
`are not a valid character`
`for a REXX */`
`/* variable, we have to`
`translate into a mnemonic`
`*/`
	Documentation remarks.

`if ((FlagName < 'A') |`
`(FlagName > 'Z')) then`
`do`
	If the second character of the switch is not a letter, then do the following variable transformations.

`select`
`when FlagName = '?' then`
`FlagName = 'SYNTAX'`
`when FlagName = '!' then`
`FlagName = 'BANG'`
`when FlagName = '*' then`
`FlagName = 'STAR'`
`when FlagName = '#' then`
`FlagName = 'POUND'`
`when FlagName = '$' then`
`FlagName = 'DOLLAR'`
`when FlagName = '%' then`
`FlagName = 'PERCENT'`
`when FlagName = '^' then`
`FlagName = 'HAT'`
`when FlagName = '&' then`
`FlagName = 'AMP'`
`when FlagName = '(' then`
`FlagName = 'LPAR'`
`when FlagName = ')' then`
`FlagName = 'RPAR'`
`when FlagName = '-' then`
`FlagName = 'DASH'`
`when FlagName = '=' then`
`FlagName = 'EQUAL'`
`otherwise /* Force a`
`syntax message */`
`FlagName = 'SYNTAX'`
	Convert symbol switches to words.

`end /* select */`	End of the Select test.
`end /* if */`	End of the If test.

```FlagValue = substr(argument,```
```3)   /* Remainder of```
```string */```
	Store the remainder of switch to a variable.

```if FlagValue = '' then``` ```FlagValue = '+'```	If there is no third character, then a switch was entered without any value after the switch, like /A, to indicate that with a plus symbol.
```Opt.Flag.FlagName =``` ```FlagValue```	Store the third and later characters of the string to a stem variable keyed on the name of the variable.
```Opt.Flag.List = FlagName``` ```Opt.Flag.List```	Store the name of the flag to a variable. Each name is appended onto the end of this variable with a space between them.
```end```	End of the do i = 1 to words(argument) loop.

```else /* it is a positional```
```parameter */```
```do```
	If the above if ((FirstChar = '-') | (FirstChar = '/')) test failed, then this is a parameter and not a switch, so do the following.

```j = j + 1```	Increase a counter by one.
```Opt.Parm.j = argument```	Store the argument to a stem variable.
```end```	End of the if ((FirstChar = '-') | (FirstChar = '/')) test.
```end /* do i... */```	End of the Do loop.
```Opt.Parm.0 = j```	Store the stem variable count to a variable.
```return```	Exit the subroutine.

```Syntax: procedure```
```/**```
```*** Display the syntax```
```**/```
```say 'Purpose - This will```
```demonstrate the parsing```
```of the command line'```
```say 'Syntax - PARSEOPT```
```[anything]'```
```exit```
	Display a message and exit when the user requests help.

PATHLIST.CMD

REXX Commands	Explanation
```/* NAME: PATHLIST.CMD PURPOSE: List the directories in an environment variable (e.g. PATH) that is a list of directories. VERSION: 1.00 DATE: August 16, 1993 */```	Documentation remarks.
```/* Copyright (c) 1993, Hilbert Computing */```	Documentation remarks.
```BootDrive = 'C:' /* Drive where OS/2 was installed. */```	Store the boot drive to a variable. Users using the dual boot option might need to change this.
`arg EnvVariable .`	Store the command-line arguments to a variable.
```if EnvVariable = "/?" then call Syntax if EnvVariable = "-?" then call Syntax```	If the user requested help, jump to a routine to display help and then exit.
```/* Default to 'PATH' for the environment variable */```	Documentation remarks.
```if EnvVariable = '' then EnvVariable = 'PATH'```	If the user did not enter any arguments on the command line, then store a value to the EnvVariable variable.
```/* Take care of the special case for LIBPATH */```	Documentation remarks.
```if EnvVariable = 'LIBPATH' then do```	If the user requested the Libpath path, then do the following.
``` call LoadFunctions /* Load the REXX utility functions DLL */```	Call a routine to load system functions.
``` call SysFileSearch 'LIBPATH=', BootDrive'\CONFIG.SYS', 'Libpath'```	Search through the CONFIG.SYS file and see how many times the phrase Libpath occurs.
``` if Libpath.0 \= 1 then do say "Warning. Possibly more than 1 LIBPATH in CONFIG.SYS" return end```	If it occurs more than once, then the CONFIG.SYS has multiple entries, so display an error message.

`EnvValue = substr(Libpath.1,9)` `/* Remove the "LIBPATH=" */`	Libpath.1 will contain the first occurrence of LIBPATH= from the call SysFileSearch command so strip off the LIBPATH= that is at the beginning since it is not a subdirectory.
`end /* if */`	End of the Do loop for the if EnvVariable = 'LIBPATH' test.
`else`	If it reaches this point, then the user did not enter Libpath as an argument.
`EnvValue = value(EnvVariable,` `, "OS2ENVIRONMENT")`	Store the value of the environmental variable back to the variable. Thus, if EnvVariable originally contained PATH, this command would store the path from the OS/2 environment back to this variable.

`/* Create the list of directories`
`  and display them in a nicely`
`  formatted */`
`/* list.`
`*/`
	Documentation remarks.

`Count = PathSplit(EnvValue)` `/* Set DirList. */`	Count the number of subdirectories in the path.

`say "The following" Count`
`    "directories were found in`
`    the" EnvVariable`
	Tell the user how many subdirectories were found.

`say copies("-",78)`	Draw a blank line across the screen.

`do i = 1 to DirList.0`
`    say "    " DirList.i`
`end`
	Loop through the subdirectories and display them.

`return`	Exit the subroutine.
`PathSplit: procedure expose` `          DirList.`	Beginning of a procedure to break up the path list.

PATHLIST.CMD, continued

REXX Commands	Explanation
```/** *** This will create a stem variable out of the semicolon-delimited *** variable that is presumably retrieved from a PATH or DPATH *** environment. **/```	Documentation remarks.
`arg PathString .`	Store the command line arguments to a variable.
`DirList = ''`	Reset the variable.
`j = 1`	Start the counter at one.
```parse var PathString DirList.j ';' PathString```	Take everything in the path variable up to the next semicolon and store it in a stem variable while storing the remainder in the original variable. This line handles the first subdirectory and the Do loop below handles the rest.
`do while DirList.j \= ''`	Loop through the subdirectories.
`j = j + 1`	Increase the counter.
```parse var PathString DirList.j ';' PathString```	Take everything in the path variable up to the next semicolon and store it in a stem variable while storing the remainder in the original variable.
`end /* while */`	End of the Do loop.
`DirList.0 = j - 1`	Store J-1 to a stem variable.
`return DirList.0`	Return the value of this stem variable.
`LoadFunctions: procedure`	Procedure to load the functions required by this program.

REXX Commands	Explanation

<pre>/**
***   This will load the DLL
        for the Rexx system
        functions supplied
***   with OS/2 v2.0
**/</pre>
	Documentation remarks.

<pre>call RxFuncAdd 'SysLoadFuncs',
    'RexxUtil', 'SysLoadFuncs'</pre>
	Load the SysLoadFuncs function.

`call SysLoadFuncs`	Call SysLoadFuncs to load all the OS/2 functions.
`return`	Exit the subroutine.

<pre>Syntax: procedure
/**
***   Display command syntax
**/
say "Syntax: PATHLIST
    [envvar]"
say
say "Purpose: Display an
    environment variable that
    is a list of paths in
    a more"
say "   readable format.   This
    also works for the
    LIBPATH.   If 'envvar' is"
say "   omitted, it defaults
    the PATH environment
    variable."
exit</pre>
	Procedure to show help and then exit.

SENDATA2.CMD

REXX Commands		Explanation
/* NAME:	SENDATA2.CMD	Documentation remarks.
PURPOSE:	Sends Data From An External Subroutine To The Main Program Via A Private Queue	
VERSION:	1.00	
DATE:	December 3, 1993	
COPYRIGHT:	1994 McGraw Hill */	

SENDATA2.CMD, continued

REXX Commands	Explanation

`HelpCheck = ARG(1)`
`  IF HelpCheck = "/?" THEN`
`    DO`
`      SAY "Sends Data From An`
`          External Subroutine To"`
`      SAY "The Main Program Via A`
`          Private Queue"`
`    EXIT`
`    END`
	Display a help screen and exit when the user requests help.

`ExternalSubCheck = ARG(1)`	Read in the first argument.
`  IF ExternalSubCheck = "SUB"` `         THEN SIGNAL ExternalSub`	If the first argument is SUB then the program is running as an external subroutine, so jump to the section to handle that. Since it is running as an external subroutine that just started running, the SIGNAL instruction does not cause any problem.
`CALL SENDATA2 SUB`	Call itself as an internal subroutine. If the line above did not jump past this line, it would get stuck in an endless loop when first called as an external subroutine.
`CALL RxQueue "Create","Ronny2"`	Create an external queue.
`CALL RxQueue "Set","Ronny2"`	Make that queue the active queue.
`DO FOREVER`	Loop forever.
`  Info = LineIn("QUEUE:")`	Read a line from the external data queue and store it to a variable.
`  IF Info= "TERMINATE" THEN EXIT`	If that variable has the value of TERMINATE then it flags the end of the data, so exit the program.
`  SAY Info`	Display the data.
`END`	End of the DO FOREVER loop.

REXX Command	Explanation
`EXIT`	This instruction is added just for completeness before the external subroutine portion. The program should never reach this line.
`EXTERNALSUB:`	This is a label used by the SIGNAL instruction to jump to when the program is running as an external subroutine.
`CALL RxQueue "Create","Ronny2"`	Create a new queue.
`CALL RxQueue "Set","Ronny2"`	Activate the new queue.
`DO I = 1 TO 100`	Loop through one hundred times.
`    Info = "Line Number " I || ":` `Random Number" RANDOM(1,100)`	Create a variable.
`    CALL LineOut "QUEUE:", Info`	Write that variable to the queue.
`    SAY "Writing Line #" || I "Of` `100 Back To Main Program` `Via External Data Queue"`	Display a message on the screen so the user can tell something is happening.
`END`	End of the DO loop.
`CALL LineOut "QUEUE:", "TERMI` `NATE"`	Add one more line to the queue to signal the end of the data.
`EXIT`	Exit the external subroutine.

SHOWSORT.CMD

REXX Command	Explanation
`/* NAME:      SHOWSORT.CMD` `   PURPOSE:   Illustrate Simple` `              Sorting` `   VERSION:   1.00` `   DATE:      October 8, 1993` `   COPYRIGHT: 1994 McGraw Hill */`	Documentation remarks.
`HelpCheck = ARG(1)` `IF HelpCheck = "/?" THEN` `   DO` `      SAY "Sample Program Showing` `           Sorting"` `      EXIT` `   END`	Display a help screen and exit when the user requests help.

SHOWSORT.CMD, continued

REXX Command	Explanation
`Example.1 = "0123456789"` `Example.2 = "daaskjlfds"` `Example.3 = "a0kjldfdff"` `Example.4 = "aAaskjldfs"` `Example.5 = "alkjldfewe"` `Example.6 = "DFASKJLFDF"` `Example.7 = "FJDASKLDFA"` `Example.8 = "EWRPIOVSDD"` `Example.9 = "pZZZZZZZZZ"`	Create the variables to be sorted. If you want to experiment, there is no requirement that the variables be the same length. You can also increase or decrease the number of variables as long as the next line is adjusted and the stem numbers use sequential numbers.
`Example.0=9`	Variable storing the number of variables to sort.
`DO J = 1 TO Example.0` `  Before.J = Example.J` `END`	Store the unsorted variables to another name so the sorted and unsorted values can be shown side by side.
`DO J = 1 TO Example.0 - 1`	Start at the top of the list of variables and loop down to the next-to-last variable.
`  DO K = J+1 TO Example.0`	Start just after the position defined by the loop above and loop to the end of the file.
`    IF Example.J > Example.K` `        THEN DO` `    /* Swap Variables */`	Compare the variable defined by the first loop (it will be on top) to the variable defined by the second loop (it will be on bottom). If the top one is larger, then they are out of order and need to be swapped. Since the second variable needs to stay below the first, that is why the first loop ends at Example.0-1.
`      Temp = Example.K`	Store the first variable to a temporary variable.
`      Example.K = Example.J`	Copy the contents of the second variable to the first variable.

REXX Commands	Explanation
`Example.J = Temp`	Replace the contents of the second variable with the contents of the first variable as they were stored in the temporary holding variable.
`END`	End of the THEN DO loop.
`END`	End of the DO K = J+1 TO Example.0 loop.
`END`	End of the DO J = 1 TO Example.0 - 1 loop.

`SAY "Before Sorting`
`    After Sorting"`
`SAY "————`
`        ————"`
	Print headers to the screen.

`DO J = 1 TO Example.0`
`  SAY Before.J "`
`        Example.J`
`END`
	Loop through the variables and print the before and after values.

SPACE.CMD

REXX Commands	Explanation

`/* NAME:      SPACE.CMD`
`   PURPOSE: Create a report of`
`            the space used by`
`            directory.`
`   VERSION: 1.00`
`   DATE:     August 16, 1993 */`
	Documentation remarks.

`/* Copyright (c) 1993, Hilbert` `   Computing */`	Documentation remarks.

`/* We use a stem variable to hold`
`   the report since the recursion`
`   we use */`
`/* creates the report "upside`
`   down".`
`*/`
	Documentation remarks.

`if arg(1) = "/?" then`
`   call Syntax`
`if arg(1) = "-?" then`
`   call Syntax`
	If the user requested help, jump to a section that handles that and then exit.

`call LoadFunctions    /* Load the` `     utility DLL functions */`	Call a routine to handle loading the OS/2 functions.
`Report.  = ''` `   /* Clear the report variable */`	Clear the variable.
`Report.0 = 0`	Initialize the variable.

SPACE.CMD, continued

REXX Commands	Explanation

`DriveList = SysDriveMap('C:',`
`    'LOCAL')   /* Report for`
`    all local drives */`
	Create a string containing all local drives, starting with drive C:.

`do i = 1 to words(DriveList)`	Loop through all the drives.
`    Drive = word(DriveList, i)`	Strip out the drive from the list of drives.
`    BytesDrive = SpaceDirectory(` `         Drive'\*.*', 0)`	Run the SpaceDirectory procedure and pass it the drive to process.
`end`	End of Do loop.

`say center("File", 10) center(`
`    "w/ Child", 12) center(`
`    "Directory", 54)`
	Print headings.

`say copies('-', 10)     copies`
`    ("-", 12)          copies`
`    ("-", 54)`
	Underline headings.

`/* Display the space utilization` `    report */`	Documentation remarks.
`do i = Report.0 to 1 by -1`	Loop through all the reports.
`    say Report.i`	Display the report.
`end`	End of the Do loop.
`return`	When the Return command is used in the main routine, its function is identical to the Exit command.
`SpaceDirectory: procedure` `        expose File. Report. Pgm.`	Beginning of the SpaceDirectory procedure. The stem variables File., Report., and Pgm. are exposed, so changes to them in the procedure will be reflected in the main routine.

`    /**`
`    ***   This will generate a`
`        space utilization report`
`        for a given drive`
`    **/`
	Documentation remarks.

`    arg Directory, Level`
 	
`        .`
	Strip out the subdirectory and level in tree that are passed to the subroutine as arguments.

`    /* Sum the size of all files` `        in this directory */`	Documentation remarks.

`call SysFileTree Directory,` `        'Current', 'F'`	Use the SysFileTree to get the total of all the files in this subdirectory. This is passed back in the Current. stem variable, one file per variable, with the count in Current.0.
`BytesDir = 0`	Reset the total to zero.
`do i = 1 to Current.0`	Loop through all of the file sizes reported back by SysFileTree.
`    parse var Current.i . .` `        BytesFile . FileName`	Strip off the file size and name.
`    BytesDir = BytesDir +` `        BytesFile`	Increment the size variable.
`end`	End of the Do loop.

`/* Determine the size of all`
`   the files in all the`
`   subtrees under this */`
`/* directory.`
`*/`
	Documentation remarks.

`call SysFileTree Directory,`
`        'Current', 'D'`
`BytesChildren = 0`
`do i = 1 to Current.0`
`    parse var Current.i . .`
`        BytesFile . SubDirName`
`    SubDirName = strip(`
`        SubDirName, 'Both')`
`    BytesChildren =`
`            BytesChildren +`
`            SpaceDirectory(`
`            SubDirName'`
`            \*.*', (Level+1))`
`end`
	Obtain information on the subdirectories branching off this subdirectory in a similar fashion.

`/* Generate the statistics for`
`   this directory and its`
`   descendants */`
	Documentation remarks.

`BytesSum = BytesDir +` `            BytesChildren`	Total the size of the files in the subdirectory and its subdirectories.

`/* Format the line for column`
`   output and add to the`
`   report */`
	Documentation remarks.

`BytesDirFmt = FormatComma(`
`                BytesDir)`
`BytesSumFmt = FormatComma(`
`                BytesSum)`
	Format the data.

SPACE.CMD, continued

REXX Commands	Explanation

`Report.0 = Report.0 + 1`
`q = Report.0`
`Report.q = right(BytesDirFmt,`
`    10) right(BytesSumFmt, 12)`
`    copies(" ", Level*3)`
`    Directory`
`return BytesSum`
	Add to the report.

`LoadFunctions: procedure`	Procedure to load the functions required by this program.

`/**`
`***    This will load the DLL`
`       for the Rexx system`
`       functions supplied`
`***    with OS/2 v2.0`
`**/`
	Documentation remarks.

`call RxFuncAdd 'SysLoadFuncs',` `    'RexxUtil', 'SysLoadFuncs'`	Load the SysLoadFuncs function.
`call SysLoadFuncs`	Call SysLoadFuncs to load all the OS/2 functions.
`return`	Exit the subroutine.
`FormatComma: procedure`	Beginning of a routine to add commas to numbers.

`/**`
`***    This will take a string`
`       (that is presumably`
`       numeric, but not verified`
`***    to be) and insert commas`
`       after groups of three`
`       digits`
`**/`
	Documentation remarks.

`arg Raw .`	Bring in the number passed to this routine.
`Formatted = ''`	Reset this variable.
`do while Raw \= 0`	Loop through all the characters in the variable.
`    Formatted = right(Raw,` `            3)','Formatted`	Take the right three characters and add a comma.
`    Raw = Raw % 1000`	Remove those three characters.
`end`	End of the Do loop.
`if Formatted = '' then` `    Formatted = 0`	If the variable is a null variable, substitute a zero.

REXX Commands	Explanation
```else``` ```do```	Otherwise, do the following.

```Formatted = Strip(Formatted```
       ```,'Trailing',',')```
```Formatted = Strip(Formatted```
       ```,'Leading',' ')```
	Strip off leading and trailing commas.

```end```	End of Do loop.
```return Formatted```	Return the formatted number.

```Syntax: procedure```
  ```/**```
  ```***   Display the syntax and```
      ```purpose of the program.```
  ```**/```
  ```say "Syntax: SPACE"```
  ```say```
  ```say "Purpose: Display the disk```
     ```space used by subdirectory```
     ```on all local"```
  ```say "disks"```
  ```exit```
	Procedure to display help and then exit when help is requested by the user.

SPAUSE.CMD

REXX Commands	Explanation

```/* NAME: SPAUSE.CMD```
   ```PURPOSE: External Subroutine```
           ```To Pause Screen```
   ```VERSION: 1.00```
   ```DATE: October 8, 1993```
   ```COPYRIGHT: 1994 McGraw Hill */```
	Documentation remarks.

```HelpCheck = ARG(1)```
```IF HelpCheck = "/?" THEN```
  ```DO```
    ```SAY "External Subroutine To```
       ```Pause Screen"```
    ```SAY "Run From REXX Program```
       ```With CALL SPAUSE"```
    ```EXIT 1```
  ```END```
	Display a help screen and exit when the user requests help.

```CALL RxFuncAdd 'SysLoadFuncs',``` ```'RexxUtil', 'SysLoadFuncs'```	Load the SysLoadFunc function from the RexxUtil dynamic link library using the RxFuncAdd command.
```CALL SysLoadFuncs```	Run the SysLoadFuncs function to load all the external functions in the RexxUtil DLL.

SPAUSE.CMD

REXX Commands	Explanation

Message = Arg(1)
      /* Any Character String */
Row = Arg(2)
      /* Number 0-23 Or Blank */
Column = Arg(3)
      /* Number 0-79 Or Blank */
 /* Must Be Blank If Row Blank */
ClsBefore = Arg(4)
    /* Yes|No Case Not Assumed */
ClsAfter = Arg(5)
    /* Yes|No Case Not Assumed */
	Bring in the arguments using the Arg internal function.

CALL CheckArg	Call a subroutine to check the arguments.
IF ClsBefore = "YES" THEN CALL SysCls	If the calling program requested that the screen be cleared before pausing the program, then do so.
IF Row <> "" THEN CALL SysCurPos Row, Column	If the calling program requested the cursor be positioned, then do so.
SAY Message	Display the message.
Character = SysGetKey(NoEcho)	Pause the program.
IF ClsAfter = "YES" THEN CALL SysCls	If the calling program requested that the screen be cleared when the pausing was done, then do so.
EXIT 0	Exit the subroutine and flag that it terminated normally.
CHECKARG:	Beginning of the subroutine to check the arguments.

IF Message = "" THEN
    Message = "Press Any Key
           To Continue..."
	If the calling program did not send a message, use the default message.

IF Row = "" THEN IF Column <> "" THEN DO	If the Row variable is empty and Column variable is not empty, then the calling program made a mistake, so do the following.

` SAY "Column Position`
`        Specified As" Column`
`SAY "But Row Position Not`
`        Specified"`
`SAY "Must Specify Both`
`        Or Neither"`
	Display an error message.

` CALL BEEP 500,500`	Beep the speaker.
` EXIT 1`	Exit the program and flag that it terminated with an error.
` END`	End of the DO block of commands.

`IF Column = "" THEN IF`
`                Row <> "" THEN`
`   DO`
`     SAY "Row Position`
`          Specified As" Row`
`     SAY "But Column Position`
`          Not Specified"`
`     SAY "Must Specify Both`
`          Or Neither"`
`     CALL BEEP 500,500`
`     EXIT 1`
`   END`
	Perform the same steps if the calling program specified a Row variable and not a Column variable.

`IF Row <> "" THEN CALL CheckNos`	If the calling program specified a Row variable, then call a subroutine to check the numbers.

`IF ClsBefore <> "" THEN`
`     ClsBefore = CheckYes(`
`     ClsBefore, "ClsBefore")`
	If the calling program specified a ClsBefore argument, then call a subroutine to check its value.

`IF ClsAfter  <> "" THEN`
`     ClsAfter  = CheckYes(`
`     ClsAfter,   "ClsAfter")`
	If the calling program specified a ClsAfter argument, then call a subroutine to check its value.

`RETURN`	Return from the subroutine to check the arguments.
`CHECKNOS:`	Beginning of the subroutine to check the numbers entered for the Row and Column arguments.
` PROCEDURE EXPOSE Row Column`	Hide all the variables except the Row and Column variables.

SPAUSE.CMD, continued

REXX Commands	Explanation
IF Row > 23 THEN CALL BadRow IF Row < 0 THEN CALL BadRow IF Row <> Trunc(Row,0) THEN CALL BadRow	If the Row variable is too large, too small, or not a whole number, then call a subroutine to handle this error.

IF Column > 79 THEN
        CALL BadColumn
IF Column < 0 THEN
        CALL BadColumn
IF Column <> Trunc(Column,0)
        THEN CALL BadColumn
	If the Column variable is too large, too small, or not a whole number, then call a subroutine to handle this error.

RETURN	Exit the subroutine.
BADROW: SAY "Row Must Be A Whole Number 0 - 23" SAY Row "Is An Invalid Number" CALL BEEP 500,500 EXIT 1 RETURN	Display an error message, beep the speaker, and exit the external subroutine with an error flag when the Row variable is an invalid number.

BADCOLUMN:
SAY "Column Must Be A Whole
        Number 0 - 79"
SAY Column "Is An Invalid
        Number"
CALL BEEP 500,500
EXIT 1
RETURN
	Display an error message, beep the speaker, and exit the external subroutine with an error flag when the Column variable is an invalid number.

CHECKYES:	Beginning of a subroutine to check the two clear screen parameters to make sure they are a Yes or No.
PROCEDURE	Hide all the variables.
ToCheck = Arg(1) PARSE UPPER VAR ToCheck ToCheck	Get the string to check and convert it to uppercase.
Variable = Arg(2)	Get the name of the argument being checked so it can be displayed in an error message if needed.

IF ToCheck = "YES" THEN
        RETURN "YES"
IF ToCheck = "NO" THEN
        RETURN "NO"
	The main routine simply replaces the value of the variable with the string returned by this subroutine, so if the string is a Yes or No then return that string to the program.

| SAY Variable "Parameter Must Be
      Yes Or No"
SAY Arg(1) "Is An Invalid
      Input"
EXIT 1 | If the program reaches this point then the string is invalid, so display an error message and exit the program. |
| RETURN " " | The subroutine will never reach this point; this is just added for completeness. |

SPELLING.CMD

REXX Command	Explanation

/* NAME: SPELLING.CMD
   PURPOSE: Spelling Test
   VERSION: 1.00
   Date: August 8, 1993
   COPYRIGHT: 1994 McGraw Hill */
	Documentation remarks.

HelpCheck = ARG(1)
IF HelpCheck = "/?" THEN
  DO
    SAY "Ask User To Spell Words"
    SAY "Checks The Answers"
    SAY "And Keeps Score"
    EXIT
  END
	Display a help screen and exit when the user requests help.

CALL RxFuncAdd 'SysCls',
      'RexxUtil', 'SysCls'
CALL RxFuncAdd 'SysCurPos',
      'RexxUtil', 'SysCurPos'
CALL RxFuncAdd 'SysSleep',
      'RexxUtil', 'SysSleep'
	Load functions from the RexxUtil dynamic link library using the RxFuncAdd command.

Count = 5 /* Must Equal Number Of Variables */	Stores the number of spelling words to a variable.
OldNumber = 0	The OldNumber variable is used to store the last word used, so the same word is not used twice in a row. This command initializes it, so the logic tests that follow work properly.
Use = RANDOM(1,Count)	The Use variable is used to store the number of the word to use. This command initializes it, so the logic tests that follow work properly.

SPELLING.CMD, continued

REXX Command	Explanation
`Attempts = 0` `Correct = 0`	Initialize the counters used to store the results.

`/* Enter New Words Here,`
`  Keeping The`
`  Numbers In Numeric Order`
`  Be Sure To Increase Value Of`
`  The Count Variable To Match */`
	Documentation remarks.

`Spelling.1 = "OBVIOUS"`
`Spelling.2 = "APPROPRIATE"`
`Spelling.3 = "DEVELOPMENT"`
`Spelling.4 = "TRANSLATE"`
`Spelling.5 = "FINANCE"`
	Store the spelling words to a stem variable. The words must be upper-case and no numbers should be skipped.

`DO FOREVER`	Start of a loop that will continue until the user exits the program. This loop is used to ask the user to spell the words.

`  DO WHILE Use = OldNumber`
`    Use = RANDOM(1,Count)`
`  END`
	This loop selects the next word-number to use. It uses a random number generator and a DO loop to prevent using the same number as last time.

`  OldNumber = Use`	Store the current number to the old number variable so it will be skipped next time.
`  Check = ""`	Reset the variable used to store the user input. This is required for the logic testing that starts the DO loop that follows.
`  CALL Display Spelling.Use`	Call a subroutine to display the spelling word on the screen and pass it the word to display.
`  DO WHILE Check <> Spelling.Use`	Loop until the user enters the correct spelling.
`    PARSE UPPER PULL Check`	Get the spelling from the user in all uppercase.
`    IF Check = "" THEN` `      CALL Shutdown`	If the user just pressed return then jump to the exit routine.
`    IF Check = "QUIT" THEN` `      CALL Shutdown`	If the user entered QUIT, then jump to the exit routine.

Code	Description
IF Check = "EXIT" THEN CALL Shutdown	If the user entered EXIT, then jump to the exit routine.
Attempts = Attempts + 1	At the point, the user tried to spell the word, so increment the counter.
IF Check = "AGAIN" THEN CALL Display Spelling.Use	It the user entered AGAIN, he could not remember the word, so redisplay it.
END	End of the loop that continues until the word is spelled properly.
Correct = Correct + 1	At this point, the word is spelled correctly, so increment the counter.
EXIT	Exit the program. The EXIT command is always used before the start of subroutines.
DISPLAY:	Subroutine to display the spelling word for one second.
CALL SysCls	Call a function to clear the screen.
CALL SysCurPos 12,35	Position the cursor.
SAY Arg(1)	Display the spelling word.
CALL SysSleep 1	Pause for one second.
CALL SysCls	Clear the screen to erase the spelling word.
CALL SysCurPos 22,53	Position the cursor.
SAY "Enter The Correct Spelling"	Display instructions.

CALL SysCurPos 23,44
SAY "Enter 'AGAIN' To See
    The Word Again"
CALL SysCurPos 24,47
SAY "Enter 'QUIT' To
  · Exit The Program"
	Display more instructions.

CALL SysCurPos 00,00	Position the cursor at the top of the screen for the user to enter the spelling.
RETURN	Exit the subroutine.
SHUTDOWN:	Routine to handle the user leaving the program.
SAY	Skip a line.

SPELLING.CMD, continued

REXX Command	Explanation
SAY "Attempts: " Attempts SAY "Correct: " Correct SAY "Score: " (Correct / Attempts) * 1.00 SAY "Goodbye"	Display the score.
EXIT	Exit the program.
RETURN	Exit the subroutine. This is included only for completeness since the EXIT command on the line above means the program will never reach this line.

TODO.CMD

REXX Commands	Explanation

/* NAME: TODO.CMD
  PURPOSE: Maintain TODO List
  VERSION: 1.00
  DATE: October 3, 1993
  COPYRIGHT: 1994 McGraw Hill */
	Documentation remarks.

HelpCheck = ARG(1)
  IF HelpCheck = "/?" THEN
     DO
       SAY "Todo Program"
       EXIT
     END
	Display a help screen and exit when the user requests help.

CALL SetUp	Run the subroutine that configures all the variables.
CALL ReadData	Run the subroutine that initially reads data from the disk.
DO FOREVER	This is the main loop that lets the user select options over and over. It has an Exit option to leave the program; otherwise, the user never leaves this loop.
CALL Display	Run a subroutine to display the screen.
Character = SysGetKey(NoEcho)	Get a single keystroke from the user.

`SELECT`	Select an option based on the character received by the SysGetKey command.

`WHEN Character = "A"`
`    THEN CALL Add`
`WHEN Character = "a"`
`    THEN Call Add`
	If the user selects A, then jump to a subroutine to add records.

`WHEN Character = "B"`
`    THEN CALL Backward`
`WHEN Character = "b"`
`    THEN Call Backward`
	If the user selects B, then jump to a subroutine to move the screen backwards.

`WHEN Character = "C"`
`    THEN CALL Change`
`WHEN Character = "c"`
`    THEN CALL Change`
	If the user selects C, then jump to a subroutine to let the user change a record.

`WHEN Character = "D"`
`    THEN CALL TaskDone`
`WHEN Character = "d"`
`    THEN CALL TaskDone`
	If the user selects D, then jump to a subroutine to handle a finished task.

`WHEN Character = "E"`
`    THEN CALL Delete`
`WHEN Character = "e"`
`    THEN Call Delete`
	If the user selects E, then jump to a subroutine to handle erasing a record.

`WHEN Character = "F"`
`    THEN CALL Forward`
`WHEN Character = "f"`
`    THEN CALL Forward`
	If the user selects F, then jump to a subroutine to move the screen forwards.

`WHEN Character = "P"`
`    THEN CALL Print`
`WHEN Character = "p"`
`    THEN CALL Print`
	If the user selects P, then jump to a subroutine to print the todo list.

`WHEN Character = "S"`
`    THEN CALL Save`
`WHEN Character = "s"`
`    THEN CALL Save`
	If the user selects S, then jump to a subroutine to save the file.

`WHEN Character = "Q"`
`    THEN CALL EXIT`
`WHEN Character = "q"`
`    THEN CALL EXIT`
	If the user selects Q, then jump to a subroutine to handle quitting. This is required to give the user the option of saving the records if they have been modified.

`OTHERWISE ErrorMessage` `    = "Invalid Selection"`	If the character was not one of the above characters, it was an invalid menu selection, so create an error message for the screen display subroutine to use.

TODO.CMD, continued

REXX Commands	Explanation
`END`	End of the SELECT loop.
`END`	End of the DO FOR-EVER loop.
`EXIT`	Since the Exit option is the only way to exit the DO FOREVER loop, this line is never reached and is added only for completeness.
`SHOWSCREEN:`	Subroutine to display the to-do records scheduled to be shown.
`  CALL SysCls`	Clear the screen.
`  /* Displays One Screen Of` `     Information */`	Documentation remarks.
`  DO I = Start To MIN(Start +` `     ScreenLength,Count)`	Loop through the to-do records, beginning with the start record and showing the minimum of the remaining records or the screen length.
`    SAY I || "." "(" ||` `       Priority.I || ")" Todo.I`	Display a line number, period, the priority (one character) inside parentheses, and the to-do text.
`  END`	End of the loop to display the screen.
`  SAY`	Display a blank line.
`RETURN`	Exit the subroutine.
`DISPLAY:`	Routine to display the screen.
`  CALL SHOWSCREEN`	Call another routine to display the to-do records scheduled to be shown.
`  CALL FigureOutMessage`	Call a subroutine to display menu options. This is required so it does not display the option to move forward at the end of a file, move backwards at the beginning of a file, or delete or edit records when there are no records.
`  SAY Message`	Display the menu options decided on in the FigureOutMessage subroutine.

`SAY ErrorMessage` `ErrorMessage = " "`	Display the error message variable then reset it. Unless an error has occurred, this variable will contain a single space.
`RETURN`	Exit the subroutine.
`FIGUREOUTMESSAGE:`	Routine to display menu options.
`SAY "A = Add Item   Q = Quit` `    S = Save File"`	Since you can always add records, quit, and save a file, display these options.
`Message = ""`	Clear the message variable.

`IF Count > 0 THEN Message =`
`    "D = Item Done  C = Change`
`    Item  E = Erase Item  P =`
`    Print " || Message`
	If there are records, then give the user options to mark a record as done, edit a record, erase a record, or print all records.

`IF Start + ScreenLength`
`    < Count THEN`
`    Message = "F = Forwards  "`
`    || Message`
	If there are more records, then give the user the option to move forwards.

`IF Start > 1 THEN Message =` `    "B = Backwards   " || Message`	If the display started after the first record, give the user the option to move backwards.
`RETURN`	Exit the subroutine.
`FORWARD:`	Subroutine to move the screen forwards.

`IF Start + ScreenLength >`
`    Count THEN`
`    ErrorMessage = "At End`
`    Of File"`
	If the current starting position plus the screen length is more than the length, it's at the end of the file and cannot move forwards, so create an error message. While the forwards menu option is not displayed in this case, the menu is not restricted, so this test is required.

`ELSE Start=Start+ScreenLength`	Otherwise, move the screen forwards by increasing the starting point. When it returns to the control loop, the screen will be redisplayed using this new starting point.

TODO.CMD, continued

REXX Commands	Explanation
RETURN	Exit the subroutine.
BACKWARD:	Subroutine to move the screen backwards.
IF Start - ScreenLength < 1 THEN ErrorMessage = "At Top Of File"	If the current starting position less the screen length is less than one, it's at the start of the file and cannot move backwards, so create an error message. While the backwards menu option is not displayed in this case, the menu is not restricted, so this test is required.
ELSE Start=Start-ScreenLength	Otherwise, move the screen backwards by decreasing the starting point. When it returns to the control loop, the screen will be redisplayed using this new starting point.
RETURN	Exit the subroutine.
READDATA:	Subroutine that initially reads the to-do list from the disk.
CALL SysCls	Clear the screen.
SAY "Reading In File, Please Wait"	Display a message. On slow systems this can take a few seconds.
/* Read In File */	Documentation remarks.
DO WHILE LINES(InFile)	Loop as long as there are lines in the file.
Count = Count + 1	Increase the counter by one. Since it starts at zero, the first line goes in while Counter equals one.
Priority.Count = LineIn(InFile) Todo.Count = LineIn(InFile)	Each record is stored on two lines. The first has the priority and the second has the text. Read both lines.
END	End of the loop.
CALL SysCls	Clear the screen.
/* Close Input File */	Documentation remarks.

`CALL LineOut InFile`	Close the to-do file so it does not remain open while the program is running.
`RETURN`	Exit the subroutine.
`SETUP:`	Subroutine to configure all the variables.

`CALL RxFuncAdd 'SysCls',`
`    'RexxUtil', 'SysCls'`
`CALL RxFuncAdd 'SysGetKey',`
`    'RexxUtil', 'SysGetKey'`
`CALL RxFuncAdd 'SysFileDelete',`
`    'RexxUtil', 'SysFileDelete'`
	Load external function.

`Count = 0`	Count stores the number of to-do records. This line sets its initial value to zero.

`BakFile  = "C:\TODO\TODO.BAK"`
`DoneFile = "C:\TODO\TODO.DUN"`
`InFile   = "C:\TODO\TODO.DO"`
	Define the files to use with the program.

`ErrorMessage  = " "`	Create a blank error message variable. The screen display routine always displays this variable and then resets it to a space. That way, it's easy for any routine to create an error message that will be displayed only once.
`Modified       = "NO"`	Store an initial value to the variable used to track when the list has been modified since the last save.
`Printer = "LPT1"`	Define the printer port.
`ScreenLength  = 18` `ScreenWidth   = 70`	Define the screen length and width.

`/* ScreenLength Needs To Allow`
`   Room For Instructions At The`
`   Bottom Of The Screen. Users`
`   Running TODO.CMD In A Window`
`   Should Adjust ScreenWidth`
`   And ScreenLength`
`   Accordingly. Length Of Todo`
`   Items Is Adjusted According`
`   To Screen Width. */`
	Documentation remarks.

TODO.CMD, continued

REXX Commands	Explanation
Start = 1	Initialize the variable used to mark the first line to display on the screen.
RETURN	Exit the subroutine.
ADD:	Subroutine to add records.
DO FOREVER	Loop forever, allowing the user to enter multiple records. There is an option to exit the loop.
CALL SysCls	Clear the screen.
LoopOK = "NO"	Create a variable that is used to see if a valid priority is entered.
DO WHILE LoopOK = "NO"	Continue looping until a valid priority is entered.

SAY "Enter Priority 1
    (High) — 9 (Low)"
SAY "Enter Q To Quit
    Entering Todo Items"
	Tell the user what to do.

Character=SysGetKey(NoEcho)	Get a character from the user.

IF Character = "Q"
    THEN RETURN
IF Character = "q"
    THEN RETURN
	If the user enters Q, then exit this routine.

DO I = 1 TO 9
    IF Character = I
        THEN LoopOK = "OK"
END
	Only priorities 1-9 are valid. Loop through these possibilities and if what the user entered matches one of these, set the check variable to OK.

IF LoopOK = "NO" THEN SAY "Invalid Priority"	If the user did not enter a valid priority, display an error message. Due to looping, the user will have to enter a valid priority before passing this point.
END	End of loop to check validity of priority.
Count = Count + 1	With the user entering a new record, increment the counter variable by one.
Priority.Count = Character	Store the priority just entered to a stem variable.

` DROP LoopOK`	Drop the extra variable.

`SAY "Enter Todo Item"`
`SAY "Entry Will Be Truncated`
`    To" ScreenWidth "Length"`
	Tell the user what to do.

`PARSE PULL Todo.Count`	Get text from the user.

`IF LENGTH(Todo.Count) >`
`    ScreenWidth THEN`
`    Todo.Count=SUBSTR(`
`    Todo.Count,1,ScreenWidth)`
	If the text is too long, truncate it.

`Modified = "YES"`	Change the flag to indicate that the to-do list has been modified since its last save.
`END`	End of the DO FOREVER loop used to enter new to-do records.
`RETURN`	Exit the subroutine.
`DELETE:`	Subroutine to delete a record.

`IF Count = 0 THEN`
`    DO`
`        Errormessage = "No Items`
`                To Delete"`
`        RETURN`
`END`
	If there are no records, create an error message for the screen display subroutine to display and return. While the delete option is not displayed in the menu where there are no records, this test is required because the menu does not restrict options.

`CALL ShowScreen`	Display the screen.

`SAY "Enter Item To Delete 1`
`    To " Count`
`SAY "Enter Q To Quit Deleting"`
`PARSE PULL ToDelete`
	Ask the user for the record number to delete.

`IF ToDelete = "Q" THEN RETURN` `IF ToDelete = "q" THEN RETURN`	If the user selected Q, then return.
`DO I = 1 TO Count`	Loop through all the record numbers.

`IF ToDelete = I THEN`
`    DO`
`    SAY "Delete? (Y/N)"`
`    SAY Priority.I Todo.I`
`    Character=SysGetKey(NoEcho)`
	If the string entered by the user matches a record number, then ask the user about deleting that record.

`IF Character = "Y"`
`        THEN CALL KillIt`
`    IF Character = "y"`
`        THEN CALL KillIt`
	If the user answers Y, then jump to a subroutine to delete the record.

`END`	End of the IF ToDelete = I section.

TODO.CMD, continued

REXX Commands	Explanation
`END`	End of the DO I = 1 TO Count loop.
`RETURN`	Exit the subroutine.
`KILLIT:`	Subroutine to delete a record.

`IF ToDelete = Count THEN`
`   DO`
`      Count = Count - 1`
`      RETURN`
`   END`
	If the record number of the record to delete is the last record, it can be deleted simply by decreasing the counter variable by one and returning.

`DO I = ToDelete TO Count`	If it reaches this point, then the done record to be deleted from the to-do list is not the last record. Loop through the records, beginning with the record just deleted and going to the end.

`   J = I + 1`
`   Priority.I = Priority.J`
`   Todo.I = Todo.J`
	Move the record after this record into the current slot.

`END`	End of the DO I = ToDelete TO Count loop.
`Count = Count - 1`	At this point, the done record has been over-written and all the active records moved down one number, so decrease the counter by one.
`Modified = "YES"`	Mark the data file as being modified.
`RETURN`	Exit the subroutine.
`SAVE:`	Subroutine to save the file.
`CALL SysFileDelete BakFile`	Delete the backup file.
`COPY InFile BakFile`	Copy the input file to the backup file.
`CALL SysFileDelete InFile`	Delete the input file.
`CALL SysCls`	Clear the screen.
`SAY "***Sorting***"`	Tell the user what is happening. With a large file on a slow computer, sorting can take several seconds.
`CALL Sort`	Call a subroutine to sort the records.

Modified = "NO"	Reset the modified flag.
DO I = 1 TO Count	Loop through all the records.
CALL LineOut InFile,Priority.I	Write the priority to the input file.
CALL LineOut InFile,Todo.I	Write the to-do text to the input file.
END	End of the loop.
CALL LineOut InFile	Close the file.
RETURN	Exit the subroutine.
SWAP:	Subroutine to swap two records that are out of order.
Temp = Todo.K	Store the first record to a temporary variable.
Todo.K = Todo.J	Set the first variable equal to the second variable.
Todo.J = Temp	Set the second variable equal to the temporary variable.
Temp = Priority.K Priority.K = Priority.J Priority.J = Temp	Swap the priorities in the same fashion.
DROP Temp	Release the temporary variable.
RETURN	Exit the subroutine.
SORT:	Subroutine to sort the records.
DO J = 1 TO Count - 1	Start at the first record and go to the next-to-last record. This loop represents the starting point for the next loop.
DO K = J+1 to Count	Start one record below the first record and continue to the end of the records
First = Priority.J‖ Todo.J	Construct a temporary variable consisting of the priority and to-do text for the record from the first loop.
Second = Priority.K‖Todo.K	Construct a temporary variable consisting of the priority and to-do text for the record from the second loop. This record physically is always after the record from the first loop.

TODO.CMD, continued

REXX Commands	Explanation
IF First > Second THEN CALL Swap	If the first record should come after the second in a sort, then call a subroutine to swap them.
END	End of the DO K = J+1 to Count loop.
END	End of the DO J = 1 TO Count - 1 loop.
RETURN	Exit the subroutine.
EXIT:	Subroutine to handle quitting the program.
IF Modified = "NO" THEN EXIT	If the records have not been modified, then exit.
CALL SysCls	Clear the screen.
SAY "File Has Been Modified!!!" SAY "Do You Want To Save It Before Leaving (Y/N)" Character = SysGetKey(NoEcho)	Issue a warning.
IF Character = "N" THEN EXIT IF Character = "n" THEN EXIT	If the user elects not to save the records, then exit.
CALL Save EXIT	If it reaches this point, the user did not press N, so save the records then exit.
RETURN	Exit the subroutine. Since the user always exits from this subroutine, this is not needed and is added just for completeness.
CHANGE:	Subroutine to let the user change a record.

IF Count = 0 THEN
  DO
    Errormessage = "No Items
      To Change"
    RETURN
END
	If there are no records, create an error message for the screen display subroutine to display and return. While the change option is not displayed in the menu where there are no records, this test is required because the menu does not restrict options.

CALL ShowScreen	Display the screen.
SAY "Enter Item To Change 1 To " Count SAY "Enter Q To Quit Changing" PARSE PULL ToChange	Ask the user for the record number to change.

`IF ToChange = "Q" THEN RETURN` `IF ToChange = "q" THEN RETURN`	If the user selected Q, then return.
`DO I = 1 TO Count`	Loop through all the record numbers.
`IF ToChange = I THEN` `    DO`	If the string entered by the user matches a record number, then let the user edit that record.
`LoopOK = "NO"`	Create a variable that is used to see if a valid priority is entered.
`DO WHILE LoopOK = "NO"`	Continue looping until a valid priority is entered.

`SAY "Enter New Priority`
`    1 (High) — 9 (Low)"`
`SAY "Enter Q To Quit`
`    Entering Todo Items"`
	Tell the user what to do.

`Character=SysGetKey(NoEcho)`	Get a character from the user.

`IF Character = "Q"`
`          THEN RETURN`
`IF Character = "q"`
`          THEN RETURN`
	If the user enters Q, exit this routine.

`DO J = 1 TO 9`
`  IF Character = J THEN DO`
`    LoopOK = "OK"`
`    Priority.I = J`
`  END`
`END`
	Only priorities 1-9 are valid. Loop through these possibilities and if what the user entered matches one of these, set the check variable to OK and store the new priority.

`IF LoopOK = "NO" THEN` `  SAY "Invalid Priority"`	If the user did not enter a valid priority, display an error message. Due to looping, the user will have to enter a valid priority before passing this point.
`END`	End of loop to check validity of priority.
`Todo.I = INTERACT(Todo.I)`	Call an external REXX program (INTERACT.CMD) and pass it to the to-do text for editing. This program allows the user to interactively edit the contents of the variable and then pass the changes back to this program.
`END`	End of the IF ToChange = I loop.

TODO.CMD, continued

REXX Commands	Explanation
`END`	End of the DO I = 1 TO Count loop.
`RETURN`	Exit the subroutine.
`PRINT:`	Subroutine to print the to-do list.
`CALL LineOut Printer,` `        "Priority    Task"`	Print a header.
`DO I = 1 TO Count`	Loop through all the records.
`    LineToPrint = Priority.I` `          "        " Todo.I`	Construct a variable consisting of a priority and to-do text separated by spaces.
`    CALL LineOut Printer,` `        LineToPrint`	Print that variable.
`END`	End of the loop that goes through all the records.
`CALL CharOut Printer, '0C'x`	Send a form feed character to the printer.
`RETURN`	Exit the subroutine.
`TASKDONE:`	Subroutine to handle a finished task.

`Size = STREAM(DoneFile,'C',`
`        'Query Size')`
`IF Size > 0 THEN NOP`
	Check the size of the output file and do nothing if it is larger than zero. This is one way to check to see if a file exists since it must exist if its size is greater than zero.

`ELSE DO`
`    CALL LineOut DoneFile,`
`        "Date Done        Time`
`        Priority    Task"`
`    CALL LineOut DoneFile,`
`        "_____    __    ___`
`        ___ ___"`
`END`
	If the file has a zero size, it either does not exist or is a 0-length file. In either case, write header information to the file.

`IF Count = 0 THEN`
`    DO`
`        Errormessage = "No Items`
`            To Mark Done"`
`        RETURN`
`    END`
	If there are no records, create an error message and exit the subroutine. While the task done menu option is not displayed in this case, the menu does not prevent the user from selecting this option, so this test is required.

`CALL ShowScreen`	Display the current screen.

Programs in the Book

SAY "Enter Finished Item 1 To " Count SAY "Enter Q To Quit"	Tell the user what to do.
PARSE PULL IsDone	Get a record number from the user.
IF IsDone = "Q" THEN RETURN IF IsDone = "q" THEN RETURN	If the user selects Q, then exit this routine.
DO I = 1 TO Count	Loop through all available record numbers.
IF IsDone = I THEN DO	If the current record number matches that entered by the user, then perform the following steps.
SAY "Complete (Y/N)?"	Ask the user a question.
SAY Priority.I Todo.I	Display the record in question.
Character=SysGetKey(NoEcho)	Get a character from the user.

IF Character = "Y"
    THEN CALL FileIt
IF Character = "y"
    THEN CALL FileIt
	If that character is a Y, then call the subroutine to place the record in the done file.

END	End of the IF IsDone = I section.
END	End of the DO I = 1 TO Count loop.
RETURN	Exit the subroutine.
FILEIT:	Subroutine Modified = "YES"

ToSave = Date() || " " ||
    TIME('C') || "   "
    Priority.I || "   "
    || Todo.I
	Create a variable containing the date, time, priority, and to-do text.

CALL LineOut DoneFile,ToSave	Write that variable to the output file.
CALL LineOut DoneFile	Close the output file.

IF IsDone = Count THEN
    DO
      Count = Count - 1
      RETURN
    END
	If the record number of the record to delete is the last record, it can be deleted simply by decreasing the counter variable by one and returning.

DO I = IsDone TO Count	If it reaches this point, then the done record to be deleted from the to-do list is not the last record. Loop through the records, beginning with the record just deleted and going to the end.

TODO.CMD, continued

REXX Commands	Explanation
| ```
   J = I + 1
   Priority.I = Priority.J
   Todo.I = Todo.J
``` | Move the record after this record into the current slot. |
END	End of the DO I = IsDone TO Count loop.
Count = Count - 1	At this point, the done record has been overwritten and all the active records moved down one number, so decrease the counter by one.
RETURN	Exit the subroutine.

TYPING.CMD

REXX Command	Explanation
| ```
/* NAME:       TYPING.CMD
   PURPOSE:    Practice Typing
   VERSION:    1.00
   DATE:       August 8, 1993
   COPYRIGHT: 1994 McGraw Hill */
``` | Documentation remarks. |
| ```
HelpCheck = ARG(1)
IF HelpCheck = "/?" THEN
  DO
     SAY "Displays 60-Character"
     SAY "Lines For The User To"
     SAY "Try To Type Checks The"
     SAY "Answers And Keeps Score"
     EXIT
  END
``` | Display a help screen and exit when the user requests help. |
| ```
CALL RxFuncAdd 'SysCls',
      'RexxUtil', 'SysCls'
``` | Load SysCls function from the RexxUtil dynamic link library using the RxFuncAdd command. |
| ```
Attempted = 0
Correct   = 0
Wrong     = 0
``` | Initialize variables used for keeping score. |
| CALL SysCls | Clear the screen. |
| ```
SAY "Type The Line Exactly As It
     Appears"
SAY "Type 'QUIT' To Exit And
     Get Score"
SAY
``` | Print directions. |

`DO FOREVER`	Loop that gives the user lines to type until the user quits.
`    CharacterStream = ""`	Reset the variable used to store the typing line. This is required because characters are appended to it.
`    DO 60`	Loop through sixty times adding one character per loop to the typing line variable.

`        CharacterStream =`
`            CharacterStream ||`
`            Character()`
	Append a single character returned by the Character subroutine to the typing line variable.

`    END /* do */`	End of the DO 60 loop.
`    SAY CharacterStream`	Display the line to type.
`    PARSE PULL Typed`	Get the line typed by the user.
`    PARSE UPPER VAR Typed` `        Check Discard`	Convert the first word the user entered to uppercase and store it in the Check variable. This variable is used to look for instructions from the user.

`    IF Check = ""      THEN`
`        CALL Shutdown`
`    IF Check = "QUIT" THEN`
`        CALL Shutdown`
`    IF Check = "EXIT" THEN`
`        CALL Shutdown`
	If the user just presses return or enters QUIT or EXIT, then jump to the exit routine.

`    Attempted = Attempted + 60`	Since there were sixty characters on the line, increase the attempted counter by sixty.
`    CALL CheckLine`	Call a subroutine to grade the line entered by the user and return a line showing missed characters.
`    SAY CorrectedLine`	Display the line showing missed characters.
`    SAY`	Skip a line before showing the next line to type.
`END`	End of the DO FOREVER loop.

TYPING.CMD, continued

REXX Command	Explanation
EXIT	Exit the program. This line is never reached because of the DO FOREVER loop, but you should always have an EXIT command before your subroutines.
CHECKLINE:	Beginning of the line to check the line entered by the user.
CorrectedLine = " "	Reset the line used to mark mistakes. This is required because characters are appended to this variable.
DO I = 1 TO 60 BY 1	Loop sixty times to process the line one character at a time.
ToType = SubStr (CharacterStream, I, 1)	Store the character the user was supposed to type in the Ith position to the ToType variable.
DidType = SubStr(Typed, I, 1)	Store the character the user did type in the Ith position to the DidType variable.
IF ToType == DidType THEN	If the ToType and DidType variables match, then...
DO	Do the following.
CorrectedLine = CorrectedLine || " "	Append a space onto the corrected line.
Correct = Correct + 1	Increase the correct character counter by one.
END /* do */	End of the do loop.
ELSE	If the ToType and DidType variables do not match, then...
DO	Do the following.
CorrectedLine = CorrectedLine || "!"	Append a ! onto the corrected line.
Wrong = Wrong + 1	Increase the incorrect character counter by one.
END /* do */	End of the do loop.
END	End of the DO 60 loop.
RETURN	Exit the subroutine.

`CHARACTER:`	Subroutine that supervises the creation of random characters.
`Which = RANDOM(1,20)`	Create a random variable called Which. This variable is used to select between lowercase letters (Which equal to 1-16 or 80%), uppercase letters (Which equal to 17-18 or 10%), a space (Which equal to 19 or 5%), or a number (Which equal to 20 or 5%).
`IF Which < 17 THEN` `        Character = Little()`	When the Which variable is less than seventeen, call on the Little function to assign a random lowercase letter.
`ELSE IF Which < 19 THEN` `        Character = Big()`	When the Which variable is seventeen or eighteen, call on the Big function to assign a random uppercase letter.
`ELSE IF Which = 19` `        THEN Character = " "`	When the Which variable equals nineteen, assign a space.
`ELSE Character =` `        RANDOM(0,9)`	When the Which variable equals twenty, assign a random number between zero and nine.
`RETURN Character`	Return the assigned character.
`LITTLE:`	Function to assign a lowercase letter.
`Pick = RANDOM(1,26)`	Create a random variable 1-26.

`SELECT`
`    WHEN Pick = 1   THEN RETURN "a"`
`    WHEN Pick = 2   THEN RETURN "b"`
 	
Continues In A Similar Fashion For 3 - 24
 	
`    WHEN Pick = 25 THEN RETURN "y"`
`    WHEN Pick = 26 THEN RETURN "z"`
	Assign lowercase letters depending on the random number.

TYPING.CMD, continued

REXX Command	Explanation
```OTHERWISE SAY "Internal Error" EXIT```	This is included as an example as the random number generator produces only numbers 1-26. However, this section shows how to handle unexpected conditions using an OTHERWISE command.
```END /* select */```	End of the loop.
```RETURN```	End of the subroutine. Since the returning and value assignment was handled in the SELECT statement, this line is added just for completeness.
```BIG:```	Function to assign an uppercase letter.
```Pick = RANDOM(1,26)```	Create a random variable 1-26.
```SELECT WHEN Pick = 1 THEN RETURN "A" WHEN Pick = 2 THEN RETURN "B" Continues In A Similar Fashion For 3 - 24 WHEN Pick = 25 THEN RETURN "Y" WHEN Pick = 26 THEN RETURN "Z"```	Assign uppercase letters depending on the random number.
```OTHERWISE SAY "Internal Error" EXIT```	This is included as an example as the random number generator produces only numbers 1-26. However, this section shows how to handle unexpected conditions using an OTHERWISE command.
```END /* select */```	End of the loop.
```RETURN```	End of the subroutine.
```SHUTDOWN:```	The routine to handle the user leaving the program.

REXX Commands	Explanation

`SAY`
`SAY "Number Attempted: "`
`   Attempted`
`SAY "Number Correct:    "`
`   Correct`
`SAY "Number Incorrect: " Wrong`
`SAY "Final Score:       "`
`   (Correct / Attempted) * 1.00`
	Display the score.

`EXIT`	Exit the program.
`RETURN`	Exit the subroutine. Since an EXIT command precedes it, this line is never reached and is included only for completeness.

WHICH.CMD

REXX Commands	Explanation

`/* NAME:    WHICH.CMD`
`   PURPOSE: Display fully-`
`            qualified name of`
`            program in PATH.`
`   VERSION: 1.00`
`   DATE:    October 3, 1993 */`
	Documentation remarks.

`parse arg file`	Parse the argument passed to the program.

`if file = "/?" then`
`   call Syntax`
`if file = "-?" then`
`   call Syntax`
	If the user requested help, jump to a routine to display help, then exit the program.

`call LoadFunctions`	Jump to a routine to handle loading functions.
`extensions = 'COM EXE BAT CMD'`	Store allowed extensions into a variable.
`fspec = SysSearchPath(` `        'PATH', file)`	Search the path looking for the specified file and store the results in a variable.
`do i = 1 to words(extensions)` `      while(fspec = '')`	If the file was not found, loop through all of the extensions.
`   ext = word(extensions, i)`	Store the extension to a variable.
`   fspec = SysSearchPath(` `      'PATH', file'.'ext)`	Search for the file with the extension appended to the name.

WHICH.CMD, continued

REXX Commands	Explanation
`end`	End of Do loop.

`if fspec = '' then`
`  do`
`  say 'No files found that`
`      match' file`
`  exit 4`
`  end`
	If the variable is a null variable, no matching file was found, so display a message and exit.

`else`
`  say fspec`
`exit`
	Otherwise, display the file specification and exit.

`LoadFunctions: procedure`	Procedure to load the functions required by this program.

`/**`
`***    This will load the DLL`
`       for the Rexx system`
`       functions supplied`
`***    with OS/2 v2.0`
`**/`
	Documentation remarks.

`call RxFuncAdd 'SysLoadFuncs',` `     'RexxUtil', 'SysLoadFuncs'`	Load the SysLoadFuncs function.
`call SysLoadFuncs`	Call SysLoadFuncs to load all the OS/2 functions.
`return`	Exit the subroutine.

`Syntax: procedure`
`/**`
`***    Display command syntax.`
`**/`
`say "Syntax:   WHICH pgmname"`
`say`
`say "Purpose: This will`
`    display the fully-`
`    qualified name of the`
`    program by"`
`say "   looking through the`
`    PATH environment`
`    variable. If there is no"`
`say "   extension specified,`
`    this will append COM,`
`    EXE, BAT and CMD and"`
`say "   search again."`
`exit`
	Display help information and program syntax when the user requests help and then exit the program.

Programs on the Disk

The disk that comes with this book has two sets of programs on it: those I wrote and those written by other authors.

My Programs

A few of these programs were written as utilities for my *OS/2 Batch Files to Go* book, from Windcrest/McGraw-Hill, but most were written specifically as examples for this book. For that reason, many of them don't have a practical function. Often, it's better to write a nonsense example of a programming concept rather than a practical example. That's because the practical example generally requires a lot of additional code to make it work and that additional code gets in the way of the concept being illustrated.

To see this in action, look at TODO.CMD on the disk. This program is a functional, but simple, to-do manager that requires over 300 lines of code. TODO.CMD, and all my examples, are in the \MYSAMPLE subdirectory on the disk. Programs by others are all in the \OTHERS subdirectory.

%0.CMD

%0.CMD is a demonstration program that illustrates how a program can access its own name. Using the PARSE SOURCE instruction, a REXX program can access its name, just as a batch file can by accessing %0. The program %0.CMD demonstrates this. Try renaming it and it will still report its proper name and path.

4PMREXX.CMD

4PMREXX.CMD is a demonstration program that displays text on the screen and then asks you if you want to repeat the display. It uses the PULL instruction, rather than SysGetKey, so it can run under PMREXX.EXE without any problems.

ABBREV.CMD

ABBREV.CMD is a demonstration program that displays several different instructions using the Abbrev string function and the results of those instructions.

ALLCAPS.CMD

ALLCAPS.CMD is a filter file that takes the input source of text, reads it in unaltered, converts it to all uppercase, and writes it back out. The syntax is:

```
ALLCAPS [infile outfile]
```

where *infile* is the name of the file containing the input and *outfile* is the name of the file to contain the uppercase output. If the filenames are missing from the command line, ALLCAPS.CMD uses standard input and output. This allows you to pipe text into ALLCAPS.CMD and pipe the results that come out of the program, allowing it to act as a filter. Thus, the command:

```
TYPE C:\CONFIG.SYS ¦ ALLCAPS > C:\CONFIG.BAK
```

would convert the CONFIG.SYS file to all uppercase and store the results under the name CONFIG.BAK. Leave off the output filename and the text will be displayed on the screen. A detailed, line-by-line explanation of the code in ALLCAPS.CMD is shown in appendix A.

ALLLOWER.CMD

ALLLOWER.CMD is a filter file that takes the input source of text, reads it in unaltered, converts it to all lowercase, and writes it back out. The syntax is:

```
ALLLOWER [infile outfile]
```

where *infile* is the name of the file containing the input and *outfile* is the name of the file to contain the lowercase output. If the filenames are missing from the command line, ALLLOWER.CMD uses standard input and output. This allows you to pipe text into ALLLOWER.CMD and pipe the results that come out of the program, allowing it to act as a filter. Thus, the command:

```
TYPE C:\CONFIG.SYS ¦ ALLLOWER > C:\CONFIG.BAK
```

would convert the CONFIG.SYS file to all lowercase and store the results under the name CONFIG.BAK. Leave off the output filename and the text will be displayed on the screen.

ARG.CMD

ARG.CMD is a demonstration program that shows how REXX treats the command line the user enters after the name of the program. Users running this program should start it with at least one argument on the command line.

ARG-CMD.CMD

ARG-CMD.CMD is a demonstration program that uses the ARG instruction to display the first nine arguments passed to the program on the command line. If no arguments are passed to it, it aborts with a warning message. If more than nine arguments are passed to it, then it displays a warning message after displaying the first nine arguments.

REXX can, of course, work with many more than nine arguments. This is just an artificial limit built into this example program.

BAT-FOR.CMD

BAT-FOR.CMD is a demonstration program that displays all the .CMD files in the current subdirectory by issuing a FOR command to OS/2 rather than using a REXX instruction.

BATSHIFT.CMD

BATSHIFT.CMD is a demonstration program that shows how REXX programs can separate command-line parameters into replaceable parameters just like batch files. Run BATSHIFT.CMD from the command line with any number of parameters after the name, separated by spaces. BATSHIFT.CMD doesn't work exactly like a batch file since commas are a valid separator for batch file replaceable parameters, but they won't work for BATSHIFT.CMD as written.

BEEPS.CMD

BEEPS.CMD is a demonstration program that shows the BEEP function by playing the scales on the computer.

BIGNUM.CMD

BIGNUM.CMD is a demonstration program that shows the results of different NUMERIC DIGITS settings by running the same problem (1/7) at different settings and showing the results. Note that the large settings, such as 10,000 and 100,000, produce a lot of numbers that can take a long time to display on your screen, especially on slower computers.

BITAND.CMD

BITAND.CMD is a demonstration program to illustrate the BitAnd function. It prompts the user for two characters, displays their binary representation, and then shows the results of performing a BitAnd on those two characters.

BITOR.CMD

BITOR.CMD is a demonstration program to illustrate the BitOr function. It prompts the user for two characters, displays their binary representation, and then shows the results of performing a BitOr on those two characters.

BITXOR.CMD

BITXOR.CMD is a demonstration program to illustrate the BitXOr function. It prompts the user for two characters, displays their binary representation, and then shows the results of performing BitXOr on those two characters.

CALEDBAT.CMD

CALEDBAT.CMD is a demonstration batch file that simply displays the contents of the first three replaceable parameters passed to it. It's called by the REXX program CALL-BAT.CMD to demonstrate the technique of calling a batch file from a REXX program.

CALL-1.CMD

CALL-1.CMD is a demonstration program that shows how to pass arguments to a subroutine being executed via the CALL command.

CALL-2.CMD

CALL-2.CMD is a demonstration program that shows the problem of placing subroutines at the end of the program.

CALL-3.CMD

CALL-3.CMD is a demonstration program that takes the SHOWTEMP.CMD program that comes with this book and displays the centered titles using a subroutine.

CALL-4.CMD

CALL-4.CMD is a demonstration program that improves on the CALL-3.CMD program that comes with this book by performing the underlining in the single subroutine as well.

CALL-5.CMD

CALL-5.CMD is a demonstration program that improves on the CALL-4.CMD program that comes with this book by adding a second subroutine to display instructions and then execute them.

CALL-6.CMD

CALL-6.CMD is a demonstration program that shows that the SIGNAL instruction can be used inside a subroutine without affecting DO loops that are in the process of executing in the main program while the subroutine is active.

CALL-7.CMD

CALL-7.CMD is a demonstration program that shows two different ways a number can be returned from a subroutine: either using the automatically created variable called Result or treating the subroutine as an internal function.

CALL-8.CMD

CALL-8.CMD is a demonstration program that shows how you can easily create a programming bug by using the same variable name for a loop counter in the main program and a subroutine that will be accessed while the loop in the main program is active. CALL-8.CMD runs in an endless loop. Press Ctrl–Break to stop the program.

CALL-9.CMD

CALL-9.CMD is a demonstration program that shows how the PROCEDURE can cause subroutine variables to be local variables. It's a modified version of CALL-8.CMD.

CALL-10.CMD

CALL-10.CMD is a demonstration program that shows how you can use the EXPOSE subinstruction of the PROCEDURE instruction to make selected variables in a subroutine global, while others remain local.

CALL-11.CMD

CALL-11.CMD is a demonstration program that shows how the EXPOSE subinstruction can expose only the variables the subroutine would have had access to without the PROCEDURE instruction.

CALL-12.CMD

CALL-12.CMD is a demonstration program that shows how data can be passed to a subroutine by arguments and how this data is usable in the subroutine even though all the variables are local variables.

CALLARG.CMD

Since the Arg function always treats all the command-line arguments as a single argument, CALLARG.CMD is a demonstration program that calls ARG.CMD as a subroutine while passing it several arguments. That way, users can see how the Arg function works when used in a subroutine. When running CALLARG.CMD, ARG.CMD should be either in the current subdirectory or in your path.

CALLBAT.CMD

CALLBAT.CMD is a demonstration program that calls the batch file CALEDBAT.CMD and passes it three replaceable parameters in order to demonstrate how to call batch files from within a REXX program.

CAPITAL.CMD

When the information a batch file receive via replaceable parameters must be tested, capitalization can become a problem since batch files don't have the string-conversion abilities of REXX. If the user is supposed to enter one of several flags, like *daily*, then you have to test for *daily*, *Daily*, and *DAILY* just to catch the common capitalizations. This requires a lot of logic testing and can still miss unusual capitalization. An easier approach is to force it to be all uppercase, which is what CAPITAL.CMD does.

You call CAPITAL.CMD and pass it a word as a replaceable parameter and it converts that word to all uppercase and stores it in the environment. CAPITAL.CMD doesn't have a prompt since it runs without user intervention.

CHANGE.CMD

CHANGE.CMD is a demonstration program that shows how to use the Translate function to alter character strings.

CHARIN.CMD

CHARIN.CMD is a demonstration program that reads input from the keyboard, displays it as the CharIn function handles it, and then reads all the characters from CHARIN.CMD and displays them on the screen. Users should run CHARIN.CMD from the subdirectory containing the program and not depend on it being in the path since it won't be able to read its characters unless it's in the current subdirectory.

CHAROUT.CMD

CHAROUT.CMD is a demonstration program that creates a temporary data file called JUNK.@@!, writes data to the file using a series of instructions, overwrites the beginning of the data series, displays the resulting contents of the data file, and then erases it. It won't run if the file JUNK.@@! already exists in order to protect your data.

CHARS.CMD

CHARS.CMD is a demonstration program that shows the Chars function by using it to count the characters in the C:\AUTOEXEC.BAT and C:\CONFIG.SYS files.

CHKDRIVE.CMD

CHKDRIVE.CMD uses the SysDriveInfo external function to display information about the specified drive. The information displayed is the drive checked, the number of bytes free, the total number of bytes, and the drive label. The information is displayed much more quickly than using the DIR or CHKDSK commands. The syntax is:

```
CHKDRIVE drive
```

where *drive* is the drive to check. It also checks for a valid drive using the SysDriveMap external function to make sure the user doesn't check an invalid drive. You can enter drives with or without the colon and in upper- or lowercase. If no drive is specified, the C: drive is checked. CHKDRIVE.CMD uses COMMAS.CMD, so this program must be either in the current subdirectory or in your path.

CLASSES.CMD

CLASSES.CMD is a demonstration program that displays all the registered object classes to the screen using the SysQueryClassList external function. This listing can be piped to a disk file.

CLS.CMD

Clearing the screen under REXX requires you to load the SysCls function, and even then the screen is cleared to an ugly white on black. CLS.CMD avoids these problems by clearing the screen using ANSI. That way no external functions are required and the screen can be cleared to any color combination you like. To use it, just add a CALL CLS instruction to your REXX programs when you want to clear the screen, and make sure CLS.CMD is in your path.

COMMAS.CMD

COMMAS.CMD is a demonstration program that takes a single unformatted number as input and insert commas in the integer portion of the number, so 12345 is returned as 12,345 and 12345.6789 is returned as 12,345.6789. If a second argument with a value of "Decimal" is passed to it, then it inserts commas in the decimal portion as well, so 12345.6789 becomes 12,345.678,9. It's interesting to note that commas are inserted in the integer portion after each third character, moving from right to left, and inserted in the decimal portion after each third character, moving from left to right, which is the standard notation. The syntax to call COMMAS.CMD is:

```
Formatted = COMMAS(unformatted[,"Decimal"])
```

where *unformatted* is the number to format. COMMAS.CMD is a demonstration program and lacks adequate error checking, which would be necessary in a production environment where a robust function was needed. If you're interested in using COMMAS.CMD, consider first adding a check to make sure the number passed to the function really is a number, since passing non-numeric characters will cause the program to crash. The source code for COMMAS.CMD is explained in appendix A.

COMPARE.CMD

COMPARE.CMD is a demonstration program that performs a series of string comparisons using the Compare function and displays the results on the screen.

COMPUTE.CMD

COMPUTE.CMD takes the mathematical expression entered on the command line after the program name, evaluates it, and displays the results. Any valid REXX mathematical expression is acceptable. No syntax checking is performed, so invalid expressions or equations that result in division by zero will return REXX error messages. OS/2 users can use COMPUTE.CMD to quickly perform simple calculations.

CONCATE.CMD

CONCATE.CMD is a demonstration program that illustrates the Concate string function. It first displays the contents of several variables, and then displays several instructions using the Concate function and the results of those instructions.

COPIES.CMD

COPIES.CMD is a demonstration program that illustrates the Copies function by executing a series of Copies instructions and displaying the results on the screen.

CURSOR.CMD

CURSOR.CMD is a demonstration program that uses the SysCurState external function to turn the cursor on and off.

D2X.CMD

D2X.CMD is a demonstration program that illustrates the D2X internal function by converting a series of random numbers.

DATATYPE.CMD

DATATYPE.CMD is a demonstration program that shows the DataType internal function by displaying the data type of a series of inputs from the user.

DATES.CMD

DATES.CMD is a demonstration program that shows the internal Date function by displaying all the output available from that function.

DELBLANK.CMD

DELBLANK.CMD is a filter file that takes the input source of text, reads it in unaltered, strips off all blank lines, and writes it back out. The syntax is:

```
DELBLANK [infile outfile]
```

where *infile* is the name of the file containing the input and *outfile* is the name of the file to contain the lowercase output. If the filenames are missing from the command line, DELBLANK.CMD will use standard input and output. This allows you to pipe text into DELBLANK.CMD and pipe the results that come out of the program, allowing it to act as a filter. Thus, the command:

```
TYPE C:\CONFIG.SYS | DELBLANK > C:\CONFIG.BAK
```

would take the CONFIG.SYS file, strip off all blank lines, and store the results under the name CONFIG.BAK. If you leave off the output filename, the text would be displayed on the screen. A detailed, line-by-line explanation of the code in DELBLANK.CMD is shown in appendix A.

DELSTR.CMD

DELSTR.CMD is a demonstration program that shows several uses of the DelStr function.

DELWORD.CMD

DELWORD.CMD is demonstration program that deletes a series of words from a string using the DelWord internal function.

DESCRIBE.CMD

DESCRIBE.CMD is a demonstration program that functions as a batch file and loads the DeScribe word processor. If a file is specified on the command line, that file is passed on to DeScribe so it can be loaded automatically. For DESCRIBE.CMD to work properly, DeScribe must be installed in the C:\DESCRIBE subdirectory.

DIAL.CMD

DIAL.CMD is a REXX program that will dial a phone number for you. The syntax is:

```
DIAL number port
```

where *number* is the phone number to dial and *port* is a single digit representing the COM port to use, where 1=COM1:, 2=COM2:, and so on. The phone number can include parentheses and a dash, but can't include any spaces. For example, a local number could be entered as 555-1212 and a long-distance number could be entered as 1(800)555-1212. The parentheses and dash aren't required, so 18005551212 would also be valid.

DIGITS.CMD

DIGITS.CMD is a demonstration program that returns the current setting for NUMERIC DIGITS using the Digits internal function.

DO-1.CMD

DO-1.CMD is a demonstration program that illustrates using multiple instructions after a WHEN subinstruction of a SELECT instruction.

DO-2.CMD

DO-2.CMD is a demonstration program that illustrates a DO #/END loop by executing the same instruction 20 times.

DO-3.CMD

DO-3.CMD is a demonstration program that illustrates a DO I = *start* TO *end* BY *increment*/END loop by performing three different versions of the same loop.

DO-4.CMD

DO-4.CMD is a demonstration program that shows two ways to leave a DO loop early: the LEAVE instruction and the FOR subinstruction.

DO-5.CMD

DO-5.CMD is a demonstration program showing the DO FOREVER loop. It continues looping until the user presses Ctrl–Break or closes the session.

DO-6.CMD

DO-6.CMD is a demonstration program that shows how to use the UNTIL subinstruction to terminate a DO loop early. To understand this example, you must know that the RANDOM(100) function generates a random number between zero and 100. This random number is a whole number and the probability of it exceeding 99 is approximately one percent, so, on average, this loop should run about 100 times before it terminates.

DO-7.CMD

DO-7.CMD is a demonstration program that uses the following loop:

```
DO I = 1 TO 10
  SAY "Loop Number:" I
  IF I > 5 THEN SIGNAL SKIP
  SAY "This Line Executed Only For I <= 5"
  SKIP:
END
```

to illustrate the problems caused when the SIGNAL instruction is used like a GOTO command in a batch file to jump around the program.

DO-8.CMD

DO-8.CMD is a demonstration program that shows how to use the ITERATE instruction to skip parts of a DO loop.

DO-9.CMD

DO-9.CMD is a demonstration program that illustrates nested DO loops by counting from 0,000 to 9,999 using four nested DO loops, each of the form DO I = 0 TO 9. DO-9.CMD has a visual display that helps the user understand how different loops run a different number of times.

DO-10.CMD

DO-10.CMD is a demonstration program that shows how to use the ITERATE instruction to increment the loop counter variable for a DO loop other than the innermost loop.

DO-11.CMD

DO-11.CMD is a demonstration program that shows how the REXX feature of naming the END instructions so REXX can check to make sure the right DO loop is being terminated is not implemented in OS/2 2.1 REXX.

DOSPAUSE.CMD

DOSPAUSE.CMD is a demonstration program that runs the SPAUSE.CMD external subroutine four different times using four different sets of arguments. After running SPAUSE.CMD four times, DOSPAUSE.CMD displays the results of those four executions.

EA.CMD

EA.CMD is a demonstration program that uses the SysGetEA external function to return the file type and extended attribute information on XCOPY.EXE. In order to work, XCOPY.EXE must be installed in the \OS2 subdirectory and EA.CMD must be executed from the same drive as the one containing XCOPY.EXE.

ERRORTXT.CMD

ERRORTXT.CMD is a demonstration program that displays the REXX error messages associated with the numbers 0–99 using the ErrorText internal function.

EXCEPT-1.CMD

EXCEPT-1.CMD is a demonstration program that counts to a very large number, simulating a "hung" program. It uses a Halt exception handler to handle the condition of the user pressing Ctrl–Break. If that happens, EXCEPT-1.CMD gives the user the option of stopping the program or continuing processing.

EXCEPT-2.CMD

EXCEPT-2.CMD is a demonstration program that tries to write to the A: drive using the LineOut internal function, after suggesting that the user make sure no disk is in the drive. This raises the NotReady condition, which EXCEPT-2.CMD is prepared to handle.

EXCEPT-3.CMD

EXCEPT-3.CMD is a demonstration program that raises the NoValue condition using the DROP instruction and a variable that hasn't been defined inside parentheses. This variable is supposed to contain a list of variables to drop. EXCEPT-3.CMD has exception handling to deal with this problem. This routine displays the line number of the problem and the contents on that line, and then exits the program.

FACTORAL.CMD

FACTORAL.CMD is an external demonstration subroutine that computes the factorial of an integer zero through 92. A factorial (written as *n*!, where *n* is the number to compute the factorial of) is the product of every integer between one and the number the factorial is being computed for. So 3! is 3*2*1 or 6, and 10! is 10*9*8*7*6*5*4*3*2*1 or 3,628,800. As you can see, the numbers get large very fast, which is the reason the maximum value is 92. The syntax for calling FACTORAL.CMD is:

```
Answer = FACTORAL(number)
```

where *number* is the number to compute the factorial of. FACTORAL.CMD is interesting because it has an internal procedure called FACTORIAL that it calls recursively. That is, the procedure calls itself repeatedly. The operation of FACTORAL.CMD and this subroutine are documented in appendix A.

FF.CMD

FF.CMD is a very useful program for finding files that match a given file specification. The syntax is:

```
FF [drive] [path] filespec
```

where *drive* is the drive to search, *path* is the subdirectory to begin the search from, and *filespec* is the file specification to look for. The *drive*, *path*, and *filespec* must each be expressed as one word, for example, C:*.CMD. Multiple filespec values can be entered on the command line and FF.CMD will search for each one in turn. For example, the command:

```
FF C:\*.CMD
```

would find all the REXX programs and batch files on the C: drive, while the command:

```
FF *.TXT
```

would find all the .TXT files in the current subdirectory and below. FF.CMD starts with the drive and subdirectory specified on the command line and looks in it and all subdirectories below that subdirectory. For example, the command:

```
FF C:\REXX\*.CMD
```

would search (for example) the C:\REXX, C:\REXX\MINE, and C:\REXX\OTHERS subdirectories because the first is specified and the next two are below it. It wouldn't search C:\BAT because it isn't below the specified subdirectory. If no drive or subdirectory is specified, FF.CMD will begin its search in the current subdirectory. More than one file specification can be specified on the command line, so the command:

```
FF C:\REXX\*.CMD C:\BAT\*.CMD A:\*.CMD
```

would be valid. The operation of FF.CMD is explained in detail in appendix A.

FF2.CMD

FF2.CMD is very similar to FF.CMD, but it searches for only one file specification at a time. However, it adds the ability to search for specific text. The syntax is:

```
FF2 [drive] [path] filespec text
```

where *drive* is the drive to search, *path* is the subdirectory to begin the search from, and *filespec* is the file specification to look for. The *drive*, *path*, and *filespec* must each be expressed as one word, for example, C:*.CMD. Multiple filespec values can be entered on a command line and FF.CMD will search for each one in turn.

Text is the text to search for. The search is not case-sensitive. Multiple words can be entered, but these words must appear in the file in exactly the same order and with the exact same spacing between them as they appear on the command line.

For each file that matches the FileSpec and contains the specified text, FF2.CMD displays every line in the file containing the specified text.

FILES.CMD

FILES.CMD is a demonstration program that shows using several of the external functions for file management. It uses SysFileSearch to show all the lines in your C:\CONFIG.SYS file containing the SET instruction, SysMkDir to create the C:\JUNK.@@! subdirectory, an OS/2 ECHO command to create the file by echoing text to it, SysFileDelete to delete the file C:\JUNK.@@!\JUNK.@@!, and finally the SysRmDir function to remove the subdirectory. Along the way, it uses the OS/2 DIR command several times to show the contents of the subdirectory.

FILEXIST.CMD

FILEXIST.CMD checks to see if the file passed to it on the command line exists and sets the errorlevel accordingly. The possible errorlevel values are:

0. The specified file is a zero-length file.

1. The specified file doesn't exist.

2. The specified file exists.

FILEXIST.CMD normally displays two lines of text when it runs, telling the status of the file and the errorlevel value. FILEXIST.CMD can also be called as a subroutine by other REXX programs to quickly check to see if a file they need exists. When passed a second argument of NoShow, these two lines aren't displayed.

FILEXIST.CMD actually "cheats" when checking the second argument. Since it accepts no other arguments after the filename, it assumes that the simple existence of a second argument indicates that it's being called as a subroutine and that it shouldn't display any information on the screen. This is a valid assumption since the Arg function treats everything entered on the command line as a single argument, so FILEXIST.CMD can get only multiple arguments when called as a subroutine. The syntax to call it as a subroutine is:

```
variable = FILEXIST(file[,noshow])
```

where *variable* is the name of the variable to receive the results of FILEXIST.CMD (which is 0, 1, or 2 and corresponds to the errorlevel set by the program), *file* is the file to check to see if it exists, and *noshow* is the optional flag used as a second argument to tell FILEXIST.CMD not to display any information.

SPELDISK.CMD calls FILEXIST.CMD to make sure its spelling dictionary exists, and CHARIN.CMD calls it to make sure CHARIN.CMD is being run from the subdirectory containing the program file.

FINDLPT.CMD

FINDLPT.CMD returns the active printer port. To allow it to be used in a batch file, FINDLPT.CMD also sets a return code. The codes are 1 for LPT1, 2 for LPT2, 3 for COM1, 4 for COM2, and 5 for anything else.

FOR-LOOP.CMD

FOR-LOOP.CMD is a demonstration batch file that simulates a batch file FOR loop in a REXX program. When running the program, you should specify several items on the command line after the name for it to process. It only displays these items on the screen; no actual operations are performed on them.

FORMAT.CMD

FORMAT.CMD is a demonstration program that illustrates the Format function by showing a sequence of numbers formatted using different settings.

GET.CMD

One of the things you'll want your batch files to do is ask users for information such as their names or the name of files to erase, copy, or run. For this task, you need a utility that can accept full words. GET.CMD does just this. The entire text string is returned to the user via the environment under the environmental variable name RETURN.

GET-ONE.CMD

GET-ONE.CMD is a batch file utility designed to get a single character from the user and return that character to the batch file via a return code equal to the ASCII code of the character.

GET09.CMD

If you want the user to be able to pick from only a few alternatives, a number works better than a letter since there are only ten (0–9) of them. Plus, it's easier to reduce the number of choices available, e.g., 0–4, since numbers rarely have any meaning to the user. GET09.CMD does just this.

GETA2Z.CMD

Testing all 256 possible values is a lot of testing for most of the questions you want to ask the user. GETA2Z.CMD reduces the testing by restricting the user to entering just a single letter. When the user enters a letter, it exits and sets errorlevel to the letter's position in the alphabet. Thus, A is returned as 1, B is returned as 2, and so on. GETA2Z.CMD is case-insensitive.

GETDATA.CMD

GETDATA.CMD is a demonstration program that reads data from an external queue. It expects to have SENDATA.CMD to run either before it or after it in another session in order to place data into the external queue named RONNY. Until SENDATA.CMD runs, GETDATA.CMD will be in an endless loop.

HIWORLD.CMD

HIWORLD.CMD is a demonstration program that displays one line of text on the screen.

INSERT.CMD

INSERT.CMD is a demonstration program that shows how to use the Insert internal function to insert one string inside another.

INTERACT.CMD

REXX doesn't support interactive editing of variables. That is, it doesn't allow you to display a variable containing a value and have the user scroll around making changes. Since REXX doesn't support this directly, I wrote INTERACT.CMD to simulate interactive editing.

INTERACT.CMD displays the variable on the screen, moves the cursor to the first position of the variable, and then uses the SysGetKey function to get a keystroke from the user. If the keystroke is a cursor-movement key, such as the left arrow or Home key, it computes a new location for the cursor and moves it there. If that causes the cursor to move beyond the end of the variable, it pads the variable with spaces to make it extend to the current cursor position. Pressing the Ins key toggles it between insert and overstrike mode.

If the user presses the backspace key, it moves the cursor one position to the left, deletes that character from the variable, repositions each character to the right of the cursor one position to the left, and redisplays the variable. If the user presses Enter, the current value of the edited variable is accepted.

If the user presses any other keystroke, that keystroke is added into the variable at the current cursor position. In overstrike mode (the default), it just replaces the current character at that position and moves the cursor one position to the right. In insert mode, the character is entered at the current cursor position and the remaining characters are moved one position to the right to accommodate the new character.

As written, INTERACT.CMD is a function that accepts just the variable to edit and returns it to the calling program. It works with a specific location on the screen and restricts variables to 60 characters or less. It could be easily modified to accept the screen position and record length as an input, and then all of your REXX programs could call it for variable editing. If you do this, TODO.CMD will also need to be modified since it calls INTERACT.CMD and depends on it running with its default values.

ISITANUM.CMD

ISITANUM.CMD is a utility program designed to perform error checking for other REXX programs. It takes a single number and returns a code to indicate if the argument passed to is a number. The syntax is:

```
resultvariable = ISITANUM(variable)
```

where *resultvariable* is the name of the variable to contain the results and *variable* contains the data to check. The return codes are:

0. More than one piece of data was passed to ISITANUM.CMD. The program is designed to test only one number at a time. If you need to check more than one number, pass them to ISITANUM.CMD one at a time.

1. The data passed to it was not a number.

2. The data passed to it was a whole number.

3. The data passed to it was a number but not a whole number.

4. An unexpected error occurred.

ISITANUM.CMD is an excellent way to quickly check numbers before using them in programs that require numbers from the user. ISITANUM.CMD is explained in detail in appendix A.

ISITZERO.CMD

Occasionally, it's useful to test a file to see if it's a zero-length file. ISITZERO.CMD does just that. For easy testing in batch files, it sets the return code to one for a zero-length file and zero otherwise.

KEYVALUE.CMD

KEYVALUE.CMD shows the value the SysGetKey external function sees for any keystroke you press. KEYVALUE.CMD will continue asking you for different keystrokes to report on. Press Enter (which has a value of 13 to SysGetKey) to exit the program. For extended keystrokes, KEYVALUE.CMD reports both values. KEYVALUE.CMD can be very useful when your program needs to get input using the SysGetKey external function and you aren't sure of the codes for the characters your program is expecting.

LASTPOS.CMD

LASTPOS.CMD is a demonstration program that shows using the LastPos function in a program.

LEFT.CMD

LEFT.CMD is a demonstration program that shows using the Left function in a program.

LENGTH.CMD

LENGTH.CMD is a demonstration program that shows using the Length function in a program.

LINEIN.CMD

LINEIN.CMD is a demonstration program that shows how to use the LineIn function to read data from a data file. This program uses itself as the data file so it must be run from the subdirectory containing the LINEIN.CMD file. The program checks for this and will abort if it's run from another subdirectory.

LINEOUT.CMD

LINEOUT.CMD is a demonstration program that shows how to use the LineOut function to write data to a file. It creates a data file called JUNK.@@!, writes data to it, uses OS/2 to TYPE the file to the screen, and then erases the file. LINEOUT.CMD will refuse to run if the file JUNK@@! already exists.

LISTCALL.CMD

The program LISTIT.CMD is designed to list ASCII files for easy viewing. However, LISTIT.CMD is limited in that it allows you to list only one file on the command line and that one file cannot contain wildcards. LISTCALL.CMD overcomes these disadvantages. It allows you to enter multiple sets of wildcards on the command line, and LISTCALL.CMD feeds the files to LISTIT.CMD one at a time. The syntax is:

```
LISTCALL wildcard1 wildcard2 wildcard3 ...
```

where *wildcard1*, *wildcard2*, and so on are wildcard specifications to view. For example, the command:

```
LISTCALL A*.CMD E*.CMD X*.CMD
```

will list all the REXX programs (or batch files) starting with A, E, or X.

LISTIT.CMD

LISTIT.CMD is an ASCII file viewer. You must list the name of the file to view on the command line, and wildcards are not supported. To view your CONFIG.SYS file, you would enter the command:

```
LISTIT C:\CONFIG.SYS
```

on the command line. LISTIT.CMD allows you to scroll forwards and backwards. Lines too long to be displayed on the screen are automatically wrapped to the next line. If you usually run LISTIT.CMD from a window that isn't the full screen, the code will adjust to any length and width of window.

While LISTIT.CMD doesn't directly support wildcards, you can use the OS/2 command line to add wildcard support to the program by using a FOR loop. For example, to view every .TXT file, use the OS/2 command:

```
FOR %J IN (*.TXT) DO LISTIT %J
```

You can also use the LISTCALL.CMD program, discussed previously. A detailed, line-by-line explanation of the code in LISTIT.CMD is shown in appendix A. You might want to modify LISTIT.CMD to call FILEXIST.CMD first to make sure the file specified by the user exists.

LOGIC.CMD

LOGIC.CMD is a demonstration program that shows how different logical comparisons work in a REXX program by performing a series of logical tests, and displaying the tests and their results.

MAP.CMD

MAP.CMD is a demonstration program that uses the SysDriveMap external function to display all available drives.

MATH.CMD

MATH.CMD is a demonstration program that shows a number of REXX mathematical functions in operation.

MATHTEST.CMD

MATHTEST.CMD is a simple math test program for younger children. It offers tests on addition, subtraction, multiplication, and division, as well as mixed problems.

There are three levels: easy, moderate, and hard. At the easy level, the numbers used for addition and multiplication and the answers for division and subtraction never exceed 10. The limit for moderate is 15 and the limit for hard is 20.

The problems are generated randomly and are controlled so subtraction answers are never negative and division answers are always whole numbers. MATHTEST.CMD keeps score and displays the results when the user quits the program.

A detailed, line-by-line explanation of the code in MATHTEST.CMD is shown in appendix A.

MESSAGE.CMD

MESSAGE.CMD is a demonstration program that shows using the RxMessageBox external function running under PMREXX to display a message box on the screen. It reacts differently depending on which button the user selects.

MULTI-IF.CMD

MULTI-IF.CMD is a demonstration program that shows how IF statements can be embedded inside other IF statements. It prompts the user for a word and then uses four embedded IF statements to display the word entered by the user.

OBJECT.CMD

OBJECT.CMD is a demonstration program that uses the SysCreateObject external function to create a new folder called REXX Example on the desktop. It then creates a shadow of this folder on the desktop. It then uses the SysDestroyObject external function to delete that folder—which automatically deletes the shadow.

OS2PAUSE.CMD

OS2PAUSE.CMD is a demonstration program that shows how to place a PAUSE instruction in a REXX program by accessing the OS/2 shell PAUSE command with @PAUSE.

OVERLAY.CMD

OVERLAY.CMD is a demonstration program that shows how to use the Overlay function.

PASSWORD.CMD

PASSWORD.CMD is a demonstration program that gives the user five chances to enter a password. If the correct password is entered, the program continues execution; otherwise, it terminates. The password is Ronny and capitalization matters.

PASSWORD.CMD is just a demonstration program and has several major flaws. First, the password is hardcoded into the program, which is an ASCII file, so anyone could look at the file and easily figure out the password. Second, the password is displayed on the screen so anyone looking over the user's shoulder could easily see the password. So the program does not offer much security.

PAUSE.CMD

Unfortunately, REXX doesn't offer a simple PAUSE command like the OS/2 and DOS batch languages do. To remedy that situation, I wrote PAUSE.CMD. When called with the instruction:

```
CALL PAUSE
```

it functions exactly like the batch PAUSE command. It displays a "Press Any Key To Continue . . ." message on the next line of the screen, waits for the user to press any key, and then returns control to the calling program. If it's passed a CLS argument, it clears the screen before returning control.

Of course, users can also include the PAUSE command, which would be passed to the OS/2 shell program and then execute it as though it had been issued by a batch file.

PC-1.CMD

While writing this book, I was also working on a project at the school were I teach to perform a statistical analysis on the evaluations the students complete of each course at the end of the semester. The data was supplied to me in ASCII files, one per semester. The file had fifteen entries for each student evaluation, a code for the instructor's name, the period number, and responses to thirteen questions. These were stored with one entry per row. I needed to convert the data file so it had one evaluation per line. I also needed to make sure the responses on each line were directly below the same responses on the line above so I could move this data into a database. The codes were all the same length, but the period number could be either a one- or two-digit number. Additionally, the student responses to the thirteen questions were A–E, where A=4, B=3, C=2, D=1, and E isn't applicable and is converted to zero.

PC-1.CMD is a quick-and-dirty program I put together to reformat the data. You'll notice that I didn't pay a lot of attention to internal documentation, capitalization, or form in general—which is the nature of a quick-and-dirty program. PC-1.CMD was designed to convert eight data files. After that, it would never be used again. If I spent too much time getting everything perfect, I could have manually converted the data files more quickly. Since I needed PC-1.CMD to work correctly only eight times, I put it together as quickly as I could.

POS.CMD

POS.CMD is a demonstration program that shows using the Pos function in a program to find the position of one string inside a second string.

POSITION.CMD

POSITION.CMD is a demonstration program that demonstrates the SysCurPos function by using it to position the cursor at different locations on the screen and then display those coordinates on the screen.

PRECEDE.CMD

PRECEDE.CMD is a demonstration program that illustrates mathematical precedence by working through a complex equation one step at a time.

PRECISE.CMD

PRECISE.CMD is a demonstration program that demonstrates the NUMERIC DIGITS by performing the same instruction (1/3) at precision levels varying from 1 to 40.

QUEUE-1.CMD

QUEUE-1.CMD is a demonstration program that demonstrates external data-queue management using the RxQueue function.

QUEUE-2.CMD

QUEUE-2.CMD is a demonstration program that uses the RXQUEUE.EXE OS/2 filter to pipe the results of an OS/2 DIR command into an external data queue. It then reads and processes this queue using REXX commands.

QUEUE-3.CMD

QUEUE-3.CMD is an external demonstration subroutine that's called by QUEUE-4.CMD. It uses the PARSE PULL instruction to get three pieces of information: first name, last name, and age. When run as a stand-alone program, it reads these from the keyboard and then displays them. When called as an external subroutine by QUEUE-4.CMD, QUEUE-4.CMD has already placed a first name of Ronny and last name of Richardson into an external data queue, so QUEUE-3.CMD reads these and prompts the user for only his age.

QUEUE-4.CMD

QUEUE-4.CMD is a demonstration program that places a first and last name, Ronny and Richardson respectively, into an external data queue before calling QUEUE-3.CMD as an external subroutine. QUEUE-3.CMD reads the first and last name from the external data queue using the PARSE PULL instruction and then automatically switches over and reads the age from the keyboard using the same PARSE PULL instruction.

QUEUE-5.CMD

QUEUE-5.CMD is an external demonstration subroutine that's called by QUEUE-4.CMD. It uses the LineIn internal function to get three pieces of information: first name, last name, and age. When run as a stand-alone program, it waits forever on the first use of the LineIn function since no data is waiting in the queue. (Press Ctrl–Break to abort.)

When called as an external subroutine by QUEUE-4.CMD, QUEUE-4.CMD has already placed the first name of Ronny and last name of Richardson into an external data queue, so QUEUE-5.CMD reads these and waits forever on the third line. (Again, press Ctrl–Break to abort.)

RANDOM.CMD

RANDOM.CMD is a demonstration program that shows how to use the Random function to draw a series of random numbers. By using a seed, the program also shows how to generate a sequence of random numbers at any time.

RC.CMD

OS/2 maintains a single byte of memory that batch files, programs, and REXX programs can save a number to in order to transfer information between them. About half the time the OS/2 documentation refers to this as the *errorlevel*, and the test in a batch file is IF ERRORLEVEL. The other half of the time, the OS/2 documentation refers to it as a *return code*. REXX takes the latter approach. Rather than testing the errorlevel value directly, REXX stores its value automatically in the variable RC. You can test this value or simply display its contents, as the program RC.CMD illustrates. RC.CMD tries to copy a file called ZZZZZZZZ.999 to the A: drive using XCOPY. Usually, this file won't exist, which will generate an errorlevel value that's displayed by RC.CMD.

REVERSE.CMD

REVERSE.CMD is a demonstration program that shows how to reverse character strings with the Reverse function.

REXX-1.CMD

REXX-1.CMD is a demonstration program that simply displays two lines of text on the screen.

REXX-2.CMD

REXX-2.CMD is a demonstration program that displays two lines of text on the screen. Unlike REXX-1.CMD, part of that text is stored inside a variable.

REXX-3.CMD

REXX-3.CMD is a demonstration program that stores two numbers in variables, adds those two numbers, and then displays the results.

REXX-4.CMD

REXX-4.CMD is a demonstration program that asks the user for his first and last name, individually, stores that information in variables, and then displays that information.

REXX-5.CMD

REXX-5.CMD is a demonstration program that asks the user for his first and last names together, stores that information to two variables by automatically splitting it, and then displays the results.

REXX-6.CMD

REXX-6.CMD is a demonstration program that asks the user for two numbers and then uses logic testing to tell the user whether or not the sum is over 20. The program doesn't perform any error checking to see if the user actually entered numbers. If the user responds with anything other than valid numbers, REXX will abort the program.

REXX-7.CMD

REXX-7.CMD is a demonstration program that gives the user a simple math test. First it asks the user for two numbers. Then it continually asks the user for the sum of those two numbers until the correct sum is entered. Like REXX-6.CMD, this program lacks error checking to make sure the user enters numbers for each step.

REXX-8.CMD

REXX-8.CMD is a demonstration program that replaces REXX-7.CMD. It works the same way, only it gives the user the option of entering STOP and exiting the math test loop.

REXX-9.CMD

REXX-9.CMD is a demonstration program that uses a loop to display a message 100 times.

REXX-10.CMD

REXX-10.CMD is a demonstration program that, like REXX-9.CMD, uses a loop to display a message 100 times. This program also displays a counter, counting from 1 to 100.

REXX-11.CMD

REXX-11.CMD is a demonstration program that gives a math test like REXX-7.CMD, only this program uses subroutines to get the information and give the test.

REXX-12.CMD

REXX-12.CMD is a demonstration program that, like REXX-10.CMD, counts to 100 on the screen, only this program uses a subroutine and passes it two parameters.

REXXECHO.CMD

REXXECHO.CMD is a demonstration program that shows how different commands are sent to OS/2 depending on the usage of quotation marks. Because / always causes a problem when it's outside of quotation marks, the messages use OS2 rather than OS/2.

RIGHT.CMD

RIGHT.CMD is a demonstration program that shows how to use the Right function.

SAMPLE.CMD

SAMPLE.CMD is a demonstration program that displays four lines of text on the screen.

SCREEN.CMD

SCREEN.CMD is a demonstration program that shows using the SysTextScreenRead function to read the contents of the screen and store it to a variable to allow the program to later restore the screen, and the SysTextScreenSize function to report the size of the screen.

SENDATA.CMD

SENDATA.CMD is a demonstration program that places data into an external queue named RONNY. This data is read by GETDATA.CMD. SENDATA.CMD can be run before GETDATA.CMD in the same session or a different session, or it can be run in a different session after GETDATA.CMD is running. GETDATA.CMD remains in an endless loop until SENDATA.CMD runs.

SENDATA2.CMD

SENDATA2.CMD is a demonstration program that uses an external data queue to transfer a large volume of data from an external subroutine to the calling program. SENDATA2.CMD calls itself as an external subroutine. SENDATA2.CMD is explained in detail in appendix A.

SHOW-POS.CMD

SHOW-POS.CMD is a demonstration program that uses the SysCurPos external function to report the current position of the cursor.

SHOWCAP.CMD

SHOWCAP.CMD is a demonstration that asks the user for the same string twice, only with different capitalization. It then converts the two strings to uppercase before comparing them.

SHOWRX.CMD

SHOWRX.CMD is a demonstration program that shows how to use the RxFuncAdd, RxFuncQuery, and RxFuncDrop functions in a program.

SHOWSAY.CMD

SHOWSAY.CMD is a demonstration program that displays a series of text lines on the screen with the SAY instruction to show how text scrolls off the screen once it reaches the bottom of the screen.

SHOWSORT.CMD

SHOWSORT.CMD is a demonstration program that illustrates a simple sorting algorithm in REXX. It sorts ten-digit character strings from right to left, one column at a time.

SHOWTEMP.CMD

SHOWTEMP.CMD is a demonstration program that shows the various forms of templates that can be used with the PARSE instruction to control how strings are parsed.

SIGN.CMD

SIGN.CMD is a demonstration program that uses the Sign internal function to return the sign of a series of random numbers.

SLEEP.CMD

SLEEP.CMD is an external subroutine designed to be called by other programs. It pauses execution for the number of seconds specified when it's called. The syntax to call the program is:

```
CALL SLEEP seconds
```

where *seconds* is the number of seconds to pause execution. SLEEP.CMD calls ISITANUM.CMD to perform limited error checking for it.

SOURCE.CMD

SOURCE.CMD is a demonstration program that shows how to use the SourceLine function to print out lines of the current program.

SPACE.CMD

SPACE.CMD is a demonstration program that shows how to use the Space function to pad words with a fixed number of spaces.

SPAUSE.CMD

SPAUSE.CMD is an external demonstration subroutine designed to pause the screen. The syntax is:

```
SPAUSE [message, row, column, clsbefore, clsafter]
```

where *message* is the message to display while the program is pausing. The default message if none is entered is "Press Any Key To Continue . . . ." *Row* is the row number to position the cursor on, and *column* is the column number to position the cursor on. If the row and column arguments are both left blank, the cursor is left in its current position.

Clsbefore is a flag to indicate if the screen should be cleared before displaying the message and pausing the program. Valid inputs are Yes and No. Capitalization doesn't matter. The screen should be cleared if the cursor is being positioned, but the routine doesn't enforce this. *Clsafter* is a flag to indicate if the screen should be cleared after the pausing and just before control is returned to the calling program. Valid inputs are Yes and No. Capitalization doesn't matter.

SPAUSE.CMD is a well-designed external subroutine that performs extensive error checking to make sure only valid parameters are supplied to the subroutine.

SPELDISK.CMD

SPELDISK.CMD is a spelling test program. It reads the words you enter in a disk file into memory and constructs a dictionary. As written, that file is C:\TODO\SPELWORD.TXT, but that can easily be changed. It uses that dictionary to display randomly selected words on the screen for one second. It then asks you to enter the spelling of the word. Once you correctly spell the word, it selects another word and continues. If you can't successfully spell the word, SPELDISK.CMD has an option that lets you view the word again.

SPELDISK.CMD keeps track of your score and displays the results when you quit the program. SPELDISK.CMD is an excellent way for readers with children to give them spelling tests.

SPELLING.CMD

SPELLING.CMD is a modified version of SPELDISK.CMD that has the words built into the program rather than stored in a separate file. That makes it easier to transport the program but harder to add and delete words. When adding or deleting words, you must remember to update the counter variable. A detailed, line-by-line explanation of the code in SPELLING.CMD is shown in appendix A.

STEM.CMD

STEM.CMD is a demonstration program that illustrates the use of complex stem variables in programs. It first prompts you for five first names and stores these in the stem variable Name.First.I, where I takes on values 1–5. For each first name, it then prompts you for the last name and age and stores these in the stem variables

Name.Last.I and Name.Age.I, respectively. It then issues a report showing the full name and age of each person on a separate line.

While this demonstration program makes no further use of the data, an operational program could then write the data to a disk file as part of a database. The next time you run the program, it could read this data from the disk and allow you to add to it, alter it, or create reports based on it, thus forming the basis of a REXX database system.

STRCONVT.CMD

STRCONVT.CMD is a demonstration program that performs and displays a number of string format conversions.

STRINGBK.CMD

STRINGBK.CMD is a demonstration program that returns one of 11 different sayings, depending on what argument is passed to it. It demonstrates how a string can be returned from an external subroutine.

STRINGDO.CMD

STRINGDO.CMD is a demonstration program that calls STRINGBK.CMD in a randomly generated argument to show how a string returned by an external subroutine can be used.

STRIP.CMD

STRIP.CMD is a demonstration program that shows how to use the Strip function to remove leading, trailing, or both sets of spaces or a single other character.

SUBSTR.CMD

SUBSTR.CMD is a demonstration program that shows how to use the SubStr function in a program to return portions of a character string or number.

SUBWORD.CMD

SUBWORD.CMD is a demonstration program that shows how to use the SubWord function in a program to return words from a character string.

SYMBOL.CMD

SYMBOL.CMD is a demonstration program that shows how to use the Symbol function in a program to return the status of a symbol.

TEMPLATE.CMD

TEMPLATE.CMD is a template file that contains spaces for the information that I enter at the top of each REXX program and a template of the help section I use in each REXX program.

THETIME.CMD

TIME.CMD is a demonstration program that shows how to use the Time function in a program to display the time in different fashions.

TODO.CMD

TODO.CMD is a simple to-do program. The items and associated priorities you enter are stored in a disk file. TODO.CMD allows you to enter new items, interactively edit existing items, delete items, and send finished items to a done file. The data is automatically sorted when it's saved. A detailed, line-by-line explanation of the code in TODO.CMD is shown in appendix A.

TRACE-1.CMD

TRACE-1.CMD is a demonstration program that runs through a series of calculations three times, once with each of the passive tracing modes.

TRACE-2.CMD

TRACE-2.CMD is a demonstration program that runs through the same calculations as TRACE-1.CMD once using the tracing mode specified on the command line. It lacks error checking for the user input, so it's up to the user to make a valid input.

TRUNC.CMD

TRUNC.CMD is a demonstration program that shows how to use the Trunc function in a program to round numbers.

TYPING.CMD

TYPING.CMD is a typing drill program. Sixty randomly selected characters are displayed on the screen. The cursor is then placed below that line for the user to type in the same line. Once the user presses Return, the program compares the two lines and marks any positions where the user made a typing mistake. It then displays another line. TYPING.CMD keeps score and displays the results when the user exits the program. A detailed, line-by-line explanation of the code in TYPING.CMD is shown in appendix A.

VALUE.CMD

VALUE.CMD is a demonstration program that shows how to use the Value function to read and alter both the value of REXX variables and OS/2 environmental variables.

VERIFIED.CMD

VERIFIED.CMD is a demonstration program that shows how to use the Verify function to test and see if one string has all its characters contained in a second string.

WORDS.CMD

WORDS.CMD is a demonstration program that shows how to use several word-related functions in a program. The Word function returns a single word from a string. The WordIndex function returns the starting character position for a specified word. The WordLength function finds the length of specified words. The WordPos function specifies the starting position of a specific word. Finally, the Words function returns the number of words in a string.

XRANGE.CMD

XRANGE.CMD is a demonstration program that shows how to use the XRange function to return all the characters between two characters.

YESORNO.CMD

YESORNO.CMD is a batch file utility that prompts the user for a Yes or No response and waits until a correct response is entered. The response is returned to the batch file via a return code, where Yes is a zero and No is a one. This is very useful for asking questions in a batch file.

Programs from Others

These programs are ones I collected to give you additional programming examples. In all cases, I obtained the appropriate permission to include the programs on the disk. These programs are stored in the \OTHERS subdirectory on the disk that comes with this book.

Including example programs from other authors lets you see more programs than I could write by myself. I'm convinced that the more programs you have to look at and refer back to when you get stuck, the easier you'll find learning to use REXX—or any language for that matter. As an additional bonus, I think it helps for you to see different programming styles and different approaches to solving programming problems.

BACKCONF.CMD

BACKCONF.CMD was written by Gary Murphy of Hilbert Computing. It checks the CONFIG.SYS on your boot drive. If it has been modified, it makes a backup copy under a name like CONFIG.282. The extension is determined by the Julian date, so multiple backups on the same date will overwrite one another. BACKCONF.CMD has the following line in it:

```
call SysFileTree BootDrive'\CONFIG.SYS', 'Found', 'F', '+****', '-****'
```

and the '-****' mask is supposed to turn off the archive bit for the files that match. However, there was a bug in the RexxUtil DDL that shipped with OS/2 version 2.0

that prevented the archive bit from being turned off. For that reason, the program has this second line:

```
'@attrib -A' BootDrive'\CONFIG.SYS'
```

to make sure the archive bit is turned off.

CHKCONF.CMD

CHKCONF.CMD reads in your CONFIG.SYS file and verifies as much of the file as it can. It actually does a very good job of checking it. It only checks the file and makes suggestions to you. No modifications are made, so you can safely run it any time.

EAPREP.CMD

EAPREP.CMD was written by Mercer H. Harz. It creates command files for you to execute before backing up in order to create a copy of the extended attributes that DOS can copy and, after running a restore, use to reattach the extended attributes. This is useful if you need to make a backup during a DOS session. The command files produced by EAPREP.CMD make use of the EAUTIL.EXE OS/2 utility to create the command files. The syntax is:

```
EAPREP drive dir
```

where *drive* specifies the drive to process and *dir* specifies the name of the subdirectory in which to store the extended attribute files. EAPREP.CMD produces two files: x_BKP.CMD to prepare the extended attributes for backup and x_RST.CMD to reinstall them after a restore, where x is the drive letter being processed.

In order to make sure that all the files are backed up in an up-to-date fashion, you should run EAPREP.CMD just before performing a backup. EAPREP.CMD doesn't back up and restore the workplace shell desktop, even though some of its information is stored in extended attributes.

REXX has no native function to determine if a file has extended attributes. To overcome this, EAPREP.CMD simply checks every file for a nonzero entry in the extended attributes file. For each nonzero entry it finds, it adds an associated entry in the back up and restore command files. EAPREP.CMD processes each file it finds; no selective processing is available. Any files currently being used by OS/2 will generate an error message during this process.

Extended attributes take up a lot of space. EAPREP.CMD makes a second copy of the extended attributes for backup/restore purposes while maintaining the original undisturbed copy for use by OS/2. Since two copies of the extended attributes exist after running EAPREP.CMD, a lot of hard disk space is used. Users who are hard-disk constrained won't be able to use EAPREP.CMD. If you're concerned, run CHKDSK.EXE to find out how much extended attribute space your system has and then make sure you have that much free space plus a little extra.

MKCMD.CMD

MKCMD.CMD was written by Gary Murphy of Hilbert Computing. It automates batch file creation. The syntax is:

```
MKCMD filespec [before after]
```

where *filespec* is the file specification for MKCMD.CMD to use, *before* is the optional command to enter before each file (it's limited to a single word), and *after* is the optional command to enter after each file.

MKCMD.CMD loops through each of the files in the current subdirectory that match *filespec*, expanding the filename as it goes to its full name with the drive and subdirectory. It appends the before command before the filename and the After command after the filename. Notice that the arguments aren't separated by commas.

Output is sent to the screen so you can review the operation of MKCMD.CMD before creating a batch file with it. Once you're satisfied, you can pipe the results to a batch file. If you started MKCMD.CMD with the command:

```
MKCMD *.CMD COPY A: /V
```

then your output might look like this:

```
COPY F:\OTHERS\BACKCONF.CMD A: /V
COPY F:\OTHERS\CHKCONF.CMD A: /V
COPY F:\OTHERS\MKCMD.CMD A: /V
COPY F:\OTHERS\PARSEOPT.CMD A: /V
COPY F:\OTHERS\PATHLIST.CMD A: /V
COPY F:\OTHERS\SPACE.CMD A: /V
COPY F:\OTHERS\WHICH.CMD A: /V
```

Of course, the specific files that appear in your list will depend on the files in the current subdirectory matching the filespec file specification. You'll see the following lines in MKCMD.CMD:

```
do j = 1 to Found.0
   say Before Found.j After
end
```

The Found.0 variable contains the number of files found that match the wildcard specified on the command line. When none match, this first line becomes:

```
do j = 1 to 0
```

which would generate an error, except REXX allows the lower bound to exceed the upper bound. When that happens, it simply skips the loop.

PARSEOPT.CMD

PARSEOPT.CMD was written by Gary Murphy of Hilbert Computing. It's a demonstration program that shows how to parse the command line into multiple parameters. The PARSEOPT.CMD routine was written to allow the command line to be separated into positional parameters and command-line flags. PARSEOPT.CMD also converts some of the arguments passed to it on the command line when they're symbols like $ or *. The command to run PARSEOPT.CMD is:

```
PARSEOPT anything
```

where *anything* is any command line you want parsed. PARSEOPT.CMD has two lines you might wonder about at first. Near the top of the program, you'll see the line:

```
parse arg arguments
```

You'll also see an identical line near the top of the ParseOptions procedure, which might cause you to wonder why the program needs the same command twice. REXX provides the ability for procedure scoping. The main routine has an implicit initial scope. The argument string that's given to that procedure are the arguments on the command line. If you follow a REXX label with the keyword Procedure, then there's a new variable scope created. The scope means that the procedure can see no variables in the caller's scope except those listed after the Expose keyword. The first Parse line gets the string from the command line for the main routine. Since this isn't exposed by ParseOptions, that procedure must reread the command-line arguments, thus the second Parse line.

PATHLIST.CMD

PATHLIST.CMD was written by Gary Murphy of Hilbert Computing. It lists the subdirectories in your path in a very readable format. The syntax is:

```
PATHLIST [searchpath]
```

where *searchpath* is a path list. If omitted, it defaults to PATH, but it can handle DPATH, HELP, BOOKSHELF, and so on.

PREPROC.CMD

PREPROC.CMD was written by Gary Murphy of Hilbert Computing. This program will parse a source file for #include and #define statements, and resolve them in a manner similar to the preprocessor found in many C compilers. The support is simple string substitution, which won't handle macro expansion. Those included files surrounded by double quotation marks (") must be in the current directory, and the filename must include the extension. Those with angle brackets (<,>) must be the subdirectory found in the INCLUDE environment variable. The syntax is:

```
PREPROC infile outfile
```

where *infile* is the name of the file to process and *outfile* is the name of the file to receive the results. For example, the following line:

```
#INCLUDE "TODO.CMD"
```

would cause the TODO.CMD file to be read in and replace this line in the outfile. The original infile is not modified. For this to work, TODO.CMD must be in the current subdirectory. The following line:

```
#INCLUDE <TODO.CMD>
```

would cause this line to be replaced in the outfile by the TODO.CMD file located in the subdirectory specified in the Include environmental variable. Finally, the line:

```
#DEFINE X1 CurrentMarketPrice
```

would cause each occurrence of the character string X1 in the InFile to be replaced by the character string CurrentMarketPrice in the OutFile.

If you write a set of external subroutines that you tend to include in different programs as you write them, PREPROC.CMD can save you a lot of time you'd spend cutting and pasting. It also allows you to assign short variable names in the program and expand them to more meaningful names later.

RCD.CMD

RCD.CMD is a program by Robert D. Reynolds to quickly change subdirectories. Rather than entering the entire path to a given subdirectory, RCD.CMD allows you to enter just the first couple of characters of the subdirectory name or even a few characters out of the middle of the name. The syntax is:

```
RCD [-r] [-s] dirname
```

where -r is an optional switch that tells RCD.CMD to reread the directory structure. This is required after subdirectories are added or deleted. The subdirectory structure is stored in a database called RCD.DB that's stored as a hidden file in the root directory of the current drive. The optional -s switch tells RCD.CMD to match the characters in *dirname* to any characters in the subdirectory name and not just the starting characters. *Dirname* stands for the characters to match in the subdirectory. For example, the command:

```
RCD MY
```

on my D: drive causes OS/2 to change to the D:\BOOK12\DISK\MYSAMPLE subdirectory. As you can see, entering RCD MY is much shorter and quicker than entering CD\BOOK12\DISK\MYSAMPLE on the command line.

Anyone using the command line of OS/2 will find RCD.CMD very useful even if they never do any REXX programming. RCD.CMD is freeware, so you can modify it and pass copies on to friends. The author asks that you write him with any improvements you make to the program. His address is given in RCD.TXT, which you'll also find on the disk that comes with this book. Anyone passing along copies of RCD.CMD should include RCD.TXT.

RXSUMRY.CMD

RXSUMRY.CMD was written by Gary Murphy of Hilbert Computing. It's an excellent program for tracking your REXX programs and OS/2 batch files. In order for RX-SUMRY.CMD to work properly, you must construct your REXX programs and OS/2 batch files in a certain manner. For your REXX programs, I recommend you begin each program with something like the following:

```
/* NAME:
   PURPOSE:
   VERSION:
   DATE:
   COPYRIGHT: */
HelpCheck = ARG(1)
  IF HelpCheck = "/?" THEN
    DO
      SAY ""
      EXIT
    END
```

You'll notice that most of the batch files that come with this book start in this fashion. For batch files, I recommend you begin each one with the following:

```
@ECHO OFF
REM NAME:
REM PURPOSE:
REM VERSION:
REM DATE:
IF (%1)==(?)  GOTO HELP
IF (%1)==(/?) GOTO HELP
IF (%1)==(/h) GOTO HELP
IF (%1)==(/H) GOTO HELP
```

RXSUMRY.CMD uses this information to find the file you're looking for. Enter RX-SUMRY.CMD by itself on the command line and it will display the name of every .CMD file along with all the text following the PURPOSE: line. If you have a lot of files, you can narrow the search by entering a word or two that you know is on that line of the files you're looking for on the command line after the program name, and it will display only those filenames and lines containing the word or words you entered.

RXTIME.CMD

RXTIME.CMD is a program by Jerry am Ende that will dial the Naval Observatory and set the system clock to their time. It isn't precisely accurate in that it doesn't take into account the time lag associated with sending the time over the telephone time. That is, it assumes the time that arrives via the modem is accurate without any delays. It should set the system clock to within a second of Naval Observatory time. RXTIME.CMD is an excellent example of using the SIGNAL ON instruction in a program and using a REXX program to control the COM port.

SPACE.CMD

SPACE.CMD is a program by Gary Murphy of Hilbert Computing that lists the space used by each subdirectory on all your local drives. To run it, simply enter its name on the command line. The report is displayed on the screen and scrolls by fairly fast. If you want a more permanent record, you can easily pipe it to a file or the printer. Depending on the speed of your computer and size of your hard disk, SPACE.CMD can take several seconds to several minutes to generate its report, so don't get impatient if you don't see output right away.

WHICH.CMD

WHICH.CMD is a program by Gary Murphy of Hilbert Computing to search your path to find a program or batch file. You start the program with the command:

```
WHICH filename[.extension]
```

where *filename* is the name of the file to search for (wildcards aren't supported) and *extension* is the optional extension. The extensions allowed are .COM, .EXE, .BAT, and .CMD. If you don't specify an extension, it searches for all of them.

Error no.	Error text	Explanation	Correction
REX0001	***File Table full***	There are currently too many files open for this session.	Close files that are open but no longer in use.
REX0003	***Program is unreadable***	An attempt was made to access a program that was either nonexistent or locked by another process.	Verify file's existence and make sure no other process has it locked.
REX0004	***Program interrupted****	The system interrupted execution of a program because of some error, or by user request.	Trap interrupts via CALL ON HALT or SIGNAL ON HALT.
REX0005	***Machine resources exhausted***	While attempting to execute a program, the language processor was unable to obtain the resources it needed to continue execution.	Close other sessions.
REX0006	***Unmatched /* or quote***	A comment or literal string was started but never finished. This can be detected at the end of the program (or the end of data in an INTERPRET instruction) for comments, or at the end of a line for strings.	Add the closing symbol.
REX0007	***WHEN or OTHERWISE expected****	Within a SELECT construct, at least one WHEN construct (and possibly an OTHERWISE clause) is expected.	Look for any instruction other than WHEN (or no WHEN construct before the OTHERWISE) in the SELECT construct.
REX0008	***Unexpected THEN or ELSE***	A THEN or an ELSE has been found that does not match a corresponding IF (or WHEN) clause.	Look for a missing END or DO...END in the THEN part of a complex IF... THEN...ELSE construction.
REX0009	***Unexpected WHEN or OTHERWISE***	A WHEN or an OTHERWISE has been found outside of a SELECT construct. It might have been	Correct program logic.

Error no.	Error text	Explanation	Correction
		enclosed unintentionally in a DO...END construct by the user leaving off an END instruction, or an attempt might have been made to branch to it with a SIGNAL instruction.	
REX0010	***Unexpected or unmatched END***	There are more ENDs in the program than DOs and SELECTs, or the ENDs are wrongly placed so they do not match DOs and SELECTs. This error will also be generated if an END immediately follows a THEN or an ELSE.	Try using TRACE Scan to show the structure of the program and hence make it more obvious where the error is. Putting the name of the control variable on ENDs that close repetitive loops can also help locate this kind of error. A common mistake that causes this error is attempting to jump into the middle of a loop using the SIGNAL instruction. Since the previous DO will not have been executed, the END is unexpected. Also, since SIGNAL deactivates any current loops, it cannot be used to jump from one place inside a loop to another.
REX0011	***Control stack full***	An interpreter limit of levels of nesting of control structures (DO...END, IF...THEN...ELSE, etc.) has been exceeded. This could be due to a looping INTERPRET instruction, which could loop forever. Similarly, a recursive subroutine or internal function that does not terminate correctly could loop forever.	Correct program logic.
REX0012	***Clause too long***	The length of the internal or external representation of a clause has exceeded the interpreter's limit.	Shorten the clause.
REX0013	***Invalid character in program***	The program includes a character outside of a literal (quoted) string that is not a blank or one of the valid alphanumeric/special characters.	Remove the invalid character.
REX0014	***Incomplete DO/SELECT/ IF***	On reaching the end of the program (or end of the string in an INTERPRET instruction), it has been detected that there is a DO or SELECT without a matching END, or an IF that is not followed by a THEN clause to execute.	It may be helpful to use TRACE Scan to show the structure of the program and hence make it more obvious where the missing END should be. Putting the name of the control variable on ENDs that close repetitive loops can also help locate this kind of error.
REX0015	***Invalid hexadecimal or binary string***	Hexadecimal strings cannot have leading or trailing blanks, and can have embedded blanks only at byte boundaries. Only digits 0–9 and the letters a–f and A–F	Use the explicit concatenation operator, ‖, in situations where the X or B is intended to represent a variable.

Error no.	Error text	Explanation	Correction
		are allowed. Similarly, binary strings can have blanks added only at the boundaries of groups of four binary digits, and only the digits 0 and 1 are allowed. This error can also be caused by following a literal string by the one-character symbol X (for example the name of the variable X) when the string is not intended to be taken as a hexadecimal specification, or by the symbol B when the string is not intended to be taken as a binary specification.	
REX0016	***Label not found***	A SIGNAL instruction has been executed (or an event for which a trap was set has occurred), and the label specified cannot be found in the program.	Add the appropriate label.
REX0017	***Unexpected PROCEDURE***	A PROCEDURE instruction was encountered which was not the first instruction executed after a CALL or function invocation.	Check for the possibility of "dropping through" into an internal routine rather than invoking it properly.
REX0018	***THEN expected***	All IF clauses and WHEN clauses in REXX must be followed by a THEN clause. Some other clause was found when a THEN was expected.	Add the THEN clause.
REX0019	***String or symbol expected***	Following either the keyword CALL or the sequence SIGNAL ON or SIGNAL OFF, a literal string or a symbol was expected but neither was found.	Add the appropriate literal string or symbol.
REX0020	***Symbol expected***	In the clauses CALL ON, END, ITERATE, LEAVE, NUMERIC, PARSE, PROCEDURE, and SIGNAL ON, a symbol can be expected. Either it was not present when required, or some other token was found. Alternatively, DROP and the EXPOSE option of PROCEDURE expect a list of symbols. Some other token was found.	Add the appropriate symbol.
REX0021	***Invalid data on end of clause***	A clause such as SELECT or NOP is followed by some token other than a comment.	Remove the invalid data.
REX0022	***Invalid character string***	This error results if a literal string contains character codes that are not valid in the interpreter. This might be because some characters are "impossible," or because the character	Correct the character string.

Error no.	Error text	Explanation	Correction
		set is extended in some way and certain character combinations are not allowed.	
REX0023	***Invalid data string***	This error results if a data string (result of an expression, etc.) contains character codes that are not valid in the interpreter. This might be because some characters are "impossible," or because the character set is extended in some way and certain character combinations are not allowed.	Correct the data string.
REX0024	***Invalid TRACE request***	The setting specified on a TRACE instruction starts with a character that does not match one of the valid TRACE settings (i.e., A, C, E, F, I, L, N, O, R, or S). This error is also raised if an attempt is made to request TRACE Scan when inside any kind of control construct.	Change to a valid TRACE setting.
REX0025	***Invalid subkeyword found***	An expected token has been found in the position in an instruction where a particular subkeyword was expected. For example, in a NUMERIC instruction, the second token must be DIGITS, FUZZ, or FORM, and anything else is an error.	Correct the subkeyword.
REX0026	***Invalid whole number***	One of the following did not evaluate to a whole number: the positional patterns in parsing templates, the power value (right-hand operand) of the power operator, the values in a DO instruction after the FOR modifier, the values given for DIGITS or FUZZ in the NUMERIC instruction, and the number used in the TRACE setting. This error is also raised if the value is not permitted (for example, a negative repetition count in a DO instruction), or when the division performed during an integer divide or remainder operation does not result in a whole number.	Correct to a whole number.
REX0027	***Invalid DO syntax***	Some syntax error has been found in the DO instruction. This might be by using BY, TO, or FOR twice, or using BY, TO, or FOR when there is no control variable specified, etc.	Correct program logic.

Error no.	Error text	Explanation	Correction
REX0028	***Invalid LEAVE or ITERATE***	A LEAVE or ITERATE instruction was encountered in an invalid position. Either no loop is active, or the name specified on the instruction does not match the control variable of any active loop. Note that since internal routines and the INTERPRET instruction protect DO loops, they become inactive, and therefore a LEAVE in a subroutine cannot affect a DO loop in the calling routine. A common cause for this error message is attempting to use the SIGNAL instruction to transfer control within or into a loop. Since SIGNAL terminates all active loops, an ITERATE or LEAVE would then be in error.	Correct program logic.
REX0029	***Environment name too long***	The environment name specified by the ADDRESS instruction is longer than permitted for the system under which the interpreter is executing.	Correct the environment name.
REX0030	***Name or string too long***	A variable name or a label name (or the length of a literal string) has exceeded the interpreter's limit.	Shorten the variable or label name.
REX0031	***Name starts with number or period ***	A value cannot be assigned to a variable whose name starts with a numeric digit or a period (since if it were permitted you could redefine numeric constants).	Correct the variable name.
REX0033	***Invalid expression result***	The result of an expression in an instruction was found to be invalid in the particular context in which it was used.	Check for an illegal FUZZ or DIGITS value in a NUMERIC instruction (FUZZ cannot become larger than DIGITS).
REX0034	***Logical value not 0 or 1***	The expression in an IF, WHEN, DO WHILE, or DO UNTIL phrase must result in a 0 or a 1, as must any term operated on by a logical operator.	Correct program logic.
REX0035	***Invalid expression***	This is due to a grammatical error in an expression, such as ending it with an operator or having two operators adjacent with nothing in between. It might also be due to an expression that is missing when one is required.	Check for special characters (such as operators) in an intended character expression that are not enclosed in quotes.
REX0036	***Unmatched (in expression***	This is due to not pairing parentheses correctly within an expres-	Add the appropriate parentheses.

Error no.	Error text	Explanation	Correction
		sion. There are more left parentheses than right parentheses.	
REX0037	***Unexpected , or)***	Either a comma has been found outside a function invocation, or there are too many right parentheses in an expression.	Remove the extra comma or add the appropriate parentheses.
REX0038	***Invalid template or pattern***	Within a parsing template, a special character that is not allowed (for example, %) has been found, or the syntax of a variable pattern is incorrect (i.e., no symbol was found after a left parenthesis). This error can also be raised if the WITH subkeyword is omitted in a PARSE VALUE instruction.	Correct the template.
REX0039	***Evaluation stack overflow***	The expression is too complex to be evaluated by the language processor.	Check for too many nested parentheses, functions, etc.
REX0040	***Incorrect call to routine***	The specified built-in or external routine does exist, but it has been used incorrectly. Either invalid arguments were passed to the routine, the program invoked was not compatible with the language processor, or more than an implementation-limited number of arguments were passed to the routine.	Correct program logic.
REX0041	***Bad arithmetic conversion***	One of the terms involved in an arithmetic operation is not a valid number, or its exponent exceeds the implementation limit (often 9 digits).	Correct the number.
REX0042	***Arithmetic overflow/ underflow***	The result of an arithmetic operation requires an exponent that is outside the range supported by the interpreter. This can happen during evaluation of an expression (commonly an attempt to divide a number by 0), or possibly during the stepping of a DO loop control variable.	Correct the mathematics.
REX0043	***Routine not found***	A function has been invoked within an expression (or a subroutine has been invoked by a CALL), but it cannot be found. No label with the specified name exists in the program, it is not the name of a built-in function, and the language processor has been unable to locate it externally.	Check for: a mistyped label or name, or a symbol or literal string adjacent to a (when it should have been separated by a blank or some other operator (this would be understood as a function invocation).

Error no.	Error text	Explanation	Correction
REX0044	***Function did not return data***	An external function has been invoked within an expression, but even though it appeared to end without error, it did not return data for use within the expression.	Correct the external data.
REX0045	***No data specified on function RETURN***	The program has been called as a function, but an attempt is being made (by RETURN) to return without passing back any data. Similarly, if an internal routine is called as a function, then the RETURN instruction that ends it must specify an expression.	Correct program logic.
REX0046	***Invalid variable reference***	Within a DROP, PARSE, or PROCEDURE instruction, the syntax of a variable reference is incorrect. This might be due to a missing parenthesis or an incorrectly coded variable within the parentheses.	Correct the variable reference.
REX0047	***Unexpected label***	A label appeared as part of the instructions executed by an INTERPRET instruction.	Remove the label from the interpreted data.
REX0048	***Failure in system service***	A system service used by the language processor (such as stream input or output, or manipulation of an external data queue) has failed to work correctly and hence normal execution cannot continue.	Restart OS/2.
REX0049	***Interpretation error***	Some kind of severe error has been detected within the language processor or execution process during internal self-consistency checks.	Restart OS/2. If that does not correct the problem, contact IBM technical support.
REX0102	January	Displays The Month of January.	Serves no useful purpose.
REX0103	February	Displays The Month of February.	Serves no useful purpose.
REX0104	March	Displays The Month of March.	Serves no useful purpose.
REX0105	April	Displays The Month of April.	Serves no useful purpose.
REX0106	May	Displays The Month of May.	Serves no useful purpose.
REX0107	June	Displays The Month of June.	Serves no useful purpose.
REX0108	July	Displays The Month of July.	Serves no useful purpose.
REX0109	August	Displays The Month of August.	Serves no useful purpose.
REX0110	September	Displays The Month of September.	Serves no useful purpose.
REX0111	October	Displays The Month of October.	Serves no useful purpose.
REX0112	November	Displays The Month of November.	Serves no useful purpose.
REX0113	December	Displays The Month of December.	Serves no useful purpose.

Error no.	Error text	Explanation	Correction
REX0114	***Interactive trace. Trace Off to end debug, ENTER to Continue.***	Information message.	No correction needed.
REX0115	The RXSUBCOM parameters are incorrect.	RXSUBCOM accepts the following parameters: To register a subcommand environment RXSUBCOM REGISTER ENVIRONMENT_NAME DLL_NAME ENTRY_POINT To query a specific subcommand environment for existence RXSUBCOM QUERY [ENVIRONMENT_NAME [DLL_NAME]] To drop a subcommand environment handler RXSUBCOM DROP ENVIRONMENT_NAME [DLL_NAME] To load a subcommand environment from disk RXSUBCOM LOAD ENVIRONMENT_NAME [DLL_NAME]	Check the RXSUBCOM parameters and retry the command.
REX0116	The RXSUBCOM parameter REGISTER is incorrect.	RXSUBCOM REGISTER requires all of the following parameters: RXSUBCOM REGISTER ENVIRONMENT_NAME DLL_NAME ENTRY_POINT ENVIRONMENT_NAME is the name of the subcommand environment. DLL_NAME is the Dynalink Module name. ENTRY_POINT is the name of the function to be executed when called.	Check the RXSUBCOM parameters and retry the command.
REX0117	The RXSUBCOM parameter DROP is incorrect.	RXSUBCOM DROP requires the environment name be specified. RXSUBCOM DROP ENVIRONMENT_NAME [DLL_NAME] ENVIRONMENT_NAME is the name of the subcommand environment. DLL_NAME is the Dynalink Module name (optional).	Check the RXSUBCOM parameters and retry the command.

Error no.	Error text	Explanation	Correction
REX0118	The RXSUBCOM parameter LOAD is incorrect.	RXSUBCOM LOAD requires the environment name be specified. RXSUBCOM LOAD ENVIRONMENT_NAME [DLL_NAME] ENVIRONMENT_NAME is the name of the subcommand environment. DLL_NAME is the Dynalink Module name (optional).	Check the RXSUBCOM parameters and retry the command.
REX0119	The REXX queuing system is not initialized.	The REXX queuing system is not initialized. The queuing system requires a housekeeping program to run. This program usually runs under the Presentation Manager shell. The program is not running.	Report this message to your IBM service representative.
REX0120	The size of the data is incorrect.	The data supplied to the RXQUEUE command is too long. The RXQUEUE.EXE program accepts data records containing 0 - 65472 bytes. A record exceeded the allowable limits.	Use shorter data records.
REX0121	Storage for data queues is exhausted.	The queuing system is out of memory. No more storage is available to store queued data.	Delete some queues or remove queued data from the system. Then retry your request.
REX0122	The name *** is not a valid queue name.	The queue name contains an invalid character. Only the following characters can appear in queue names: A-Z, 0-9, ., !, ?, and _.	Change the queue name and retry the command.
REX0123	The queue access mode is not correct.	An internal error occured in RXQUEUE. RXQUEUE.EXE tried to access a queue with an incorrect access mode. Correct access modes are LIFO and FIFO.	Report this message to your IBM service representative.
REX0124	The queue *** does not exist.	The command attempted to access a nonexistent queue.	Create the queue and try again, or use a queue that has been created.
REX0125	The RXSUBCOM parameter QUERY is incorrect.	RXSUBCOM QUERY requires the environment name be specified. RXSUBCOM QUERY ENVIRONMENT_NAME [DLL_NAME] ENVIRONMENT_NAME is the name of the subcommand environment. DLL_NAME is the Dynalink Module name (optional).	Check the RXSUBCOM parameters and retry the command.

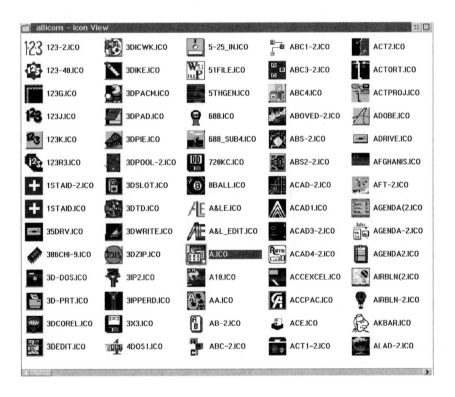

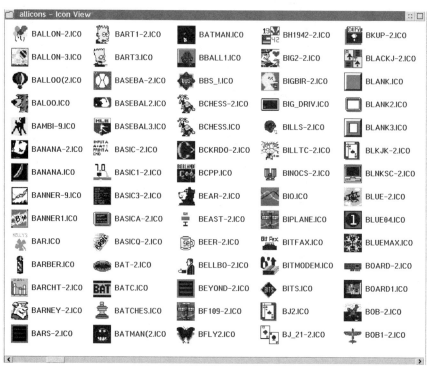

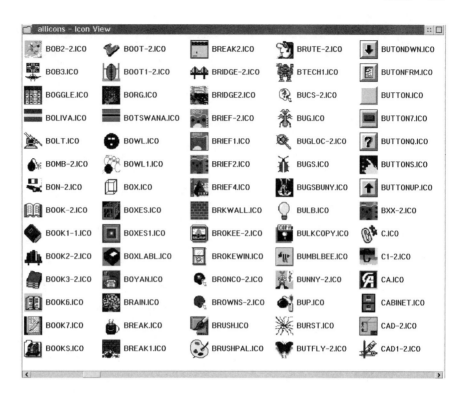

allicons - Icon View

BOB2-2.ICO	BOOT-2.ICO	BREAK2.ICO	BRUTE-2.ICO	BUTONDWN.ICO
BOB3.ICO	BOOT1-2.ICO	BRIDGE-2.ICO	BTECH1.ICO	BUTONFRM.ICO
BOGGLE.ICO	BORG.ICO	BRIDGE2.ICO	BUCS-2.ICO	BUTTON.ICO
BOLIVA.ICO	BOTSWANA.ICO	BRIEF-2.ICO	BUG.ICO	BUTTON7.ICO
BOLT.ICO	BOWL.ICO	BRIEF1.ICO	BUGLOC-2.ICO	BUTTONQ.ICO
BOMB-2.ICO	BOWL1.ICO	BRIEF2.ICO	BUGS.ICO	BUTTONS.ICO
BON-2.ICO	BOX.ICO	BRIEF4.ICO	BUGSBUNY.ICO	BUTTONUP.ICO
BOOK-2.ICO	BOXES.ICO	BRKWALL.ICO	BULB.ICO	BXX-2.ICO
BOOK1-1.ICO	BOXES1.ICO	BROKEE-2.ICO	BULKCOPY.ICO	C.ICO
BOOK2-2.ICO	BOXLABL.ICO	BROKEWIN.ICO	BUMBLBEE.ICO	C1-2.ICO
BOOK3-2.ICO	BOYAN.ICO	BRONCO-2.ICO	BUNNY-2.ICO	CA.ICO
BOOK6.ICO	BRAIN.ICO	BROWNS-2.ICO	BUP.ICO	CABINET.ICO
BOOK7.ICO	BREAK.ICO	BRUSH.ICO	BURST.ICO	CAD-2.ICO
BOOKS.ICO	BREAK1.ICO	BRUSHPAL.ICO	BUTFLY-2.ICO	CAD1-2.ICO

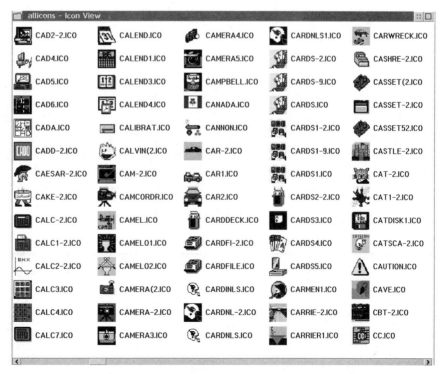

allicons - Icon View

CAD2-2.ICO	CALEND.ICO	CAMERA4.ICO	CARDNLS1.ICO	CARWRECK.ICO
CAD4.ICO	CALEND1.ICO	CAMERA5.ICO	CARDS-2.ICO	CASHRE-2.ICO
CAD5.ICO	CALEND3.ICO	CAMPBELL.ICO	CARDS-9.ICO	CASSET(2.ICO
CAD6.ICO	CALEND4.ICO	CANADA.ICO	CARDS.ICO	CASSET-2.ICO
CADA.ICO	CALIBRAT.ICO	CANNON.ICO	CARDS1-2.ICO	CASSET52.ICO
CADD-2.ICO	CALVIN(2.ICO	CAR-2.ICO	CARDS1-9.ICO	CASTLE-2.ICO
CAESAR-2.ICO	CAM-2.ICO	CAR1.ICO	CARDS1.ICO	CAT-2.ICO
CAKE-2.ICO	CAMCORDR.ICO	CAR2.ICO	CARDS2-2.ICO	CAT1-2.ICO
CALC-2.ICO	CAMEL.ICO	CARDDECK.ICO	CARDS3.ICO	CATDISK1.ICO
CALC1-2.ICO	CAMELO1.ICO	CARDFI-2.ICO	CARDS4.ICO	CATSCA-2.ICO
CALC2-2.ICO	CAMELO2.ICO	CARDFILE.ICO	CARDS5.ICO	CAUTION.ICO
CALC3.ICO	CAMERA(2.ICO	CARDINLS.ICO	CARMEN1.ICO	CAVE.ICO
CALC4.ICO	CAMERA-2.ICO	CARDNL-2.ICO	CARRIE-2.ICO	CBT-2.ICO
CALC7.ICO	CAMERA3.ICO	CARDNLS.ICO	CARRIER1.ICO	CC.ICO

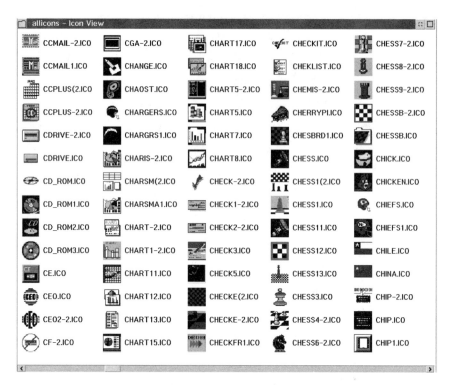

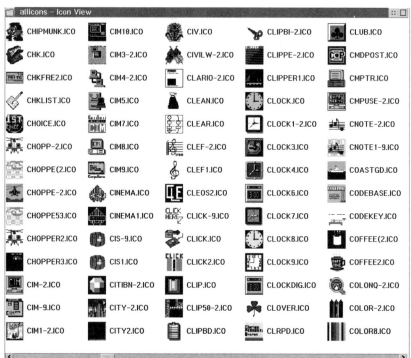

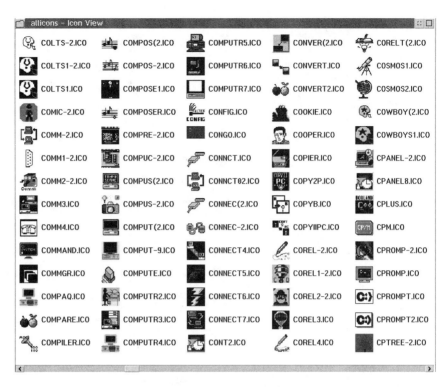

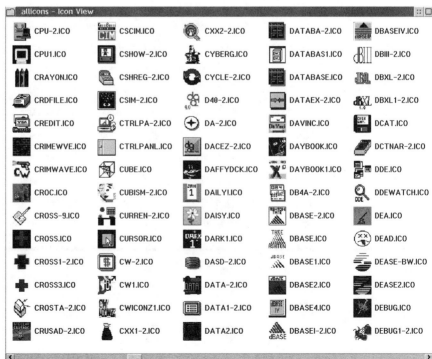

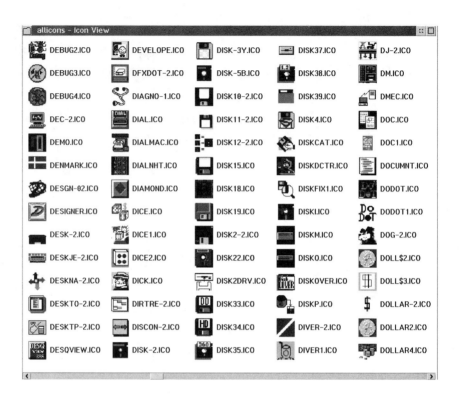

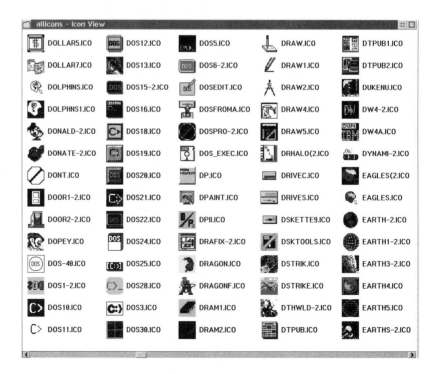

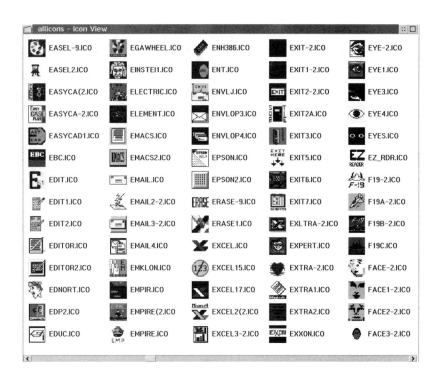

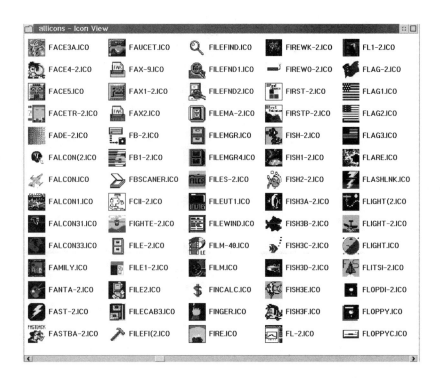

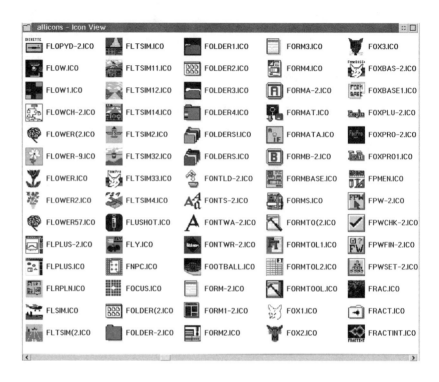

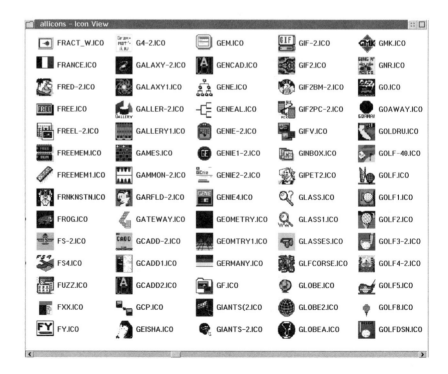

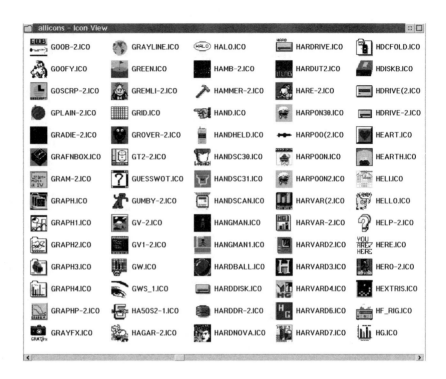

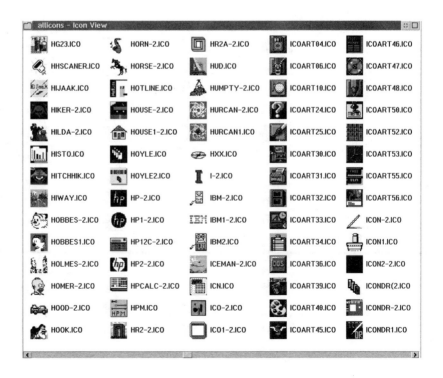

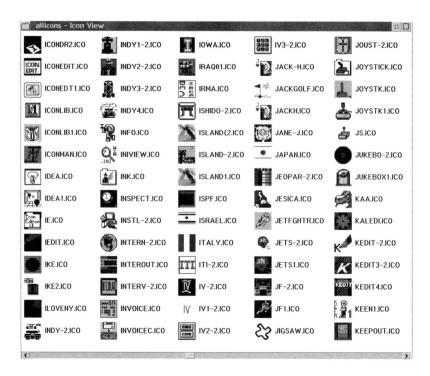

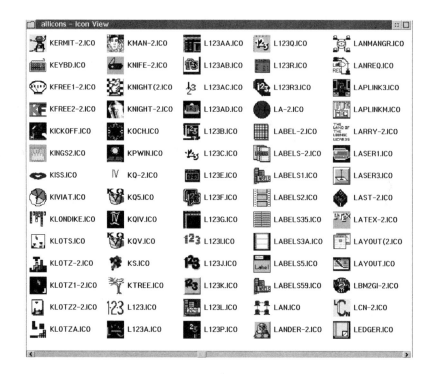

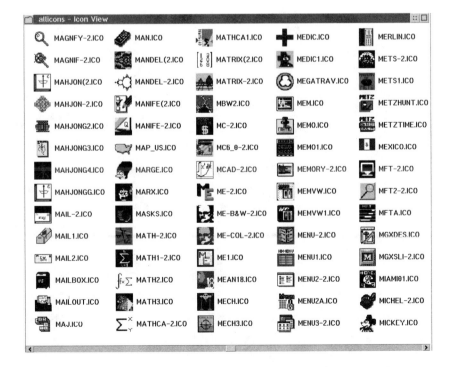

allicons – Icon View

LEONAR-2.ICO	LIGHTNIN.ICO	LIST3-2.ICO	LOGITECA.ICO	M1-2.ICO
LETTER-2.ICO	LINER.ICO	LISTB.ICO	LOGITECH.ICO	M1A-2.ICO
LETTER1.ICO	LINK-2.ICO	LISTC.ICO	LOGO.ICO	M2ZMODEM.ICO
LETTERS.ICO	LINK1-2.ICO	LISTIC(2.ICO	LONGHORN.ICO	MACE-2.ICO
LEWP.ICO	LINK2.ICO	LISTIC-2.ICO	LOOM.ICO	MACE1-2.ICO
LEXIS-2.ICO	LINK4.ICO	LISTICO1.ICO	LOTS123.ICO	MACE2.ICO
LEXIS1-2.ICO	LIONS-2.ICO	LL2-2.ICO	LOTTO-2.ICO	MACOLA-2.ICO
LHARC-2.ICO	LIONS1-2.ICO	LMC.ICO	LOTUS-2.ICO	MACRO-2.ICO
LHX-2.ICO	LIPS-2.ICO	LOBSTER.ICO	LS.ICO	MAG-2.ICO
LIBRARY.ICO	LIPS1.ICO	LOCK-2.ICO	LSL.ICO	MAG1-2.ICO
LICO.ICO	LIPS2.ICO	LOCK1.ICO	LURCH-2.ICO	MAGELL-2.ICO
LIFESA-2.ICO	LIST-2.ICO	LOCK2.ICO	LUXEMBOU.ICO	MAGELLAN.ICO
LIGHT-2.ICO	LIST1-2.ICO	LOGICO-1.ICO	LYS.ICO	MAGGIE-2.ICO
LIGHT1-2.ICO	LIST2-2.ICO	LOGITE-2.ICO	LZH-2.ICO	MAGIC.ICO

allicons – Icon View

MAGNFY-2.ICO	MAN.ICO	MATHCA1.ICO	MEDIC.ICO	MERLIN.ICO
MAGNIF-2.ICO	MANDEL(2.ICO	MATRIX(2.ICO	MEDIC1.ICO	METS-2.ICO
MAHJON(2.ICO	MANDEL-2.ICO	MATRIX-2.ICO	MEGATRAV.ICO	METS1.ICO
MAHJON-2.ICO	MANIFE(2.ICO	MBW2.ICO	MEM.ICO	METZHUNT.ICO
MAHJONG2.ICO	MANIFE-2.ICO	MC-2.ICO	MEMO.ICO	METZTIME.ICO
MAHJONG3.ICO	MAP_US.ICO	MC6_0-2.ICO	MEMO1.ICO	MEXICO.ICO
MAHJONG4.ICO	MARGE.ICO	MCAD-2.ICO	MEMORY-2.ICO	MFT-2.ICO
MAHJONGG.ICO	MARX.ICO	ME-2.ICO	MEMVW.ICO	MFT2-2.ICO
MAIL-2.ICO	MASKS.ICO	ME-B&W-2.ICO	MEMVW1.ICO	MFTA.ICO
MAIL1.ICO	MATH-2.ICO	ME-COL-2.ICO	MENU-2.ICO	MGXDES.ICO
MAIL2.ICO	MATH1-2.ICO	ME1.ICO	MENU1.ICO	MGXSLI-2.ICO
MAILBOX.ICO	MATH2.ICO	MEAN18.ICO	MENU2-2.ICO	MIAMI01.ICO
MAILOUT.ICO	MATH3.ICO	MECH.ICO	MENU2A.ICO	MICHEL-2.ICO
MAJ.ICO	MATHCA-2.ICO	MECH3.ICO	MENU3-2.ICO	MICKEY.ICO

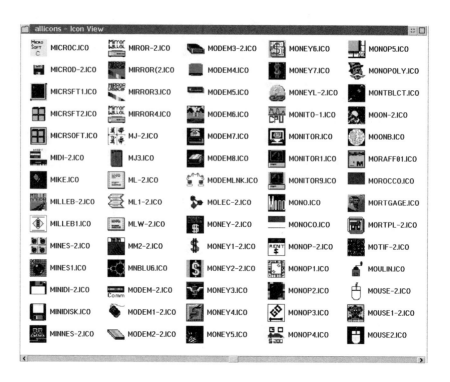

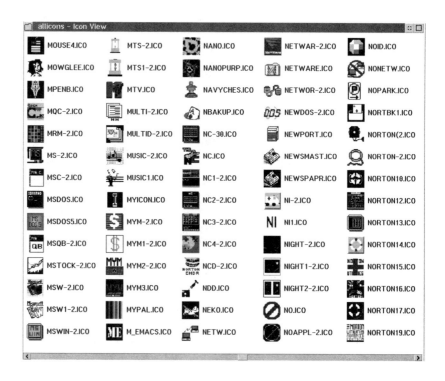

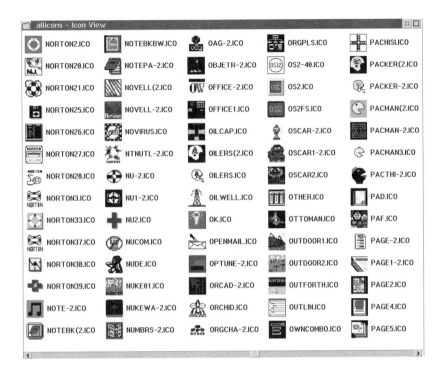

allicons - Icon View

NORTON2.ICO	NOTEBKBW.ICO	OAG-2.ICO	ORGPLS.ICO	PACHISI.ICO
NORTON20.ICO	NOTEPA-2.ICO	OBJETR-2.ICO	OS2-40.ICO	PACKER(2.ICO
NORTON21.ICO	NOVELL(2.ICO	OFFICE-2.ICO	OS2.ICO	PACKER-2.ICO
NORTON25.ICO	NOVELL-2.ICO	OFFICE1.ICO	OS2FS.ICO	PACMAN(2.ICO
NORTON26.ICO	NOVIRUS.ICO	OILCAP.ICO	OSCAR-2.ICO	PACMAN-2.ICO
NORTON27.ICO	NTNUTL-2.ICO	OILERS(2.ICO	OSCAR1-2.ICO	PACMAN3.ICO
NORTON28.ICO	NU-2.ICO	OILERS.ICO	OSCAR2.ICO	PACTHI-2.ICO
NORTON3.ICO	NU1-2.ICO	OILWELL.ICO	OTHER.ICO	PAD.ICO
NORTON33.ICO	NU2.ICO	OK.ICO	OTTOMAN.ICO	PAF.ICO
NORTON37.ICO	NUCOM.ICO	OPENMAIL.ICO	OUTDOOR1.ICO	PAGE-2.ICO
NORTON38.ICO	NUDE.ICO	OPTUNE-2.ICO	OUTDOOR2.ICO	PAGE1-2.ICO
NORTON39.ICO	NUKE01.ICO	ORCAD-2.ICO	OUTFORTH.ICO	PAGE2.ICO
NOTE-2.ICO	NUKEWA-2.ICO	ORCHID.ICO	OUTLIN.ICO	PAGE4.ICO
NOTEBK(2.ICO	NUMBRS-2.ICO	ORGCHA-2.ICO	OWNCOMBO.ICO	PAGE5.ICO

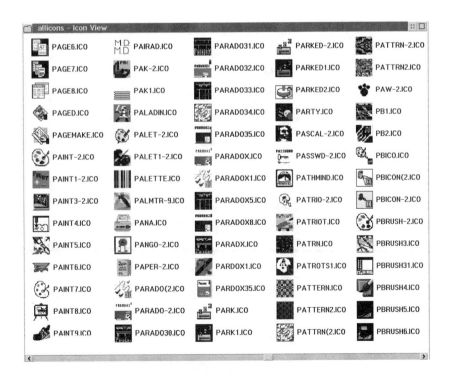

allicons - Icon View

PAGE6.ICO	PAIRAD.ICO	PARADO31.ICO	PARKED-2.ICO	PATTRN-2.ICO
PAGE7.ICO	PAK-2.ICO	PARADO32.ICO	PARKED1.ICO	PATTRN2.ICO
PAGE8.ICO	PAK1.ICO	PARADO33.ICO	PARKED2.ICO	PAW-2.ICO
PAGED.ICO	PALADIN.ICO	PARADO34.ICO	PARTY.ICO	PB1.ICO
PAGEMAKE.ICO	PALET-2.ICO	PARADO35.ICO	PASCAL-2.ICO	PB2.ICO
PAINT-2.ICO	PALET1-2.ICO	PARADOX.ICO	PASSWD-2.ICO	PBICO.ICO
PAINT1-2.ICO	PALETTE.ICO	PARADOX1.ICO	PATHMIND.ICO	PBICON(2.ICO
PAINT3-2.ICO	PALMTR-9.ICO	PARADOX5.ICO	PATRIO-2.ICO	PBICON-2.ICO
PAINT4.ICO	PANA.ICO	PARADOX8.ICO	PATRIOT.ICO	PBRUSH-2.ICO
PAINT5.ICO	PANGO-2.ICO	PARADX.ICO	PATRN.ICO	PBRUSH3.ICO
PAINT6.ICO	PAPER-2.ICO	PARDOX1.ICO	PATROTS1.ICO	PBRUSH31.ICO
PAINT7.ICO	PARADO(2.ICO	PARDOX35.ICO	PATTERN.ICO	PBRUSH4.ICO
PAINT8.ICO	PARADO-2.ICO	PARK.ICO	PATTERN2.ICO	PBRUSH5.ICO
PAINT9.ICO	PARADO30.ICO	PARK1.ICO	PATTRN(2.ICO	PBRUSH6.ICO

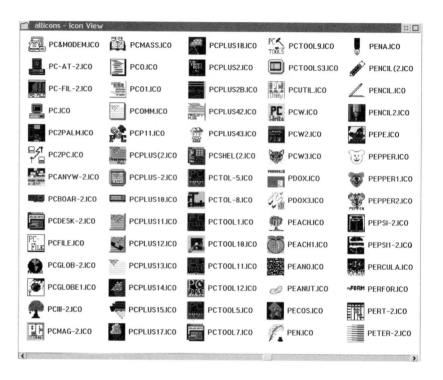

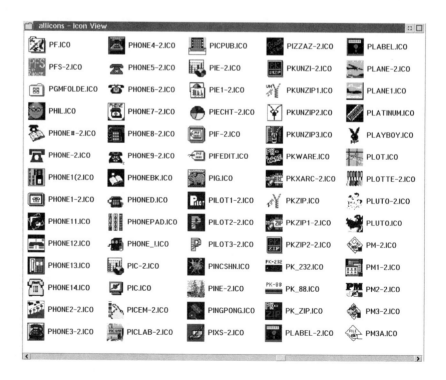

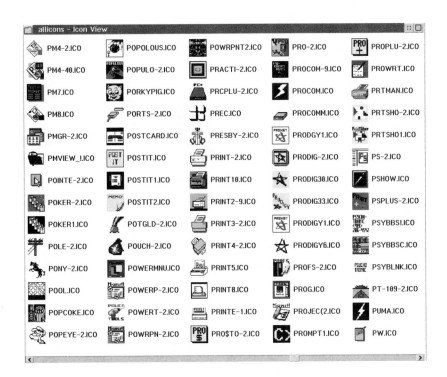

allicons - Icon View

PM4-2.ICO	POPOLOUS.ICO	POWRPNT2.ICO	PRO-2.ICO	PROPLU-2.ICO
PM4-40.ICO	POPULO-2.ICO	PRACTI-2.ICO	PROCOM-9.ICO	PROWRT.ICO
PM7.ICO	PORKYPIG.ICO	PRCPLU-2.ICO	PROCOM.ICO	PRTMAN.ICO
PM8.ICO	PORTS-2.ICO	PREC.ICO	PROCOMM.ICO	PRTSHO-2.ICO
PMGR-2.ICO	POSTCARD.ICO	PRESBY-2.ICO	PRODGY1.ICO	PRTSHO1.ICO
PMVIEW_!.ICO	POSTIT.ICO	PRINT-2.ICO	PRODIG-2.ICO	PS-2.ICO
POINTE-2.ICO	POSTIT1.ICO	PRINT10.ICO	PRODIG30.ICO	PSHOW.ICO
POKER-2.ICO	POSTIT2.ICO	PRINT2-9.ICO	PRODIG33.ICO	PSPLUS-2.ICO
POKER1.ICO	POTGLD-2.ICO	PRINT3-2.ICO	PRODIGY1.ICO	PSYBBSI.ICO
POLE-2.ICO	POUCH-2.ICO	PRINT4-2.ICO	PRODIGY6.ICO	PSYBBSC.ICO
PONY-2.ICO	POWERMNU.ICO	PRINT5.ICO	PROFS-2.ICO	PSYBLNK.ICO
POOL.ICO	POWERP-2.ICO	PRINT8.ICO	PROG.ICO	PT-109-2.ICO
POPCOKE.ICO	POWERT-2.ICO	PRINTE-1.ICO	PROJEC(2.ICO	PUMA.ICO
POPEYE-2.ICO	POWRPN-2.ICO	PRO$TO-2.ICO	PROMPT1.ICO	PW.ICO

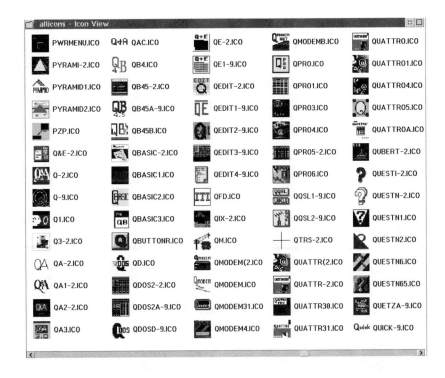

allicons - Icon View

PWRMENU.ICO	QAC.ICO	QE-2.ICO	QMODEMB.ICO	QUATTRO.ICO
PYRAMI-2.ICO	QB4.ICO	QE1-9.ICO	QPRO.ICO	QUATTRO1.ICO
PYRAMID1.ICO	QB45-2.ICO	QEDIT-2.ICO	QPRO1.ICO	QUATTRO4.ICO
PYRAMID2.ICO	QB45A-9.ICO	QEDIT1-9.ICO	QPRO3.ICO	QUATTRO5.ICO
PZP.ICO	QB45B.ICO	QEDIT2-9.ICO	QPRO4.ICO	QUATTROA.ICO
Q&E-2.ICO	QBASIC-2.ICO	QEDIT3-9.ICO	QPRO5-2.ICO	QUBERT-2.ICO
Q-2.ICO	QBASIC1.ICO	QEDIT4-9.ICO	QPRO6.ICO	QUESTI-2.ICO
Q-9.ICO	QBASIC2.ICO	QFD.ICO	QQSL1-9.ICO	QUESTN-2.ICO
Q1.ICO	QBASIC3.ICO	QIX-2.ICO	QQSL2-9.ICO	QUESTN1.ICO
Q3-2.ICO	QBUTTONR.ICO	QM.ICO	QTRS-2.ICO	QUESTN2.ICO
QA-2.ICO	QD.ICO	QMODEM(2.ICO	QUATTR(2.ICO	QUESTN6.ICO
QA1-2.ICO	QDOS2-2.ICO	QMODEM.ICO	QUATTR-2.ICO	QUESTN65.ICO
QA2-2.ICO	QDOS2A-9.ICO	QMODEM31.ICO	QUATTR30.ICO	QUETZA-9.ICO
QA3.ICO	QDOSD-9.ICO	QMODEM4.ICO	QUATTR31.ICO	QUICK-9.ICO

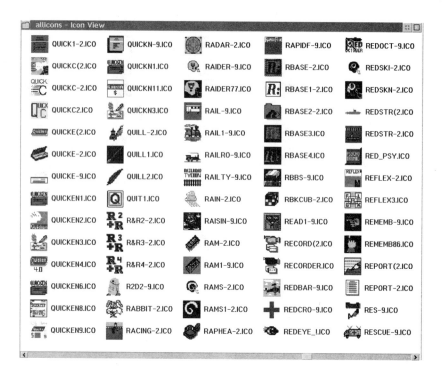

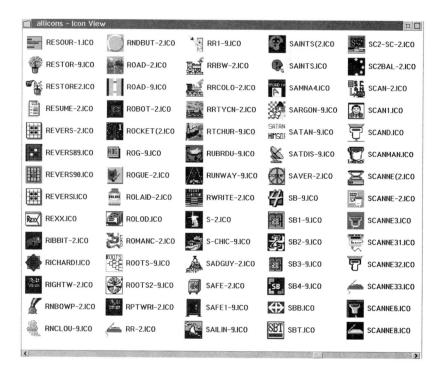

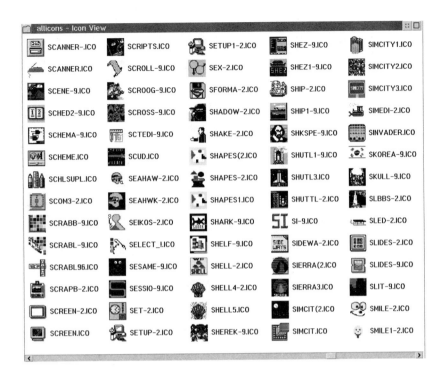

allicons – Icon View

SCANNER–.ICO	SCRIPTS.ICO	SETUP1–2.ICO	SHEZ–9.ICO	SIMCITY1.ICO
SCANNER.ICO	SCROLL–9.ICO	SEX–2.ICO	SHEZ1–9.ICO	SIMCITY2.ICO
SCENE–9.ICO	SCROOG–9.ICO	SFORMA–2.ICO	SHIP–2.ICO	SIMCITY3.ICO
SCHED2–9.ICO	SCROSS–9.ICO	SHADOW–2.ICO	SHIP1–9.ICO	SIMEDI–2.ICO
SCHEMA–9.ICO	SCTEDI–9.ICO	SHAKE–2.ICO	SHKSPE–9.ICO	SINVADER.ICO
SCHEME.ICO	SCUD.ICO	SHAPES(2.ICO	SHUTL1–9.ICO	SKOREA–9.ICO
SCHLSUPL.ICO	SEAHAW–2.ICO	SHAPES–2.ICO	SHUTL3.ICO	SKULL–9.ICO
SCOM3–2.ICO	SEAHWK–2.ICO	SHAPES1.ICO	SHUTTL–2.ICO	SLBBS–2.ICO
SCRABB–9.ICO	SEIKOS–2.ICO	SHARK–9.ICO	SI–9.ICO	SLED–2.ICO
SCRABL–9.ICO	SELECT_I.ICO	SHELF–9.ICO	SIDEWA–2.ICO	SLIDES–2.ICO
SCRABL96.ICO	SESAME–9.ICO	SHELL–2.ICO	SIERRA(2.ICO	SLIDES–9.ICO
SCRAPB–2.ICO	SESSIO–9.ICO	SHELL4–2.ICO	SIERRA3.ICO	SLIT–9.ICO
SCREEN–2.ICO	SET–2.ICO	SHELL5.ICO	SIMCIT(2.ICO	SMILE–2.ICO
SCREEN.ICO	SETUP–2.ICO	SHEREK–9.ICO	SIMCIT.ICO	SMILE1–2.ICO

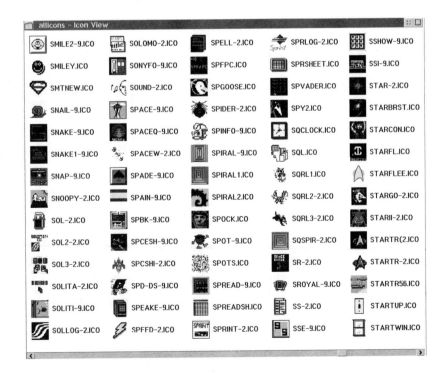

allicons – Icon View

SMILE2–9.ICO	SOLOMO–2.ICO	SPELL–2.ICO	SPRLOG–2.ICO	SSHOW–9.ICO
SMILEY.ICO	SONYFO–9.ICO	SPFPC.ICO	SPRSHEET.ICO	SSI–9.ICO
SMTNEW.ICO	SOUND–2.ICO	SPGOOSE.ICO	SPVADER.ICO	STAR–2.ICO
SNAIL–9.ICO	SPACE–9.ICO	SPIDER–2.ICO	SPY2.ICO	STARBRST.ICO
SNAKE–9.ICO	SPACEQ–9.ICO	SPINFO–9.ICO	SQCLOCK.ICO	STARCON.ICO
SNAKE1–9.ICO	SPACEW–2.ICO	SPIRAL–9.ICO	SQL.ICO	STARFL.ICO
SNAP–9.ICO	SPADE–9.ICO	SPIRAL1.ICO	SQRL1.ICO	STARFLEE.ICO
SNOOPY–2.ICO	SPAIN–9.ICO	SPIRAL2.ICO	SQRL2–2.ICO	STARGO–2.ICO
SOL–2.ICO	SPBK–9.ICO	SPOCK.ICO	SQRL3–2.ICO	STARII–2.ICO
SOL2–2.ICO	SPCESH–9.ICO	SPOT–9.ICO	SQSPIR–2.ICO	STARTR(2.ICO
SOL3–2.ICO	SPCSHI–2.ICO	SPOTS.ICO	SR–2.ICO	STARTR–2.ICO
SOLITA–2.ICO	SPD–DS–9.ICO	SPREAD–9.ICO	SROYAL–9.ICO	STARTR56.ICO
SOLITI–9.ICO	SPEAKE–9.ICO	SPREADSH.ICO	SS–2.ICO	STARTUP.ICO
SOLLOG–2.ICO	SPFFD–2.ICO	SPRINT–2.ICO	SSE–9.ICO	STARTWIN.ICO

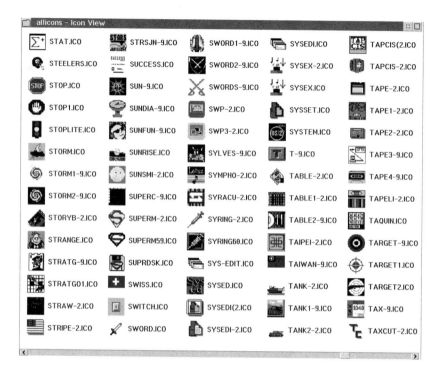

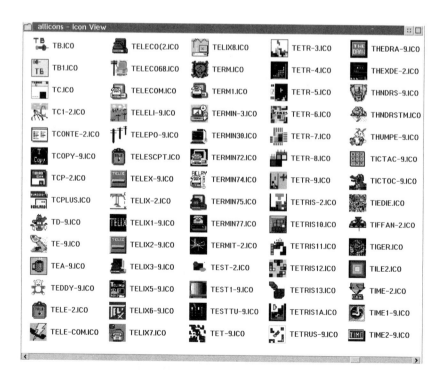

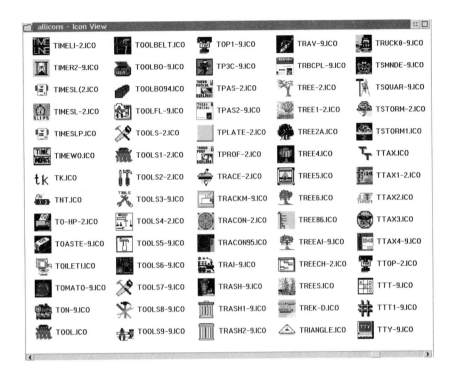

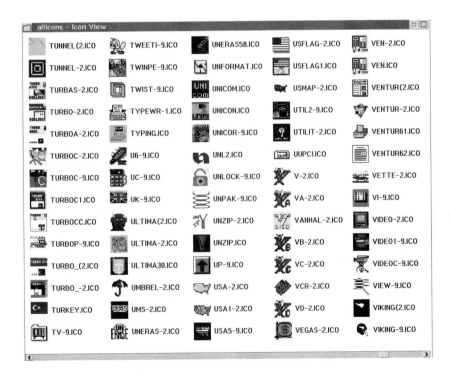

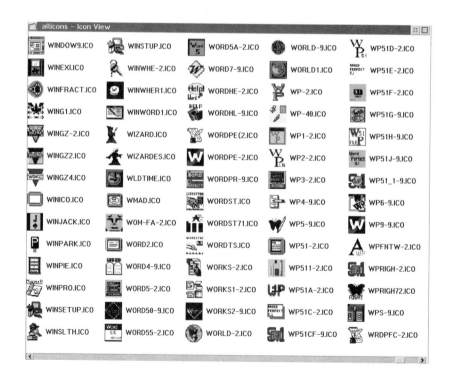

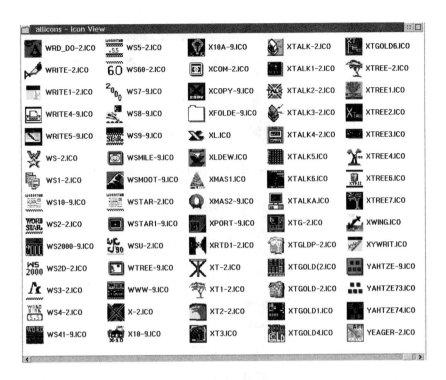

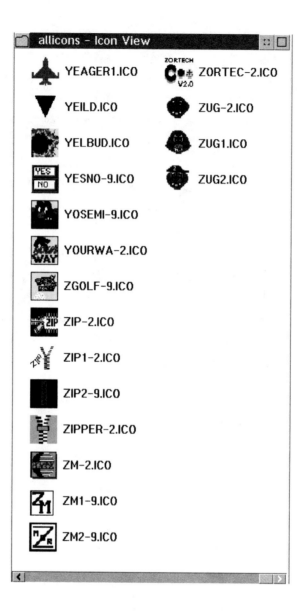

Glossary

argument Information being passed between a main program and a subroutine, or between a program and a function.

array variable A type of variable found in many programming languages. It allows multiple data values to be stored to the same variable name by using a row and column counter to address different cells within the variable name, much like a spreadsheet row and column number allows the addressing of different cells in a worksheet. The REXX version of array variables are called stem variables.

assignment The process of associating a piece of data with a variable name. This is done initially when the variable is created and again any time the contents of the variable are changed.

binary A method of counting in base 2. Since binary has only two digits, only 0 and 1 are used. To count from 0 to 16 in binary, you would have 0, 01, 10, 11, 100, 101, 110, 111, 1000, 1001, 1010, 1011, 1100, 1110, 1111, and 10000.

bug A programming mistake.

built-in function A function that's defined to be part of the REXX language.

class A class defines the behavior, graphical appearance, and information content used to represent something that exists in the real world.

clause Several clauses combined together to form a complete REXX instruction. However, not all REXX instructions are complete when made up of just a single line.

command A character string that's sent to an external environment for additional processing.

command language A language designed to issue a series of commands to the operating system, just as the batch file language does.

comments Text added to a program that the computer doesn't execute, but that helps explain and document the operation of the program. In REXX, these start with a /* and end with a */, and can be placed anywhere in the program.

compound variable *See* **stem variable**.

concatenation *See* **string concatenation**.

condition An unpredictable event outside a program that causes the program to behave in an unintended manner. Also called an exception.

data queue A generic term that includes the session queue, detached session queue, and external data queue.

delayed state The state of a condition trap after the condition has been raised but before the trap has been reset.

detached session queue A session queue for a REXX program when the program is started with the OS/2 DETACH command.

dynamic link library (DLL) A file that can be attached to a main program to add functionality. In REXX, this is the RexxUtil library.

embedded IF statement When one IF statement is used as the instruction portion of another IF statement.

endless loop A loop that will continue running forever.

engineering notation A method of writing very large or very small numbers. Numbers are written like 1.2e+3, where the 1.2 is a number greater than –1000 and less than +1000. For numbers greater than 1000, you continually divide by 1000 until the number is between –1000 and +1000. For numbers less than –1000, you continually multiply by 1000 until it's between –1000 and +1000. The sign following the e represents the operation used to convert the first number. A plus sign stands for dividing by tens, and the minus sign stands for multiplying by tens. A plus sign is generally dropped, so 1.2e+3 is the same as 1.2e3. The number after the e represents the number of tens used in the conversion, so 1.2e3 represents 1200 and 1.2e–3 would represent .0012. A type of exponential notation; *see also* **scientific notation**.

error number The number assigned by REXX to a specific error or bug. A description of each error number is available using the built-in ErrorText function.

exception *See* **condition**.

exception handling The ability of a program to respond to unexpected problems.

exec Another name for a REXX program. It's more common on other platforms.

exponential notation *See* **engineering notation** and **scientific notation**.

expression A portion of a REXX clause containing an explicit mathematical, string, logical, or relational operation to be performed.

extended attributes Additional information that the system or program associates with a file. For example, REXX stores a tokenized version of a .CMD program file in extended attributes the first time it runs the program.

external data queue A stream of characters that's stored by OS/2 external to any active REXX program. It can be accessed by any REXX and non-REXX program.

external command A command that's passed by REXX to the operating system.

external subroutine A separate .CMD program that the main program calls when needed.

function A built-in or external program that returns a single number of character strings to the calling program.

global variable A variable that can be read and modified by the main program and all its internal subroutines.

hardwiring Using the actual value in a program rather than storing the value to a variable in one spot and then using that variable everywhere you need the value.

hexadecimal A method of counting in base 16, where A–F are used to represent the extra digits. So 1–33 would be 0, 1, 2, 3, 4, 5, 6, 7, 8, 9, A, B, C, D, E, F, 10, 11, 12, 13, 14, 15, 16, 17, 18, 19, 1A, 1B, 1C, 1D, 1F, 20, and 21.

instruction   A REXX clause containing a keyword.

integer   A number that can be expressed without a decimal.

internal function   *See* **built-in function**.

internal subroutine   A subroutine that's completely self-contained within the main program.

keyword instruction   One or more clauses where the first word of the first clause is a keyword. That keyword tells REXX what instruction to execute for that clause.

label   A symbol followed by a colon, e.g., END:. A label is used to mark a location in a program; the line itself doesn't execute.

literal string   A phrase inside of quotation marks that cannot be modified by REXX.

local variable   A variable that's active only within the subroutine and has no impact outside the subroutine.

logical statement   A statement that can be evaluated by REXX as either true or false.

looping   Repeating the same sequence of instructions more than once.

message file   A message file contains character strings and associated numbers. Any application can reference the text by the associated number. This provides national language support (NLS).

nested   When one type of code is contained inside another section of that same type of code. For example, a DO loop can be nested inside another DO loop.

node   A stem or compound variable is divided into two or more segments by one or more periods. Each segment is a node.

normal logical comparison   Pads strings to equal length and strips off leading and trailing spaces and zeros from numbers.

null character   A character having an ASCII value of zero.

number   A character string containing: one or more digits 1–9, a decimal point located anywhere in the number, possibly a leading sign, spaces before and/or after the number, no commas, or an optional letter e followed by an optional sign and a whole number.

object   A working copy of something defined by that object's class.

operators   Character like –, +, and * that tell OS/2 to perform a mathematical operation.

operating character   Characters like + and – that indicate mathematical operations, and also logical characters like < and >.

packed number   A number with leading zeros.

parsing   Breaking down a character string into two or more substrings.

precision   The level of accuracy used to perform REXX calculations.

private data queue   *See* **external data queue**.

procedure   Another name for a REXX program.

production software   A program that's ready for use by the general public.

punctuation characters   Characters like the comma and semicolon that indicate REXX punctuation.

recursive   A program or subroutine that calls itself.

reserved word   A special token, a word REXX reserves to itself and doesn't allow you to use. Typically, reserved words are reserved only when they occupy a particular spot in an instruction. Most reserved words must be the first token to be reserved.

return code   A number returned by many programs and internal commands to indicate how well they performed their assigned task. Under DOS, this is called an errorlevel.

SAA   *See* **system application architecture**.

scientific notation   A method of writing very large or very small numbers. Numbers are written like 1.2e+3, where the 1.2 is a number greater than –10 and less than +10. For numbers greater than 10, you continually divide by 10 until the number is between –10 and +10. For numbers less than –10, you continually multiply by 10 until it's between –10 and +10. The sign following the e represents the operation used to convert the first number. A plus sign stands for dividing by tens, and the minus sign stands for multiplying by tens. A plus sign is generally dropped, so 1.2e+3 is the same as 1.2e3. The number after the e represents the number of tens used in the conversion, so 1.2e3 represents 1200 and 1.2e–3 would represent .0012. A type of exponential notation; *see also* **engineering notation**.

session queue   The default queue created by REXX, which is available to all processes.

simple variable   The opposite of a compound or stem variable, this is any variable without a period in its name.

statement   The basic unit of code in a REXX program. Unless a statement begins with an IF, DO, or SELECT instruction, a statement and clause are identical. When a statement begins with an IF, DO, or SELECT instruction, that statement can extend across multiple lines and thus include multiple clauses.

stem   The first node of a stem or compound variable. This is the part of the variable name up to the first period.

stem variable   The REXX version of an array variable, this is any variable with a period in its name, which allows multiple data values to be stored to a single variable name using a "stem" with different numeric or string values to keep the various data values separate. Also called a compound variable.

stream   A series of characters from a device such as a keyboard, file, or serial port.

string   A series of characters.

string concatenation   Combining two or more strings together to form a single string.

strict logical comparison   Doesn't allow padding of character strings, nor leading spaces, trailing spaces, and zeros to be stripped off numbers.

subroutine   A special block inside a program that functions very much like a stand-alone program. It has its own starting and ending point and, while it's running, the main program is suspended. When the subroutine is finished, control is passed back to the main program, which continues from the line after where it passed control to the subroutine.

symbol characters   These are characters like A–Z that you can use in a variable name.

system application architecture (SAA)   A set of rules and guidelines that IBM uses for creating applications that are portable (or transportable) across their entire line of computer hardware. REXX is the SAA command language.

tail   Everything after the stem, or first period, in a stem or compound variable. A tail can consist of one or many nodes.

template A pattern used when splitting up a string. The ARG, PARSE, and PULL instructions allow for a template.

token The smallest unit of a REXX program.

tokenization The process of converting a REXX program into a series of symbols understood by the computer.

trace The action of debugging a REXX program.

two's complement form A way of storing negative numbers. The negative form of a number is formed by taking the positive binary representation of that number and changing all the 1s and 0s in that number to 0s and 1s, respectively, and then adding one to the number.

typing The process of assigning a particular classification to a variable, for example, assigning Var1 to store numeric data and Var2 to store string data. REXX doesn't require, and indeed doesn't support, variable typing. Any variable can contain any type of data.

uninitialized variable Any variable that hasn't been assigned a value.

unpacked number A number that has had its leading zeros removed.

user-designed function A special type of subroutine that uses only local variables, gets all the data it needs to run from arguments, and returns a single value to the calling program.

variable A computerized version of a mailbox. It stores data under a name. The name won't change while the program runs, but the data stored under the name might change many times while the program runs.

whole number A number that can be expressed as an integer without using exponential notation.

word A portion of a character string with a space on both sides.

Index

%, 96
%0.CMD, 315
& (logical and), 97, 105
&& (exclusive or), 97, 106
*, 96
**, 96
+, 96
/, 96
//, 96
\ (logical not), 105
\< (greater than or equal to), 103
\= (not equal), 102
\== (strictly not equal), 104
\> (less than or equal to), 103
\>> (strictly greater than or equal to), 105
\>> (strictly less than or equal to), 105
¦ (inclusive or), 105
¦¦, 97
< (less than), 97, 103
<< (strictly less than), 97, 98, 104
<<= (strictly less than or equal to), 105
<= (less than or equal to), 103
<> (not equal), 102
−, 96
= (equal), 49, 102
== (strictly equal), 97, 98, 103-104
>, 97
> (greater than), 102
>< (not equal), 102
>= (greater than or equal to), 103
>> (strictly greater than), 97, 104
>>= (strictly greater than or equal to), 105
?, 49
4PMREXX.CMD, 315

A

ABBREV.CMD, 316
Abbrev function, 90, 145-146
Abs function, 98, 135-136
Address function, 139
ADDRESS instruction, 178-180, 193

AEOM (*see* Apple Macintosh Apple Events Object Model)
ALLCAPS.CMD, 239-240, 316
ALLOWER.CMD, 316
Apple Macintosh Apple Events Object Model (AEOM), 163
application programming interface (API), 118, 159
ARG.CMD, 316
ARG-CMD.CMD, 317
Arg function, 48, 63-64, 67, 90, 145-147
ARG instruction, 180, 193
ASCII, 7-8
assignments, 34-35, 41

B

B2X function, 90, 98, 131-132
BACKCONF.CMD, 240-242, 343-344
batch commands, 78
BAT-FOR.CMD, 317
BATSHIFT.CMD, 317
Beep function, 76, 139-140
BEEPS.CMD, 317
BIGNUM.CMD, 317
binary number system, 40, 59-60
BITAND.CMD, 317
BitAnd function, 121
BITOR.CMD, 317
BitOr function, 122-123
BITXOR.CMD, 318
BitXOr function, 123-124
branching, variables and, 44-46

C

C command, 130
C2D function, 91, 131-133
C2X function, 91, 131, 133
CALEDBAT.CMD, 318
CALL-1.CMD, 318
CALL-2.CMD, 318
CALL-3.CMD, 318
CALL-4.CMD, 318

CALL-5.CMD, 242-247, 318
CALL-6.CMD, 318
CALL-7.CMD, 318
CALL-8.CMD, 319
CALL-9.CMD, 319
CALL-10.CMD, 319
CALL-11.CMD, 319
CALL-12.CMD, 319
CALLARG.CMD, 319
CALLBAT.CMD, 319
CALL command, 77, 78
CALL instruction, 117, 180-182, 193
CALL show, 49
CALL Tell, 50
CAPITAL.CMD, 319-320
Center function, 90, 145, 148
CHANGE.CMD, 320
characters
   invalid, 39-40
   operational, 39
   punctuation, 39
   special, 33
   symbol, 39
character string literals, 40
CHARIN.CMD, 320
CharIn function, 90, 126-127
CHAROUT.CMD, 320
CharOut function, 91, 127-128
CHARS.CMD, 320
Chars function, 91, 127
CHKCONF.CMD, 344
CHKDRIVE.CMD, 320
CHOICE command, 77, 78
CLASSES.CMD, 321
clauses, 33-34, 37-39
CLEAR command, 26
CLS.CMD, 321
command line
   getting information from, 61-64
   using, 18
commands, 41 (*see also* specific command names)
   batch, 78

non-REXX, 77-84
OS/2, 35
COMMAS.CMD, 247-249, 321
communication, 72-76
COMPARE.CMD, 321
Compare function, 91, 145, 148
COMPUTE.CMD, 321
CONCATE.CMD, 249-250, 322
Condition function, 124-125
conditions, 225
COPIES.CMD, 322
Copies function, 91, 145, 148-149
COPY command, 26
Cowlishaw, Mike, 1
CURSOR.CMD, 322
CUT command, 26

D

D command, 130
D2C function, 99, 131, 133
D2X function, 131, 134
D2X.CMD, 322
data queues, external, 216-222
DATATYPE.CMD, 322
DataType function, 98, 139, 141-142
Date function, 91, 139-141
DATES.CMD, 322
DateType function, 91
debugging, 234-238
default exception handling, 226
DELBLANK.CMD, 251, 322
DELSTR.CMD, 323
DelStr function, 91, 145, 149
DELWORD.CMD, 323
DelWord function, 91, 145, 149
DESCRIBE.CMD, 323
detached session queue, 218
DIAL.CMD, 323
DIGITS.CMD, 323
Digits function, 99, 135-136
directories, sub-, 18
disk management, 167-173
DO instruction, 47, 193, 182-184
DO loop, 114-116
DO END loop, 108-111
DO UNTIL statement, 46-47
DO WHILE statement, 46-47
DO-1.CMD, 323
DO-2.CMD, 323
DO-3.CMD, 323
DO-4.CMD, 324
DO-5.CMD, 324
DO-6.CMD, 324
DO-7.CMD, 324
DO-8.CMD, 324
DO-9.CMD, 324
DO-10.CMD, 324
DO-11.CMD, 325
documentation, 3-4
DOSPAUSE.CMD, 325
DROP instruction, 184, 193

E

EA.CMD, 325
EAPREP.CMD, 344
ECHO command, 73, 77, 79
editing, 10-13 (see also Enhanced
  Editor)
  advanced, 16-17
  icons, 24-27
  intermediate, 13-16
endnum, 109
Enhanced Editor, 4-7
  ASCII files and, 7-8
  getting started with, 8-10
Error condition, 225
ERRORLEVEL command, 77, 79
error messages, 350-358
errors
  debugging, 234-238
  exception handling, 223-233
ErrorText function, 121, 125
ERRORTXT.CMD, 325
EXCEPT-1.CMD, 228-229, 325
EXCEPT-2.CMD, 230, 325
EXCEPT-3.CMD, 230-231, 325
exception handling, 124-125, 223-233
  defining, 227-228
  description, 224
  enabling/disabling, 227
  information available to, 232
  selecting between Type I and II, 231
  types of, 226-227
exceptions, types of, 225
EXIT instruction, 48, 184-185, 193
exitnum, 112
EXPAND command, 17
exponential notation, 95
extended attributes, 173-174
external data queues, 216-222
  avoiding conflicts with, 222
  creating new, 218-219
  deleting, 221-222
  demonstrations of, 217-218
  finding active, 221
  getting data from, 220-221
  making active, 219
  putting data into, 219-220
  understanding, 217-218

F

FACTORAL.CMD, 252-253, 326
Failure condition, 225
FF.CMD, 326-327
FF2.CMD, 253-255, 327
file management, 167-173
file management functions, 125-131
files, 36
FILES.CMD, 327
FILEXIST.CMD, 327-328
FINDLPT.CMD, 328
FOR command, 77, 80
FOR-LOOP.CMD, 328

Form function, 135, 137
format-conversion functions, 131-135
FORMAT.CMD, 328
Format function, 99, 135, 137
functions (see also specific function
  names)
  built-in, 117-157
  external, 158-177
Fuzz function, 99, 135, 138

G

GETA2Z.CMD, 329
GET.CMD, 328
GETDATA.CMD, 217, 329
GET-ONE.CMD, 328
GET09.CMD, 329
global variables, 205-207
GOTO command, 77, 80-81

H

Halt condition, 225
hardware, requirements, xvii
hexadecimal number system, 40, 58-59
HIWORLD.CMD, 329

I

Icon Editor, 24-27
icons, 23-24, 358-380
  commands for, 26
  creating new, 30
  drawing, 24
  dropping and dragging, 30
  installing, 27-30
  modifying existing, 24
  pasting an existing, 30
  using, 18-23
IF command, 77, 81
IF instruction, 185
IF statements, 106-108
IF THEN ELSE statement, 46
IF THEN statement, 46
IMPORT command, 14
Independent Color Form, 25-26
INSERT.CMD, 329
Insert function, 91, 145, 150
installation
  icons, 27-30
  REXX, 1-2
instructions, 35
  keyword, 41, 178-194
INTERACT.CMD, 329-330
interactive tracing, 237-238
INTERPRET instruction, 185, 193
invalid characters, 39-40
ISITANUM.CMD, 255-257, 330
ISITZERO.CMD, 330
ITERATE instruction, 185, 194

K

KEYVALUE.CMD, 331
keyword instructions, 41, 178-194

L

labels, 34, 41
LASTPOS.CMD, 331
LastPos function, 91, 145, 150
LEAVE instruction, 186, 194
LEFT.CMD, 331
Left function, 91, 145, 151
LENGTH.CMD, 331
Length function, 91, 145, 151
LINEIN.CMD, 331
LineIn function, 126, 128-129
LINEIN instruction, 67
LINEOUT.CMD, 331
LineOut function, 126, 129
Lines function, 126, 130
LISTCALL.CMD, 331-332
LISTIT.CMD, 257-264, 332
literal strings, 32
local variables, 204-207
logical statements, 101-106
LOGIC.CMD, 332
logic testing, 101-108
    looping and, 46-47
looping, 108-116
    altering the counter, 114
    counting the, 109-111
    fixed number of times, 108-109
    forever, 113-114
    leaving it early, 111-113
    logic testing and, 46-47
    nesting, 114-115
    until condition is met, 114

M

MAP.CMD, 332
MATH.CMD, 332
mathematical calculations, variables
    and, 68
mathematical functions, 135-139
mathematical operations, 96
mathematical precedence, 96-97
MATHTEST.CMD, 264-268, 332-333
Max function, 99, 135-136
MESSAGE.CMD, 333
Min function, 99, 135-136
MKCMD.CMD, 269-271, 345
mouse elevator, 12
MULTI-IF.CMD, 333

N

NEW command, 14, 26
NOP instruction, 186, 194
normal comparisons, 101
NotReady condition, 225
NoValue condition, 225
number systems
    binary, 40, 59-60
    hexadecimal, 40, 58-59
numbers, 40, 93-100
    display rounding, 94
    errors, 98-99

exponential notation, 95
mathematical operations, 96
mathematical precedence, 96-97
power with functions, 99-100
precision, 94-95
whole, 95
NUMERIC DIGITS instruction, 98
NUMERIC FUZZ instruction, 98
NUMERIC instruction, 186-187, 194
numeric variables, 86

O

OBJECT.CMD, 333
objects, 164-167
OPEN command, 26
operational characters, 39
operators, 32, 40, 96-98
OPTIONS instruction, 187, 194
OS/2 commands, 35
OS2PAUSE.CMD, 333
OVERLAY.CMD, 333
Overlay function, 91, 145, 151-152

P

PARSE instruction, 66, 187-191, 194
PARSEOPT.CMD, 271-275, 345-346
passive tracing, 235-237
PASSWORD.CMD, 333
PASTE command, 26
path, modifying, 18
PATHLIST.CMD, 276-279, 346
PAUSE.CMD, 334
PAUSE command, 74-75, 78, 81
PC-1.CMD, 334
PMREXX.EXE, 53-54
POS.CMD, 334
Pos function, 91, 145, 152
POSITION.CMD, 334
PRECEDE.CMD, 335
PRECISE.CMD, 335
PREPROC.CMD, 346-347
PRINT command, 14
PROCEDURE instruction, 191, 194
programs and programming
    including non-REXX commands, 77-84
    running external, 82-83
    writing simple, 44-48
PULL instruction, 45-47, 67, 191, 194
punctuation characters, 39
PUSH instruction, 191, 194

Q

queue
    external data, 216-222
    session, 217
QUEUE instruction, 191-192, 194
QUEUE-1.CMD, 335
QUEUE-2.CMD, 335
QUEUE-3.CMD, 335
QUEUE-4.CMD, 335
QUEUE-5.CMD, 335-336

Queued function, 139, 142
QUIT command, 14

R

RANDOM.CMD, 336
Random function, 135, 138
RC.CMD, 336
RCD.CMD, 347
REM command, 78, 81-82
RENAME command, 14
reserved words, 33
RETURN instruction, 48, 192, 194
REVERSE.CMD, 336
Reverse function, 91
REXX
    background/history, xvi-xvii
    executing programs, 18
    installing, 1-2
    interactive, 49-55
    overview, 31-43
REXX function, 117
REXX-1.CMD, 336
REXX-2.CMD, 336
REXX-3.CMD, 336
REXX-4.CMD, 336
REXX-5.CMD, 337
REXX-6.CMD, 337
REXX-7.CMD, 337
REXX-8.CMD, 337
REXX-9.CMD, 337
REXX-10.CMD, 337
REXX-11.CMD, 337
REXX-12.CMD, 337
REXXECHO.CMD, 338
REXXTRY.CMD, 49-52
RIGHT.CMD, 338
Right function, 92, 145, 152-153
RxFuncAdd function, 120, 159-160
RxFuncDrop function, 120, 160
RxFuncQuery function, 120, 160
RxMessageBox function, 161-162, 177
RxQuery function, 120
RXSUMRY.CMD, 348
RXTIME.CMD, 348

S

S command, 130
SAA (see Systems Application Archi-
    tecture)
SAMPLE.CMD, 338
SAVE AS command, 14, 26
SAVE command, 26, 50
SAY command, 12
SAY instruction, 45, 72-73, 192, 194
screen
    clearing the, 76
    controlling, 161-164
SCREEN.CMD, 338
search and replace, 15-16
searching, functions, 121, 160-161
SELECT ALL command, 26

SELECT command, 26
SELECT instruction, 192, 194
SELECT statement, 107
SENDATA.CMD, 217, 338
SENDATA2.CMD, 217, 338
SENDATA2.CMD, 279-281
session queue, 217
  detached, 218
SHIFT command, 78, 82
SHOWCAP.CMD, 338
SHOW-POS.CMD, 338
SHOWRX.CMD, 339
SHOWSAY.CMD, 339
SHOWSORT.CMD, 281-283, 339
SHOWTEMP.CMD, 339
SIGN.CMD, 339
Sign function, 99, 135, 138
SIGNAL instruction, 45, 112, 192-193,
  194, 200
SLEEP.CMD, 339
software, requirements, xvii
SOM (*see* System Object Model)
source code
  ALLCAPS.CMD, 239-240
  BACKCONF.CMD, 240-242
  CALL-5.CMD, 242-247
  COMMAS.CMD, 247-249
  CONCATE.CMD, 249-250
  DELBLANK.CMD, 251
  FACTORAL.CMD, 252-253
  FF2.CMD, 253-255
  ISITANUM.CMD, 255-257
  LISTIT.CMD, 257-264
  MATHTEST.CMD, 264-268
  MKCMD.CMD, 269-271
  PARSEOPT.CMD, 271-275
  PATHLIST.CMD, 276-279
  SENDATA2.CMD, 279-281
  SHOWSORT.CMD, 281-283
  SPACE.CMD, 283-287
  SPAUSE.CMD, 287-291
  SPELLING.CMD, 291-294
  TODO.CMD, 294-308
  TYPING.CMD, 308-313
  WHICH.CMD, 313-314
SOURCE.CMD, 339
SOURCE instruction, 67
SourceLine function, 121, 125
SPACE.CMD, 283-287, 339, 349
Space function, 145, 153
SPAUSE.CMD, 287-291, 340
special characters, 33
SPELDISK.CMD, 340
SPELLING.CMD, 291-294, 340
startnum, 109
statements, 36
STEM.CMD, 340-341
stem variables, 70
STRCONVT.CMD, 341
Stream function, 126, 130-131
strict comparisons, 101

STRINGBK.CMD, 341
string concatenation, 88-90
STRINGDO.CMD, 341
string manipulation, variables and, 68
string variables, 86
strings, 85-92
  definition, 87-88
  functions, 145-157
  literal, 32
  literal character, 40
  power with functions, 90-92
Strip function, 92, 99, 145, 153-154
STRIP.CMD, 341
subdirectories, creating, 18
subroutines, 47-48
  advantages of external, 210-211
  advantages of internal, 199
  anatomy of external, 212
  calling the external, 213-214
  examples of, 196-199, 201-203
  external, 210-215
  internal, 195-209
  leaving, 200
  returning a value, 214
  rules of internal, 201
  saved data and, 201
  types of, 195
  variable management in internal,
    203-209
SUBSTR.CMD, 341
SubStr function, 92, 99, 145, 154
SUBWORD.CMD, 341
SubWord function, 92, 145, 154
symbol characters, 39
SYMBOL.CMD, 341
Symbol function, 139, 142-143
symbols, 33, 40
  syntax, 41
syntax, 118
Syntax condition, 226
syntax symbols, 41
SysCls function, 161-163, 177
SysCreateObject function, 165-166, 177
SysCurPos function, 74, 161, 163, 177
SysDeregisterObjectClass function,
  165-166, 177
SysDestroyClassList function, 165-166
SysDestroyObject function, 177
SysDriveInfo function, 167-168, 177
SysDriveMap function, 167-169, 177
SysDropFuncs function, 160, 177
SysFileDelete function, 167, 169, 177
SysFileSearch function, 167, 169-170,
  177
SysFileTree function, 167, 170-171, 177
SysGetEA function, 173, 177
SysGetKey function, 68, 75, 174-175,
  177
SysGetMessage function, 161, 174,
  175, 177
SysIni function, 161, 174-177

SysMkDir function, 167, 171, 177
SysOS2Ver function, 161, 174, 176, 177
SysPutEA function, 173-174, 177
SysQueryClassList function, 165-166,
  177
SysRegisterObjectClass function, 164,
  167, 177
SysRmDir function, 167, 171-172, 177
SysSearchPath function, 167, 172, 177
SysSetIcon function, 174, 176, 177
SysSetObjectData function, 164, 167,
  177
SysSleep function, 174, 176, 177
System Object Model (SOM), 163
SysTempFileName function, 167, 172-
  173, 177
Systems Application Architecture
  (SAA), 1
SysTextScreenRead function, 161,
  163, 177
SysTextScreenSize function, 161, 163,
  177
SysWaitNamedPipe function, 161,
  174-177

T
tail variables, 70
TEMPLATE.CMD, 341
THETIME.CMD, 342
Time function, 139, 143-144
TODO.CMD, 294-308, 342
tokens, 32, 39-41
Trace function, 121, 125
TRACE instruction, 193, 194
TRACE-1.CMD, 342
TRACE-2.CMD, 342
Translate function, 92, 145, 155
TRUNC.CMD, 342
Trunc function, 99, 135, 139
Type I exception handling, 226
Type II exception handling, 226-227
TYPING.CMD, 308-313, 342

U
UNDO command, 26
users
  asking for variable data from, 65-68
  communicating with, 72-76

V
VALUE.CMD, 342
Value function, 92, 99, 139, 144
VALUE WITH instruction, 67
VAR instruction, 67
variable arrays, 68-71
variables, 56-71
  asking user for data, 65-68
  assigning binary values to, 59-60
  assigning hexadecimal values to, 58-
    59
  assigning values to, 56-58

variables, *continued*
  branching and, 44-46
  creating, 56
  getting information from command
   line, 61-64
  global, 205-207
  local, 204-207
  managing in internal subroutines,
   203-209
  mathematical calculations, 68
  numeric, 86
  stem, 70
  string, 86
  string manipulation, 68

  tail, 70
  taking information from other, 64-65
variable typing, 86
VERIFIED.CMD, 342
Verify function, 92, 145, 155-156
VERSION instruction, 67-68

W

WHICH.CMD, 313-314, 349
Word function, 92, 145, 156
WordIndex function, 92, 145, 156
WordLength function, 92, 146, 156-157
WordPos function, 92, 146, 157
WORDS.CMD, 343

Words function, 92, 146, 157
WPFolder, 164
WPProgram, 164
WPShadow, 164

X

X2B function, 92, 99, 131, 134
X2C function, 92, 99, 131, 134
X2D function, 92, 99, 131, 135
XCOPY command, 179
XRANGE.CMD, 343
XRange function, 139, 144-145

Y

YESORNO.CMD, 343

DISK WARRANTY

This software is protected by both United States copyright law and international copyright treaty provision. You must treat this software just like a book, except that you may copy it into a computer in order to be used and you may make archival copies of the software for the sole purpose of backing up our software and protecting your investment from loss.

By saying "just like a book," McGraw-Hill means, for example, that this software may be used by any number of people and may be freely moved from one computer location to another, so long as there is no possibility of its being used at one location or on one computer while it also is being used at another. Just as a book cannot be read by two different people in two different places at the same time, neither can the software be used by two different people in two different places at the same time (unless, of course, McGraw-Hill's copyright is being violated).

LIMITED WARRANTY

Windcrest/McGraw-Hill takes great care to provide you with top-quality software, thoroughly checked to prevent virus infections. McGraw-Hill warrants the physical diskette(s) contained herein to be free of defects in materials and workmanship for a period of sixty days from the purchase date. If McGraw-Hill receives written notification within the warranty period of defects in materials or workmanship, and such notification is determined by McGraw-Hill to be correct, McGraw-Hill will replace the defective diskette(s). Send requests to:

> Customer Service
> Windcrest/McGraw-Hill
> 13311 Monterey Lane
> Blue Ridge Summit, PA 17294-0850

The entire and exclusive liability and remedy for breach of this Limited Warranty shall be limited to replacement of defective diskette(s) and shall not include or extend to any claim for or right to cover any other damages, including but not limited to, loss of profit, data, or use of the software, or special, incidental, or consequential damages or other similar claims, even if McGraw-Hill has been specifically advised of the possibility of such damages. In no event will McGraw-Hill's liability for any damages to you or any other person ever exceed the lower of suggested list price or actual price paid for the license to use the software, regardless of any form of the claim.

McGRAW-HILL, INC. SPECIFICALLY DISCLAIMS ALL OTHER WARRANTIES, EXPRESS OR IMPLIED, INCLUDING, BUT NOT LIMITED TO, ANY IMPLIED WARRANTY OF MERCHANTABILITY OR FITNESS FOR A PARTICULAR PURPOSE.

Specifically, McGraw-Hill makes no representation or warranty that the software is fit for any particular purpose and any implied warranty of merchantability is limited to the sixty-day duration of the Limited Warranty covering the physical diskette(s) only (and not the software) and is otherwise expressly and specifically disclaimed.

This limited warranty gives you specific legal rights; you may have others which may vary from state to state. Some states do not allow the exclusion of incidental or consequential damages, or the limitation on how long an implied warranty lasts, so some of the above may not apply to you.

If you need help with the enclosed disk . . .

The enclosed disk contains all the REXX programs referenced in the book and contained in appendix A. It also includes all the icons listed in appendix D. The files are contained in three subdirectories: ICONS, MYSAMPLE, and OTHERS.

IMPORTANT

Read the Disk Warranty terms on the previous page before opening the disk envelope. Opening the envelope constitutes acceptance of these terms and renders this entire book-disk package nonreturnable except for replacement in kind due to material defect.